The Trojan War as Military History

Dedicated to the ghost of my father, Manolis, who introduced me to the Heroes and their world when he did; and it did matter.

The Trojan War as Military History

Manousos E. Kambouris

Pen & Sword
MILITARY

First published in Great Britain in 2023 by
Pen & Sword Military
An imprint of
Pen & Sword Books Ltd
Yorkshire – Philadelphia

Typeset by Mac Style
Printed in the UK by CPI Group (UK) Ltd, Croydon, CR0 4YY.

Pen & Sword Books Limited incorporates the imprints of Atlas,
Archaeology, Aviation, Discovery, Family History, Fiction, History,
Maritime, Military, Military Classics, Politics, Select, Transport, True
Crime, Air World, Frontline Publishing, Leo Cooper, Remember
When, Seaforth Publishing, The Praetorian Press, Wharncliffe Local
History, Wharncliffe Transport, Wharncliffe True Crime, White Owl
and After the Battle.

For a complete list of Pen & Sword titles please contact

PEN & SWORD BOOKS LIMITED
47 Church Street, Barnsley, South Yorkshire, S70 2AS, England
E-mail: enquiries@pen-and-sword.co.uk
Website: www.pen-and-sword.co.uk
or
PEN AND SWORD BOOKS
1950 Lawrence Rd, Havertown, PA 19083, USA
E-mail: Uspen-and-sword@casematepublishers.com
Website: www.penandswordbooks.com

Contents

Plates

1. *Axine* pickaxe, as a sidearm of a warrior
2. Studded club, as a sidearm of a warrior
3. Slashing axe combined with scale body armour
4. Old-time, small metal greaves over soft fabric full-length leg-guards combined with a collection of axes
5. Dendra-type armour
6. To the left, a collection of offensive weapons, with spears and different types of axes. To the right, the long *pakana* longsword, combined with non-metal armour, greaves over leg-guards and a single epaulette from Dendra-type armour
7. The Dendra-panoplied warrior carries a scaled-down naval spear like the one described by Homer for Ajax and the Greeks for naval engagements
8. Close-quarters first-strike attack with a sidearm, here a pickaxe, once the opponent has closed with the enemy armed with a shafted weapon
9. Close-quarters second-strike attack with a sidearm, here a pickaxe, once the opponent has thrust and missed with a shafted weapon
10. Dirk-type swords in the hands of armoured and unarmoured/light infantry
11. A prehoplite/early hoplite
12. Find of a stabbing dirk
13. Find of a cut-and-thrust dirk
14. Different Mycenaean sword types reconstructed
15. Find of a helmet;
16. Find of bronze greaves of the early type
17. The use of the two-handed infantry pike by an unarmoured bearer of the full-size figure-of-eight shield

Illustrations

Maps

Preface

I was introduced at the age of four to the world of Homer; my father thought that the values of that time were a good moral compass for his son. Especially the Heroic Code, found throughout the *Iliad*, about striving for excellence (i.e. in XI-783). I never left such company. At the time, mid 70s, it was an oddity but still taught in school. Considered a myth, it was taught as essential for a young Greek to *Know Oneself*. And then it vanished. A new, dynamic generation of scholars was expected to look upon the epics with fresh eyes, less prejudice, inquisitive mind and new technology and re-start its study as had happened with Biblical Archaeology. But the Epics went to the recycle bin; the Greek Universities would gladly burn them as anachronistic or reactionary and ideological nests of warmongering. Saying they are something other than fairy tales, of course, would invite the Inquisition. Thus I never followed that road of academicism and scholarship. Nor did any compatriots and friends; one session of browsing to Bronze Age warfare would reveal very few Greek academic contributions; if instead of the neutral and acceptable 'Bronze Age' one substitutes 'epics' or 'Homer/ Iliad', the results are telltale. And not a fairy tale.

Some five decades later, I pay my debt to the glorious shadows that formed the basis of the Greek Psyche for the best part of three millennia by trying to bring them to history from the shades of lore.

Introduction

This book is not fiction. It uses imagination and deduction to paste into the realm of History something slandered as fiction. It is not an academic work; it is based on original sources, and contemporary scholarship is used only to make clear which ideas are borrowed, adopted or rejected, and which ones are original. No extensive discussion on centuries of scholarship is intended, especially since the Bronze Age came into vogue once more in the last 30 years. Homer did not, but the Bronze Age did.

The Trojan War was always considered a fact for the ancient Greeks and it was their defining moment; the first time they were Greeks against foreigners as such (Thuc I.3,1). Actually, it was the very last episode of the early days of Greece and the only one of which an accurate account has survived. The war and the world recounted in the *Iliad* is much more similar to other Levantine civilizations than the Archaic and Classical Greek one, which diverted dramatically (Hanson 1999). Still, this was the defining moment; the relatively standard and conformist world was what inspired the novelty once the Total Reboot was enacted in the beginning of the first millennium BC.

The historicity of the Trojan War is an issue. The jihadi mission of conventional scholarship to erase it or to reduce it to fiction continued for centuries. Fiction it cannot be; the detail and cohesion show a reporting element being of cardinal importance (Scott 1909). Fiction may exist where there is literary abundance; where there is scarcity, fiction is not needed, nor is it possible. The shreds of literacy need something very spectacular to be primed, and this is, usually, a fact of notoriety or renown; emphasis on *fact*. This became painfully obvious with the digs of Schliemann, which unearthed the ruins of ancient cities. Frustrating as this was, the digs showed no road sign saying 'Troy'; no doorbell of Priam, to paraphrase a Greek philologist. Thus, it *may* have been the Troy, but it was not *unequivocally* the Troy. Moreover, there was no proof of a war, much less of *the* war recounted by Homer. It was a matter of ideology and prejudice, and this makes archaeological evidence, arguments and conclusions on the subject debatable even to this day. The issue of ideology was concealed, or camouflaged, as a matter of methodology and ethics. Schliemann was sloppy, compromised the area and was unethical, as someone else (Frank Calvert) had identified the site of Hissarlick and told him where to look. That he went to Troy when everybody said that he should not, that he unearthed some other Bronze-Age Greek *metropoleis* without the help of Calvert, including *the* Mycenae, is obviously of minor or no importance.

Well, yes, but Schliemann revealed it, and without him the skilful and methodical archaeologists who followed would have never dug there, blinded by the dogma. Schliemann believed and succeeded. He kicked Bronze-Age Greece into history, followed by Ventris, and this has never been forgiven. But it is also not forgotten.

While the facts are debatable, everyone may claim their share. The antagonists of the Trojan field may be Celts (Wilkens 1990), areas in the midst of SW Asia Minor (Pantazis 2006) or even extraterrestrials for as long as they are not identified as Greeks and their opposite numbers. But a VERY unpleasant reality enters here: the Classical Greeks, whose identity and existence is by now uncontested, thought that they were the descendants of the Homeric Greeks. And with much more fervour than the European Christianity considered the truth of the Dogma of the Holy Trinity; or at least with the same fervour and conviction. There were views and there were diversions. Both literary and representation sources show us that there were other episodes and versions of the *Iliad* than the one we are familiar with. It is an edited corpus, produced in mid-sixth-century Athens by Onomacritus, a scholar and seer who was serving a (pair of) tyrants, the sons of Peisistratus of Athens. This scholar was a strange person: he was persecuted for corrupting another corpus and exiled (Hdt VII.6,3); once his liege was exiled too, they both sought refuge at the Persian court and the scholar-seer kept swelling the ego, ambition and greed of their host sovereign with omens that Greece was going to succumb (Hdt VII.6,4); which never happened.

This man could well have corrupted the corpus we inherited; some decades earlier a true sage, Solon of Athens, reportedly did so for propaganda purposes (Plut, *Vit Solon* 10); and there is at least one very suspect piece in the Iliad which seems out of context, but very much within the context of sixth- to fifth-century Athens. An ionization of the language can be detected, for example by the use of the suffix '-ides' for patronymics, instead of '-idas' in Dorian and possibly Aeolian (*-ijo* in Linear B tablets); an imperfect one, thus implying a process somehow paused. And one cannot but wonder: if there was such corruption and additional versions and material in reference to the official 'cut' in Athens, what about Lacedaimon or any other mainland metropolis which participated, such as Chalcis?

The Greeks of the classical age knew there was the possibility, if not the certainty, of corruption, although the issue in oral tradition is the fidelity of transmission through generations, as maintained by different tribes that still pass such oral traditions from mouth to ear. The extent – and the cause – of such corruption was an issue. Some philosophers rejected the core of the epics, their morality and their moral instructiveness (Xenophanes, *Poet Phil Frag* 12.3). Some others, especially the narrow-minded Thucydides, doubted some of the practical aspects, such as the size of the fleet or the duration of the siege (Thuc I.11,1). Not for any good reason; imperial Athens was habitually undertaking two-year-long sieges, as at Potidaea (Thuc II.70,5). The Phoenician metropolis, Tyre, endured the 586–573 BC siege by Nebuchadnezzar II of Babylon and *nobody* doubts the length of said siege. They also knew that the Trojan War was the epilogue of their Heroic Age and the only one for which they had some cohesive corpus. There were many more epics than the Homeric ones; the *Fall of Ilium* and *Aethiopis* being just two examples, both created by Arctinus the Milesian, allegedly a student of Homer. These two, plus the *Little Iliad* of Lesches, Arctinus' student, which kind of bridges them together, are sequels to the *Iliad*. On the other hand, *Oedipus, Thebais, Successors* and *the Cyprian Epics* contain information that makes them prequels to the *Iliad*, while *The Returns of the Heroes* is the prequel to the *Odyssey*, following the *Fall of Ilium*.

The epic legends of previous generations, such as Hercules and Theseus, have reached us by compilations produced during the classical age and later; Apollodorus is one important though late source. They may have been corrupted, as such material was *interpreted* by the Classical Greeks themselves, especially in terms of geography (Arrian, *Anab* II.16,5–6) and geopolitics; the collapse of the Mediterranean in the dawn of the first millennium eliminated records and knowledge. And there *was* corruption for propaganda: Periclean Athens edited and circulated versions of the mythology, adding their arch-hero Theseus *everywhere*, which became proverbial (Plut, *Vit Thes* 29). It is no small wonder that some of the ancient Greeks were indeed pondering over the issue of the interpretation of the myths and epics, in terms of figures of speech and in any other way conceivable by their inquisitive nature (Arrian, Anab II.16,5; Palaephatus, *De Incredibilibus; Philostratus, Heroic*). They did question the authority of Homer, as well as his objectivity. They did not question the facts of the Trojan War as it was narrated (the timeline was always an issue) nor the existence of Homer; of *one* Homer having authored the Epics assigned to him. The American E.A. Poe is one man who wrote prodigiously. The Poes are many men and women. The latter are not the true, collective nature of the former. That simple.

It is true that the Homeric Epics show a prominent pastoralism and, more to the point, a heavy preponderance of livestock (Pantazis 2006). It is a society living around livestock, with raids and all, with the princelings helping in herding these assets. But this does not mean a substandard material culture: in the Far West, technology, from the railway to the telegraph to the revolver, was in abundance; still, cattle were the essential commodity and the rich ranchers participated, with their sons and nephews, in conducting or supervising such work, mainly performed by cowboys. The Far-Westerner rich rancher was not a tied yuppy. He was working hard, getting dirty and gory. This is the same with the world of Homer. It has industrial scale production in fabric, transportation and some crude telecoms by beacons, but the livestock was of paramount importance and the value of things was assessed in oxen (Peacock 2017), although precious metals were reportedly counted by weight (Brown 1998); the weights being supposedly the invention of Palamedes (Phil, *Her* 33,1). Whether this was a unit of currency, similar to the European Currency Unit/ECU before the latter became the Euro, or some kind of coin with an ox imprinted, may not be determined with certainty; coinage was supposedly invented later, by the Lydian empire, but as with literacy, a hiatus could suggest another reality. Whether Palamedes, the sage-inventor, can be possibly credited with standard coin (Phil, *Her* 33,1) or some other system of comparative value is debatable.

The limitations and pitfalls

These reasons compel the enhancement of the narrative of the Homeric epics as undertaken in this book, in order to try to present a possible, or rather plausible, reality in a geopolitical context centred on the ten-year campaign. Other epics and ancient literary sources are taken into account and expand the timeline and the horizon of events, although in cases of ambiguity there is no set algorithm. Gaps are filled and interpretations are based on material evidence unearthed by archaeology, especially regarding the Hittites, the Mycenaean citadels and Bronze-Age artefacts reminiscent of the Homeric text; but a healthy scepticism is recommended in all cases. And last, comparative historical accounts, with similar practices from other timelines of similar regimes, are occasionally used to bridge gaps. In any case, one should remember that the epics, especially the Homeric ones (being the only intact ones) are, in terms of narrative, a great advancement towards history, compared with middle-eastern practices exemplified by the commemorative Egyptian accounts carved on state propaganda inscriptions. The practice continued all the way to the late fourth century by the Achaemenids, as in Behistun and Persepolis, at a time the Greeks had securely entered the realm of scientific history. The *Songs of Homer* are the progenitors of Herodotean history and although containing features such as the prosaic accounts for alpha-males weakens any arguments for historicity, tactical and technical context, reasoning and complexity create an integrated and cohesive account of events. The detailed accounts they contain suggest different sources, but the cohesion of the synthesis suggests just one mastermind; they were most probably written to be created, so as to integrate the details and continuity, but orally transmitted ever afterwards, similarly to all popular songs of the music industry in the twentieth century. The first written version of the epics being lost for centuries, they were collected and written down as a project which would gain the family of Peisistratus and the city of Athens great fame within the Greek world.

The contractor for the project, as mentioned earlier, is well-known, a sage of sorts: Onomacritus, friend to Hipparchus, the younger son of the Tyrant Peisistratus. His career was chequered: after collating the Homeric Poems to produce the versions we currently possess (other versions *did* exist) he was commissioned to do the same with the *Orphics*, especially the *Hymns of Musaeus*. But he was caught counterfeiting them and was summarily sacked. Weirdly, Herodotus does not mention the … misunderstanding, nor that he had the responsibility for editing the *Iliad* and the *Odyssey*. This story says a lot: there were people with sufficient knowledge to intercept such practices, but also the sanctity of the oral transmission, which is supposed to be memorized and communicated verbatim by carefully selected, gifted individuals, seems to have been compromised. Some decades before, Solon the Wise had done the same for political reasons. The forger sage was approached anew by the surviving clan of Peisistratus sometime after 510, probably after 505, and possibly as late as 485 BC, in their quest to petition Persian help from Xerxes so as to be reinstated in Athens (Hdt VII.6,3), but this was after the perturbed Hipparchus, who had recruited him and then sacked him, had been murdered by a dissident faction sometime around 520 BC.

Thus, the Homeric poems may have been corrupted by intention as well; there are scenes in decorated pottery and tragedy that clearly belong to the context of the *Iliad* but are not present in our version of it. Additionally, there were a number of further compositions developing the subject, or expanding it. The latter referred to the lore of different lands of the heroic age, and episodes known from the existing epics but loosely associated with them, such as the siege of Thebes. The former comprises epics directly referring to the Trojan War and its aftermath, possibly some events before it and leading to it. Importantly, before the Trojan War, not merely before the context of the *Iliad*, which is narrating just a few days of the last year of a ten-year campaign (not war). Further works from different sources (and, obviously, schools) are also there to highlight some issues and provide additional coverage: The works of Diktys the Cretan, nominally a soldier of the Greeks, and of Dares the Phrygian, a Trojan priest, were unearthed much later, something in the order of half a millennium later than the latest versions of the epics. Both works gained notoriety in the West at times when Homer was lost and out of vogue. Dares, being the only source from the Trojan side, must have existed in more than one version, as some secondary sources mention scenes and events not included in the existing, fairly complete version of this work (Zangger 2016).

For many reasons Dares was considered an authority in medieval, Roman-obsessed Europe, setting a fashion of Trojan lineage in different royal houses. The fact though is that being considered an eyewitness, and his name being mentioned in the *Iliad* (V-910), his ethnic name is out of context. From the time of the Trojan War there is not one mention of Phrygians. It is true that our sources for the ethnology of the area are Hittite, and not strictly native ones, but for someone to sign his work as 'Dares the Phrygian', then the term is not a Greek invention; the word *Phrygian* must have been used in some language alien but known to the Geeks, and that did happen many years, nay, centuries later than the events reported. Thus, either our knowledge of the ethnology of that era is sorely limited and perhaps erroneous, or there is an issue with the genuineness of this work. After all, other works on the subject were composed much later, and prototype works, not compilations, including the *Aeneid* of Virgil.

Thus, there are three insurmountable obstacles in a historical approach: the first is the timeline; the Greek lore is problematic, and in cases inconsistent, and there are few solid estimates, counted in years – and these present an uncertainty of some 70 years, too much for a historical account. Archaeology is even worse: dating is performed using a number of methods, each with some givens, but both their linearity and correctness are somewhat overstated. These methods seemed obvious and solid, but this was rather PR and wishful thinking, as insinuated by the repeated revisions. True, one can only do his best, but there is an interesting Greek saying that 'fairly good and the best are enemies'. Thus, when the Greek lore is not in accordance with archaeology, this does not mean a priori that the former is mistaken or corrupted.

Similarly, meticulously kept archives are also not without mistakes, both spontaneous (due to the level of knowledge) and intentional (propaganda).

The volumes of archives of both sides in the Second World War are a very nice example of such manipulation, and falsification of archives is a favourite for a corruption and special operations' Olympics…

Politics is the second issue. In here, religious matters must be included; religion is by definition policy, as it sets a framework of social conduct and way of life. The vitriolic comments of some academics onto anything corresponding to Homeric archaeology, which would be the equivalent of Biblical archaeology, show a mysterious zest reeking of prejudice, only superficially disguised as academicity. The Homeric Archaeology is contested both by the said academics as accounting to different tradition verging on the reconsideration of the past, and the adamant atheists, as any highly religious version of science is extremely unwelcome. Science and reason *must* be the prerogative of atheism, and reverent open-mindedness is a most unwelcome pole in the universal fight for the proper lifestyle (*Eu Zein*) as coined by the Greeks. Similarly, ardent Christians of many doctrines are by default hostile to any non-Christian tradition being proven true in any sense: these were the 'lies of the Pagans'. The Christian intolerance even to monotheistic doctrines, including some Christian ones that are considered as heresies, is monumental; it is with very great effort and through the Enlightenment that such fervour was appeased, but the painstakingly new-found tolerance was reserved first of all for other Christians and then for monotheistic religions. The very science of the West being initially nurtured in church-sponsored universities of the Catholic church means the open-mindedness always has its limitations, congenital ones, and accepting a pagan lore of intense religiousness, with divine interventions as prominent as in the Bible, is naturally out of the question.

This is not pure religion: in many countries the 'Creationists' are considered a scientific position, similar to the 'Evolutionists', despite dating the world to 4004 BC. If this preposterous idea still claims support and scientific status, other, less preposterous ones do too, and traditions and archaeology promoting myths, history, beliefs and ways of life competing with a given set of principles – a doctrine – are eagerly if not fanatically discouraged.

There is a tripartite ideological caterpillar. It consists of the different aspects of Western atheism and capitalism, Eastern atheism in the form of communism, and the East–West consensus that monotheism is the way to go and a superior system of worship (the differences amongst the three most popular Monotheistic systems notwithstanding). This caterpillar is meant to mow down anything devoted to any other religion and seems unstoppable as it moves to it.

And then, there are the current key-masters: especially after the creation of Israel in 1948, which leveraged historic arguments of belonging, but actually after the historic rebirth of Greece in 1821 (factually in 1829) in much the same terms, the Turks, current dwellers and inhabitants of the theatre of the Trojan War, are not very fond of the idea of having large parts of Asia Minor excavated only to unearth monuments showing the recent nature of their presence therein; especially if such findings, directly or indirectly, favour claims from their enemies just to the west, the Greeks, the previous owners of such estates for at least 3,000 years – or a bit less.

The Greeks on the other hand do have some issues within the EU that follows a strict pro-Roman protocol, as it is its thesis that Europe was created by the Roman Empire and that European history starts with the Romans (a fact that infuriates the Greeks, since the term *Europe* comes from their ancient lore). This problem is amplified by their own Greek Orthodox Church, which really dislikes ancient lore, especially if rich in pagan religion, and is criticized – actually, savagely accused – by the Russian Orthodox Church for being less attached to Christian dogma and verging towards leniency to pagan and also to atheist practices. Although religious freedom is a constitutional prerogative in Greece, this does not extend to natives that believe in the pagan gods; ancient religious sites are not returned to their proper use as places of worship when requested. The very high proportion of leftish bureaucracy, with a hostile attitude towards all things ethnic and national but for ethnic cookery and attire, creates a very unhelpful and adverse environment, underlined by (the lack of) any research of note for the era, especially in terms of military achievements. It must be stressed that, in a fit of intolerance, access to archaeological sites is conditional on attire style, not coverage. It is forbidden for people dressed in the ancient Greek way to approach even for the secular use of such places. Modern attire (with an allowance for local colour) is mandatory. In the 90s, there was an urban legend (*legend*, as it is difficult to trace it today in the Internet) that a Kalash committee invited by some concern or other to the ancient cradle in a set of exchanges, after being re-discovered by modern Greece, tried to visit an archaeological site. Since they had no standard Muslim attire, as Afghan or Pakistani citizens, nor European, and their own traditional one was rather ancient(ish), they were not admitted!

Third and last, but not least, is the issue of infighting amongst different scientific communities. There have been books, one from a distinguished archaeologist deeply involved in excavations in Asia Minor, referring to other locations and civilizations that demanded redirecting resources (both material and immaterial; very few people make movies about the Hittites) away from the scientifically unsubstantiated issues of Troy. This was of course to be redirected towards his own area of expertise, which was producing actual and actionable results.

In this work there are clear priorities: anything related to war, from geopolitics and religion to metallurgy, is taken seriously. The Homeric issue, referring to the identity, origin and age of the poet, or the Homeric geography are not. Homer is considered as an excellently informed, very capable and inspired, individual man who may have witnessed the war, but most probably not. He must have come into possession of something like the heraldic accounts of battles, as was the custom in medieval Europe, where the antagonists formally signed the account of a battle and the deeds naming victor and vanquished. And, of course, he composed in writing a single corpus for each epic poem. It is thus understood that at the time of the events there was writing. The Greek hero who Homer never speaks about, Palamedes (Phil, *Her* 43,1), was credited with the invention of letters, and this may refer to the transition from the Linear B to alphabetic writing. Temporal anomalies are irrelevant when the timelines are this confused; as the biosciences insist, in issues methodological, one's methods should have better discriminatory power than one's conclusions – and this is seldom taken as a rule in humanities. In this case, no one can say when alphabetical writing was introduced; we may have found indications of its use, but nothing precludes earlier introduction and parallel use with the Linear B script, as was the case with the Egyptian inscriptions in two different native writing systems, as in the Rosetta Stone.

The author understands the impact of geography on military operations, but this has been exaggerated by many researchers, scholars or not. Actually, geography becomes crucial for military history only when it becomes restrictive to the events: if the footprint of the protagonists, taken as the functional sizes of all of them (i.e. the spatial extent of their deployment and their prospective mobility) extends the limits of a homogeneous and well-defined geographical area. For example, the terrain is irrelevant for the Battle of Marathon. The battle, not the campaign, could have occurred in many other locations and develop similarly or identically, with few possible deviations. On the contrary, the Battle of Thermopylae would have never developed as it did if it were to occur elsewhere; the use of available forces was adapted and took advantage of the terrain as a key factor of the actual battle. There are indeed some very interesting cases of doubting conventional wisdom, prominent amongst which is Pantazis (2006) *Homer and Troy* (in Greek). Still, the present work sees the Troy of Priam in Hissarlik, following in many aspects Zangger's work of 2016 about the Luwian hypothesis and does not dwell upon the arguments of Pantazis. The solution is fraught with problems; this is the curse of Homeric archaeology and history. It has not been resolved for millennia. Here, trying to understand better the fighting and support elements and procedures exhausts the ambition of the author. Extensive dwelling on the myths and archaeogeography are kept to a minimum, so as to form the background for understanding the *military history* of the Trojan War.

Some symmetry is always nice in the context of Ancient Greece. This introduction started with what this work is; it should end with how this work is set out. The book is divided into three parts: the protagonists, where the two enemies are described in one section each, and, in a separate section, the Heroes – of both sides – as a social and military entity and as people. The second part describes Homeric warfare in the conventional Bronze Age context, but also taking into account less conventional aspects, particular to the era or of ubiquitous historical relevance. And the third part reappraises the Greek/Achaean campaign against Troy. Both ancient and modern sources are used; for the *Iliad* and the *Odyssey*, references include Roman numbers for the books; uppercase for the *Iliad*, lowercase for the *Odyssey*. The numbers in Arabic digits refer to the line, in the case of poetry. All other – prose – sources are referenced by writer, work if the writer has authored more than one, then book by Roman numbers and then, in Arabic digits, section and paragraph where applicable.

Part I

The Lore Thus Far

Section 1

Who is Who – the Mycenaeans

Chapter 1

Revisiting the Myths

A) The distant past for the glorious days

Greek mythology presents many gaps and issues of chronological order. But if read without prejudice and with an open mind, it seems to offer accurate and coherent historical data. It should be emphasized from the beginning that historians, in order to accept lore as history, require it to be written. But when it is written, and Herodotus is an excellent example, more rules apply to deny historicity on request. Thus, there is no good reason not to consider a myth as history; written history is accepted on a provisional basis. It is a given, of course, that uncertainties in myth are manifold and of considerable impact, worse than in written history. Nevertheless, it is a quantitative, not qualitative difference. Written sources in many cases lie blatantly due to prejudice and other restrictions; but they are generally considered as 'sources'. The errors in historicity may be due to the composer of the epics, if he were much too late, or to the editors, or to both.

There is no creation myth for the Mycenaean world. The introductory myths of the Greeks do not contain a chapter about arrival, either. They never admitted arriving from anywhere else. They were born from the land. After the Deluge, and with Mount Parnassus as the epicentre, the sole surviving couple, within an ark, Deucalion and his wife Pyrra, asked the Gods for subjects. They were advised to throw stones behind them and, when they did, humans emerged (Apollod I.7,2). There is another such myth, for a much later instance, just two generations before the Trojan War, where ants became men to populate the kingdom of Aiacus, son of Zeus (Paus II.29,2), grandfather to Achilles. In both cases, the subterranean and local attributes should be noted as characteristics of the new populations. Underdogs of the previous status quo, hitherto hiding, or survivors from a natural disaster, may be inferred. However, interpreting the myths through symbolism is a very poor scientific practice and, even when there is no alternative, it should be avoided.

The main lore for the ancient Greeks is the five generations of the heroes, one of the five iterations of the human presence on earth (Hes,

Works 110/170). One can track in these the Age of the Heroes, after the Bronze and before the Iron Age. Their tale starts in NE Peloponnese, in the plain of Argolis, where two siblings, Acrisius and Proitus, rule neighbouring cities (Argos and Tiryns), and occasionally fight amongst themselves. They are the twin sons of Avas (Apollod II.2,1), progenitor of a Greek clan, or warrior brotherhood, the Avandes, who in the years of the Trojan War reside in the island of Euboea (II-536/43), just opposite Boeotia and thus away from the Argolid.

This happens some five generations after Danaus arrived at the Argolid, wresting the kingship from the local ruler by public vote (Paus II.19,3–4). It is the first name we hear for this area. Danaus, who gave his name to the Peloponnesian Greeks for centuries – and in Homer – came from Egypt. But he actually was *returning* to his roots after a sojourn in Egypt (Paus II.16,1), with his 50 daughters and his brother Aigyptos (the exact word in Greek for Egypt), who sired 50 sons (Apollod II.1). The family had emigrated to Egypt in a previous generation; they were repatriating émigrés in the Argolid. They came back by sea: Danaus is credited with being the first to build a ship (Apollod II.1,4), and the Egyptians had very questionable relations with the blue element.

The lore does not report the foundation of the city of Argos in the Argolid by the newcomers; that had been founded generations earlier by Phoroneus and named after him 'City of Phoroneus' (Paus II.15,5). Not by a single word, which is very untypical for the Greeks throughout the ages. At the time, what is now the Peloponnese was named by other progenitors Apia and Pelasgia (thus the abode of Pelasgians), while the City of Phoroneus was similarly named Argos by a hero bearing this name (Apollod II.1,2). The Greek lore assigns toponyms to humans, a very old practice seen throughout Eurasia. Usually, recurring toponyms indicate migrations and/or colonization, as exemplified by the Alexandrias in the classical world, but it is possible that some toponyms are descriptive in meaning and thus, as such, identity is irrelevant to the origin of the inhabitants.

The lore does not record the ethnic or tribal name of the natives of Argolis at the time of Danaus; Argives must have been a valid name for the inhabitants of the city, but this remains controversial for the wider area. Pelasgians might come to mind, as one of the two older names of the Peloponnese was Pelasgia (from Pelasgus, a hero born in Arcadia though, definitely outside of Argolis). The other was Apia (Apollod II.1,1; Paus II.5,7). That the Danaids simply ruled over local inhabitants, who then took the name of the ruling Danaus, is evident. No matter how numerous the two households had been, the sons of the one brother were betrothed to the daughters of the other, who murdered their husbands – but for one. The offspring of this single happy couple was Avas (Apollod II.2,1). Thus, there is no way the people over whom Avas' sons ruled were progeny of Danaus.

Enter the twin sons of Avas (Apollod II.2,1). One of them, Acrisius, first of all tries to get rid of his brother Proitus, but the latter escapes to Lycia in SW Asia Minor, marries into the court of Iobates, the local ruler and finally returns with a vengeance with Lycian troops to assist him. He takes half the kingdom from his brother and founds and fortifies the city of Tiryns to rule (Apollod II.2,1; Paus II.16,2). Said Acrisius has some problems with the succession, because an oracle warns that his grandson will slay him; it is the myth of Perseus. After some soap-opera scenes, Perseus, sired by Zeus, is growing up peacefully with his mother Danae (a name in honor of Danaus) in Seriphos, an island of western Cyclades, as guests of Dictys, a fisherman (Apollod II.4,1). Polydectes, the brother of Dictys, was the local King. The title accounts for the Mycenaean petty chief *basireus* rather than any fairytale kingling with crown, castle, gardens and knights.

Lust-stricken for Danae, Polydectes tries to get rid of the lad by machinating impossible tasks that are causally related with the enthronement and marriage of Pelops (Apollod II.4,2), beyond the narrow sea lane *and* the whole width of Peloponnesus! This sets the stage for the first of the heroes, an offspring of Zeus, who gains his fame by his courage, skill, wits and divine protection through the Goddess Athena. His adventures initiate the geopolitics of the dawn of the heroic age of the Greek Lore.

A diversion is needed. Perseus is the first *Hellene*, *Greek* or whatever, known to us. With Perseus we start *knowing* things, despite some reluctance to admit it. He is the first human offspring of Zeus in the Peloponnese. He is the first hero; the five generations of the heroes start with him and end with the sons of Hercules. For him we have information about the kit and weapons he used in his adventures; we know he was under the wing of Athena and of other Gods. He founded the city of Mycenae (Paus II.15,4; Apollod II.4,4), he invented the throwing of discus/quoit as a pastime (Paus II.16,2). His myth is entangled with another hero, Bellerophon and the two must have been roughly contemporaries, as King Proitus features in both cases.

Perseus came of age when Pelops acquired the kingdom of Pisa (Apollod II.4,2), which means actually *before* the Peloponnese took its current, historic name. Two generations before, during his grandfather's reign, the Greeks started using shields (Paus II.25,7), and in his day they were using chariots; Pelops won his bride at a chariot race, and against a fully armed enemy, King Oenomaus of Pisa, outfitted by Ares in person, and operating in a two-man crew with his driver being the son of Hermes (Diod IV.73; Apollod E.2,3–7). This suggests fully fledged chariot warfare. Thus Perseus must be considered the first hero. There were other personalities in Greece before him, such as the two founding Theban dynasties. The term hero starts with him, though. And this term has nothing to do with what we understand now. It is rather a social distinction; a knight would be a good parallel, as knightly behaviour was introduced much later than the orders and institutions of knights. Thus, obscure figures in the *Iliad* are mentioned as 'heroes'; they had done nothing memorable, they had shown no great courage or devotion beyond their duty, or anything else. They were simply members of a warrior caste; Samurai may be just as good a parallel. They had the heroic code, their lineage was chequered but important; God(esse)s routinely intervened for their conception. Rather than supposing simply embellishing bastard origin, this lineage should be interpreted as offspring of the priesthood, similar to the Boys of the Temple of other ancient civilizations; the female offspring under similar conditions of constitutional 'father unknown' bastardhood were probably designated 'nymphs'. The concept of heroes will be further discussed later on. Here, it will suffice to say that god-born heroes were in line for any throne and, should they kill their grandfather, they were free of guilt of patricide; just manslaughter, for which ritual purification was more than enough (Apollod II.1,5). Understandably, a very cruel Acrisius was mortally infuriated with his daughter Danae being impregnated by 'Zeus', no less (Apollod II.4,1) – a coup in the making, literally.

Back to Perseus. It is important that slightly to the south-west of Seriphos lies the island of Melos, with established late-Stone-Age maritime contacts with the Argolid, due to the extra-hard obsidian stone found even as a surface deposit there. A neolithic settlement has been discovered there, at Philakopi. The Western Cyclades are proven to have traded by sea with the Argolid. Moreover, despite some lame excuses from conventional archaeology, some pyramidal structures discovered in the Argolic plain defy conventional archaeology's wisdom and preconceptions and are very old, which corroborates the report that these were the tombs of the fallen during the civil war between two brothers: Acrisius, ruler of Argos (grandfather to Perseus) and Proitus, actual founder and king of Tiryns (Paus II.16,2). This was reportedly the first battle where shields were used (Paus II.25,7) – or, at least, the first such use in Greece, perhaps implying a distinct Greek model invented/developed in converging evolution and not adopted/transplanted by other civilizations and cultures. Still, the shield type is not reported, but the figure-of-eight shield (see below) could fit the description.

At the same time, the myth of Perseus introduces some very enlightening elements. The first is the near and far geography of a more or less interacting world, which will be discussed later. Second comes the kit: in his quest to slay Medusa, he uses a god-issued three-piece kit. The helmet of invisibility, of unknown style. Then, a shield of polished bronze which was used as a mirror (Apollod II.4,2). This item differs from anything Egyptian and indicates something like the later Herzsprung all-bronze, central-grip shields *but* for the lack of any decoration hammered or incised on its surface as this would mar its use as a mirror. Assyrian models may be related to this piece, although dating is elusive both in absolute and relative terms. Of course, bronze-faced shields are also a possibility; these models are ubiquitous in the *Iliad* and earlier in technology and use than the Herzsprung.

The third piece is of immense interest. It is described as a scythe or rather sickle in Greek, and the term '*harpe*' (Apollod II.4,2) is the same used for the asymmetrically curved stringed musical instrument (*harp*), most typical of the Egyptian musical and cultural environment. But the weapon must have been a typical (Egyptian or oriental) *kopesh* curved blade, a type which might have evolved to similar sickle-like hand weapons used by Hittites and Luwians; i.e. Lycians (Sekunda 1992) and Carians (Hdt V.112,2).

In the continuation of the lore centred on Perseus, there is Bellerophon, who faces problems similar to those of Perseus but this time with Proitus. Reading the myth further, with Bellerophon being sent by Proitus to Iobates, his father-in-law, one finds that the Greeks of that era used writing (VI-168/70) but the ability to read was limited and perhaps the prerogative of royalty, whether through education or through the use of scribes; the myth is not specific but mentions execution directives along with an incriminating report, written from one king to another. Along with the sparse mention of horses, centred on Pegasus (Hes, *Theog* 280/1 & 325), one feels like one is witnessing the birth of Greek warfare of the heroic age. Additionally, Perseus is credited with the invention of the discus/quoit, a sporting contraption so lethal (Paus II.16,2) that it could have been nothing short of a missile weapon, given that *all* the Greek sports were simulating warlike drills and exercises with direct usefulness in warfare. The specifics of weaponry, though, are discussed elsewhere.

At some point, two forces, perhaps related dynasties, begin to emerge. Thebes in Central Greece, and Mycenae in the Peloponnese, founded by the bloodline of Danaus, who named the people of the Argolic plain after himself (Danaans), despite being a foreigner in all but origin. His bloodline had been abroad for generations as emigrants.

But across the Gulf of (yet-to-be) Corinth, in the north, other events where unfolding. An expeditionary mission from the Levant was wandering, searching princess Europe, the sister of its headman. Actually, it might well have been sent to *explore* Europe. After some wandering they established themselves at Thebes, with divine intervention. It is the Myth of Cadmus (Apollod III.1). The deities of Olympus were always temperamental and somehow favoured the newcomer (Apollod III.4,2) against the natives, who were under the patronage of the war god Ares and dubbed 'The Sowed Ones', meaning the nativity as opposed to arrival/immigration (Apollod III.4,1). These were mostly massacred but *some* preferentially integrated into the new state of affairs (Apollod III.4,1). This obviously refers to the aristocracy; the newcomers, once firmly established, founded a city. One should rather understand a citadel, named after their chieftain, Cadmeia, a must in order to barricade themselves amongst the natives who lived dispersed, in a pre-urban manner. They were right to do so. They were expelled, and resumed wandering (Apollod III.5,4); their chief died old and happy away from his citadel, while the natives, under Zethos and Amphion, took over. They proceeded with the urbanization and walled the city, practically miraculously. The reality behind the miracle is of little consequence; the important thing is that the city of Thebes emerged, walled and ready for magnificence, under a local royal family that named the city 'Thebes' (Apollod III.5,5–7) and with matrimonial ties through Niobe, the bride of one of the brothers, Amphion (Apollod III.5,5), with the Hittites.

However, said family was exterminated by divine intervention again (Apollod III.5,6), and the bloodline of Cadmus (the name sounds oriental, *Cadmon*) was re-established thanks to the integrated locals who proved faithful to their acquired allegiance (Paus IX.5,3). Polydorus, son of Cadmus (Apollod III.4,2), and Polydorus' son Labdakus reigned before the throne went to the local dynasty (Apollod III.5,5). It finally rebounded to Laius, son of Labdakus (Apollod III.5,7) after he returned from his self-exile to the court of King Pelops, whose son Chrysippus he raped (Apollod III.5,5), thus incurring the curse of the Labdakids. Given that the third generation of the offspring of Cadmus was directly involved with Pelops and one of his sons, the synchronization with Danaus is possible, as Perseus was a youth when Pelops married. It follows that Cadmus must have been roughly contemporary with the daughter of Danaus and her husband Lynceus (Apollod II.19,6).

Two brothers, on the other hand, were reigning over two miraculous cities. The first was Sisyphus, the wisest and most cunning man ever to live, and he founded Ephyra (Apollod I.9,3), which would become Corinth.

The other city was Orchomenus, near Thebes, run by Athamas, brother to Sisyphys (Apollod I.9,1). Possibly an older establishment, it came to prominence and its wealth was legendary even after its decline, as is obvious by Achilles' assertion comparing it with the Thebes of Egypt (IX-381/4). Probably such wealth was directly or indirectly accounted for by trade with the east. Niobe, the daughter of Tandalus (Tudaliya?) and sister of Pelops (Diod IV.74,3) had been married to Amphion (Apollod III.5,6), establishing contacts with the Hittites while Ino, daughter of Cadmus (Apollod III.4,2) and thus of Levantine pedigree was married to Athamas (Apollod I.9,1), linking Orchomenus with the Levantine trade.

The lore with the successive marriages and the soap-opera drama of the house of Athamas resulted in his firstborn, Phrixus, finding refuge at the extremities of the earth, in Colchis run by the Mage-King Aeates. Thus the Golden Fleece is introduced into Greek lore (Apollod I.9,1–2). The Argonauts will claim the prize some two generations later or less: the grandsons of King Athamas are mentioned as participating in the quest (Apollod I.9,1), but they were young, perhaps teenagers.

King Athamas, ejected from his realm, trekked north-east to the north of the Gulf of Malis and carved an area, Athamantia (Apollod I.9,2), for himself, his followers and their kin, leaving Orchomenus to Clymenus and his son Erginus, who imposed authority and reparations in the form of tribute upon Thebes. Given that Hercules will literally bust their skulls (Apollod II.4,11), this change of regime must have coincided with the decline of Orchomenus causally; though, if a cause or result, remains debatable.

The other important issue with Corinth is that it produced, through the line of Sisyphus, one of the two first Greek heroes: the grandson of Sisyphus, Bellerophon (Paus II.4,3). The timeline is always hazy, but Bellerophon belonged to the lifespan of Perseus, although he must have been somewhat older. Thus Sisyphus and Athamas are contemporary with Acrisius and Proitus and coincide with the fortification of Tiryns and the establishment of the second Greek–Oriental axis, the one between Argos and Lycia by Proitus and Iobates (Apollod II.2,1), as opposed to the one of Thebes–Hatussa by Amphion and Tandalus, while there was also the Orchomenus–Levant by Athamas and Ino.

Greek fortunes in the east were declining: the line of Bellerophon succumbed to neighbours of the natives in Lycia (VI-190/205); Ilus in north-west Asia Minor, in the Troad, had long ago ejected Pelops and thus severed the links of Tandalus with central Greece (XX-230/2; Diod IV.74–5), which must have been compromised by the gimmicks of Athamas (Apollod I.9,2) and the Theban brawls (Apollod III.6,1). Thus, the developing Greek states that flourished by commerce had only the western option and the northern, to the north coast of the Aegean, made accessible by Hercules. The Levant was always challenging at the very least, including any trade concessions with Egypt. In this light, the kings of such cities and the (private) concerns that were quite powerful as seen in the *Odyssey* (ii-1/80) would do anything to open the route to the Black Sea and the main European waterway, the Danube. Pelias, king of such a city, Iolcus, tasked Jason to do exactly that (Hes, *Theog* 995/6), betting on the impossible. But the concerns were such, and so powerful, that it resulted in an exploratory campaign of the whole of Greece (Apollod I.9,16): the quest for the Golden Fleece, with the Argonauts meticulously selected by the advice of Cheiron, the sage Centaur (Apollonius Rhod, *Argon* I.33).

B) Mycenae ascending

Perseus, son of Zeus and maternal grandson of King Acrisius of Argos, son of Av(ant)as, took the throne by right of succession but exchanged it with that of Tiryns, ruled by Megapenthes, son of Proitus, brother of Acrisius. Perseus founded, after becoming king of Tiryns, the city of Mycenae, which guarded the entrance to the Argolic plain from the north. Thus, his part of the kingdom had two major cities, Tiryns and the newly established Mycenae.

Proitus won Tiryns by carving out half of the kingdom from his usurping brother with the help of his father-in-law Iobates of Lycia (VI-166/80), where he had taken refuge when ejected by Acrisius (Apollod II.2,1). Proitus, who first hosted and then sent the first human hero of Greek lore, Bellerophon, to Lycia on a suicide mission, seems to have been establishing cordial trans-Aegean relations, as mentioned earlier, which would be disrupted after many years, in the time of, and due to, king Priam of Troy and Sarpedon of Lycia. The Hittite records corroborate the Greek myth: the Hittite Madawatta headed an insurgency of the south-western provinces from the central authority of Hattusa and developed cordial relations with the Achaeans. After many phases and adventures, the realm was brought back under the Hittite imperial control. The myth of Bellerophon (VI 150–205) says exactly this: that Iobates became a close friend, bonded by hospitality and matrimony with the Kings of Tiryns, who repaid his assistance in winning the throne by dispatching heroic warrior(s), possibly expendables, to assist in his struggle with his embittered ex-overlord and other local enemies.

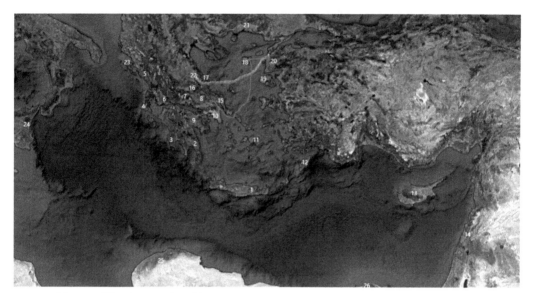

Map 1.1: The theatre of the Trojan War and its world

The itinerary to Troy was well-known, by the time of the Argonauts (thick line connecting numbers 22 to 20) and Hercules' campaign. But possible defences, or alterations due to the pharaonic projects of Priam, port facilities and shore improvements would have been something new and have affected the landing. Additionally, the massive 1,200 vessels of Agamemnon's fleet (thin line connecting numbers 15, 18 and 20) needed to locate shores to call in at night, so as to reassemble in the morning to continue, enemy islands that had to be subdued and itineraries that allowed proximity of the vessels, in order to support each other and keep some distance to not hinder each other, especially in choppy seas or if under attack by the Trojan navy. Such a fleet negotiating the currents of the Hellespont was not an easy proposition, exacerbated by the need to manoeuvre to assault positions, coordinate and keep formation so as to implement a contested landing.

1: Crete; 2: Sparta; 3: Pylos; 4: Ithaca in Cephalonia; 5: Ephyra in Thesprotia; 6: Calydon in Aetolia; 7: Delphi in Phocis; 8: Boeotia; 9: Mycenae, Argos, Tiryns in Argolid; 10: Athens; 11: The Cyclades Isles; 12: Rhodes; 13: Cyprus; 14: The Levant/Phoenicia; 15: Euboea; 16: Phthia; 17: Pelion Mt; 18: Lemnos; 19: Lesbos; 20: Troad; 21: Thrace; 22: Iolcus; 23: Corfu; 24: Sicily; 25: Libya ; 26: Egypt.

Eventually, though, the locals in SW Asia Minor prevailed; by killing Isander, the eldest son of Bellerophon, they brought the area back to Hittite loyalism. Such locals are mentioned in the *Iliad* as *Solymoi* (VI-184); they were probably under the suzerainty of the Hittites and accomplished the *reconquista* of the area.

It must be stressed that Bellerophon was most probably the first Greek warrior to use a horse in combat (Hes, *Theog* 325), and *riding* it at that; then again, this horse, Pegasus, was of divine origin (meaning it was exceedingly fast, big and strong, so as to carry a warrior on his back, not pull a vehicle) and came into existence at the time of Perseus miraculously (Hes, *Theog* 280/1), in faraway lands; possibly in Libya (Apollod II.4,2) but certainly *not* in Greece, as it was spawned from the blood of the slain Medusa. The steed was related by blood to the sea god Poseidon, lord of the herds, and bound by lore to Corinth (Paus II.3,5), the double port par excellence, for both western and eastern trade. Thus the rulers and sovereigns – and overlords – of the area had in their hands a novel asset for warfare, and this asset must have been imported by sea.

Perseus and Bellerophon were of the same generation; the first found and tamed Pegasus, the second used it in combat. Still, the latter must have been younger, as the second generation of his offspring, Glaucus and Sarpedon (VI-196/206) fought at Troy, compared to Perseus' fourth, Tlepolemus of Rhodes, the son of Hercules (II-657/8).

When Perseus founded Mycenae, he sired some legitimate and some illegitimate children, but two of these became Kings; Electryon in Mycenae (Apollod II.4,6) and Alceus in Tiryns; this double kingdom may be the secret meaning of the two lions of the kingdom's blazon, over the main gates, although other possibilities abound: the duality with Thebes, under later Perseids, or with Crete, under the Pelopids; or the Eastern and Western interests and expansion of the Mycenaean power. The legitimate sons of Electryon (but not Licymnius, the illegitimate one that could lay no claim to the throne) were slain in a raid, and the son and successor of Alceus, Amphitryon, married to the daughter of Electryon (and his own first cousin), Alkmene. After 'accidentally' killing Electryon with a club (reminiscent of the similar 'accident' of his grandfather Perseus, who had slain his own grandfather Acrisius) the signature weapon of his future son, Hercules, Amphitryon attempted to inherit his throne through his wife and reunite the kingdom of Perseus (Apollod II.4,6). It was not to be. Another son of Perseus, going by the name of Sthenelus, throneless, exiled the slayer, probably by projecting another version of the events that survived (Hes, *Sh* 80/5), and proposed a falling-out as the prelude to the murder. Sthenelus in any case questioned the legitimacy of a female liege – betrothed to the Kingslayer – and took the combined throne for himself and his firstborn son, Eurystheus, who became the next king (Apollod II.4,5), as he married into the emerging Pelopids (Apollod II.4,5). Amphitryon and Alcmene found refuge in Thebes (Apollod II.4,6), where Alcides was born to them, later to become Hercules.

Who is Hercules? He was probably a historical figure, but his identity is an issue, especially due to indications that the name was actually a title (similarly to the regal titles of *Pharaoh*, *Minos*, the eastern *Buddha*, religious prodigies, and the Jewish war leaders, *Messiah*), endowed to one prodigious person in a generation, either as a normal or as an ad hoc measure (meaning once in a number of generations). With the exception of the non-Greek namesakes or corresponding dignitaries, such as the Semitic Melkart, the Egyptian equivalent, etc. (Arr, *Anab* II.16,2–3), Pausanias distinguishes one Cretan Hercules (VIII.31,3), belonging to the clan of the Digits of Ida (Idaean Dactyls), and one from Thebes/Tiryns, the son of Amphitryon and Alcmene (IX.27,8). The latter was reportedly named Alcides when born, before being *recognized* as Hercules. Alcides was born in Thebes, a Boeotian by birth and was raised in the Kithairon mountain nearby, so he qualified as a shepherd. His mortal father, Amphitryon, was the heir of the throne of Tiryns, as mentioned already. His mother Alcmene, granddaughter to Perseus, kept her maternal lineage from the family of Pelops (Diod IV.9,1).

Alcides, as a young prince in exile, took an elaborate course of education, although he did not excel in all fields. He actually killed in a fit of rage his teacher of lyre and music in general, a competency necessary for both martial and princely education. This murder was partly an accident due to his excessive strength (Apollod II.4,9). Others were to follow, the result of a violent character and a lack of progress on the issue of harmony and self-constraint.

On the contrary, he excelled in other areas of knowledge. He became excellently versed in highly specialized areas, such as land improvement projects, practical toxicology, and some others and was particularly cunning. Therefore the Goddess Athena, originally a Boeotian divinity, 'born' to the south of Lake Copais, in Alalkomenai (IV-8), grew very fond of him and became his personal guardian goddess. Alcides as Hercules was a veritable strongman, a highly gifted wrestler with a typical basic sense of justice, but also with murderous fits of rage and a taste for the gentlemanly activities of stealing, kidnapping, and considering the easiest way of solving a problem the way the Mafia does, occasionally overstepping the not-very-fine line of sacrilege. Cutting off the noses of the dignitaries of Orchomenus (Apollod II.4,11) after overthrowing its supremacy was an act of sacrilege that no other Greek would ever dare to commit, and would surely have paid a steep price if he had.

This character defines the protégés of the wargod Mars (Ares) and not Athena, and thus raises some flags. Discipline had never been Hercules' strong point, even as a warrior. He did not employ the standard weaponry of the gentleman, like spear, sword and shield. Instead, he is bearded, wears an animal skin (lion skin to be exact), and uses a club and a bow with poisoned arrows (a formally forbidden practice in battle, as implied in Homer, amongst the civilized bourgeoisie). The use of poisoned arrows, on the other hand, was the prerogative of the divine archer, Apollo, the death-dealer ('Sminteus') and not of Athena. Apollo, with whom Hercules was to have some spectacular face-offs, like the one about the oracle at Delphi (Apollod II.6,2); obviously the newly strengthened Thebes wanted to control the oracle and its revenue.

All the above illustrate the view of the sophisticated inhabitants of cities (e.g. Mycenae) of the mountain people and the rural population on the fringes of their territories: somewhat like the Morlocks of *The Time Machine*. Gifted in matters of technology, such as construction, controlled incineration/arson, poisons, etc., they were uncultured savages, as depicted in the frescoes of Pylos, and with little respect for, if not actually hostile to the institutionalized idea of the family, as they were polygamous and with tendencies to kidnap and rape women, resulting in the deep dislike of the Goddess Hera who presided over marriage and marital sex – at least in the classical-era interpretation of the myths.

The club and the lion skin indicate more than the 'urban folklore'. The latter indicates leather outfits, from the sheepskin used as everyday dress to thick leather armour: cheap, affordable to shepherds, light and absolutely effective in shock and impact, especially of bronze-tipped arrows. The club is no unique feature, neither. Amphitryon had slain (accidentally, of course) his father-in-law with one, as already noted (Apollod II.4,6). Homer refers to a great warrior who fights with an 'iron' mace (unknown if this means fully iron, iron-headed or iron-studded), but is wearing armour: he is Arithous (or Arithoos), nicknamed '*korynitis*', i.e. the club-bearer (VII-137/41). Pausanias calls Arithous an Arcadian (Paus VIII.11,4), but in Homer his son Menesthius starts off for Troy from the Boeotian city of Arne (VII-8/10). He must have been the same man who had changed places of residence (Hercules had changed three times). The alternative, a namesake with a similar, exotic weapon preference is far-fetched. It is possible that clubs were specialized weapons and not the crude pieces of wood illustrated to account for the folklore of the bourgeoisie. Additionally, Periphetes, one of the brigands slain by Theseus, was armed with a bronze club/mace (Plut, *Vit Thes* 8,1), i.e. a specialized, expensive and demanding in manufacture, and thus rare, weapon. In Egypt the mace was a favoured weapon, issued to entire units. It does not mean that it was imported to Greece; if anything, the opposite is implied by some of the lore surrounding Hercules and more specifically his adventures in Egypt. But the mace was, after all, a favoured weapon at that time, and it re-emerged in prominence in the Middle Ages.

Finally, the bow of Hercules is a special weapon, a gift of the archer-God Apollo (Apollod II.4,11) for a special archer (Apollod II.4,9) who uses vile, trilobate (V-393) poison-smeared arrows. Hercules was also superhumanly strong: he shot with it at the sun, an act of insolence at the very least; but the sun god (*not* Apollo; this should be taken into account) was unnerved (Apollod II.5,10). This bow is clearly of composite construction, a technology that armed the Heraclids like Philoktetes and obviously his entire unit in Troy (II-718/20). This technology seems to be commonplace in western central Greece, namely Aetolia, from where Odysseus has one, a gift of Iphitus, who was murdered by Hercules (xxi-22/40). The mountain people and shepherds (as with the Mongols) made good archers, with ample time and opportunity to practise and access to the animal-derived raw materials required for decent composite bows.

In all, Hercules is the opposite of later Greek warriors, showing the prestige of light, unarmoured infantry in the Mycenaean world, which is evident in the frescoes of Pylos and in many other representations, including ringstones. The skin survived to the Roman age, where it was used (as an overcoat) by standard-bearers, the club and the bow were weapons often shown in Egyptian and Assyrian reliefs, and the concept fits well with light infantry units of these kingdoms and cultures.

The myths regarding Hercules vividly describe most eloquently the events preceding the Trojan War; after all, the first fall of Troy was credited to Hercules (V-637/43; Apollod II.6,4). The time frame is somewhat unclear, especially in absolute chronology, but occasionally in relative as well. Amphitryon leads an expedition west to exterminate the Taphian raiders who wiped out his in-laws (Apollod II.4,6). Some years later Thebes, thanks to Hercules, a prince of Tiryns born in exile, reversed the bond of servitude imposed on the city by the neighbouring – and declining – Orchomenus of King Erginus (Apollod II.4,11). In this way, Thebes became the main centre of power north of the Isthmus, and since Hercules was the offspring of the bloodline of Perseus, this must have occurred with full Mycenaean support.

Then, to return the favour, Hercules was pressed into Mycenaean service (Diod IV.10,6); the religious reasons that underlined the help he offered to his cousin and sovereign Eurystheus are indicative of the deep involvement of the priesthood and the power struggle and balance amongst those from different areas. The priesthood of Mycenae enjoyed precedence over that of Thebes. Priestly supremacy at that time meant informational, technological and scientific dimensions, which create superpowers to this day. It is no coincidence that the main patron deity of the mainland was Hera. She protects the Greeks in Troy, is the patron goddess of three mainland cities, Argos, Mycenae and Sparta (IV-51/2), watches over the progress of Jason in Thessaly (i.e. of Mycenaean Hellenism) in the Argonaut campaign, and does not *pursue* Hercules (indicatively Diod IV.9,4), but makes him a bondsman of the Mycenaean throne. She is glorified in the very name of Hercules (the Greek form is Heracles, meaning 'Glory of Hera'), and by persecuting him she pressed the hero into the service of Mycenae to spearhead the aggrandizement of the city while atoning for his family's behaviour in Tyrins, which must have equalled high treason.

Hercules always operated with the active assistance of the Goddess Athena, who presided over technology, wit and knowledge. Since the time of Diodorus at the latest, Hercules is understood not to have performed his feats alone, as reported by the lore (actually this was reported in *most cases*), but heading a (war)band (Diod IV.19,1). Regarding his legendary first capture of Troy, tradition reported him leading a raiding force of 18 ships of 50 oars each (Apollod II.6,4), equalling less than 900 warriors – and this at the very most. These troops were to gain notoriety as the Heraclids. In Greek, the suffix '-ids' (actually '-*idas*' in Dorian, '-*ides*' in Ionian, '-*ijo*' in linear B) equals the '-*sson*' in Scandinavian and "*bin*" in Arabic and means 'son of'. But the meaning is not always taken literally; in the next generation, it may imply the successors, the ones who continue the trade and carry the brand-name; and these were many.

It is no coincidence that Amphitryon, a distinguished general, is reported by the lore to have been the mortal father of Hercules: perhaps the legend alludes to the massive use of mountain warriors by the civilized, urbane but weak Thebes, who adopted them and thanks to them suddenly grew in power, overthrowing the – declining – superpower of the day, the Orchomenus. Hercules would ally himself with such ilk in the form of the Dorians, while he has Arcadian troops under his orders on an almost permanent basis (Apollod II.7,7). The civilized Athens of Pericles was promoting its own champion Theseus as a great hero, and it is important that he bears the elements of civilization as a trademark: sandals (instead of hide/lionskin) and sword as the main weapon (instead of the club and bow).

The patron deity of Thebes was Dionysus, a bucolic deity similar to Apollo; a son of Zeus and Semele; a grandson of Cadmus (Apollod III.4,2). The similarity with the Theban Hercules, who was despised by Hera because of Zeus' indiscretion with Alcmene, is obvious: her feelings towards Dionysus were similar. The enmity of Hera-Argos towards Thebes and its proxies and deities is well attested: the myth of the strangling by the baby Alcides of two snakes sent by Hera (Diod IV.10,1), suggests that the Melambodidae priestly family who usurped power in Argos (Apollod I.9,12), the city of Hera (IV-8), tried a high-handed policy: their aim was either to suffocate early the growing power of Thebes, or, alternatively, to neutralize an opposition-in-exile. The successor of the defector/traitor Amphytrion, who had legitimate claims on the usurped throne of Tiryns/Mycenae, was targeted for assassination. The connecting link of the Herculian myth and dynastic status in the Argolid is the appearance in the role of the villain of the official Melambodidae symbol, the serpent-dragon. The anti-Theban campaign implied by the myth of the snakes developed to multiple episodes of intense clashes in successive generations. From the campaign of the Seven-Against-Thebes, pro-Mycenaean Thebans and Boeotians face 'loyalist' Theban offspring and allies for two generations. The sons of the Seven conquer and destroy Thebes (IV-405/8); during the campaigns that led to the Trojan War, Telephus, son of Hercules, kills one of the Sons of the Seven, Thersander, the son of Polynices in Mysia (Apollod E.3,17). During the Trojan campaign, the elected commander of the Boeotians, Peneleus, is killed by Eurypylus, the son of Telephus and grandson of Hercules (Dikt IV.17)! The war between Mycenae and Thebes was fought by proxies in Asia, after its conclusion on the mainland. Pausanias speaks of the transfer of Hector's bones from Troy to Thebes under the guidance of the oracle of Delphi (Paus IX.18,5). Thebes became a standard-bearer for anti-Hellenism, hosting the bones of the greatest personal enemy of the archetypal Greek, Achilles, to match the siding of the city with the Persians both during the invasion of Xerxes and during the reign of Alexander the Great.

Looking at the map

The geography of the lore of Hercules, given the shreds of the political map of the time, produces a coherent picture: a concentric, radial expansion is obvious. Mopping the mountain range of Kithaeron near Thebes initiates the adventures of Hercules. The local lion is slain, most probably a real beast (Apollod II.4,9), but tribal chieftains and brigands named after predatory animals, as might have been the case with the Scylla monster of the *Odyssey* (Palaeph, *De Incred* 20), are a concept that must always be considered in the myths surrounding Hercules. Especially given the use of animals as shield blazons/emblems/coats-of-arms of the era (Apollod III.6,1).

The next step is the defeat and subjugation of Orchomenus, resulting in special honours by the Theban ruler, Creon (Diod IV.10,6). He is the uncle/brother-in-law of Oedipus, and he held the regency thrice. The first time was after the slaying of Laius and before the crowning of Oedipus, for a brief time. A second time may be understood after the demise of Oedipus and before his offspring reached the yearly rotation agreement, and the third was after the demise of the twins and the repulse of the Argive campaign of the Seven. The third time, after the repulsed Argive campaign against Thebes, the city was too powerful and prestigious to be under foreign overlordship, to produce a Hercules and lease him to Mycenae. The timeline of the life of Hercules is very problematic; he seems to have been one generation before the Trojan War, but some ancient writers tend to believe rather that it was two generations at least (Arr, *Anab* II.16,2). In any case, the lore suggests that these events happen before the ascendancy of Oedipus and after the slaying of Laius, one of the two times Creon held the regency proper.

Nevertheless, vested in glory, Hercules gives in to a fit of rage and murders his family, possibly denoting the incompatibility of the bellicose and uncivilized mountain people with the settled bourgeoisie of Thebes, however grateful and indebted the latter had been towards the former. The Delphic oracle suggests employment in Mycenae as atonement (Apollod II.4,12).

This says nothing other than the acknowledgement of the ruler of Mycenae (it was a newly founded city, just two generations old) as the/his/their liege for a standard contract, especially once Alcides was an offspring of the Royal House of Mycenae. He might have been, or become, an equivalent of the lord of the hosts, at the very least commander of the light infantry. This arm of the armed forces can be observed in frescoes and appears in Homeric context, both in name, *Pryleis* (XXI-90), and in description (XIV-519/20 and possibly III-16/8). The lore indicates that admission to the city was at some time suspended (Apollod II.5,1) due to the fear the hero inspired in his liege, King Eurystheus, son of Sthenelus, a relative of his (probably an uncle, although of the same age). This implies that the warband of Alcides (most probably it was now that he became Hercules, in the service of the city of Hera) was considered a risk factor within the city. The reasons vary; from fear of a coup by his loyal troops, who were bound with personal rather than institutional bonds of loyalty, through events of public (dis)order perpetrated by his savages, all the way to a possible legal dynastic insurrection, as Alcides had a valid claim on the throne of Perseus; he was his great-grandson from both parents.

The tasks laid upon the warband were clearly extending the territorial footprint of Mycenae. No matter whether true monsters and beasts or competitors/antagonists with the respective blazons/symbols/totems or coats-of-arms (let us not forget that the symbol of Mycenae was the pair of lions in the Lion Gate), the geography is clear: Nemea is first to be pacified or annexed, then Lerna and Stymphalos, all in the north-east Peloponnese. Then there is the expansion outside the Argolic plain, in central and western Peloponnese: Kyrenia, more or less in the middle of the distance between Corinth and Patras, but in the mountains, and Erymanthos in northern Arcadia both extend to the west of the Argolid. This means that the whole of the northern Peloponnese, with the exception of the area near contemporary Patras, slides under the sovereignty of Mycenae in a few years (Apollod II.5,4). The area bristles with archaeological findings, presented in the Museum of Patras.

Other Peloponnesian areas follow suite and bend the knee to the Mycenaean overlord, or, at the very least, sphere of influence. Elis is 'liberated' from the dung of Augeas, (Apollod II.5,5), a risk to public health; but also from Augeas, its king and owner of the great herds of cattle. The dynasty of Neleus at Pylos is exterminated, Neleus included, except for the youngest, Nestor (Apollod II.7,3), who will prove to be a faithful ally of the Mycenaean rulers to the end. According to Homer, both Nestor and Neleus had survived Hercules' attack (XI-681/92). The demise of Pylian power might have predated the demise of Elis, or it may have been the other way round, as there was friction between the two neighbours for two generations, starting with the quarrel between Neleus of Pylos and Augeas of Elis (XI-695/701). In Sparta, Tyndareus will be installed on the throne by Hercules, instead of his naughty brother Hippokoon (Apollod II.7,3).

Hercules slays the kings and their male offspring, except for the youngest, who becomes a king under the overlordship of Mycenae. It is the motif of the expansion of the Mycenaean power of the Perseids and the way Nestor in Pylos, Tyndareus in Sparta and later Priam in Troy got their thrones; only the latter will secede from the embrace of Mycenae after many years and many events. The next Mycenaean dynasty, the Pelopids, would follow a different pattern, based on holy matrimony and foreign aristocrats bred to rule.

With almost the entire Peloponnese under the sceptre of Mycenae (the exception was the north-west corner of Patras), the sphere of influence widens: Aetolia will be added later and then, with the assistance of Athens, under Theseus, Crete will become a client. Some three campaigns were needed plus a disastrous Cretan campaign to Sicily (Apollod E.1,14–15) to end the supremacy of the Minoans: Hercules (Apollod II.5,7), the Argonauts (Apollod I.9,26) and, last, Theseus (Apollod E.1,7–9) brought the island to its knees, so that in the next generation, in Troy, it was one of the many areas considering the ruler of Mycenae as their liege and overlord (IV-255/64). In these three campaigns the issue had twice to do with bulls, the symbol of the Minoans and an animal sacred to Poseidon. Only the Argonauts were implicated not against something reminiscent of or associated with a bull, but with the brazen robot Talus (Apollod I.9,26), the guardian of the Cretan coastline, which they readily destroyed.

The Mycenaean expansion through Hercules continues at a frantic pace far beyond the Peloponnese. In the northern Aegean Mycenaean bases and interests are established, as implied by the Herculean feat regarding the Mares of King Diomedes (Apollod II.5,8). A minimum of four campaigns then open the way to the Black Sea. The Argonauts pave the way, to be followed by Hercules and then Theseus, both venturing into the land of the Amazons (Apollod II.5,9 and Plut, *Vit Thes* 26,1–2 respectively). The first fall of Troy by Hercules (Apollod II.6,4) concludes the project.

Hercules next seems to push expansion to the Western Mediterranean, with the feats of the Apples of the Hesperides (Apollod II.5,10) and the cattle of Gheriones (Apollod II.5,11), traditionally located around the Atlas range in Morocco and the Iberian peninsula respectively. Arrian, in the second century AD, has his doubts about the issue of Iberia and gives an alternative location in north-west mainland Greece for the cattle (Arr, *Anab* II.16,5–6). He most logically maintains that the lore of Hercules in Iberia (and possibly in Gaul), including the renowned Pillars, must refer to the Semitic Melcart after the western expansion of Carthage. These events somehow interfered with the lore of Greek Hercules. Still, the latter refers to the Golden Apples of the Hesperides (in Greek *Western Girls*), which may have been lemons or oranges, and then there is the meeting of Hercules with Atlas the Giant (father of the Hesperides). After all, the advent of the Sardinian, Tyrrhenean and some Italian cultures (Hdt I.94) some years later shows that trans-Mediterranean travel was less of a challenge than Arrian was prepared to believe (Arr, *Anab* II.16,7) while supplanting the Greek cult of Hercules with the Semitic one once Carthage established control over Iberia (definitely after its founding in the mid-eighth century BC) is by no means impossible; it is the reverse procedure than the one suggested by Arrian, as mentioned above.

Actually, Homer, who presents different versions even for theology, with Zeus being the elder of the three divine siblings (XIII-354/5), seems to suggest, involuntarily, different versions for the last three labours of Hercules, locating them in Greece. The name Gheriones in Greek sounds much like the usual adjective in Homer for Nestor, meaning 'of Gherenia' (XI-839), some distance to the east of Pylos. If one takes into consideration that Hercules exterminated the sons of Neleus due to their stealing the cattle of Gheriones from Hercules (Phil, *Her* 26,3), one may suppose that it is two different mythic expressions of the same lore. The triple-headed, three-torso Gheriones (Apollod II.5,10) might refer to a three-person chariot team, as used by the Hittites (Bryce 2007; Fields 2006) and also by the Assyrians occasionally (Dezső 2012); the prodigy may imply the ultimate crew, operating as one with the highest degree of cooperation and coordination.

Considering the Golden Apples of the Hesperides, *Golden* in Greek means also beautiful, perfect, and shiny; the Greek word for apples is the same for the Homeric word for sheep (Palaeph, *De Incred* 18), thus the Golden Apples of the Hesperides may have been a flock of sheep in the west; the keeper Eurytion sounds suspiciously near to 'son of Eurytus', meaning Iphitus, murdered by Hercules over some herds.

Last but not least, in north-west Greece there was King Aidoneus of the Molossians, so named from the god of the underworld. A nickname or not, he had kennels with large, vicious hounds (named after this tribe) and fed to them king Perithous, son of Zeus, when the latter tried to kidnap his daughter with the help of Theseus (Plut, *Vit Thes* 31,4). Hercules saved the other half of the criminal duo, Theseus, who was chained in prison (Plut, *Vit Thes* 35,1–2). This would account for Hercules going to the realm of Ades (Aidoneus in Homer) and conquering the terrible hound, Cerberus (Apollod II.5,12).

Taking the above into consideration, it seems that during that time the Mycenaeans became deeply involved in Asia Minor, as could be inferred from the Herculean lore concerning his being sold slave to the Queen Omphale of Lydia in western Asia Minor (Apollod II.6,3). Although the national name might be anachronistic, the fact remains that the kingdom was under Mt Tmolus and the slavery is obviously a closed contract for a shepherd of people (XI-841), the standard Mycenaean attestation for the leader of a warband (the Greek word for 'people' in Homeric means 'troops') and possibly also in the *Torah*, in the case of Abraham. Hercules' band, most probably both warband and engineers, would have been duty-bound to their Shepherd and followed him in exile, or rather, servitude abroad. After all, the contract was closed, and this further suggests simple servitude for a price rather than anything else; a contract of sorts, with terms favouring the contracting authority, something very modern in concept after all.

A measure of exchange with Egypt is also attested: if the lore does not belong to the Egyptian Hercules, one of the twelve-member pantheon of the land (to whom this referred exactly remains unclear), the lore mentions a visit by the Greek hero and the murder of the tyrannical pharaoh Bousiris who tried to sacrifice him (Apollod II.5,11; Diod 4.18.1). This part of the lore may refer to the Cretan Hercules (Cretans were not very reputable in Egypt) and/or imply some Mycenaean involvement in the ejection of the Hycsos, although this is indeed unnecessarily complicated. Contrary to Herodotus' beliefs (II.45,2), and given the distrust, to say the least, of the Egyptians for any strangers (Hdt II.179), ritual extermination is not a preposterous proposition for the people and culture.

C) Dominance in Greece

Within one or at most two golden generations, the Mycenaeans have created a world empire. Although many believe – for excellent reasons – that Greek mythology tends to 'telescope' the timeline, this is not proven. It is not at all improbable that, for ease of memorization, events of many generations have been combined into just a few and incorporated into the lore of Greek mythology. But in terms of plausibility, it is unwarranted. Many times in history a prodigious generation achieves in a short time achievements that would take centuries. Alexander's generation amongst the Greeks is an excellent case; one only has to look at the map to compare the first five years of his campaigns to the twenty years of his father, King Philip II, to put the issue into perspective. Genghis Khan's generation for the Mongols and Napoleon's generation for the French are equally illustrative examples.

At its peak, the Mycenaean world almost collapsed and disappeared, like a new Atlantis, due to two events, the temporal sequence of which is uncertain. The first is the massive campaign of the Seven against Thebes, and the other became known as the 'Amazon War'. For the first, there is more than one interpretation of the events: one possibility is that the Argive constituent of

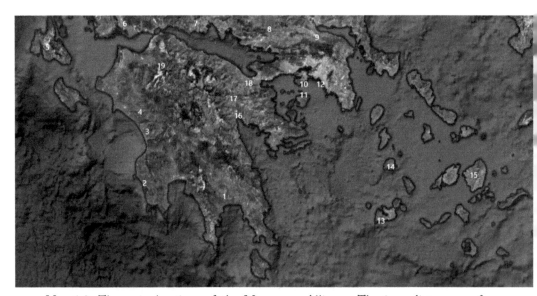

Map 1.2: The main locations of the Mycenaean Alliance. The immediate sway of Agamemnon was between Mycenae (17) and Erymanthus (19); Diomedes, between Aegina (11) and Argos (16).

1: Sparta; 2: Pylos; 3: Pisa; 4: Elis; 5: Cephalonia; 6: Calydon; 7: Phocis; 8: Thebes; 9: Aulis; 10: Salamis; 11: Aegina; 12: Athens; 13: Melos; 14: Seriphos; 15: Naxos 16: Argos; 17: Mycenae; 18: Corinth/Ephyra; 19: Erymanthus.

the north-east Peloponnesian superpower saw a good opportunity to extend its grasp northwards, while Mycenae through Hercules was doing the same in the central Peloponnese and, further east, across the Aegean.

Perhaps the developing might of Thebes was not sitting well. Thebes was mighty: if not the most powerful city in the Mycenaean world, clearly the most powerful city north of the isthmus after the decline of the Boeotian Orchomenus.

The campaign of the Seven – against Thebes – was the first check on the Argive expansion after the subjugation of the Peloponnese and involved contingents from different areas, not only from Argos; Messene and Arcadia being examples (Paus II.20,5). The war left both sides exhausted, but Thebes survived with its prestige skyrocketing, as it did so with no intervention from its arch-hero Hercules. Almost simultaneously, a Mycenaean attack against Athens would end in disaster: King Eurystheus, moving against the menacing Heraclids, possibly Thebans but definitely the warband of Hercules that included troops from other places, notably Arcadians (Apollod II.7,7), and also against the somewhat annoying Athenians of King Theseus, is defeated and slain in battle – or shortly after (Apollod II.8,1).

Theseus was second cousin to Hercules (Plut, *Vit Thes* 7,1), both being maternal great-grandchildren of Pelops. Under him, Athens and Troezen, his maternal estate, do not belong to the nuclear Perseid Mycenaean sphere of influence. They have Pelopid allegiances. Theseus' grandfather belongs to the second-most-prestigious family in Peloponnese, the Pelopids of Pisa, a family of émigrés – actually filthy rich political refugees – from Assuwa, or, in classical Greek parlance, Lydia in western Asia Minor. These were gaining prestige, power and notoriety in Peloponnese; so much so that the peninsula was renamed by the patriarch. Under Theseus, a Pelopid and protégé of Poseidon (the patron god of Troezen), Athens enjoyed a newly acquired greatness and an unprecedented increase of prestige and imperium, from the islands and Crete all the way to Thessaly. The latter was the realm of Lapithes, governed by Peirithus, son of Zeus (II-741).

Poseidon, the god of Troezen (Plut, *Vit Thes* 6,1) and patron of Theseus, favours Athens against his other favourite kingdom, Crete. As a result, Theseus, after metaphorically cropping the horns of the Cretan Bull, i.e. the executive, hard power of the Minoans, intervenes either through prestige or through raw strength (Apollod III.7,1) to enforce piety upon the victorious Thebans; to allow proper funeral rites for the slain invaders in the army of the Seven. Athens rises to the status of a buffer, a third pillar.

With the King of Mycenae slain and the King of Argos, with his host, destroyed under the walls of Thebes, the island of Pelops was open for any invader and ready to be renamed once again. The immediate danger was the Heraclids. But, from the ashes, a personality of some esteem came forth and saved the day. He was Atreus, who won the crown of Perseus by divine intervention and public vote (Apollod E.2,12). Atreus, allegedly expelled by his father Pelops for murdering Phocus, one of his half-brothers, but possibly deployed into position in Midea, another citadel of Argolis, together with Thyestes, his brother and accomplice in the fratricide, and his mother Hippodameia (Paus VI.20,7). They were established there by Sthenelus (Apollod II.4,6), father of Eurystheus, who was already married into the family, wedded as he was to Nicippe, daughter of Pelops (Apollod II.4,5). The house of Atreus sits on the throne of Perseus, and stabilizes the realm. Under Atreus, the victorious Heraclids are repulsed (Diod IV.58,1–3). The infighting that runs in the family, though, is bitter and entangles kingdoms in Peloponnese (such as Sparta) and north of the Gulf of Corinth for two generations, ending with the absolute power of Agamemnon and the rebirth of the awe and prestige of Mycenae.

The Peloponnesians being absorbed in the *camarilla* and actual warfare with different frenemies, their northern counterparts are left alone. Not necessarily perceived as a blessing. The Amazon War shakes Athens from the bottom up. It is very interesting that there is absolutely no myth or lore in the rest of Greece on the subject, as if the Amazons, from the Black Sea, appeared suddenly in Attica (Apollod E.1,16). There may be some archaeological substantiation for the event. Destruction layers identified by archaeologists may have to be attributed to this very invasion instead of the usual explanation as the 'coming of the Greeks' or the Indo-Europeans. The Ancient Greeks acknowledged no Indo-Europeans or other ingress events. Given that Hercules, Theseus, Perseus and Bellerophon faced different tribes of Amazons at some time, the return of the favour was well-deserved. Implying that the Greeks confused long-haired men of the Hittite empire, or some of its subjects, with women, as some have suggested, is an untenable proposition, especially because the Greeks wore long hair at that time (II-11), and were probably shaving as seen in the fresco of Pylos. In any case, the invasion, perhaps the first in Greek history, will be stopped before the Peloponnese, in Athens proper; it is the Amazonomachy, the War with the Amazons (Plut, *Vit Thes* 27). The fate of central Greece and the degree of desolation are unknown, but while operations took place elsewhere (Plut, *Vit Thes* 27,5–6) the main urban centres were probably spared as archaeology and, most importantly, the lore have no record of a major disaster and urban devastation. One cannot resist the temptation to associate this invasion with the western campaign of the Luwians (Trojans and Maeonians, meaning

Lydians) as described by Classical authorities (Hdt VII.20,2). The Amazons may have been part of this host and their horde turned south to exact vengeance, while the main forces were going west, to the Ionian sea.

The conclusion of the campaign is that Theseus survived but was shaken and finally ejected from Athens and the control of the Pelopids over Athens became solid with the installation of Menestheus, a native of the land and of a clan virulently antagonistic to Aegeus, the alleged father of Theseus (Apollod III.15,6–7) and possibly an impostor (Apollod III.15,5). The dynastic change ousted Theseus to seek refuge in Scyros, where he held estates, only to be treacherously slain by the local king Lycomedes (Apollod E.1,23); no mistake or accident there, although this might have been Athenian propaganda of the classical era, once more. The catalyst for these events was the first abduction of Helen of Sparta by Theseus (Apollod III.10,7). The king of Athens hoped to acquire dynastic rights in Sparta, but this time Theseus had overstepped, overestimating his powers. The Dioscuri (literally 'Sons of Zeus'), brothers of Helen and sons of Tyndareus, a king established by Hercules (Apollod II.7,3) invaded Attica and crushed the Athenians (Apollod E.1,22), retrieved their sister, and established Menestheus to the throne of Athens (Apollod E.1,23) – who declared Theseus an outcast (Apollod E.1,24). The Dioscuri had their hands full: guarding the virtue of their sister and being Argonauts (Apollod I.8,16) was only part of their CV. They also assisted the young Atreids to claim their birthright in Mycenae after the bloody feud between Atreus and Thyestes (Apollod E.2,13–16). Sparta, a client state, now had a say in the power struggle of Mycenae. Initially, the Perseid influence was imposed on Sparta by Hercules through establishing Tyndareus. Once it found its position vastly enhanced, Sparta came under direct Mycenaean control by matrimony, as the kingship was ceded to Menelaus by Tyndareus (Apollod E.2,16) since the sons of Tyndareus very conveniently – and divinely – came out of the way, in a brawl over … cattle (Apollod III.11,2).

Crete slipped under Mycenaean influence after the demise of Minoan rule, effected by three campaigns: Hercules' (Apollod II.5,7), Jason and the Argonauts' (Apollod I.9,26) and Theseus' (Apollod E.1,7–9), while the death of the sovereign in the west, in Sicily, (Apollod E.1,14–15) destroyed both armed forces and the island-empire's prestige and aura. His son Deucalion marries his sister Phaedra with Theseus (Apollod E.1,17), thus giving him access to the succession. Under Idomeneus, son to Deucalion (XII-117), its allegiance changed from the failing Athenian power to that of Mycenae, either directly as insinuated in the *Iliad* (IV-257/64) or through Pylos (Zangger 2016). The dreams of Theseus for his own network of client rulers by installing his bastard sons were shattered utterly when his birthplace, Troezen, was detached from any semblance of Athenian dependence – or independence – and given to Argos (II-559/63), now ruled by Diomedes under Mycenaean overlordship in a reshuffle of the spheres of influence of the two major powers of the Argolic plain.

Sparta also slid, rather progressively, under Mycenaean control: Menelaus and Agamemnon marry the two Spartan princesses: Agamemnon Clytaemnestra and Menelaus her young and beautiful sister, the famed Helen of Sparta, after she had been reclaimed by her brothers from Theseus (Apollod III.10,7). With Helen goes the crown of Sparta (Apollod E.2,16), despite the line not being maternal; Helen's mother, Leda, was not from Sparta (Apollod III.10,5), but Clytaemnestra was married off to Mycenae and the two male siblings were slain (Apollod III11,2). This episode, which implicated almost all of the Greek princelings in the honour of the husband of Helen (Apollod III.10,8–9) concludes the Atreid ascendancy. Simultaneously, after the second war on Thebes is won by the sons of the Seven (IV-405/10), the city is razed and Mycenae, taking advantage, wrestles the kingship of Argos from the campaigning rulers, Diomedes and Sthenelus, only to reinstate them as dependent rulers under the overlordship of Agamemnon, once they took the pledge.

After the demise of Thebes by the sons of the Seven, the Boeotian Orchomenus, previously brought to its knees by Hercules and King Creon, flourished anew and sent 30 ships to Troy (II-511/6; Dikt I,3). Originally, under Athamas, Orchomenus had become comparable in wealth with the Egyptian Thebes (IX-3801/4). This is an important lead on the concurrency of Egyptian affairs with the events in Greece. Together with Iolcus, they formed the epicentres of the Minyans, the foremost power in central Greece before the Achaeans. They were part of a network as has already been mentioned: Ephyra, to become Corinth, was the throne of Athamas' brother, Sisyphus, while Iolcus, under Pelias, had established an interest in Pylos through the reign of Neleus, brother to Pelias (Apollod I.9,8). The relations between the relatives are unimportant. What is important is that the four cities were naval and commercial superpowers. Orchomenus of Athamas had ties with the East, the Luwian states – or the Hittite empire – and with its decline (in two steps, the second and most fatal being the blow dealt by Hercules in the name of Thebes) these contacts died out. Corinth, founded by Sisyphus (Apollod I.9,3), the brother of Athamas of Orchomenus (Apollod I.9,1), bred Jason, to wrest the seat of Iolcus from Pelias and reopen eastern trade; it was a mission of utter importance, where all of Greece took part: the campaign of the Argonauts (Apollod I.9,16).

Even Hercules joined in, with the explicit task to make friends (in any way he saw fit) with the gate-master, the Troy of Laomedon, that had shaken the Hittite control by ejecting Pelops. The Golden Fleece finally came back not to Iolcus, as agreed, but to Corinth, signalling its ascendancy in commerce (Apollod I.9,27–28). Corinth had been securely under the sceptre of Agamemnon (II-569/77), while Pylos and Crete offered him their allegiance, creating a vast trade empire.

Well, not so vast, nor firmly established. The successive dynastic clashes in Mycenae and the implications for the power structure in Greece, including the meteoric career of Theseus, gave some people a break. The Trojans of Priam, who had experienced the terror of the Mycenaean campaign under Hercules, would have loved to lead a retaliatory campaign. Thanks to the Mycenaean ebb, the Trojan network extended to the whole of the north-western Asia Minor, and all the Thracian lands, mainly, but not necessarily exclusively, west of the Hellespont. This brought the Trojans to the Ionian Sea (Hdt VII.20,2). While Egypt, a trade partner of the Greeks was recovering in the south, the Trojan alliance and its Hittite frenemies (the status at the time is a bit hazy) blocked the traffic to the Black Sea once more. The Trojan expansion in Europe, though, blocked the land and river routes of the Northern Balkans. As a result, the Mycenaeans were suffocating politically, commercially and militarily. Their import economy, left only with a westward opening, could collapse, and it was only a matter of time before they suffered another invasion. The Trojans did not hide their intentions. If the Amazon invasion was not proof enough, one of the most stalwart Trojan politicians, Alexander/Paris challenged the Mycenaeans in the Aegean by building a fleet, and coupling it with bold campaigns. In one of these, he advanced claims to one of the most important thrones of the Mycenaean commonwealth: that of Sparta.

D) The Numbers Two

At the time of the Trojan War and slightly before it, there were two second-grade powers, one north and one south of the Gulf of Corinth, where important developments were taking place. In the shadow of Mycenae, Argos, the much older city, was finding its footing after the disaster that was the Campaign of the Seven. Mycenae, prudently, had not taken any part in it (IV-376.81) and was thus spared any casualties and saw its prestige and power increased, at least comparatively. On the north, Calydon in Aetolia, at the western exit of the Gulf of Corinth, was increasing in importance as it guarded the egress of vessels from the Gulf for trade with the west. King

Oeneus was a devoted believer of Dionysus and thus taught winemaking (Apollod I.8,1); his name is the same root with *wine* in Greek (*oinos*). His son Meleagrus, the greatest warrior of his time (Apollod I.8,2), organized the Hunt for the Calydonian Boar – the most prestigious event after the Argonautic campaign – that ended ingloriously in bloodshed over spoils and ultimately in a round of pleasantries between neighbours that culminated with Meleagrus dead (Apollod I.8,2–3) and his father Oeneus deposed by his nephews (Apollod I.8,6). Another son of Oeneus, Tydeus, was exiled and found refuge at the same time with Polynices, son of Oedipus, in Argos, at the court of King Adrastus. This king made the refugees his in-laws (Apollod III.6,1). Ruling the south shore of the Gulf of Corinth, he embraced their causes and campaigned first against Thebes, with Arcadian and Messenian assistance (Paus IX.9,2) but, importantly, not Mycenaean (IV-376/81). The disastrous defeat of his host by the Theban forces reinforced by Phocians and, unexpectedly, Phlegyans (Paus IX.9,2) became proverbial. But the next generation, the sons of the Seven, succeeded, assisted by Corinthian, Megarian, Arcadian and Messenian troops (Paus IX.9,4). After Thebes, they proceeded to embrace the cause of Tydeus, or rather, now, of his son, Diomedes, married to the daughter of King Adrastus, Aigialea.

One complication is that, after the success in Thebes, the sons of the Seven went to Calydon and reinstated Oeneus; his grandson Thoas, by his daughter (Apollod I.8,1), was the commander of the Aetolians at Troy (II-638/43). The sons of the Seven took the opportunity to expand their operations into Acarnania and carve another kingdom, Ampilochia (Apollod III.7,7); during their absence, Mycenae invaded Argos, Agamemnon took the throne and suggested to the deposed kings returning it, along with other estates, in exchange for their allegiance; and so it happened.

The other complication was that, after exchanging the throne of Tiryns for that of Argos with Perseus, Megapenthes sired Argeus who sired Anaxagoras. The latter faced a dire challenge to his authority: a massive psychosis of the women of the realm (Apollod II.2,2). The unsolicited saviour, the diviner Melambus from Messene, fixed the issue for two-thirds of the kingdom; one for him and another for his brother Bias (Paus II.18,4–5). Melambus son of Amythaon was from the Pylian branch of the royal family who founded Iolcus in Thessaly (Apollod I.9,11). Cretheus was the founder of Iolcus and had three sons: the later King Aeson, alleged father of Jason, Pheres, who founded the city of Pherai and Amythaon, who moved to Pylos and sired Melambus and Bias. This migration would account for the establishment of the Achaeans, originating north of the Malian Gulf (Hdt VII.173,1), to south-west Peloponnese.

This triple kingship, due to the intervention of Melambus, resulted in the complex command structure of the Argives of Argolid in Troy. Diomedes had a claim from both the Melambodidai and Biantidai, through his wife Aigialea, daughter of Adrastus (Apollod I.8,6), the reigning king, son of Talaus and grandson of Bias; Talaus was married to the granddaughter of Melambus (Apollod I.9,13). Diomedes was regent to the boy Cyanippus, son or brother to the slain Aigialeus (Apollod I.9,13; Paus II.30,10). His friend Sthenelus was an Anaxagorid claimant, as son of Kapaneus and nephew of Iphis; the latter had inherited the claim from his father Alector, son of Anaxagoras (Paus II.18,4–5). And then Euryalus was son of Mecisteus (II-565/6), brother to Adrastus and thus co-regent to the boy Cyanippus, holding a partial claim from the Biantidai (Apollod I.9,13).

Chapter 2

The International *Status Quo*

A crash course in geography and religion

In the Greek lore, it seems that a much wider picture should be envisaged in terms of Mediterranean voyage and commerce. Quintessential chapters of the myths concerning the Gods, like the duel of Athena and Arachne and of Apollo against Marsyas (Hittite *Murisilis?*), take place in western Asia Minor, either under the guise of Assuwa/Asia, or under the guise of Arzawa, terms to be explained later. Our undertones from the classical era use the then-current toponyms, as Lydia and Phrygia, but this false chronology does not refute the facts of the lore. In the Odyssey, on the other hand, western trade is a given (i-183/5); this trade is the only way to explain the Pylos of Nestor, a small south-west principality of insignificant size and resources on the ground, contributing a massive fleet of 90 vessels in the Catalogue of Ships in the second book of the *Iliad* (II-494/759), second only to Agamemnon, the high king, and more numerous than the Spartan one of Menelaus, who rules over more than three times the footprint. It is through western trade, and this accounts for the wealth implied in the *Iliad* by the description of Nestor's armament (VIII-192/3) and the extremely intimate relationship of the liege and the princes with chariotry (XXIII-301/50). Western Greece and Sicily, in particular, seem to be connected by standard shipping lanes (xv-307; xxiv-307), with some characters dwelling in Ithaca but originating from Sicily (xxiv-211) or further up the coast (xv-405).

The Phoenicians are routinely mentioned in the same context, either in general (xv-415) or specifically by the metropolis of Sidon (xv-425; VI-290/2). The name 'Phoenician' in Greek implies something red. It may refer to the dye for crimson cloth, an amenity later massively available in classical Sparta – hence the luxury in a monetarily poor state to field its army in a uniform crimson outfit, as 'red cloaks' (Xen, *Const Lac* 11.3). Or it might refer to a physical feature, some phenotype of reddish colour (perhaps beard and hair) and thus apply also to the populations of north-west Africa, like the Cabylians and their brethren to the east. Whether in the Levant this population is the one later known as the Phoenicians, of Semitic stock, is a matter of conjecture: Herodotus clearly reports a Semitic migration from Mesopotamia/the Gulf Region (Hdt VII.89,2) which fits well with the Biblical story of Abraham coming from Chaldea to Palestine, a trek to be repeated some 2,000 years later by the Muslim Arabs. But the early lore insists upon an eastward migration of the early Phoenicians from Libya nonetheless (Apollod II.1,4).

Another digression is needed. The Greek tribes campaigning against Troy were many, but the main ones were the 'Danaans' of the Peloponnese (strictly speaking from the Argolid) and the Achaeans of the area north of the Isthmus – initially from the area just north of the Malian Gulf (Hdt VII.173,1). An important set of differences has been identified by scholars, from as early as the nineteenth century, and the arguments may fit well into the Homeric saga (Drews 1979).

There were also the Minyans in central Greece, from where the crew of *Argo* was raised. The core of Greece revolves around the Gulf of Corinth; there lies the cultural centre of Delphi, and important fleets are raised, from such states, which is unexplained if later formats of power geography are followed. There was international, long-range commerce, but the core was the Gulf of Corinth and the balance of north versus south. And then there were the eastern islands.

Many Mycenaean lords did not participate in the campaign in person but sent contingents, being duty-bound by the oath of Helen's suitors – and hard-pressed, no doubt, by the high-handed Atreid authority with steep penalties for no-shows (Scott 1909). They could have been simply reluctant and recalcitrant. But if the combined notions of Plutarch (*Vit Thes* 34,2) and Herodotus regarding the eastern aggression (Hdt VII.20,2) are taken as valid, some of them may have been left behind to guard the strategic rear, especially from the European allies of Troy, Thracians and Paeonians just north-north-east and on continental soil (II-848/50 & 844/5). The latter interpretation, although not very convincing, could offer an alternative explanation for the absence of contingents from the Cyclades and the northern Sporades, just east of Thessaly. Such naval contingents were to intercept any seaborne Trojan counter-offensive. Actually, at least regarding the Cyclades, different interpretations, that they are included amongst the territories of Agamemnon (Argos–Arzawa) are more convincing.

The Catalogue of the Ships in the *Iliad* (II-494/759) makes the geography of power clear. The Homeric directory is perhaps meant to be compared with some other list, e.g. the one that would refer to the fleet assembled in Aulis. In any case, the large island of Euboea, inhabited by the tribe of Avantes and including the cities of Chalkis, Eretria, Styra, Istiaia, and Karystos furnishes ships for the Greek cause although the father of the ruling king

(II-536/42) had been slain by the father of Hercules in a conflict in Boeotia (Paus IX.19,3); something implying a most questionable attitude amongst the Heraclids as a whole towards Mycenae and the campaign. The Cyclades, the Sporades and the islands of the eastern Aegean north of Kos do not send ships to Troy. A central island in the Cyclades, Tenos, had been conquered by Achilles and was obviously hostile; other islands of the Cyclades did contribute vessels to the War but not in the final campaign (Dikt I.17).

On the contrary, Kos, Kasos, Karpathos, Nisyros, Kalymnos, Rhodes and Symi at the south-eastern corner of the Aegean do so (II-653/4 671/80). Lesbos and Tenedos, in the north-eastern Aegean, just across Troad, are conquered by Achilles (Apollod E.3,26 & 33) – so they are hostile. The Achaeans are supplied with wine from Lemnos, ruled over by Euenus the son of Jason (IV-468) and grain from Thrace. The latter obviously refers to areas conquered by some Achaean expeditionary forces under Ajax the Great (Dikt II.18) and both these amenities are also commandeered from Delos (Dikt I.23).

Samothrace, Imbros and Thasos are not mentioned in any account of operations, and it is possible that they were not attacked, although obviously under Trojan influence, or neutral (especially Samothrace, a holy island). For Chios, Samos, that is the mid-eastern Aegean, there is no comment whatsoever; Icaria though, just some metres west of Samos had been conquered by Hercules and renamed to honour the dead son of Daedalus (Apollod II.6,3), but its allegiance during the days of the Trojan war is far from clear.

It is of interest that, in Homer, Agamemnon is accredited with Corinth, with the whole southern coast of the Gulf of Corinth (II-569/75) which was originally under the control of Argos, and with 'many islands'. The latter cannot be Hydra and Spetses; the south-western Cyclades at the very least should be considered part of his territory, since the realm of Agamemnon included part of today's Arcadia, especially its coastal strip, and one of these islands, Seriphos, is where Perseus grew up (Apollod II.4,1). A king of Cyclades, Dionysus, on the other hand, led an invasion to the Argolid with an army of women (Maenads), and was repulsed by Perseus (Paus II.20,4), which led them to eventual reconciliation.

This story explains perhaps Perseus' decision to found Mycenae very far from the sea and perched on mountains. It also gives a precedent and an antithesis to the lore of the all-women armies of the Amazons: there are seemingly more of this pedigree than the famous horse-dependent tribe of Asia Minor, from Themiscyra at the river Thermodon (Diod II.45–6). This ilk comes from a different area and element, the sea (possibly reflecting the matriarchal Cycladian civilization), and opens the question of the identity of Dionysus. There are two such Gods, the Theban, son of Zeus and Semele, and the mystical one, Bacchus, presiding over the mysteries (Arr, *Anab* II.16,3). The name in Cyclades emerges anew three generations later with the myth of Theseus, as the latter dumped the abducted Minoan princess Ariadne in Naxos, sacred island of (a) Dionysus who married the scorned princess (Diod IV.61,5), implying there was still some degree of independence on the island of Naxos.

The epics clearly suggest that 'steep Scyros' was also conquered by Achilles, and a slave girl is reported taken during said operations against King Eunias, her father (IX-662/4). The tradition with Achilles hiding amongst the daughters of King Lycomedes (the slayer of Theseus) suggests that the latter may have been neutral, a fact that changes when Achilles joins the Greek army. He leads Scyrian forces in the first trans-Aegean campaign that ended in Mysia, some distance south from the beaches of the Troad. Lycomedes' keeping Achilles concealed (Apollod III.13,8) means that Scyros was beyond the sway of the recruiters of Agamemnon, and Neoptolemus, son of Achilles and Lycomedes' daughter, remained there (XIX-326/7) as heir to the throne of Phthia (XIX-326/33) – and obviously that of Scyros – until he came of age and was called to Troy. Slaying the maverick Theseus, rapist of princess Helen of Sparta (before she became the wife of Menelaus), and thus spontaneous contender for the throne of Sparta and consequently of two-thirds of the southern Peloponnese, must have been instrumental for the opinion – and thus tolerances – of the Atreids towards Lycomedes. It is the easiest to assume the island had two kings, Eunias and Lycomedes, but it still leaves room for a number of doubts.

Different sources assign some states to different sides, as is the case with the city of Kolophon. This may be attributable to shifts of allegiance, seen throughout the ages, as with Italy in the Second World War; the map of alliances by Homer reflects a snapshot in time of the tenth year of the war. Mysia and Lycia were also recalcitrant in their allegiances, Cyprus was friendly to the Greeks, with Greek cities already flourishing there, and lavish presents of King Kinyras to Agamemnon (XI-19/23), but no expeditionary participation in the end phase, as is evident from its total absence from the Catalogue of Ships (II-494/759); thus the wider picture remains unclear. The raid of Paris against Sidon (VI-290/1) vividly demonstrates events mentioned in Semitic archives about incursions in the Levant (Zangger 2016). Paris must have called at Cyprus during said raid (Apollod E.16,4 & E.3,4), and perhaps Egypt, where his advances obviously found no willing listeners (Hdt II.112–20); the Egyptians remained steadfast with the Mycenaeans as vividly implied by the reports of King Menelaus in the *Odyssey* (iv-125/37), a solid trade partner for the Greeks in times of need. Moreover, this differential Egyptian attitude towards Menelaus and Paris fits well to the theory that Luwians, including the novice Trojan navy, were the adventurous and aggressive raiders known as the Sea Peoples, rather than the Mycenaeans (Zangger 2016) – at least in their majority (Moreu 2003), as occasional Mycenaean raiders took the southern route to Egypt (xiv-245/72).

The divine frenemies: Hera–Athena–Poseidon and the priestly geography of the Achaean world

The three deities so set against Troy (I-400) drew together against a mortal enemy. This was an opportunistic approach. Generally speaking, there was some bickering amongst them in Greece.

Starting with Pelias and Neleus, seed of Poseidon, the former hated Hera (Apollonius Rhod, *Argon* I.10–18); an excellent reason for the Goddess to assist Jason at every step to overthrow Pelias. Whether Jason was a long-lost son of Aeson, or a Pelopid reared and bred to take a throne of opportunity is open to question. The other brother, Neleus, moved to Pylus where he carved for himself a nice kingdom and his city and bloodline came under the protection of Poseidon (iii-3/6; XIII-554/5 respectively). Hera had her minion, Hercules, to change all that and install Nestor; who, prudently, considers Athena his personal guardian deity (VII-153/5), not Poseidon. Still, his son Antilochus was under the direct protection of the sea god (XIII-554/5); incidentally the same goes for Idomeneus (XIII-434/5) and the whole bloodline of Minos. Once Jason fails at Iolcus, the Golden Fleece goes to Corinth (Apollod I.9,27–28). The ancient tradition though may have mentioned *Ephyra*, which may be either Corinth or opposite to Corfu. Along with the fleece one acquired supremacy over the waves. Corinth did so, in Archaic and Classical Greece and it was the Allied Greek headquarters during the invasion of Xerxes (Hdt VII.172,1).

More interestingly, Troezen and thus Theseus were also under the auspices of Poseidon (Apollod III.15,7 & Apollod E.1,19), which made Theseus a very capable and dexterous pirate/sea raider; so much so that he brought the power of Minoan Crete to its knees after conquering the bull sacred to the sea god (Apollod E.1,5–6). One may assume that Athena, the goddess of Athens since its renaming from Cecropia (Apollod III.14,1), would have been more than a little upset. No wonder that her favourite hero, Odysseus (XXIII-782/3), was persecuted relentlessly by Poseidon (Phil, *Her* 25,15) and she was machinating at Poseidon's absence with the whole pantheon to deliver him (i-22/75).

In the case of Hercules, Athena and Hera were on the same page; most probably the same was true with Perseus, as Sparta, Argos and Mycenae were the three main cities of Hera (IV-51/2). The same can be said of Palamedes; his father Nauplius is son of Poseidon and the man is eliminated by Athena's minions, Odysseus and Diomedes, supported at every turn by Hera's favorite, Agamemnon (Apollod E.3,8). Athena and Poseidon were also on the same page, because the goddess presided over shipbuilding, as directly mentioned for both the building of *Argo* (Apollod I.9,16) and the Trojan master shipbuilder, Phereclus (V-59/62).

The Homeric world is one of the divine being literally an everyday issue, pertaining to every expression of the life and piety is of paramount importance as the political/administrative authorities are intermingled with the religious service and the issue of piety equals to discipline. Still, the Greeks, but not the Trojans, do question the gods. The historical onset of their signature inquisitive spirit. Agamemnon generally considers Calchas to be clearly unreliable, (I-105/10) and he is probably right; whatever the Mycenaean ruler was, he was not a fool and he held priestly office as god-ordained ruler of his people. Besides, several sources state that Calchas was a Trojan defector (Dares 15). The most pious Greek, even towards Apollo, his declared enemy and preordained Nemesis, is Achilles, who protects Calchas from bullying by Agamemnon (I-85/91). This is why he was immensely successful at war; he is always reported as someone beloved by the Gods; Zeus himself quarrels with other gods, his siblings included, to avenge the affront to him (I-551/67). This, of course, as long as he respects the gods and does not exaggerate and press his own will and ego when they try to intervene softly, i.e. by saving some opponent of his, like Aeneas (XX-320/50); the man is not even trying to change his fate, impending death; he has made his peace with his fate (XXII-365/6). But when he confronts Apollo, after the death of Patroclus, Achilles seems, or sounds, as if having understood 'something' unsettling despite his pious behaviour. The detailed record of the demise of Patroclus (XVI-94 & 703/4) might have sounded suspicious and not simply 'unexplained' to the son of a goddess (XVIII-33/6) and the student of Cheiron (XI-829/31); he instantly ceases to be so dear to the gods.

Despite the fact that Achilles succumbs to the divine will (XXIV-133/7) and surrenders the body of Hector (XXIV-139/40), he perishes a little later (Apollod E.5,3) and this is long preordained (XIX-326/33; XXIII-140/52). He shall be killed by an arrow from Paris, guided by Apollo; or near the temple of Apollo, the issue is a bit confusing in various traditions but Apollo is always involved – or perhaps his priest(s). One may wonder: if he did not return Hector's dead, something very logical as Hector wanted to feed the corpse of Patroclus to the vultures and dogs (XVII-125/7), what more did he have to worry about?

Section 2

Who is Who – the Orientals

Chapter 3

The Luwian Connection

The political geography of the Bronze Age Aegean is not sufficiently understood – and approached – to say the least. There are several reasons for this. Different policies regarding excavations from the Turkish authorities are just one issue (Pantazis 2006; Zangger 2016). Different policies and priorities, not to say preconceptions of the European academic establishments, are a far more impactful one. By insisting that the discoveries in Central Europe denote a culture or even a civilization that no-one has heard of, a civilization that has been sending technology in the form of Naue II swords and copper breastplates south-eastwards, and mercenaries to the most warlike Mycenaeans, and by plotting the Sea Peoples' cradle north-east of Tunis, requires a geographic and historical vacuum, where these candidacies may be inserted. The Greek peninsula is unavailable, so is central Asia Minor, where the Hittites are solidly established.

The Hittites are absent from the Greek epics, but for some exceptions (xi-519/21). On the contrary, the Greeks, or Achaeans, feature prominently in the Hittite records. There are many names and toponyms that may be identified, with some imagination. But still, a proper alignment is very difficult, especially in terms of chronology. And there is a hole in the map. What was there, between the Aegean and the central part of Asia Minor? The Hittites occupied (some of) that area for a brief time during the Age of Bronze. There must have been something else, someone else. Despite their might, the Hittites, when compared with the Mycenaeans and other contemporary cultures seem backward, unpretentious and underdeveloped in material culture, especially as seen in representational art.

The view that Homer's society is far from the stratified and bureaucratic Mycenaean palatial society (Pantazis 2006) is perhaps unwarranted; different aspects of the same entity would be a plausible interpretation of the difference between records and archaeology. After all, the literary evidence for the twenty-first century would never mention the bureaucracy of our states, especially that of the treasury/IRS. In Homer, the industrial character of the Mycenaean economy is amply demonstrated by the mention of captive women of skills (IX-12/30). Their number is not for domestic tasks, but for

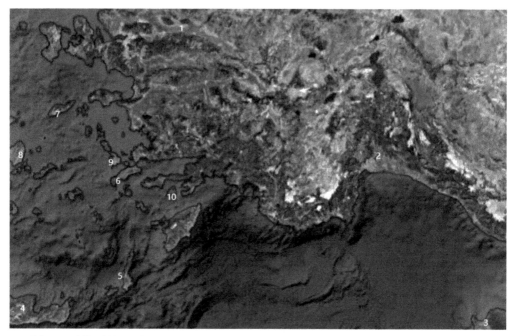

Map 3.1: The SW border.
Hercules served as a slave (i.e. his warband and he had a closed contract of servitude) of Queen Omphale, daughter of Tmolus, in Lydia. This would have stabilized the Asian Arzawa, the seeds of which were sown in Lycia (2) of Iobates, five generations before Hercules. Two grandsons of Hercules brought to Troy thirty ships from a group of islands (5, 6, 9), whereas only nine were brought by the great island of Rhodes, headed by a son of Hercules. Still, these, along with the tiny island of Symi (10) to the north of Rhodes, which contributed three vessels under an independent ruler, were creating a veritable island chain, especially since Icaria (7) had been reduced by Hercules himself beforehand.

1: Mount Tmolus, Lydia; 2: Lycia; 3: Cyprus; 4: Crete; 5; Kasos & Karpathos; 6: Kos; 7: Icaria; 8: Naxos; 9: Kalymnos; 10: Symi.

the renowned textile industry of the Achaeans. Not having mastered the power of steam, as the English textile factories of that maritime empire did, their Mycenaean predecessors used raiding to obtain slaves to power their facilities with manual labour.

On the other hand, the Greek lore transmitted not by poets, but by historians, Herodotus and Thucydides, implies a long-flourishing culture in this environment, a culture interacting intensely with the Greeks and also with the Pelasgians, the alleged pre-Greeks as yet unidentified by science in location, artefacts or remains. The deluge and continuous motion were the order of the day in the southern Balkans in the first quarter of the first millennium BC. But still, this flourishing culture, mother to the very closely related historic peoples of Lydia, Mysia, Caria and other ethnic names known to the classical world, seems to be there, lying hidden. It is the Luwians, mentioned by the Hittites as Luwiya (Zangger 2016) and engulfing all these nations; a mother culture that Herodotus suspects (Hdt I.171,6) but fails to put in context. Possibly there was *no* context; them sharing common consciousness due to their *culture, not origin*, is a projection of the culture-heavy anthropology of the nineteenth century onwards.

There are some issues with the Luwian hypothesis, none of them major, but issues nonetheless. Prominent names in Greek epic cannot be identified in foreign texts and Hittite names cannot be detected in the Greek lore. Given that the Mycenaeans reverted to oral transmission of their history once the bureaucracy seemed unsustainable, less detail is expected; verbal transmission is laborious and less comprehensive, but more sustainable. The Hittites did not make the transition and were deleted from history; archaeology vindicated them, though. The term *Luwiya* (Zangger 2016) is the most prominent example of Hittite terms not encountered or suspected in Greek, and the toponyms Ahiyawa, Arzawa follow. Although, in Herodotus, the Lydians as such are dated a few brief generations before the Trojan War, in Homer they can be identified under their older name, Maiones (X-431); the association is secured by Herodotus (Hdt I.7,3). Greek lore implicates a Lydian queen, Omphale, near Mount Tmolus, consorting with Hercules, possibly retroprojecting the national name in the Bronze Age. So, the possibility that Luwia may be hiding behind Lydia gains some credibility.

The other association, not necessarily mutually exclusive with the above mentioned, is Libya. If a migration from the east was part of the Libyan nation-building (the time remains to be argued convincingly), Herodotus' tip that the Greeks learnt of and adopted Poseidon from the Libyans, along with other information, may be better understood: as with Carthage, it was a transplanted civilization from the East, in this case from the Luwian cradle in Asia Minor, whereas Carthage was a colony of the Semitic Levant; the Greeks were quick to do the same to Italy, Sicily and Cyrenaica, as did the Minoans; a tidal wave of westward migration by sea, exemplified by the mention of *Enetoi*, Greek for Venetians, as allies of Troy and established in Asia (II-851/2).

As mentioned elsewhere, much of the early Greek lore concerning the Olympian deities and their interactions with humans takes place on Asian soil, despite the belief of Herodotus that most of them may be understood as of Egyptian origin (Hdt II.4,2). This implies the worship of the same pantheon in Greece and western Asia Minor rather than projecting one pantheon onto another, as is done habitually by Herodotus (Hdt IV.59) and perhaps occasionally by Homer. It is a valid question whether the Homeric pantheon is the same as the Mycenaean one (Castleden 2005), but this is irrelevant; drifting of religious ideas could explain many things, as the Homeric Pantheon is different to the version projected by Hesiod and the main ideology of Classical Greece.

Given that linguistics had not been invented, one may also surmise that a common tongue was spoken and intense association was the order of the day. Repeated Greek adventurism to Asia was reciprocated by the 'Lydian' Tandalus (Hittite 'Tudaliya'). He sent or otherwise dispatched his son Pelops by sea to Greece, where he carved a kingdom for himself in Western Apia, or, rather, acquired it with a coup (Diod IV.73), and renamed Apia to Peloponnese (Thuc I.8,2) by marrying his offspring to almost all petty royal houses. The episodes of heroic lore occurring in Asia perhaps denote temporal windows of extreme Mycenaean influence and dynamic expansion and then a drastic shrinkage of such territories and influence. Thus, geographical overlap of realms and toponyms is well explained in a temporal context. Such areas under Greek influence may well be called with a name precisely denoting the national core of the empire, much like the British Empire being present with colours and troops in India, and an incursion against any such territory was indeed an affront, or hostility, against Britain. This concept would explain the use of the word Ahiyawa by the Hittites in contexts fitting Asian, not European, territory. It may be referring to the metropolitan lands (the Argolid in Peloponnese), to the empire of the Mycenaeans/Achaeans, or to their Asian lands, whatever their extend, according to context and time. This could possibly resolve the issue of Arzawa as well. It may be explained as stemming from the word Argos and thus being the Hittite equivalent for the 'Land of Argos'. The suffix syllable -*wa* may mean the land (Greek *Ga* or *Ge* and *Gaia*) as in Assuwa (Land of Asia or of Asius, the latter being a common Trojan name), Ahiyawa (land of the Achaeans-Ahiyia) etc. The Assuwa would have been a larger confederacy centred on the NW corner of Asia Minor with a local, native nucleus and expanding or contracting according to the political conditions, possibly to Europe if Homer and Herodotus are to be believed. The Arzawa was a competing or opposing formation (much like the opposing blocks in Europe throughout modern times), including Asian lands under Mycenaean sovereignty; at the time the term Mycenaeans meant only the inhabitants of the city and the political identifier was Danaans, Argives and Achaeans. There is some indirect corroboration in the *Iliad*: it is very difficult to interpret any other way (but for poetic licence) the explicit mention that Agamemnon 'ruling the whole of Argos and many islands (II-107/8)'. Thucydides focused on the identification of islands (Thuc I.9,4), partly due to their then-non-Greek population component, especially Carian (Thuc I.6,1) – that is, Luwian; Carian prominence in the Aegean islands is attested both before the Trojan War (Diod V.51) and after the Trojan War (Diod V.84), a fact that places them among the Sea Peoples and corroborates the Egyptian description of the '… many islands of the Sea Peoples …'.

But the other part of the statement of Thucydides is just as important. Being himself the ruler of Mycenae, with Argos proper (the city) and eastern Argolis being represented by the commanding trio of Diomedes, Sthenelus and Euryalus (II-559/68), although in a subordinate capacity (Str X.2,25), Agamemnon must have been directly ruling a much more extended area. The emphatic phrase 'whole of Argos' refers to something wider than the plain of the Argolid, and this realm encompasses 'many islands'. This potentially explains the prominent lack of any but the most remote Aegean islands in the SE Aegean (II-653/80) from the list of ships. The north-east Aegean islands were neutral or sided with the Trojans, as was Tenedos and Lesbos. Or it may not; Naxos was under Carian rule before Theseus (Diod V.51). In any case, Agamemnon was the sovereign of an area called *Argos*, being much wider than the Argolid and not governed by subordinate rulers over which he was overlord, but by him directly; something not applicable to the city of Argos, which was ruled by Diomedes *et al*. If Arzawa was the expanded 'colonies of the Mycenaean Crown/Sceptre', the Ahiyawa occasionally understood as on or near Asian soil, possibly an island complex, must have been the islands governed by allied but independent rulers, that would be the complex of Cos, Kasos, Karpathos, Nisyros, Syme and Kalyndae, the latter being modern-day Kalymnos (II-653/80). More or less today's Dodecanese.

On the Greek mainland, there were at least four cities named Argos (Argos Orestikon in Macedon; Argos Amphilochikon in Western Greece; Argos Pelasgikon in Phthia, south of Thessaly; and of course the original Argos in the Argolid). The location of Argos Pelasgikon in Phthia is secure, but strange; the name of Peloponnese before Pelops had been *Apia* at one time and *Pelasgia* at another.

This tradition of planting cities with the same name has a later parallel in history with the scores of Alexandrias, but also with the different 'New' colonial lands (New York, New England, New Zealand etc). Thus, the whole of Argos might have implied, not exclusively to what has already been suggested, the different 'secondary' Argos cities and their surrounding areas, including an Argos in western Asia Minor.

Additionally, the innovative identification of the *Attarisiya* of the Hittite archives not with *Atreus*, as usually suggested but with *Atreid* (Giannakos 2016) is very plausible since the Hittite suffix *-iya* sounds similar to the

Linear B -*ijo*, later Greek -*ides*, meaning 'son of'. If this hypothesis is correct, it follows that Agamemnon, or some army/ies of his, had been operating in the area for quite some time and pressing for a relapse of the Asian part of Arzawa. This corroborates with the lengthy campaigns of the Trojan war before the fall of Troy, as Nestor recounts in the *Odyssey* (iii-105/8); after all, before the landing at Troad, at least one great amphibious operation had been carried out, resulting in turning (parts of) Mysia for the Achaeans or, at least, neutralizing it (Apollod E.3,17–20).

In Homeric geography there are some candidates that qualify for the Hittites. The cradle of the latter is east of Halys river, where in classical times the Cappadocians were located (Hdt I.172,2). Phrygia lay on the west bank of the Halys, as does Paphlagonia (possibly *Pala* in the Hittite records) and then to the west is Lydia, south of which were Caria and north Mysia and the Troad; Homer mentions all these people but for the Lydians, for whom he uses the older name, Maeonians (Hdt I.7,3). For Herodotus, Lydians, Carians and Mysians were related (Hdt I.171,6), and these were obviously the Luwian core. The Phrygians were the most ancient people for him (Hdt II.2); as a consequence, Homer's locating them in the environs of the Sagarius (III-185/7), due west of Halys, is compatible with such traditions and incompatible with a western origin for the Phrygians in Macedon, during the times of King Midas (Hdt VIII.18,2). In turn, this suggests that a massive incursion to the west, which brought the Brugi in the northern part of the Greek Peninsula should be taken instead, which corroborates the non-Homeric tradition in Herodotus (Hdt VII.20,2) for Trojan – Luwian invasions in Europe all the way to the Adriatic just before the known Trojan War, which would account for the very extended network of Trojan allies in Europe, at the very least to the River Axius (II-848/50).

There are two more issues to tackle. One is the Trojan allies under the name of Halizones. They are mentioned in Homer (II-856/7), as residents of a land called Halibe; the Greek spelling implies they are near the river Halys, and their land would be in Hittite Haliwa, 'the land of Halys'. The Halizones, similarly to the Cappadocians (or even the Phrygians), are candidates for the Homeric memory of the Hittites. Other candidate Homeric references are the Solymoi (VI-184), enemies of the renegade prince Iobates/Mudawata of Lycia (VI-171/85); but they are rather local players and not the national Hettaeans. But the most prominent candidacy for a Hittite track are the *Cetiaeans* (very near to the alternative word *Hettaeans*, especially soundwise), led in battle against the Greeks by a ruler of Mysia, Eurypylus, the son of Telephus (xi-519/21; Dikt IV.14). The whole issue reads intriguingly like the events of the Seha river valley insurgency as recounted in the Hittite archives.

As a result, the Homeric epics may well untangle the very extensive ethnographic data of Herodotus, which include contradictory traditions and perhaps official storylines. For example, Herodotus mentions the Carians as dwellers of the Anatolian peninsula, or as islanders expelled by the Minoans who found refuge to the Anatolian coast (Hdt I.171). Thucydides establishes a Carian presence in the Central Aegean, specifically in Delos, in dates where their characteristic armour was identifiable to the classical Athenians, and the inhumation procedures still practised and known (Thuc I.8,1). This suggests a Luwian maritime activity of some extent, possibly before their expulsion from the Aegean by the Minoans and the Mycenaeans; but this activity could be identified also after the Trojan War, as suggested by the list of thalassocracies (Diod VII.11) but also stated directly (Diod V.84). Herodotus' version for his Carian compatriots, with an origin leading to the Leleges (Hdt I.171,2) is very improbable, as the Hittite records mention *Karkisa* and Homer produces both Carians and Leleges (X-429). The Homeric Kaukones (II-429 & XX-329) may be identified with the *Kaska* of the Hittite records.

Herodotus, as mentioned earlier, on the one hand reports that the patriarch of the Lydians was Lydus, the brother of Tyrrhenus, and named as Lydians the hitherto Maeonians who did not migrate to Italy (Hdt I.94); this, by Homer, seems more probable than the alternative tradition of Herodotus, where Lydus is sibling to Car and Mysus. This latter tradition rather speaks for the close relationship of the three nations (Hdt I.171,5). The Pelasgians, on the other hand, are attested on both sides of the Aegean and in Italy (Hdt I.57 and I.56,2 respectively) and are mentioned in Homer (II-840/2); they *could* be identified as Luwians, but Herodotus, excellent in ethnography and culture/linguistics, takes care to differentiate them from Lydians and any other culture (Hdt I.57,3). Thus the Lydians are the best candidates for the Luwian name, along with their siblings. Contrary to the expansion of the term Hellas/Hellene and the identity declared by its use, which expanded from a small backward area to the whole of Greece, and its many colonies, to the whole Mediterranean basin and beyond, the collective Luwian identity contracted geographically and ethnologically to Lydian as time passed.

A number of events and names are cross-referenced between Greek lore and Hittite records, as mentioned above. Namely the Madawatta insurrection of Lukka (Moreu 2003), i.e. the close relationship and mutual military assistance between Iobates of Lycia and Proitos, the King of Tiryns (including the events involving Bellerophon) is such a case. The sedition was finally contained by the Hittites, a fact that resulted in Lycia supporting the Trojans during the Trojan War (II-876/7). The Seha river incident may be corroborated with the Greek landing at Mysia, in Classical Greek parlance

(Moreu 2003). It is important that although the Greek abortive operation befriended the Mysian ruler Telephus to a pro-Greek neutrality, in Homer Mysian forces are present amongst the Allies of Troy deployed for battle (II-858); obviously coming from other areas and not from the affected part of Mysia. In the end, the Hittite intervention of any kind established an anti-Greek regime and Eurypylus the son of Telephus led not just Mysians, but Hittites/Het(t)aeans to assist Troy (xi-519/21).

To this list, some more must be added. First, the cruelty, cunning and efficiency of Tandalus, who may be identified with Tudaliya I of the Hittites, was not lost to the Greeks (Diod IV.75). The ejection/persecution of his offspring, Pelops (Diod IV.73), resulted in a well-understood enmity against the agent of his ejection, Ilus, founder of the city of Ilium/Wilusa (Diod IV.75). This enmity led to the venomous hatred and ill-will of the Pelopids (both Hercules, who was second-generation, and Agamemnon, third or fourth-generation) against Troy, the capital city of Ilion/Wilusa. The name of Tandalus became embedded in the Greek lore, and this far beyond the proverbial Tandalian Tasks; Agamemnon murdered Tandalus the Younger, son of Thyestes, and thus his cousin, and brother to Aegisthus, and appropriated his realm in the western Peloponnese and his wife, Clytaemnestra (Apollod E.2,16), who later reclaimed her husband's blood with said Aegisthus as her consort. Insertion of such a name in the Greek local aristocracy implies a royal name. Pelops, the father of Atreus and Thyestes, had been mistreated in the extreme by his own father Tandalus (Apollod E.2.3). The lore does not need to be repeated, but under this light the use of the name Tandalus by Thyestes for his son can be considered as a direct spurn to his father Pelops who – allegedly – disowned the two brothers and their mother. Alternatively though, it might be considered as the use of a 'power name', a regal name from the original clade and dynasty to denote the ancestral prerogatives of the new king(s) of Pisa, their affiliation to the Asian dynasties and perhaps their claim to their original homeland, from where they had been ejected by none other than Ilus, the founder of the city of Troy (Diod IV.75) as already mentioned.

Then, the Achaean occupation of Miletus (Milawata), associated with the Hittite renegade prince Piyamaradus (the only fitting character of the Greek epic might be Priam but this is a *very* long shot), which was also contained by the Hittites, is unknown from Greek epic; as a result, during the Trojan War Miletus is counted in the Carian lands that support Troy (II-877/8). This incident must refer to the expansion of Arzawa and its eventual ebb. The initial phase of this Arzawa on Asian soil must have been incorporated into the Herculean myths of events unfolding in Asia/Lydia. The events unfolding between the *Iliad* and *Odyssey* show that the Aegean was a Greek sea at the time, but possibly either before or after a Luwian presence was strong and could account for the Egyptian mention of the Sea Peoples 'conspiring in their many islands…', corrected of course for the very poor Egyptian geographical understanding of things Mediterranean.

The Hittite King name Murisilis is very similar to the Greek Myrsilus (but also to the Marsyas of the myth of Apollo). Myrsilus is son of Myrsus, who is the last Heraclid king of Lydia (Hdt I.7,2–4), before the native dynasty of five generations that ended with Croesus in the mid-sixth century BC. The Heraclids reigned 'for 22 generations, 500 years …' (Hdt I.7,4), starting with the fifth descendant of Hercules, which means three generations after the Trojan War. But there is more; Myrsilus is the name of the driver of the chariot of King Oenomaus of Pisa, involuntary father-in-law of Pelops, who caused his master's demise and thus the ascent to the throne of the rich easterner. The tragic figure, who was murdered by Pelops subsequently, obviously to silence him, changed the course of the history of the Peloponnesus – literally (Apollod E.2,4).

Last but not least, the first fall of Troy to Hercules might account for the problems mentioned in Hittite records of Wilusan sedition, which was also contained eventually, in the Greek lore by the King Priam and his stalwart son Paris (in Homer *Alexander*, i.e. III-16), who must be referring to the Alaksandu Treaty of the Hittites, which brought back the region to the Hittite sphere of influence, but most probably, not under the sceptre of Hattusas.

Little city on the prairie

By ousting Pelops (allegedly son of Tudaliya/Tandalus, but this may refer to a loyal subject in a paternalistic autocracy scheme) Ilus made the State of Troad, around the city of Troy, a free agent. At this point the lore is more hazy than usual. Ilus had a claim by right of ancestry over Troad; in this scene the family of Tandalus and Pelops had no claim, with the possible exception of a heavy-handed overlordship demanding pledges.

Tandalus is presented by the myth as a cruel, successful and efficient king whose footprint on the ground is not well defined. This king must have annexed the north-western part of Asia Minor at a time when the Euxine trade was unknown to the Greeks.

In this mythical context, the young prince Pelops is evicted by Ilus (Diod IV.75). He is not from the land. His eviction suggests a Hittite prince that was sent to be the local ruler under the sceptre of Tandalus I of Hattusas, and the locals reacted violently. Losing the sovereignty to a local, the prince and his household feel they have better chances to migrate than to face the anger of the King for his lost province. Thus Ilus evicts foreigners. Said foreigners go to Peloponnesus, where their chief, Pelops, is challenged by the ruling king, King Oenomaus of Pisa, to a race to the death. The help of the driver of the king becomes instrumental to Pelops' coup. This driver is called Myrtilus (Apollod E.2,6), a name really close to the Hittite Murisillis, another powerful regal name of the Hittites. Myrtilus must have been an exile or emigrant, possibly from the royal household of Hattousas, who found employment as a chariotry expert: Oenomaus raced against prospective bridegrooms and speared them when catching them, Hittite-style, in terms of chariotry tactics (Apollod E.2,4–5). Myrtilus obviously assisted his compatriot Pelops, a wealthy newcomer with a great fortune and a large retinue, against his present employer, so as to wrest the kingdom (Apollod E.2,6–7).

During this time, Ilus has declared the Troad independent. The original local stock, the Teucrians, possibly recognized in the Tekker of the Egyptian texts, were beefed up by successive arrivals. Dardanus is the first to lead colonists and founds a city to the south of the area, near the Ide mountain, so as to control the southern approaches to the area and the flow of the water streams. There is no mention of a city at the time of the Teucrians, the original inhabitants of the area.

After the death of the childless king Teucer, Dardanus reigned over the whole area. His offspring found another city to the north-west, at the mouth of the Hellespont. The thing is that the new city is founded twice; by Tros and Ilus (XX-230/2), accounting for the names of Troy and Ilium both being associated with the fabled city. The only way to fit them both is to understand the one as the founder of the citadel, the eagle's nest at Hissarlik, and the other as the founder of the lower city, which has yet to emerge despite some progress in the digs (Zangger 2016). Such double ancestry can be seen in Athens and in Thebes.

The new city is strategically placed and grows fast, dwarfing the one of Dardanus, with which they form an unequal couple; an axis of power, similar to the Argos–Tiryns scheme in the Argolid. It is no accident that Aeneas, and his father Anchises, are in Troy during the war. Aeneas might have been there as head of the troops sent to assist. Why is his elderly father there? Who is viceroy at the city of Dardanus? Obviously the city had been sacked or evacuated before being assaulted by the Greeks, and the royal family had found refuge in Troy, where they might present a claim to the throne. After all, they are of a clade of the same family, and their city is older by a generation or two, (XX-215/40), which suggests seniority in the governance of the area. This antithesis, between the status of refugee and a claim to the throne, is vividly attested in the *Iliad* (XIII-459/61; XX-183).

The Wilusiad*

A Luwian princeling, Piyamaradus (Piyama meaning 'gift') was assisted in taking the Trojan throne and severing Troy from the Hittites by a Tawagalawa, brother of the King of Ahiyawa, and there was an issue with a dowry of a royal marriage between the kingdoms. By replacing the name Priam (meaning 'ransomed'), a prince originally named Podarces (meaning 'fleet of foot' in Greek) took the throne by Greek interference through Hercules, a Theban officer and citizen and thus subject of Eteocles, ruler of Thebes, son of Oedipus. Eteocles/Tawagalawa was affiliated with – or of equal status to – the emperor (*Wanaka*) of the Achaeans, obviously Eurystheus and thus considered his 'brother' (meaning fellow king, not sibling). When Alaksandu/Alexander (Paris – possibly Pariya or Paris-ziti, the latter similar in meaning to 'Alexander') became king (possibly *Basireus*, or prime minister) in Troy, he re-bound the realm to the Hittite orbit, more or less, in expanded autonomy. Since Priam had given, more or less voluntarily, his sister Hesione to marry Telamon (another lesser candidate for the name Tawagalawa) to secure some understanding with the Achaeans, there *was* an issue of dowry between Troy and them as reported in Hittite texts; the east Aegean Islands (most probably Lesbos and Tenedos) were supposed to pass to her betrothed, which did not happen (Rutherford 2020). The claim of the Achaeans could be resolved by the Trojans extracting back the bride, i.e. dissolving the marriage. The treaty of Alaksandu is overseen by the Trojan protector deities: Apaliuna (Apollo); a watercourse deity (either Scamander the river, or Poseidon); and the 'thunder-god of the Army', the Zeus revered by Priam, who was throwing lightning bolts to the Achaeans. Any of two Carian avatars may be implied: Zeus Stratius ('of the Army') or Zeus Labrandius (Hdt V.119,2), *Labarna* being an early Hittite emperor name or a title. The bearer had dismembered the Arzawa to four states, which the Hittites annexed: *Wilusa*-Ilios, *Mira* – probably Maionia, including the city *Apasa*-Ephesus after Arzawa had been destroyed, *Seha-river Country* – probably Mysia, with the river Caicus, and *Hapalla* – probably Pisidia.

* Term coined by Watkins, 1984.

Chapter 4

The Trojans

The Troy of legend had been (co)founded by tribes from the Greek mainland, especially from Arcadia and Samothrace (Dion Hal I.61), although a partial Cretan origin is also conceivable (Strab XIII.48). The fabled city was fortified during the reign of Laomedon, father of Priam, by the labour of a god in penance, Poseidon (XXI-441/55) with the help of mortals; importantly, Aeacus, the most reverent man in Greece, to become king of Aegina (Pind, *Od* 8,30/48). The city succumbed to Hercules, who was assisted by Telamon, the son of Aeacus, a most loyal companion of Hercules and an Argonaut. Telamon obviously was privy to the secrets of the city walls and the weak points of the fortification and was the first to storm the city when the wall gave way (Apollod II.6,4).

The *History of the Trojan War* of Dares states that said King Laomedon of Troy was utterly hostile to the Argonauts when they attempted to open the Black Sea trade route for the Greeks, and this was the cause of Hercules' enmity (Dares 2–3). A pure case of combined operations by the Mycenaeans to access the Black Sea, an area of geoeconomic importance, with access to rich grain-producing areas, possibly metals and, just as important, a riverine highway to Central Europe. An access denied by other, competing powers and concerns.

Legend, though, has it that it was a rescue and a feud: Hercules rescued Laomedon's daughter, who had been offered as sacrifice to a sea beast (a direct retelling of the story of his great-grandfather Perseus and Andromeda) to atone to Poseidon, builder of the walls, but the wily king did not give him the divine horses he had promised as a reward. The divinity of horses and equine bloodlines was of paramount importance at the time of chariot-borne combat, as it is evident in the *Iliad*, where the said horses figure time and again.

Troy fell to a force of no more than thirty ships (actually, from three to twenty-seven, depending on the source, but most likely eighteen), carrying no more than 3,500 warriors. This event, implicating the magnificent wall made by the gods, must account for the level of Troy VI. It was not destroyed; its royal family was exterminated as per standard Perseid SOPs but for the youngest, who was established as ruler under the overlordship of Mycenae,

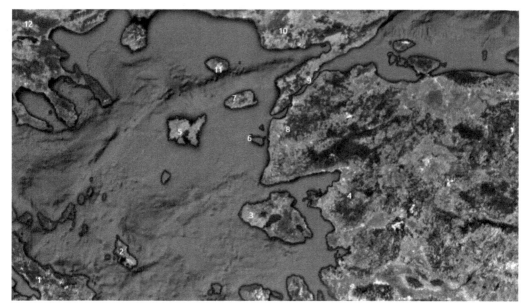

Map 4.1: Troy and surroundings.

1: Euboea; 2: Scyros; 3: Lesbos; 4: Mysia; 5: Lemnos; 6: Tenedos; 7: Imbros; 8: The Troad;
9: The Hellespont; 10: Thrace; 11: Samothrace; 12: Paeonia.

the city of Hera, whose name was glorified in *Hercules*. Thus, the Glory of
Hera brought Troy to its heels and chained it to the Mycenaean sphere while
securing the trade sea route opened by the Argonauts to the Euxine. In a while,
the deeds of Hercules in Lydia would establish the Mycenaean presence in
Asia, which must be understood as the Arzawa in Asia, with Apasa/Ephesus
as its capital city. A sea corridor to the island of Cos, and another to Lemnos
and the Hellespont bridged the Peloponnesian mainland with the new lands,
colonies and estates in Asia. Or, one may think, the correct ancient term for
what we now call the Mycenaean Empire – for the Hittites and Luwians. For
the Greeks, the Mycenaean empire is simply the Argos.

   Somewhere there, things changed and the Greek influence in Asia,
evident as mentioned before in the myths of Hercules, Theseus and
Bellerophon, seems to have been ebbing. It happened within a generation
in terms of lore, and it may have been due to the Hittite response, local
Luwian pressure and also due to internal friction. The massive infighting
between Peloponnesians and Thebans, along with the demise of Hercules,
who went out of favour in Mycenae, kick-started an avalanche of doomsday
events, mainly dynastic: the ascent, and then the affairs, of the house of
Atreus were meddlesome to the extreme and bloody, and events blew up,
exterminating a whole generation of heroes, including but not limited to

Theseus, Hercules himself, Jason, Meleager and the two pairs of siblings in southern Peloponnese, the Apharids and the Dioscuri. Lycia changed colours and was at loggerheads with the powerful Achaean island of Rhodes, a friction evident in the *Iliad*. A very obscure character, with the least Greek name, Sarpedon, commanded the Lycian forces dispatched to assist Troy (II-876/7). Sarpedon is a name that may well have Semitic origins (see Solomon, Nagmachon).

The power vested in Sarpedon, as described by himself to his second-in-command and cousin Glaucus (XII-310/20), a member of the old Greek aristocracy of the region (VI-150/206), who pledged to the new sovereign, whoever that was, is not that of a *Wanaka*. It amounts rather to a petty *Basireus* of the tablets of Linear B. Clearly collecting honours and tribute on many levels, he is ruling in the manner of the Mycenaean theocracy, implied by the stereotype 'being honoured like a god' (XII-310/2) and the sceptre of Agamemnon, forged and presented by the gods (II-100/8), a symbol of divine mandate (I-278/9). All these were achieved despite the astute Greek character, which was leading constantly to open challenges to his divine power by other commanders and commoners (I-225/31 and II-212/25 respectively); persons, by the way, who hated each other more than they hated Agamemnon (II-220).

Since the small army of Hercules could never have destroyed a powerfully fortified city, but could have assaulted and conquered it (as proven by the Viking raids centuries later), Troy VI, the magnificent, must have been the city of both Laomedon and his son, Priam. The Trojans 2.0, the ones spared by Hercules to populate the city in its new, pro-Mycenaean period, proved industrious enough to make their city within a generation much grander than it had been. Their sovereign Priam was to thank (Dares 4), but also the turmoil in Greece, spreading in both sides of the Aegean, and perhaps similar events in the east. In any case, the Troy of Priam became the navel of a Luwian confederacy, Assuwa, which grew in competition to the Greek sphere, Arzawa (similar to the expansion of NATO to former Warsaw Pact countries) and with a friendly attitude to the Hittites, although direct dependence seems not to have been the case. A realignment, as described by the treaty of Alaksandu, but not servitude.

In these conditions, there was a liability: King Priam had seen his brothers murdered by the crew of Hercules – although in Homer this is not the case, the brothers are alive and kicking. He himself was ransomed by his sister, Hesione, who was given as a prize to Telamon, the architect of the triumph of Hercules – and bore to him at least one son, Teukros, the greatest archer in Homer's Greek camp, brother to Ajax the Great. The name is an alternative ethnic for the Trojans and denotes the origin of the mother, the regal past of the family, the founding King Teucer.

It is not just that Priam loved his sister and wanted her to share in his blessings. Nor the gratitude for her ransoming him; the latter is dubious. The pattern of the regime changes effected by Hercules, as seen in Elis, Pylos and Sparta was to murder the royal line but for the youngest prince, clearly out of the race for succession, and install him in the throne. Thus, enslaving and selling overseas, as chattel, young Podarkes, who was later to become King Priam, simply does not fit the pattern; much less slaughtering him on the spot. It is possibly a poetic and perhaps desperate effort to explain the change of the name in Greek etymology, while a Luwian or Hittite linguistic approach may have been more appropriate.

Additionally, slaying all the brothers of Priam fits the usual pattern of Hercules' conduct, but in Homer there are brothers still alive (XX-237/8) who participate in the senate, nonetheless (III-146/50). This implies a more complicated series of events: perhaps the extermination of the senior siblings in line for succession, but the sparing of Podarkes and *his* selection for the puppet ruler of Troy; automatically this spared all the junior siblings.

Often hegemony gets born in the ashes and grows fast; it is hegemony that brings brilliance, and not the other way around. Typical cases are the Delian League, which was organized in the smoking ruins of Athens in less than a generation and built the Parthenon. A despoiled Athens became a world power in 30 short years (479–449 BC). Troy flourished under Laomedon, tried to deny the Greek (or rather the Mycenaean) expansion to the Black Sea under the guise of the Argonaut campaign, was put down by Hercules in a textbook case of timing, with its army possibly abroad to assist the Hittites, but then, during the reconstruction, managed to gain enormous lustre and geopolitical power, hard power, including a most aggressive navy, which did eventually bring economic prosperity again. This was probably the legacy of Paris, to be exact, although there is some tradition of Luwian naval supremacy in the Aegean before the ascent of the Mycenaeans; Naxos, the larger island of the central Aegean, is reported to have been under the Carians at the time Theseus called at it, returning from Crete (Diod V.51).

Even in Homer, a Luwian navy is explicitly mentioned, although in poor condition and dwarfing the fleet of the Greeks: the poor condition is evident because Phereclus, the chief director of the shipyards and the genius behind the shipbuilding programme of Paris, is slain in a set-piece battle (V-59/65; Apollod E.3,2), while an allied contingent from Europe crossed in ships, but left them further upstream in the Hellespont and reached the besieged city by land (XI-227/30). Still, the fact that Aeneas emigrated on deck (Paus VIII.12,8) implies they were there and kept in relatively good condition.

This was a challenge in the front yard of Mycenae: the sea. The issue was no longer limited to the remote Arzawa lands. The realm of Poseidon, second only to Zeus (XV-165 & 204), was at stake; the naval arm of the campaign of Memnon, sent to defend Troy by some Mesopotamian despot (Dikt IV.4) proves the nature of the contest and the existential level of the threat.

The prerogative of half the Greek kingdoms, from the coastal areas of Thessaly and Athens to Crete, the islands and Pylos, was the sea (Castleden 2005). Only one Greek contingent was unfamiliar with the element and not operating a naval arm: the Arcadians (II-603/14). This new Trojan policy was by definition, without anything further ado, an act of war. Pushing the frontiers all the way to Thessaly, incorporating the whole of the North Aegean, left no doubts, anyway, as it cut off the Mycenaeans from Europe by land, severing the profitable, if not vital, commercial highways that may be identified by material evidence (Castleden 2005).

The Arzawa (*sensu lato*) confronting King Priam's team led by his 'son' Paris, is very different and severely weakened; a fact that allowed massive Trojan inroads in Europe and a most impressive buildup of a power base in Asia Minor; the Assuwa federation. This power axis, from the River Axius in Europe all the way to Sagarius in Asia (II-848/50 and III-185/9 respectively) could have never been harnessed by the dwindling Hittites, but could well have co-existed with them.

When, after many years of eclipse and decline, the Arzawa was consolidated under Agamemnon, and reactivated, it was a new beast. The house of Pelops, from where Agamemnon came, had a different *Modus operandi* than Hercules and was somewhat suspicious of the offspring (not necessarily biological) of the latter, as of course, were the Trojans, too. The Pelopids were marrying into royal houses and planting their progeny on the thrones. True, Agamemnon preferred more drastic measures, planting foreign heroes and aristocrats of his own choosing on artificially or spontaneously vacant thrones. But Priam may have not had such detailed intelligence; after all, marital agreements set the Spartan throne under the direct control of the House of Atreus. Knowing the pattern from his own practices – a common pattern in aristocracies – Priam had a problem, which accounts for his concern over the return of his sister. What of the son of Hesione, had she had one? He could lay claim to the Trojan throne. Thus, Hesione should have been brought back, and by this her captive status would negate claims of her bastard son. It must have been a very nasty surprise to learn that such son would be a second-rate hero amongst the invaders. This made the abduction of Helen, to nurse similar claims by the offspring of Paris to the throne of Sparta, an overreaction. There could be no parley. The son of Hesione was a loyal Greek hero, under the sceptre of Agamemnon; not even a shepherd/leader of the army (*laagetas* in Homer, *rawaketa* in Linear B scripture) of some petty kingdom. He was a no-one. It is remotely possible, but not probable, that he was a contender for the throne of the new, all-mighty Ilios. Or was he?

The stern character of the Trojan regime, with a despot endowed supreme power and allowed constitutional polygamy (the Greeks would have nothing of the kind; see IX-341/2, although bedding slave girls and spawning bastards was seen as a valid pastime), was well beyond Greek culture. The same went for more oriental influences, brought about by the turn of the Trojan allegiances eastwards. Priam, hating the Greeks, happily effected this turn; but who engineered it?

A shepherd, on the northeastern outskirts of the kingdom, gained a reputation among his peers and neighbours for his wit, justice, judgment, hunting prowess and athletic virtues. A local, everyday boy, a direct competitor to the arrogant, high-handed authority of King Priam and his sons and officials. His fame grew so much that the lore had it that he presided over a beauty contest between three goddesses. The lore had it amongst Hera, Athena and Aphrodite, with a golden apple being the prize (Apollod E.3,2). And Paris selected the third of these.

This shepherd, a popular leader and with quite some popular support, challenged the royal authority. He vanquished all competitors, especially the princelings, on an occasion of formal religious games. In this way, he was sapping the authority of the royal family, since such proceedings made clear that the gods – who presided over the games and gave their favour so that a champion could emerge (as in the description of the funeral games in XXIII of the *Iliad*, obviously) – had rejected the royal family, who ruled by divine mandate as mentioned earlier (I-278/9).

This was a direct threat to the throne; the wise sovereign, instead of letting his sons resolve the issue by murdering the impostor, actually embraced him and adopted him literally. Most probably at this point the shepherd activist Paris became a son of Priam, with the royal name Alexander (a Greek-tongued one), or, alternatively, Alaksandu (a Hittite or Luwian one). Whether the Hittites turned the name Alexander to the phonetically similar Alaksandu (meaning 'radiant' in Hittite) or the other way around, Alexander being Alaksandu Hellenized, is of little consequence. However, the latter is less probable. *Paris* in Hittite (Pari-zitis) has the same meaning that *Alexander* has in Greek (Pantazis 2006). This implies the Greek tradition kept the original, oriental name, and its meaning in Greek, which may have been used in official correspondence, paraphrased in Hittite. Otherwise, there is no way Homer would have known of the word Paris as a translation of Alexander. After all, Troy was at the nexus of two civilizations and linguistic worlds. Luwiya was no longer mentioned in the Hittite records as a political or geographical entity (Pantazis 2006) and many Trojan aristocrats had Greek names. Antimachus (fighting-against), Archilochus (commander of the company or of the ambush), Helenus (masculine of Helen), Politis (citizen), Deiphobus (fear of Zeus). But other names are clearly oriental: Agenor, Antenor, Hector and Priam; the interpretation of the latter as 'ransomed' is least convincing. 'The ransomed one' is not a royal name and 'Priam' sounds very much oriental (*Pariya-muwa*, very brave), possibly a title rather than a first name. In this line of thought, it must be noted that in Hittite official parlance 'father' also means 'lord' or overlord, liege (a paternalistic parlance surviving to the twentieth century with Stalin and Kemal Atatürk) as implied in the royal correspondence (Zangger 2016; Pantazis 2006). Thus, Paris being adopted may mean he submitted to the authority of Priam. Moreover, the Hittite emperor is time and again referred to as the sun, and the protection of the sun god over Troy may actually imply that of the emperor-sun, although at the time Apollo was *not* the god of the Sun. He was a solar god, but the Sun was someone else, identified as *Helios* (XVIII-239/40), not Apollo.

How did Priam do this and save face? He recalled a long-lost son, exposed to the beasts so many years ago; why would a father of 49 sons have exposed a baby? Because of evil signs and omens, of course, which also explained the clandestine nature of the deed. This made it believable, less preposterous and also buffered the popularity of the populist leader. It meant he was trouble, but the sovereign adopted him into the ruling elite. It was Paris. Befriending Aeneas, the leader of the Dardanians, Paris effected the turn of Troy: he engineered the Alaksandu treaty with the Hittites; he was an astute politician first and foremost, in stark contrast to his brothers or 'brothers', the crown princes. Bold, dashing and stalwart, he brought Troy into the path of greatness by reorienting it away from the Arzawan principles and the spiritual and religious overlordship of Hera.

Godly reflections

The Greek lore is very revealing. Paris had to choose the most beautiful goddess from amongst the three contenders, each one trying to bribe him: Aphrodite by the promise of a most beautiful wife, Athena with martial excellence and wisdom and Hera with royal magnificence: he was to be lord over all Asia.

If the third promise is understood literally and in context, it means over all of Assuwa, and not of Asia in the modern sense. Consequently it denotes the promise of the rebooted, Pelopid Mycenaean Empire – or confederacy – to integrate a powerful Troy that would, in turn, become the overlord of the Assuwan states. It was a rebirth of the Arzawa from its ashes and something the Hittites would not like one bit. This would have been the ultimate step of Agamemnon across the central Aegean, already under his sway, to absorb north-western Asia Minor and the islands nearby (Lesbos, Imbros, Lemnos, Tenedos). But it was not to be.

The offer of Athena might imply an independent option for Troy and its allies. The martial prowess without the premise of greatness and wisdom imply a self-determination and self-esteem tantamount to independence on a basis of equality in an international system of power. Athena was revered in Troy and before the choice of Paris she was never seen as hostile. Even in the events of the epic, the respective priesthood seems to have been quintessential for the survival of the city: her most sacred totem had to be removed, and a public display of atonement almost changed the outcome of the war, as described elsewhere. Her personal hatred of one of the best Greek warriors, who was ostensibly doing her bidding against the city of Priam, shows complicated allegiances, too complicated for the gimmicks of a storyteller, too absurd for a god, but excellently explained by the multilayered reality of international religious practices and centres within periodically clashing geopolitical entities. In such a fluid environment, the priests, especially those of the same deity, had to make sure that, no matter the outcome, their sanctified brethren on the other, losing side, would not be harmed by the victorious troops, and reverence was the only way to ensure this. A reverence enforced sternly and savagely upon offenders, as was the case with Ajax the Lesser, who simply disrespected a refugee in the temple of the goddess, Cassandra, the youngest daughter of Priam, Agamemnon's kingly spoil of war, who would thus father successors to the Trojan royal line, underlining the victory to eternity in the most definitive manner.

This leaves the actual choice of Paris, Aphrodite. In the Greek pantheon she is the goddess of beauty, desire and sex, not a matron of geopolitics. Homer underlines this issue (V-426/30) and thus makes us consider why he takes such trouble. Some Orientals, including the Mesopotamians, assign to their counterpart of Aphrodite the mantle of war goddess, as is the case with Istar. The female battle persona in the Greek pantheon was assigned to Athena, the virgin and wise one; others preferred a female deity devoted to lust, as 'In Love and War'…

Thus the Aphrodite revered by Paris was a war goddess and a patroness of love, a safe indication of orientalism, and thus scorned and ridiculed by Homer in this capacity of hers (V-426/30). But this also confirms that Homer recognized such a divine persona for Aphrodite; it was not alien, nor even unfamiliar, to later Greece. Pausanias speaks of two such cases of religious places and artefacts in Greece consecrated to a warrior Aphrodite. She was revered in Corinth and her statue at her temple in Acrocorinth depicted her armed, although with what weapons, Pausanias fails to mention (Paus II.5.1). Additionally, the Thespians, known for their sacrifice alongside Leonidas at Thermopylae, were under the protection of *Aphrodite Melainis* ('the black'), (Paus IX.25,7) of whom there was a temple just outside Corinth (Paus II.2,4). Whether this local sect(s) were indigenous or foreign, is unknown. It is possible that these Greek personifications of Aphrodite were referring to Astarte, and were imported to the mainland along with the spoils and prisoners of the Trojan War. In concept, the case with the Artemis of Ephesus (in Hittite *Apasa*), who was (most probably) a Luwian deity renamed and adopted in Greek guise but not character or image, was similar. Furthermore, the statue of Zeus that Pausanias mentions in Argos as a spoil of Troy taken by Diomedes' buddy, Sthenelus, was supposedly a totem of the family of King Priam and had three eyes (Paus II.24,3), something incompatible with Greek myths for Zeus. This means that the Trojans had (re)introduced another pantheon, possibly in parallel with the Olympian one. Since, in the *Iliad*, Zeus is sitting on the local mountain, Ida, and is fond of the Trojans, this would account for the Trojan version of Zeus. Priam explicitly refers to Zeus inhabiting his mountain, Ida (XXIV-308), not Olympus. Other deities revered in the city may have had diverse origins, as was standard practice; Athena must have been the Greek deity. It must not be overlooked that Tarhun, the Hittite/ Luwian storm God, is as plausible an agent for throwing lightning bolts and that, in the opposite sense, when Troy was realigned to the Orient, the Greek pantheon was translated to the Hittite one. Still, the family totem of Priam being non-Greek suggests a genuine semantic association with some Oriental pantheon and, more importantly, that he was the high priest of Zeus/Tarhun; so he was vested with supreme religious power as well, most probably not unlike Agamemnon, and thus requested to vow for the city in formal duel (III-105/6).

Zeus and Aphrodite are the best examples of the alternative hypothesis on Trojan religion; that it had incorporated a dimension of Luwian or Hittite Panthea, either exclusively or inclusively to the Greek one, possibly brought by Greek colonists and imposed or recast by Hercules. This hypothesis up to now does not include some non-Greek deity that would have been translated or mutated to Athena by a Greek poet; it would have been most convenient, as it would have resolved the somewhat temperamental attitude of the goddess of wisdom and self-restraint (I-188/210), nonetheless, who offered protection to Troy and delivered punishment to Greeks while wholeheartedly supporting the latter, as they were her avengers! It is true that the more orthodox hypothesis, of local priesthoods rallying to the mission and cause of the nation/city, is also handy, as it is reminiscent of many newer examples where enemies of the same belief/doctrine fight with each other and their religious establishments support the respective secular authorities and affiliations. This is the easy approach, and if refined by the local peculiarities and preferences, it offers a nice interpretation of the Duels of the Gods (XX-33/40; XXI-328/504).

But there are two more deities that are more compatible, in their Trojan guise, with foreign rather than Greek gods. Apollo and Poseidon are referred to as having worked for the sovereign of Troy and built its magnificent walls – or Poseidon did so, while Apollo herded cattle (XXI-440/52). Building a wall is so untypical for the Greek Poseidon; as a god of tempests and earthquakes, he is more adept in bringing them down (VII-461/3; XII-27/32). In any case, the builders of the Trojan walls were, by definition, protectors if not patrons of the realm. It was the most direct way to offer everyday protection and security to their flock; building, or blessing, the wall. But, incidentally, the Alaksandu treaty mentions two deities as the protectors of Troy; a sun god and a water god (Pantazis 2006). The first is easily identified as *Apaulina*, the Greek Apollo, who is, though, *not* the sungod; Homer in the *Odyssey* is careful to talk of Helios and not of Apollo (i-6/9). Still, the solar character of Apollo made him a good translational platform for the Luwian/Hittite Sun-God.

The water deity mentioned in the Alaksandu treaty may account for the one served by the priest Laokoon. The Greek tradition assigns to him the office of Poseidon, a deity not particularly fond of the Trojans in the epic, and perhaps of little affinity: before Paris, Troy seems benign to seafaring, although not to commerce. The Trojans were a hub; there was no need to ride the waves themselves when they could collect fees and trade merchandise. Thus, the niche of a water god presiding over underground streams, hydraulic works and other freshwater resources, vital for a great Metropolis (Zangger 2016) can be identified, and the parentage of the great warrior Cycnus, engaged against Protesilaus, should be reappraised instead of being assigned to Poseidon (Ovid Met 12,64–94).

The name of Cycnus (reigned for three generations, thus a regnal name), in its Hittite version, Kukkunni, is found in the Alaksandu treaty as the forebearer of Alaksandu (Pantazis 2006). This complicates things; Paris was the protégé of Aphrodite/Istar and son of Priam; still, he was raised by a shepherd and the latter's name is unknown. Between Greek names, Hellenization of oriental names and Greek translations of oriental names, there is quite some margin. The use in occult of the son of the patron water-god (Cycnus) as forebearer of the head of state or the heir (Alaksandu) could fit Hittite beliefs well; the King of Hattusas is referred to as the sun (Pantazis 2006). Equating the king or the royal line with the protector deities of the realm is by no means implausible.

It must be stressed that Poseidon was a good choice for bringing the Trojan water god to a Greek audience: the Arcadian city-state of Mantinea is very far from the sea, its territory being landlocked; still, their patron god at least in the classical times was Poseidon and the emblem of the city, and coat-of-arms, was his trident. It probably referred to the avatar of Poseidon ruling over freshwater, and not sea or earthquakes – the region is not torn by earthquakes, as are other parts of Greece. And, a very interesting remark, the Greek Poseidon was also the god of horses (Burkert 1985). The Trojans were a people of horse-breeding above and before anything else, and Homer always uses respective adjectives to refer to them (XX-180). Still, there is no mention of Poseidon in the Iliad as being worshipped by the Trojans, even after the latter had started seafaring. The two exceptions were the case of Laokoon and Poseidon's involvement to save Aeneas from Achilles so as to continue the Trojan line (XX-291/308), a task not only befitting a patron–god, but also executed in antagonizing the recognized patron deity, Apollo (XXI-294/6)!

The choice Paris embraced was to align Troy with the Oriental powers; not with the western, nor a course of independence. The commerce of Troy was after all with the East, and there lay their allegiance before the conquest of Hercules. They had fought for the Hittites, or with the Hittites, in the Battle of Qadesh, a fact placing them against the Egyptians and thus as prime candidates for being amongst the Sea Peoples (D'Amato and Salimbeti 2015; Moreu 2003). Aeneas, son to Aphrodite and prince of Dardania, must have been instrumental in this decision and the engineering of it to a policy. A good friend of Paris, Aeneas was the second best Trojan fighter after Hector (XVII-513), followed Paris to his sea quests (Monro 1884), was distrusted deeply by Priam (XIII-459/61) and was considered as eyeing the throne; the Greeks knew the issue, and Achilles teased him on the subject (XX-179/83). The possible formula would have been to be installed by the powers that be, (personified in Aphrodite or whatever the Trojan name of the deity had been and represented by its priests) in a coup, or after the old monarch had passed away, and bypassing Priam's offspring.

Trojan politics

The position of Paris in Trojan politics is very interesting. In Homer, an aristocratic poet, one gets the impression that the successor is Prince Hector, but that may only have been part of the truth. He was the Lord of the Hosts, the *laagetas*, but his position in line for the succession is another issue. His son was called by the Trojans Astyanax – 'the Lord of the City'; his given name was to honour the great river Skamander that gave life to the plain (VI-400/3). But that may have applied to just a fraction of the citizen body. We do not read anything for any faction of Hector, but we do for a faction of Paris. Hector seems apolitical, too much so for a ruler-to-be, but, like his father, he never prays to Aphrodite; his reverence goes to Zeus and Apollo, and this says a lot for the religious allegiances of the Trojan royal family before and after Paris.

Paris was the astute politician, who gained foothold in the palace by his popularity, who reorientated Troy to the east after its rebirth, possibly as the true engineer of the Treaty of Alaksandu with the Hittites (Pantazis 2006) and launched it to prominence with his naval strategy (V-59/64). He might have been the true, or the most probable, successor of King Priam. It must be noted that Hera, i.e. Mycenae, promised supreme power to Paris in Assuwa and that included Troy; thus a formula to establish him in power was available. After all, he was recognized as second-born (Apollod III.12.6), behind only Hector in the line-up; or perhaps the status of 'second' was referring to the order of succession and not to the order of birth. This explains why alternative traditions have him as the last child of Queen Hecuba; he was the last offspring of hers to be declared a prince, *not* the youngest one in terms of age.

Hector, under this political compromise between the Trojan throne and the pastoralists to the south plus their Dardanian kin, would have remained the first prince and lord of the hosts, and perhaps his son would have been in line to rule next to Paris, reclaiming the succession for the line of Ilus, the founder. Interestingly, in this line of thought, Achilles never says to Aeneas the seemingly obvious: that the Trojan throne would go to Hector. He just mentions 'Priam's own sons' (that includes adopted ones by definition) but no favoured runner-up, no heir-apparent (XX-183). This makes Aeneas, who was a buddy of Paris, an active vector of Orientalism, and an ambitious agent. A contender for the throne under the recast Trojan power structure, as envisaged by Paris.

Aeneas was of divine lineage; son of Aphrodite/Istar to Anchises of Dardania (II-819/22), a dynastic partner in Assuwa and with a voice in public affairs (XIII-463), who does not participate in the Trojan senate, though. Two Dardanians do, the only Senators not of the bloodline of Priam (III-146/50). Two of the most prestigious families of Troy are actually Dardanians; Euphorbus, the son of Senator Panthus is explicitly called a Dardanian (XVI-807/8), and two of the sons of Senator Antenor (II-822/3) are commanding the Dardanian contingent with Aeneas (II-819/20). Thus the Dardanians *are* Trojans, the Trojans are not all of them Dardanians. There is some debate that the same goes for the Lycians (Pantazis 2006).

Indeed, the unobstructed departure of Aeneas after the fall of Troy indicates some foul play; and illustrates the chaotic picture of the westward migration. According to Diktys, the Greeks offered him a feud in Greece proper to rule, but he refused as his ambitions far exceeded the rank of petty *basireus*, either under Trojan or under Greek overlordship. He wanted to be the supreme ruler somewhere. It seems that Aeneas was very adaptable: failing to fit in the Troy of Priam, after the slaying of his friend Paris, he made successive attempts: since he could not settle there, he had a hand in its undoing (Dion Hal I.77) and tried to do so in that of Antenor, then tried to settle in Greece and then fled to Italy – like many Greeks and Trojans. Still, Aeneas founded two cities in the southern Peloponnese, or rather in Laconia, and the tomb of his father could be seen in Arcadia (Paus VIII.12,8), partly corroborating Diktys. This implies that Aeneas might have accepted the offer, but the chaos after the return of the victorious Greeks made their promises void. Agamemnon was murdered, Menelaus, on whose land he founded cities to dwell, wandered to the south, and his newfound followers and acolytes would be less than welcome, especially Trojan ones. A very wise decision was, then, to move out of the direct Mycenaean control, to the (far) west, following the lead of Greek survivors of the Trojan War who disliked the new status quo in their motherland.

If this reading is correct, the hatred of the other crown princes for Paris was well deserved; and the same goes for a large faction of the city that paid the price for the adventurism of the naval policy and the ambitious bearing in the international arena. However, this should not be taken literally: Homer is patently aristocratically minded (or his audience encouraged, passively or actively, a composition along these lines) and hated populist leaders; typical amongst the Achaeans is the case of Thersites, who is besmirched in the *Iliad* to a prodigious degree (II-212/20). On the contrary, he admires the loyal soldier and noble son Hector.

If Herodotus is right and the Trojans had reached the Ionian Sea, cutting a swath through the Greek peninsula, any Trojan claims to the throne of Sparta meant that Greece would be caught in a pincer of epic proportions.

Whether this land corridor across the Balkans allowed Luwian groups to migrate to Italy, without sailing through or around the Greek cradle, is conjectural. But the whole stage does suggest that the Golden Apple of Discord, the prize of the contest among the three goddesses, might be understood as world domination, a fitting association with The Big Apple, i.e. New York. Even at the time, there were some other fruits; the continuous use of apples in myths of paramount importance, such as The Apples of the Hesperides, the Forbidden Fruit of Paradise and the Apple of Discord show a consistent intercultural (Greek and Hebrew/Mesopotamian) association of this particular fruit with divine spheres and other planes, higher than agriculture. Paris' policy meant a great deal of trouble for the Mycenaeans, namely their exclusion from the trade routes through the Balkans, on top of losing access through the Hellespont to the Black Sea, an access brought about by successful campaigns of the Argonauts, Hercules and Theseus. If one takes into consideration that the throne of Sparta belonged to Helen and not to Menelaus, the dynastic complications are evident. Homer mentions no offspring of Helen and Paris, but Diktys' work, no matter whether original or drawing from alternative traditions at some time lost, reports three children of Helen sired by Paris (Vounomus, Korythus, Ideus). All of them were conveniently out of the way following an accident after the death of Paris. During the final round of negotiations, not long before the events of the final downfall of the city, Menelaus would have demanded the elimination of these claimants, and someone from Troy would gladly have obliged, Aeneas and the faction of Antenor being excellent candidates.

In this light, the aggressive Trojan expansion must actually have been an immensely popular enterprise, especially after the despoilment and massive loss of prestige due to the operations of Hercules. It was embraced by the king and approved by the people who became extremely rich through plunder or through commerce and influence; a fact obviously not enjoyed by some princes, especially members of the royal family who were seeing their social prerogative somewhat diminished. At its core can be found the naval programme and policy of Paris, and its ruthless aggression, detectable with some difficulty in Hector's remarks (III-46/51), which is reminiscent of classical Athens. Put in context, and given that Paris had looted Sidon in Phoenicia (VI-289/92; Apollod E.3,2), one understands that many raids must have taken place, and this on the one hand explains Menelaus' consternation in terms of Trojan bellicosity, warmongering and aggression (XIII-621/40). On the other hand, it corroborates the events recreated by archaeology, with attacks of the Sea Peoples in the Levant (D'Amato and Salimbeti 2015). Such attacks seem to have taken place before the final phase of the Trojan War and possibly instigated it, and not at its wake, as a result of it (Giannakos 2016; Zangger 2016). The Trojans were instrumental in this scheme, but other Luwians must have partaken (Zangger 2016), and perhaps the Hittites; or the latter may have been nodding with plausible deniability as their south-eastern neighbours were despoiled and levelled by their western allies or subjects (Moreu 2003).

The policy of a war to the bitter – and victorious – end was actively pursued. King Priam was fully supportive; actually he loved the project so much that he continued it to its conclusion with Paris gone. Instead of returning Helen to the Greeks and ending the war, he married the widow to one of his other sons, Prince Deiphobus (the name means 'Zeus fearing', as in 'god-fearing'). Earlier, the proposed lynching of the Greek ambassadors by a mob incensed by Antimachus, Paris' "agent provocateur" (XI-138/41), that would roll over any attempt to settle the issue without a war is conspicuously reminiscent of the execution of the Persian envoys by the Spartans before the first invasion of Greece (Hdt VII.33,1), possibly around 491 BC and might have inspired the Spartan king, Cleomenes I. In this light, Paris' political opponent Antenor, a member of the Trojan senate who advocated legitimacy in foreign affairs and observance of the Mycenaean alliance, the return of the pillage, including the abducted Helen, and atonement for the insult, found himself in dire straits, and his wife, Priestess of Athena, in a similar unenviable position. When his proposals were rejected, Antenor gave sanctuary to the Greek envoys, including King Menelaus. He deservedly secured asylum for all the members of his household and, probably, the administration of the cinders of Troy (Apollod E.3,28–9)). This would fit the blueprints of Troy VII, a post-catastrophe city of unenviable wealth and standing and in constant fear of attack, a vast difference to the power, influence, prestige and magnificence of the Homeric Troy. He was morally, religiously and politically impeccable. This was also the case of Panthus, a commoner, not of the royal clan, who also partook in the Trojan senate. Antenor and Panthus gave their sons to the Trojan army, where they fought with distinction and neither of them could be considered a traitor. Polydamas son of Panthus, perhaps the best tactical mind of Troy, clearly tells Hector that he is abusing his power and birthright in their disagreements to advance his strategy (XIII-725/35), implying a distrust of the prince to the no-blueblood elements of the – obviously constitutional – monarchy. Whether this constitutional element, centred on the senate, was the result of the reshuffling of the government effected by Paris, or corresponded with the state of affairs at least after the intervention of Hercules (or even the original form of governance in Troy), cannot be decided.

The Trojan state was positioned between the edge of the Hellespont, the Kyzicus peninsula and the Adramytic Gulf, opposite Lesbos, and divided into eight or nine 'dynasties' (Strab, *Geog* XIII.1,2), which may be the Assuwan nucleus. The dynasties could be understood as local administrative units, corresponding to the Trojan senate, which included Antenor, Panthus, Thymoites, Oukalegon, Iketaon, Klytius, and Lambus; Priam presided over it (III-146/50), making in total eight members. Alternatively, the other dynasties may have been local ones (Strab, *Geog* XIII.1,7), including some of the ones exterminated by Achilles and others mentioned in the catalogue of Trojan Allies (II-816/77). What is of interest is that the list of Trojan allies (which, however, reflects the circumstances in the tenth year of the war) does not allow for eight or nine contingents from this area; local, confederate contingents might be a maximum of four, on top of the Trojans proper. The four possibly confederate units are the Dardanians under Aeneas and two sons of Antenor (II-819/23), the (northern) Lycians under Pandarus (II-824/7), the Hellespontians under Asius (II-835/9), the name meaning 'of Asia/Assuwa' plus the 'southerners' under two chieftains of no particular weight (II-828/31). The rest are more distant allies. Since antiquity, the existence of two separate Lycian forces (Strab, *Geog* XX.8,4) has been noticed, with one contingent from the environs of the Troad under Pandarus (II-824/7) and the other from the distant south, in the south-western corner of Asia Minor, under Sarpedon (II-876/7).

An alternative setting, relocating the Trojan allies to a narrower area, roughly from the Strymon river, in the midst of the northern Aegean shore, to Cyzikus and just north of Lesbus has been proposed (Pantazis 2006). In this context, both Lycian contingents are posted in the vicinity of Troy, and the troops are considered Trojans: the Lycians of Pandarus are explicitly mentioned as Trojans (II-824/7), a national name extended in many cases to Dardanians as already mentioned. The Lycians of Sarpedon are explicitly mentioned to inhabit the vicinity of the river Xanthus (II-876/7; XII-312/4), and this is another name for the Scamander (XX-74; VI-4).

Chapter 5

The Son of the Rising Sun and the Daughters of Ares

And then there is the issue of the Aethiopians. The most intriguing presence in the Trojan War is King Memnon; he features in Homer briefly (xi-525) but the whole of the *Aethiopis*, a long-lost epic of Arctinus the Milesian, dealt with his deeds, along with other instrumental events, such as the emergence of an Amazon detachment and the demise of Achilles (Monro 1884).

The intriguing thing about Memnon is that he is the King of the Aethiopians. Identifying this people with today's Ethiopians is unwarranted; they are far to the south and could not cross Egypt to come to assist Troy, nor would they have had any motive to do so. Classical pottery occasionally, but not always, depicts King Memnon as negroid, but the epics do not refer to his complexion and it must be the classical interpretation of the toponyms, then securely assigned *par excellence* to Kush, in the south of Egypt. Given that Perseus saved Andromeda, his bride, from a sea-beast sent by Poseidon to Aethiopia, and since there is no mention of her being black of skin or complexion, the Aethiopians, meaning 'Dark', must be bronze-complexion Caucasians in these cases, residing near the sea, engaged in trade.

Memnon is the son of Eos, the deity personifying the dawn, thus he was an Easterner, as his name suggests; *Memnon* seems to come from the Oriental *Memnun*. He had armour of divine manufacture, made by the god of technology, Hephaestus, like that of Achilles; in stark contrast to the outfit of the African Ethiopians according to Herodotus (Hdt VII.69), but similar to the As(Syrians) in Herodotus (Hdt VII.63). Representations from upper Mesopotamia (Dezső 2012) corroborate the Assyrian use of armour and of nature compatible with the epic. Taken together, these two pieces of data suggest an Eastern, Levantine origin, not a southern one. The later tradition suggests that his capital was Susa, in distant Elam, the principal capital of the Achaemenids under Darius I and known as 'The City of Memnon' (Hdt V.54,2; Diod II.54 & II.22,3; Paus X.31,7). This resolves the issues of technology and bearings on the map. It also corroborates the use of the term Aethiopians in Homer's epics, and also in a passage of

Herodotus, that both suggest a non-black stock (else it would have been underlined), but perhaps of darker complexion (the Greek word Aethiops, singular nominative of the Aethiopians, means literally 'dark of sight'). Homer has the Aethiopians as devoted believers of the Greek Pantheon (I-423) but especially honouring Poseidon (i-204), seafaring, and divided into Far East and Far West cradles (i-22/4). The East is easily identified with the Levantine coast, and the Extreme West, either with Morocco/Spain or Tunis. In both locations Phoenician colonies were later established at Tartessus and Carthage respectively, which would suggest an identification of the Aethiopians of Homer and the Aethiopis with the Semite Phoenicians. However, the two terms, Aethiopians and Phoenicians are mentioned in the same epic cycle and even in the same Epic (iv-83/90); it must be surmised that Phoenicians and Aethiopians are not the same people.

Herodotus identifies Aethiopeans in India, (Dravides, obviously), south of Egypt (Kushites) and in Cyprus (Hdt VII.70,1 & VII.69 & VII.90 respectively). In the third case, he obviously means the Assyrians that colonized the island during their suzerainty, after conquering it under Sargon II in circa 700 bc (Papasavvas 2014). The area of Syria most probably was named from the mega-city and metropolis Tyre (in Semitic 'Syr' to this day). This identifies the Aethiopians of the epics, with the nation ruling supreme on the Levantine coast and far inland.

During the Bronze Age, there were a number of nations and states actually qualifying for the characterization 'empires', east of the Luwians: the Hittites in central Asia Minor, who expanded to rule all of the central and eastern part and the middle swath of the western part. Then there were the Mittani to the east, the Assyrians/ Mesopotamians in the south-east, the Egyptians due south, and then, further south-east than the Assyrobabylonians, the Elamites, including the Susians (Zangger 2016). Different political entities rose and then were eclipsed in this vast area over time, and the timing of the Trojan war, along with the inherent complexity of aligning chronologies in different cultures, does not make the compilation of a clear picture over the political situation to the far east easy. Whether, at the time, Elam and Assyria were under one sceptre, cannot be surmised, but the centuries of the alleged Assyrian supremacy and empire (Diod II.22,2) are a possible explanation.

In any case, somehow a powerful force crossed the lands in between, and arrived at Troy. Their route must have been the predecessor of the King's Road, established by the Achaemenids (Hdt V.52). Raising allies and reinforcements from such a distance means that either, at the time, Troy was vassal to these Aethiopeans – probably Assyrians (Diod II.22,2) or that something of a crusade and call of arms obsessed the most bellicose

Orientals. The latter option suggests that a kernel of truth may exist in the belief of a centuries-old feud between oriental monarchs and the Greeks, as succinctly suggested by Haubold (2012), quoting Sargon II and interpreting the sea ambitions of later Achaemenids.

The identity of this people is perplexing; Semitic stock would have been a valid guess, and corroborates Diodorus' views (Diod II.22), which give also specific numbers: 20,000 infantry, half imperial and half of Memnon's own province, and 200 chariots (Diod II.22,2), the usual ratio in later armies; although the numbers and the ratio imply a retroprojection by such late source as Diodorus.

The western affiliations at the time, and religious affiliations to the Greek pantheon, make the identification of Aethiopians with the Assyrians a bit problematic. A generalized use of the term for different peoples out of the known map, which was evidently limited to the eastern third of Asia Minor and a very narrow coastal strip at the coast of the Levant, to Egypt and westwards (at least) to Sicily, may be a reasonable approximation.

The Amazons are by far the most exotic element in the lore of the Trojan War. The Greek lore suggests another Asia Minor cradle (Diod II.45–6), not a steppe one as usually suggested (Mayor 2014), and the transition is explained competently (Hdt IV.110–15). There is no way to suggest misidentifying males for females to explain away the references; it is better to assume a culture dead and lost for many centuries, the artefacts of which have not been discovered yet, to introduce it into the recorded and materially substantiated history. From an Asian abode they emerge time and again to harass the Greeks: Hercules started the affront, Theseus did likewise and they returned the favour with a massive invasion, which may be associated with the Trojan invasion recounted by Herodotus before the Trojan War, as mentioned earlier. This event coincides squarely with the heyday of Theseus, against whom the Amazon attack was directed. The Amazon war against Theseus is a very explicit indication that, despite the crushing defeat dealt by Hercules in their own homeland, the nation was far from spent and done; the defeat in Athens and their retreat must have been much more detrimental. It is true that the belt of the queen, a piece of armour as well as a symbol, once lost to Hercules, meant a terrible blow to their prestige and cult, but it might have been an opportunistic victory, less triumphant than celebrated. The ebb from the second last step of the Greek Peninsula, Attica/Athens, must have been a nightmare.

Fighting against the Phrygians and their ally Priam (III-184/9) establishes them solidly in central Asia Minor. The culture may have been less of a prodigy: a manifestly different female army under (a) Dionysus, coming from the islands, invaded the Argolid at the times of Perseus (Paus II.20,4 & 22,1) and the cult of Athena among the Libyans, along with the alternative myths for the Sphinx of Thebes (Paus IX.26,2–4), Medusa (Paus II.21,5; Diod III.55,3) and Myrina (Diod III.53–5), suggest female warriors fitting a more aggressive branch of the matriarchal common heritage and inglorious past, as suggested by archaeological discoveries and mentioned earlier. This conclusion is supported by the interpretation of the lore of Medusa, in the focal lore of Perseus, as a warrior queen of the Western Mediterranean (Paus II.21,5; Diod III.55,3).

The insistence of Greek heroes to pursue such engagements with special fervour (Dikt IV.3; Diod III.55,3) seems unexplainable. It could have implied a degree of sexism, had there not been the opposite paradigms of Deianera, daughter of Oeneus, princess of the Aetolians and beloved of Hercules (Apollod I.8,1) and Atalanta, the female Argonaut (Apollod III.9,2). This extreme hostility, if not outright cruelty, is all the more strange since such an attitude is also evident in the classical era: fighting for their survival, in the face of utter and total physical extinction (not just political), the Athenians on the eve of the Battle of Salamis, put a price on Artemisia, a veritable bounty for her; from all the multitudes of the army and navy of Xerxes, as were, for example, their own traitors, Medizers and Quislings like the offspring of Peisistratus (Hdt VII.6; VIII.54). Why this scandalous preference? Because she was taking the field – or the seas – against them even though she was a woman (Hdt VIII.93,2)! This shows perhaps a grander scheme. It may still be of a sexist nature, which of course is the easy interpretation – and perhaps a popular one, especially in feminist studies. But it may also have been of a religious character: a crusade against the hated matriarchy, especially of its belligerent spin-offs, with their own protocols of sexist oppression (Diod III.53–5); after all, and speaking for the Athenians, they had faced extinction due to an Amazon invasion (Plut, *Vit Thes* 27); not to any other invaders.

Section 3

The Protagonists

Chapter 6

Heroes: the Status and their Culture

It is essential to ponder the exact nature of the paradigm of the Greek hero. What was a hero? Not for the Greeks of the Classical Age who transmitted their – slightly distorted, or evolved – version of a hero, as a blend of selflessness and exceptional bravery, especially before uneven odds and in pending catastrophes. The issue is, what constituted a hero in the eyes/ears of Homer, and possibly for all his peers and contemporaries? What were his characteristics and his principles? After all, heroes passed to immortality and the lore one generation after the Trojan War (Hes, *Works* 156/69), with the fall of Peloponnese to the Dorians.

Let us start by saying that it is a warrior's world, thus *hero* means a warrior/ hunter, since the fauna was at the time an issue. The Labours of both Hercules and Theseus were focused on exceptional animals of prodigious size or capabilities, distinct from creatures of myth, such as centaurs, sphinxes etc. Amongst the Labours of Hercules, there were a lion, a boar and a bull as exceptional villains. The hunt for the Boar of Calydon was one of the most massive heroic projects from all of Greece (Apollod III.9,2). Odysseus had a characteristic scar from a hunting injury (xix-390/5) and the lore is full of hunters who excelled and/or lost their lives, including but not restricted to Orion, Scorpio and Actaeon. Thus *hero* means danger, on the hunt or in war. But it does not mean achievement or prominence. There are many entries in the *Iliad* that Homer refers to as heroes, although they are conspicuously absent from any list of achievements. Maybe in their home village they were somebody, but in the epic they are not. And since nobody mentions their mettle and achievements, perhaps they never made it to prominence and it is not due to the haze of millennia that we know nothing for and of them. As a result, fame is an ambition, not a prerogative, for the hero.

This means that the entity is more social than anything else. It is impossible to track its limits; the commoners who were following the *eqeta* for his exploits, gory projects and prizes, were they heroes as well? Or was it left to the aristocracy? It sounds like the medieval knight. It took a formal recognition to be one, no matter how great a warrior; and then it was a title, without any battle merit attached to it. Was it thus for the hero? Does the word have something to do with Hera and, in this way, could he be one of the chosen ones of the highest female goddess, especially in Argolis and Laconia? A human consort?

The social stature, if exclusive, as was the case with the knights, would have some rules, laws and customs attached. The divine element is supreme. There is always a tendency to explain away the inclusion of divine progenitors in the bloodlines of heroes and demigods as an intentional effort to glorify their line or to account for illegitimate conceptions. The latter is implausible, because the policy of exposing newborns provided an excellent way to dispose of unwanted bastards and the myths concerning their salvation show a parallel wave of discreet, double or single-blind adoption of seemingly healthy babies by interested parties.

The former is also a poor bet. If it is a matter of self-aggrandizement, what exactly would stop everybody claiming divine heritage? And why being the bastard of different gods and not of the king and father of the gods, Zeus? Very prominent individuals, such as Odysseus, enjoying the scandalous support and protection of Athena, would have done so. Some of the sons of Priam, too; there were godspawns in the extended royal family, after all, see Aeneas. What was the reason and the mechanism for such selectivity?

It must have been a social event. It remains a very dubious issue whether some divine entities in Greek lore were supposed to be understood as biologically divine, or of a divine calling. The nymphs may well have been mortal women/girls selected or assigned to minister different worship elements, thus exercising some degree of control in a primitively controlled civic body. The sons of first-line gods and goddesses, and daughters also, could well have been children of the temple. As the ministers of the gods had their own legitimate sons (V-9/10), the most plausible model is the selective breeding of templars, possibly of exceptional physical qualities with selected mothers in some sort of mystery, similar to the yearly tenure of Babylonian girls or of the *prima noce* of the western lords. This selective procreation, a possible interpretation of the Jewish *Nazar* concept (Kalopoulos 1998) would furnish a breed of children of unknown father. Such children would be affiliated to the God(ess) served by the priest(ess) that begot them. On adulthood, they would perform a number of functions, from defence and enforcement to ministerial and other menial tasks and to introduction in the divine brotherhood for its continuity. The degree of sophistication of the Mycenaean and Luwian religious practices and concepts is not well understood, but contemporary Egypt might have been an example of the concept and principle, if not for the processes and details. Once they had concluded their duty to their begotten deity, such offspring, perhaps well trained and versed in political, military and social skills, would try to make an impact in society, with the help of the brotherhood and poised to increase both priestly prestige and returns in different resources, from believers to offerings.

The religion of Ancient Greece as we understand it from the archaic and classical periods is fundamentally different than the one described by Homer. It amounts, perhaps, to another doctrine, as defined by Christianity, if not a heresy. Given that the Dorians are prominent in commerce and warfare, the leading Greek deity is Apollo. Despite Athena being the patron goddess of Athens, even the Athenians take steps to secure a major sanctuary of Apollo within their empire, so as to ease the political-religious grasp of Delphi over their citizens' psyche and religious feeling since Delphi are located in the midst of the cradle of the Dorians. It was the Delos sanctuary, with its functions of divination and all the accoutrements, rites, processions and purification prerogatives, such as the official and utter purification of the land by removing all the existing graves (Thuc I.8,1). Classical doctrine is centred on Apollo; the doctrine of Homer is centred on Zeus, with Hera, Athena and Poseidon sharing second place; not Apollo. Also, Apollo has nothing to do with the sun in Homer; he is shiny, but not the sun, as evident in the *Odyssey*, where the sun god is Hyperion (i-8), not Apollo/Phoebus.

Thus the theology of Homer, very different from that of Hesiod and more primitive than that of the days of Leonidas and Socrates, should be viewed independently, possibly in the context of other, similar, great civilizations within sailing distance, and corrected for the lower yield, diversification and resources for the Greek states. This may be overestimated and much more magnificent cities and architecture, and far higher population density may have been the case, than what is usually supposed by the rather fragmented palace records.

Another intriguing issue with Greek heroes is that, for some of them, there seems to have been a sort of official schooling regime, an academy of sorts. It is not unusual: similar, even if not identical, approaches are heard for Achaemenid princes being submitted to a rite of passage (Plut, *Vit Artax* 3,1–3), Spartan youths, who had to endure the yearly commission of *crypteia*, although this might refer to a cadre of *selected* youths (Plut, *Vit Lyc* 28) and of course the usual period of meditation of Hebrew Rabbis in the desert, possibly at the colony of Qumran, but conceivably at any other location, solitary or collective, to seek purification and enlightenment. The 'Achaeans' had the sanctuary of Pelion, under Cheiron the Centaur (Phil, *Her* 32,1), where at least two generations of heroes underwent training (Apollonius Rhod, *Argon* II.508–11); very important is the fact that Perseus never did, and Hercules underwent standard princely (heroic?) training by tutors at home.

Achilles, a top-tier prince, is the most conspicuous graduate (Apollod III.13), and the other was Jason, whose status is somewhat debatable; he was raised and tutored there, but whether he was indeed who he claimed – or was told – to have been, this is another issue altogether. The curriculum is more or less known, but not the time frame, nor the solitary or collective setup of the academy.

Many of the heroes of the Trojan War are supposed to have graduated from Cheiron's academy (Phil, *Her* 32.2) but somehow, in Homer, Achilles seems to enjoy a special status as one of the very few, if not the only one that enjoyed such tutorship (XI-829/31). Cheiron's age may not be a problem; tutorship may extend through many generations and more, if instead of generations one thinks in terms of classes (Phil, *Her* 32.1). The annoying thing is that the schoolmaster is located in two different places, in Pholoe in Peloponnese and Pelion in Thessaly, and that he is accidentally slain by Hercules in his first abode (Apollod II.5,4). It is difficult to match a date of Achilles' graduation (XI-829/31) with a plausible *subsequent* date for the unfortunate event with Hercules, as suggested by some sources (Apollod II.5,4). Even if the issue with the location is resolved miraculously, one has the impression that Cheiron might be a tribal, mystical, or even professional name for such schoolmasters. If this is the case, and without getting into the precise nature of the Centaurs, the dual locality is resolved; there were (at least) two different Cheirons, and two colonies of Centaurs, one in the Peloponnese and one in Thessaly/Pelion, and possibly not both of them received students; there are no princelings in the story of Cheiron and Hercules. The Thessalian abode is well-established by the myths of Achilles, of Jason and of the fight between the Lapith clan and the Centaurs (II-742/4; Plut Theseus 30,3). The Peloponnesian one, if it did exist, is heard only through the Herculean legends. Whether this establishment has something to do with the duality of many locations in Greece, where a toponym is found both within and away from the Peloponnese, is uncertain. The thing is that as there is more than one area called Argos, in line with the 'new' prefix in toponyms from modern colonialism, other toponyms might have been used to replicate the original environment, along with customs and establishments. A very good indication is the legend that recounts the slaying (accidental of course) of Acrisius by his grandson Perseus. It happened when the old king had retired at Larissa, and Pausanias explicitly refers to the city in Thessaly, near Peneus river. The problem is that neither Acrisius nor his grandson had any connection with that location; there is a Larissa in the Argolid, a height in the environs of the city (Paus II.24,1), and this is a much more probable context for the event. As with Argos, the name may have been transplanted by colonizing/annexation, from the Argive Larissa to the Thessalian one. Or it may have been used to describe a similar locality. It is not known exactly what the meaning of Argos was in Mycenaean Greek, but the root has been used for the legendary ship *Argo*, for its designer and builder Argos and for the dog of Odysseus Argos, thus it has an everyday meaning.

In effect, there are two lines of heroic upbringing: the conventional/ standard one, of state and, more explicitly, family bonds and training syllabus seen in multiple cases even in the *Iliad*, where a hero/*eqeta*/aristocrat trains another, usually his scion (XV-525/7); and the special, sanctioned with a more advanced syllabus that may include medicine (Phil, *Her* 32,1–2), while literacy is included in both. The second programme takes longer years in isolation; one might think of the advanced programme of Aristotle for the cadre of princelings around Alexander the Great, or one might think of a version, much less advanced and more primitive, of temple upbringing, and training and testing programmes culminating in rites of passage and introduction into a society, an initiation in all but name.

So a hero is an international social entity of the time, based on permissive bloodlines. The bloodline of a hero may be through some line of heroes, longer or shorter, but somewhere a god (a priestly operative) must have been present, preferably combined with royalty or a female minister, such as naiad, dryad etc. A commoner may not enter their world. Their prerogative and their authority is god-ordained (I-277/9) and countable by size (I-281), which furthers competition amongst the heroes. Still they are expected to deliver, especially in terms of war excellence, and on that subject public opinion matters (XI-310/21). This battle excellence, best substantiated in cases of wildly uneven odds in public eyes (V-801; IV-390/9), is the aspect that survived to the modern day, long after their world turned to cinder. The status of the hero is very reminiscent of the medieval social structure of knighthood and the feudal links; the latter might be more a survival of the former than a parallel. The Trojan migration west, to Italy, might have retained the system in Latium/Rome and Etruria, which survived through the Roman *Equites*, minimally changed, to the Late Roman period and medieval knights. On the contrary, the fall of the Mycenaean *metropoleis* in Greece, the turmoil that followed and the new *polis* organization severed such lines with the past and only shadows survived, resulting in a very different feudal system in the Byzantine Empire where bloodlines were far less important.

And what is *very* important: an *eqeta* is a hero. A hero does not need to be an *eqeta*; Odysseus does not own or operate a chariot; he knows how to, knows the specifics (X-498/514) – *it is a hero's training* – but does not do so; he *is* a hero. So does Pandarus: he knows everything on the subject (V-226/32), he owns a full unit of chariotry back home, but had chosen to come in on foot and fight as an archer (V-193/205), obviously an armoured one (V-294/5); once this does not go well, he can fight at a moment's notice with the spear from a chariot (V-238 & 200/5).

Vanity always characterizes aristocracy, including aristocratic warriors. On top of arrogance pure and simple and similar mundane expressions of superfluous ego, a majestic appearance actually discourages enemies. Someone looking important may well do so for good reason, as with martial capabilities. Thus overbearing appearance has practical aspects on top of self-importance. As such, both sides pay attention to their appearance and the epic uses many adjectives to show this. Some are functional and apply to both. But others are more specific, quantitatively or qualitatively. The Greeks are called well-groomed in hair (II-11; they wore it long, obviously). They are also characterized by their greaves (XIII-51). The Trojans are mostly characterized with equestrian adjectives (XIV-472), but never mentioned as wearing greaves or as grooming their hair – at least not as a characteristic and universal feature. Occasionally, Greeks are also characterized by equestrian adjectives as well (XIV-10), but not as regularly as the Trojans, who must have been renowned for their equine livestock and capital. What is important is that there are special fashions in some tribes: the Avantes have a characteristic haircut (II-542). In the *Iliad* it is not mentioned, but being shod only to one foot – the left – was a characteristic of the warriors of Aetolia (Graves 1955). It is not mentioned for Diomedes or any of his troops and the tradition may antedate the Trojan War. If not, Jason appearing like that in front of Pelias was him sending a message: he was an Aetolian warrior (from his mother's side), and the sovereign must have been advised to mind such signs (Apollod I.9,16) that would indicate, no doubt, foreign intervention in his affairs; and a detrimental, hostile one obviously.

Chapter 7

The Jet Set: the World of Greek Heroes

Achilles

Achilles is the central personality not only in the *Iliad* but of the Trojan War. Nothing on the subject can be understood without unlocking this character. His CV is impressive: being nothing more than a great-grand-child of Zeus and the son of a lesser (sea-)goddess, he became the number two of Greek heroic lore, behind Hercules. Perseus, with a great list of achievements, the founder of Mycenaean Greece, scores nowhere near in terms of prestige, amongst the Greeks, in Greek lore. Theseus was a prodigy, a sales pitch for Periclean democracy (Plut, *Vit Thes* 35,5 & 29,3). If the Dorians had not conquered, eventually, the Peloponnese, in the name of Hercules, their very own hero, Achilles might have ranked even better. He was the paradigm for Greek warriors; Alexander the Great, who supposedly drew his bloodline from both, had Achilles, not Hercules, as his role model, despite the fact that Achilles registered fewer accomplishments than either of the other two. His shrine in the Troad was a place of pilgrimage and not only for Greeks. True, when Herodotus says that Xerxes offered sacrifices and honours to the heroes of old in the Troad (Hdt VII.43,2), he most probably insinuates that he did so to the Trojan heroes, for whom he posed as a vindicator (Zangger 2016). Achilles is the only one along with Hercules that went in line for an epiphany, although less elaborate. Achilles, allegedly resurrected and happily inhabiting the island of Leuke (Phil, *Her* 54–5), the nowadays renowned Snake Island in the Black Sea, Ukraine, served as the brand name (introduced in the *Aethiopis* of Arctinus the Milesian) under which the colonization of the Euxine (re)started, especially by the Ionian Greeks of Western Asia Minor, during and after the Dark Ages.

Achilles has been intentionally and, at times, spontaneously smeared by Western scholarship and the collective consciousness. This is due partly to the pro-Trojanism of most western royal families; Trojan descent is claimed for so many Europeans, that the scholarship and the lores developed therein could be nothing but the most hostile. Orientalists, in eastern and western context, felt and fared, understandably, the same. Achilles is the arch-enemy of oriental despotism, as the brawling Greek assemblies are contrasted to the absolute power of King Priam. Every autocrat likes the docile but murderous prince Hector, devoted to his king, his father, and dislikes the cold efficiency of the astute Achilles. Had he not been Greek, he would have been a flag for left wing and communists: his almost pacifist aversions (IX-406/9), his direct confrontation to the exploitation due to position and authority, his downright rejection of buyoffs (IX-375/91) and his material culture as a due reward for toil (IX-318/20) might have been included in a Marxist manifesto. The reason they have never been rests with the colour of the flag.

Under this (lack of) light, one should attempt what recent (and not-so-recent) scholarship has failed – or *declined* – to do. Ancient scholarship, on the other hand, has scored marginally better. The versions of the Homeric texts that have come down to us are inadequate. And there are pottery images and other representations, some reported by Pausanias and other wonderers and historians, that imply very different versions of the Homeric poems, with parts long lost or redacted from the texts of the Peisistratids that have come down to us. Not to mention other sources, including but not restricted to other epics.

The most profound, and at the same time visible, aspect of Achilles is that of a warrior. A tribal warrior. He is unanimously considered as a very fast man, and the Homeric adjectives underline that; he is fleet of foot (i.e. XIII-348). Nobody notices that, similar to Hercules (the giant who gave chase to a stag on foot!) he is exceptionally large. Ajax is portrayed as very big of stature, and presented thus in contemporary art, as in the movie *Troy* by Petersen. Homer, though, underlines that he is *second* to Achilles (II-768/9). He is very fast, but also very tall and wide, a nasty, lethal combination; the only defensive equipment he may use is the oversized shield of Ajax. Nothing else in the camp of the Achaeans fits him (XVIII-192/3)! This also shows that, fighting with the body-shield and spear(s), was considered by Achilles himself not only doable, but also familiar.

The usual interpretation is that he excels in infantry combat, being an excellent javelineer – or rather spear-fighter, fast and excellently armoured. These are true attributes, but the epic makes a point of his equestrian skills. He is time and again shown and credited as the best chariot-borne warrior, with the best team (II-770; XXIII-273/8). This is not a manoeuvring instrument; Achilles does not ride to battle so as to fight on foot. He actually does so, but this is not all. Both his original armour and his spear, of which there are many references in the epic, imply a lancer's kit (a chariot-borne lancer's) more than anything else. There is no way to consider a throwing spear, javelin or double-purpose *dory* too heavy and cumbersome for other, less powerful warriors to wield (XVI-1403). Such attributes fit well with a chariotry lance, of extreme weight and length, for which divine manufacture would have been of some importance. A cast weapon may be lost. One *may* understand, or suppose, that the lance was part of a fine set, with some javelins – or a pair of spears – from the same manufacturer, to form the complete offensive kit of a chariot-borne warrior. The real owner, Achilles' father, Peleus, is never mentioned in a war sense as anything but horseman (VII-125). Being of the age group of Nestor, the master of chariot jousting among the Greeks (XI-746/8), Peleus must have received a full charioteer's kit as a wedding gift from the Gods. And the very few things we learn about his panoply (which Achilles was using for the whole duration of the war except for the final stage) fit well with this interpretation.

Hector, the constitutional commander of the Trojan host and C-in-C of the allied oriental army, withdrew from the fighting to put on the armour of Achilles he took as prize from Patroclus. He must have had the best armour available in the Luwian hinterland, the shield included; his armour remained intact and unpierced when deflecting lethal casts from Ajax at the shield (XIII-191/4), Diomedes on the helmet (XI-349/53) and Idomeneus at the cuirass (XVII-605/6). Despite these facts, he opted for that of Achilles instead of his own (XVII-186/7). When he fought against Achilles, the latter took great pains to strike at an unarmoured spot (XXII-321/6). He doesn't seem to take such precautions in any other case. This suggests armour of superior quality. Additionally, it is stated explicitly that when charging, Hector was fully covered in metal but for one weak spot. The correct use of the shield may account for this effect, but this refers to the frontal aspect. From the side there is no shield, thus thighs and neck should have been unarmoured and functionally exposed. The sum of information implies a full suit of armour, with more parts than the standard cuirass/greaves/helmet kit, suitable for shock chariot warfare with the lance as the main weapon. On the contrary, the new suite of Achilles, obviously made by the divine coppersmiths and armourers of Lemnos, under the direct patronage of the smith god, Hephaestus (XVIII-462/7), must have been a novelty in fit, lightness (XIX-384/6), coverage and protection. It was not (only) the lavishness and quality, but perhaps also the design, the first of its kind, not witnessed by any mortals up to that moment (XIX-10/11); the best description of a panoply of new design and philosophy.

It is seldom noticed that Achilles, in his guise as a charioteer, introduces some innovative features. He uses a two-horse team, which is perhaps standard for the Achaeans; Trojans reportedly have four-horse teams, occasionally, the example being Hector (VIII-185). But Achilles added a side horse, Pedasus, he took as prize in his campaigns (XVI-152/4). There is no clue of anyone else having tried such an arrangement, and the concept may have been to make sharper turns rather than achieve higher speeds. Obviously the third horse is added at the side of the yoke facing inside the tactical turn, which ensures a tactically important asymmetry. Whether this turn is on the side of the warrior or on that of the driver is not attested and there are different possibilities. But the latter is more probable, because it protects the third horse from the heavy action expected on the side of the warrior and leaves a wider sector free for the use of the lance. Whether this format has anything to do with the Assyrian three-horse chariot teams (Dezső 2012) remains open.

The other important equestrian feature is that, on the day of reckoning, Achilles appears to be riding alone. A driver is absolutely necessary for the function of the chariot as a weapons system (XVII-461/5), though not for racing (XXIII-301/ 531), where weight is important and there is no distraction or other task to dictate the use of another crew member. Patroclus rides the chariot of Achilles with another driver, Automedon (XVI-219/20). Generally speaking, in mid-combat, when a driver is hit, care is taken to replace him; if nothing else, for expedient extraction (XV-445/56), and there is no shame whatsoever for a prestigious warrior in acting as the driver (V-226/8). But Achilles drives alone and fights at the same time (XX-498/501). When this happens, it must be noted, the third horse has long ago been killed. It must have been virtually impossible to do this with the extra horse, which could not have been harnessed directly to the yoke of the two-horse chariot. But once the team came back to normal size, some special skill should be inferred, to drive in the thick of the fight and still use at least one weapon. Of course it could be poetic licence or a figure of speech: when starting from the camp, Automedon had mounted the vehicle to drive (XIX-395/8). True, any mounted cavalryman reins with one hand and fights with the other, but doing so for a team of two horses means some arrangement of the reins verging on innovation or virtuosity.

However, there is some precedent: when facing Ares, Diomedes was alone in the chariot, accompanied by the goddess Athena, who remained invisible but added quite some weight to the vehicle (V-837/9), while his attendant and driver, Sthenelus, disembarked (V-835). This is a very poetic way to imply either a technical innovation, because Athena is the goddess of engineering, or mastery of equestrian skill, since she holds the reins (V-840), even though under the spell of invisibility (V-844/5). Diomedes, after all, won the chariot race at the funeral games (XXIII-99/514) and thus has shown himself to possess excellent equestrian skills.

Even in the context of chariot warfare, and perhaps contrary to assertions on Mycenaean chariot archery (Drews 1988; 1996) Achilles has nothing to do with archery; and it must be reconsidered whether archery was indeed a perfect match to chariot warfare, as proposed by Drews as above; in Homer, the shock action of the chariot is attested time and again, in a positive or negative way. When Hector drives his horses against Patroclus and is reported not to engage Greek troops due to his focus on this one opponent (XVI-731/2), it means that, in standard conditions, he would have engaged, dispatching opponents while mounted, and at full speed. Thus, when Hector is reported to have been thrashing heads (XI-309), most probably he does this while charging, and having a particularly long lance, eleven cubits long (VIII-494), he definitely uses it at the full gallop. Other Trojans do similarly against the Greeks, who fight them off with equally or even longer lances/pikes from their ships' decks, and of course Nestor provides the tactical guidelines for this kind of fight (IV-306/7).

The military revolution of the purpose-made javelin, as suggested (Drews 1996), is an excellent alternative for ranged weapons, and Achilles excels in casting. It is important that he is never mentioned as adept with the bow, as if he disdains the weapon, which cannot have been the case. The heroic training syllabus, like that of the knights of Christianity, made a point of familiarization with a diverse range of weapons, *including the bow* (Apollod II.4,9). Preferences were of course at play; Odysseus, a most accomplished archer (xxi-80/95), never carried his legendary bow to war (xxi-39/42). But Achilles is never mentioned as having even shot a bow. Similarly, he never reverts to stones in any of the battle scenes, as do many other heroes. After all, the Throw/Shot Put was an athletic event and he must have been trained in it as well. On the other hand, he is the most accomplished swordsman. He is the only warrior in the *Iliad* who *chose* to use the sword instead of a shafted weapon (XXI-17/21); all other cases refer to *reverting* to sword once shafted weapons are expended (i.e. XXII-290/306).

The signature choice of Achilles is the spear cast. It is so iconic that the obvious fact that his father's spear is a lance has been forgotten and corrupted to apply to a throwing – or throwable – spear. Inspiring the Petersen movie, in Homer a Trojan says in awe that whatever he throws never stops until it is sunk in flesh (XX-98/100). Given that he does miss occasionally, actually thrice in three high-profile single combat events, against Aeneas (XX-273/82), Asteropeus (XXI-171) and Hector (XXII-273/6), his fame must be considered excessive. On second thoughts, the comment might refer to hits, implying that there is no way to parry such a cast; it slices through shield and armour. This would have been a valid and most logical interpretation and remark; there is not one case in the epic that Achilles' spear cast is intercepted by shield or armour. This suggests a lethal cast that strikes dead-on, fast enough not to glance off (XXII-289/91), and a superior set of weapons, not breaking upon impact (XVII-605/7). Despite being fast, and perhaps due to his great stature, Achilles does not try to evade enemy casts but prefers to parry them, thus controlling fully the next step. A parried missile is no danger for anyone, especially unsuspecting friendlies (XVII-304/9), and the missile drops nearby, within the control sphere of the warrior. His god-made, brand-new armour, of the then standard (and understandably modern) panoply, takes most credit; still, as already mentioned, the old kit kept the man unwounded. In Homer, Achilles is slightly wounded/scratched by an enemy javelin and does not seem at all invulnerable. He does not feel nor act like it. As Palaephatus (*De Incred 11–12*) succinctly suggests for other mythical subjects of the heroic era, the Greek word *atrotos* should not be interpreted as *invulnerable* but as *unwounded*, a result attributable to the quality of his armour: Diomedes, Menelaus and Odysseus were all wounded through their cuirasses, while the new armour of Achilles fends off a direct spear cast to the greave (XXI-556/60).

The fuller picture of Achilles as a multi-purpose warrior instrument (not omni-purpose; he was no archer) explains his basic function in the epic, the one most of the – very few – military historians and researchers who ponder upon the epic and the era recognize: the unbeatable, invincible warrior. Troy was a rich city in a rich area, with a tradition in raising horses. There were myths of divine breeds (V-263/70) and many of the aristocracy were breeders; the usual adjective for the Trojans relates to horse breeding, taming and breaking. Their chariotry was their arm of choice; they had infantry, especially fast, agile infantry, obviously to support the chariots either as runners or as a static screen allowing preparations, formation and refuge. But the infantry was auxiliary, a battle support arm. The battle-winning element was the chariotry. Given that the Greeks were in an amphibious operation, it follows that they could not field many chariots, nor heavy chariots. Four-horse teams were out of the question; they were taking the space of two two-horse teams, with half the manpower. As a result, the limited chariotry the invasion fleet was to launch on the Trojan shores and mainland should have been elite, top quality that would wrestle the Trojan advantage by somehow overthrowing the quantitative edge, so as to dull the enemy battle-winning element. The Trojan chariotry was not only numerous but also of the highest quality, so the Greeks somehow had to secure an advantage, preferably qualitative. They did not have better horses and, as a whole, they did not have better charioteers. Thus there were two things they could work with: armour and weapons in general, and tactics. Excellently armoured and outfitted charioteers, such as Achilles, were few and definitely vital to thwart the Trojan advantage in numbers and, if possible, use innovative tactics to best their opponents.

And this is where the second element comes into play. The Greeks were vastly superior in infantry, in both quantity and quality. They could ferry it en masse with their vessels, and quickly, creating a strategically manouvrable force that could dislodge the Trojan defensive system, which must have been the strategy devised by Achilles. First, to neutralize the scattered Assuwan manpower in theatre, before it could be mobilized and concentrated, by launching swift, overwhelming raids all the way to Smyrna (Apollod E.3,32–4). And then to promote a patently indirect approach: by eliminating the political and economic fabric of the area, the powerful allied oriental army stationed in Troy would end up becoming more a liability than an asset for the Trojans. This approach was immensely successful, and the Trojans attempted to resolve the conflict with a decisive battle as soon as the opportunity arose. It is emphasized that this grand army deployed some 50,000 troops in 1,000 units of fifty men (IX-562) on the plain of Scamander alone, without counting isolated garrisons or the residual manpower of the allied areas out of theatre. The Achaeans, at the beginning of the campaign, totalled twice as many men (Scott 1909).

The infantry, especially the mobile infantry, no matter how heavily outfitted, was a Swiss Army knife. It was necessary for the amphibious raids, it was suitable for storming fortifications, positions and urban and rural environments and it was also an arm with potential against chariotry. If resolutely handled, it could overwhelm chariot crews with missiles and agility. If well outfitted with defensive arms, it could sustain punishment from the chariotry and deal with the very light infantry supporting chariot attacks, which was necessarily deficient in armour, so as to remain nimble and flexible. And this is the second attribute of Achilles as a warrior. He did excel in this kind of fighting, being strong, fast and trained for years on the broken ground of the glens and ridges of Pelion. He was the ultimate key to neutralize a chariot-centric force.

The third attribute is more cognitive than tactical. Achilles was the son of a sea-goddess, Thetis. The area he was coming from produced notorious pirates and seafarers, Perithous the son of Zeus and brother in crime (piracy) to King Theseus of Athens (Plut, *Vit Thes* 31,2–4), whose sons were with the invading army in a private capacity (Plut, *Vit Thes* 35,5), and of course the *Argo* of Jason. The area furnished massive naval contingents. Not so massive as the ones from the Peloponnese, but still quite impressive musters for a predominantly land area. And the assistance or knowledge of said goddess was a vital element for a purely amphibious campaign, with a distant target shore, at least three sailing days away under optimal conditions (IX-360/3). This shore would be, most probably, defended or at least protected by land forces and fieldworks, supported, or at least assisted, by naval forces. To complicate matters, there was a projected requirement of continuous and massive resupply in food (Thuc I.11,1), liquid supplies (VII-467/75) and less so, in fodder (V-199/203) – the latter being an issue partly alleviated by the small chariotry arm embarked in the invasion fleet. In this respect, a naval command – that of admiral (Apollod E.3,11), definitely an office corroborating Nestor's story (iii-105/6) – fits well with his record of amphibious raids (IX-328) and with the quality of his mother and the tradition of his land.

The above aspects elucidate the personal, individual merits of Achilles for the Greek cause and explain partly why he was indispensable. Greece had lost a generation of first-line heroes due to strife, war, expansion etc. The current generation, if not depleted, was not fully tested and reliable, although sporting some resounding successes, as will be discussed later. But what has been noticed only by novelists and not by historians, is that the focal attribute, in terms of warfare and military history, not epic and prose, of Achilles, was his tactical genius and leadership charisma. He was a war scientist *and* a most potent warrior, under the patronage of and paying his respects to Athena and not Ares, although he never shows any disrespect or tendency to clash with the latter, in stark contrast to the other one of Athena's protégés, Diomedes (V-855/60). Only this aspect may explain the fascination of Alexander the Great with the character, and this is appreciated by novelists rather than historians and philologists as already mentioned: Parroti 1986; 1988; Franklin 2002. And the indications in the epics abound. Describing the development of the campaign, such indications will become obvious and in-context. In here one must recount the most resounding ones, concerning his authority, not his genius: For example, Nestor directly mentions that the invaders were riding the waves to assault wherever Achilles was leading (iii-104/6); Nestor was senior and with more vessels than Achilles. Following the lead of the latter proves that there was a military hierarchy where Achilles was superior. To bolster this conclusion, Achilles alone, without notifying any other Greek, extends a truce and a free passage to King Priam when the latter comes to ransom the corpse of Hector. Achilles, moreover, states that if Priam's presence is detected, reported or suspected he would be unable to save the old king; this implies that he should, but the stakes are too high and evade his *established* control. That he *should* implies exactly the kind of constitutional, established power over the Greek host that allows granting a long truce. The last and more direct indication is the preliminaries of the battle royal that crushed the Trojan army. Achilles delivered a speech directing the conduct of the battle, laying down the plan, working up the morale of the troops; he is *the* leader and commanding officer. True, Agamemnon is hors-de-combat from his previous wound, but the attitude of Achilles is the one of the constitutional, undisputed, unchallenged commander of the host.

Achilles comes from a rather rich area. Nothing really magnificent, but still, as a chieftain (it is not clear whether he has assumed the throne and his father is regent, or Achilles is lord of the host and Peleus remains king), he is not deprived of the means for a comfortable life according to his standing (IX-364 & 399/400). The divine quality of his father's armour (XVII-194/7) accounts for the somewhat strange decision not to have his own; his high prestige as a warrior is somewhat diminished by that donning of armour. Much more important is the exact location of his fiefdom. As mentioned, at the time, there were important naval arsenals in the area, along with exploratory expeditions. But the most important thing is that there are two localities with toponyms central to Greek history. One is Achaia (II-685; Hdt VII.197,1), the birthplace of the Achaeans, the name for the Greeks used in Homer, that is proven by archaeology to be the best known in the international politics of the era, as Ahiyawa (Zangger 2016). The second such place is Hellas (II-683); the latter term in some centuries expanded to denote the Greeks (Hellenes) to the present day in their own tongue. There is also one, perhaps surrogate, third locality bearing an interesting toponym, the Argos of the Pelasgians (II-681); as mentioned, it could be a surrogate from the Argos in the Peloponnese, or a synonymous toponym, if there is a geographical/topological meaning of descriptive nature, as in Acropolis (citadel), Ayia (road), Tripolis (three cities) etc. As a result, by geographical origin, Achilles is also the embodiment of the Greek nation, both in his age and ever since (with the exception of the ages under Romanized Christian occupation, when Greeks called themselves 'Romans').

His bloodline is even more interesting. His mother is a sea goddess, which a priori made him a navigator of importance; after all, his training at Pelion was literally in a mountainous strip of land thrown into the blue of the Aegean and perhaps, with good visibility, discernible from the Asian coast across the Aegean. His father was Peleus, one of the sons of Aeacus, son of Zeus and the most just and pious man in Greece. Aeacus was named/appointed king at Aegina, the island in the middle of the Saronic

Gulf, between Attica, Corinth and Argolis, while the island was barren (Apollod III.12,6). How this occurred is a mystery, but the king was without subjects; an utterly unpopulated or depopulated island. The gods created subjects out of ants, the race of the Myrmidons. Whether this myth implies native underdogs, emancipated after the extinction of some aristocracy or master race, is difficult to determine. In any case, the king (who was initially ruling nothing but rocks, obviously) had two sons, Peleus and Telamon, who killed out of jealousy the third, Phocus, whose name was taken by Phocis (Paus X.1,1) and were thus banned by their father. This *mandra* happened also with the two sons of Pelops, Atreus and Thyestes, who were banned and thus found themselves well-placed for the throne of Mycenae (Thuc I.9,2).

Both sons gained thrones bereft of male successors: Telamon in nearby Salamis (Apollod III.12,7) and Peleus in faraway Phthia (Apollod III.13,2). But, in here, there are some interesting observations and questions. They were of course at a point ritually cleansed from the bloodguilt. But, before taking their thrones, they were part of expeditions. They were Argonauts and also companions of Hercules, and fought with distinction. The fact that Peleus, in such a faraway land, became king and the troops he sent with his son are called Myrmidons, the stock of his father's realm, not his father-in-law's, who was king, and thus were not natives, implies that he moved with some of his townsfolk. This was standard in colonization efforts, even if under duress and banishment. But here there is a matter of numbers: Achilles had some 2,500 troops (XVI-168/70), Myrmidons included (II-684). Was the national name of the folk of Peleus carried over in his new realm to encompass natives conscripted and trained into their midst? Were these the descendants of Peleus' followers from Aegina, that accompanied him into exile and became the martial aristocracy/social element in their new home, something tantamount to hostile takeover? And how many were these companions, to have produced 2,500 first-generation offspring? Each standard vessel was crewed by 50 men, as suggested by the number of rowers in the vessels of Achilles (XVI-169/70), but of others, too (II-719/20).

One may ponder on the possibility that, unlike medieval feudalism, in Achaean feudalism, the firstborn sons were sent away to carve their own kingdoms. Religious and secular power co-existed in one and the same person, the *wanaka/anax* who was assisted by the ministers of the gods but was the high priest of his people and a god-ordained ruler (IX-98/100). This is contrary to European feudalism, where the second son became a Man of the Cloth. Consequently, the reverse order in – some – Mycenaean states is a distinct possibility, especially if there is any notion of matriarchy. The pattern of succession, like the throne of Sparta going to Menelaus, husband of Helen, and not to the male offspring Castor and Pollux (Apollod E.2,16) supports such a notion. In such cases, the elder sons of Mycenaean lords were sent on multi-state expeditions and, if serving well, were delegated to orphan thrones, to succeed sovereigns without male offspring, so as to exclude entry into the cadre of the kings of any unwelcome foreigners, as had happened with Pelops.

Peleus and Telamon had murdered their brother on purpose, as their father clearly believed, to have them banished. Then, no matter the ritual cleansing, the crime was hideous. Despite that, Telamon becomes a central figure in Hercules' sack of Troy (Phil, *Her* 35,1). Peleus, after his marriage to the throne at Phthia, accidentally kills his predecessor (Apollod III.13,2), a pattern seen with Perseus, Amphitryon etc. He is scandalously favoured by the gods after his first wife passed away. He is no demigod, nothing but a second-rate hero getting a throne. But still he is officially wed to a goddess and his wedding is the event of the ages, attended by the gods who furnish extraordinary gifts, among which is a most complete kit for war: armour, weapons and horses (Apollod III.13,5). This kind of honour is unexplained; Peleus is no warrior of any renown by any means, and did not become one after said gifts; but he was a very efficient hunter and a decent fellow, with regard to other people's wives (Apollod III.13,3); the opposite of Paris. Still, his tour of duty under Jason was unimpressive (Apollod III.9,2). There is no coherence in these facts, especially if one takes into consideration that the source of the Trojan War lay at this wedding, with the Apple of Eris that led to the judgment of Paris (XXIV-25/30; Hyg, *Fab* 92; Apollod E.3.1–4).

The other question lies in the very weird fact that the island of Aegina, independent kingdom of Aeacus, populated with Myrmidons by the gods for his sake, and from where Peleus and Telamon were banished, ended in less than two generations within the realm of Diomedes and the sovereignty of Argos (II-559/65). This fact may well account for the bad blood between Achilles, grandson of King Aeacus and the two lords of Argos, Diomedes, the chief of the three lords, and Agamemnon, their overlord and liege who had it annexed during the Trojan War.

The character of the man is very well and accurately illustrated through Homer and distorted by modern scholarship, scientific or otherwise. Once again, novelists are occasionally less prejudiced, especially Parroti (1986; 1988) and Franklin (2002). Achilles is not a modest man, in principle. He knows very well his own value (IX-348/55). He still mentions that he is not a good orator, nor a wise or gifted speaker in the assembly (XVIII-105/6); a very modest claim, as it robs him of one of the two public virtues in the Greek socio-ideological system of the era: fighting excellence and public deliberation (II-202). And not rightly so. Achilles is actually good in public appearances; he resolves efficiently, although not graciously, the issue of the pestilence, and his bitter brawl with Agamemnon has profound, although not immediate, results, as it raises eyebrows amongst the kings and leaders (IX-104/13; XIX-181/3) and a direct wave of dissidence amongst the commoners as expressed by Thersites (II-239/42), whom Achilles despised (II-220). Most important, despite his pride or arrogance he is *very* quick to accept that Odysseus is wiser than him and gives the better advice despite his own, personal preferences (XIX-218/9), in contrast to Hector under similar conditions (XVIII-284/309).

Achilles was genuinely pious about the gods and it is a given that he will not raise a hand against a supplicant (XXIV-155/8). He reveres unconditionally Apollo, the arch-enemy god, in the incident of the pestilence, and although he knows that his death is preordained (IX-412/4) and approaching, once he slays Hector (XVIII-330/5; XIX-408/10; XIX-408/10; XXIV-131/2), he refrains from violating the divine prerogative to accept ransom for the corpse of Hector (XXIV-130/40). He never attempts to negotiate compliance to such prerogatives with his own destiny and the change of his fate. And once the deal for the ransom is set, he sends a guide to safeguard the ransom bringer (XXIV-390/404).

This kind of greatness and magnanimity is evident in the way he recognizes merit in friend and foe alike. In the former case he recognizes the supremacy of Diomedes amongst the Achaeans (XVI-74/5) and the stimulating, encouraging effect of Agamemnon's stout voice (XVI-76/7). He passes the correct judgment, despite public feeling, to declare Diomedes, with whom he shared no mutual appreciation, the winner in a mock combat event (XXIII-824/5) over his dear cousin Ajax, who had also saved the corpse of Patroclus from outrage. Regarding the latter case, he is quick to pay dividends to a bold and courageous, worthy opponent, his arch-enemy Hector included (XXI-279/80). Hector, contrary to the popular – and secondary – lore, shows no signs of true nobility anywhere in the *Iliad*, and is much more arrogant (XIII-725/36; XII-210/4) than Achilles; an arrogance turning to sudden disposition for parleys (XXII-111/3) and peaceful resolution of the whole issue of the war (XXII-114/21) that never crossed his mind in his zenith (VIII-180/3; XV-718/20). Achilles is much more chivalrous than any other warrior in the *Iliad*, to say nothing about the *Odyssey*. He not only allowed the dignity of a decent burial to a slain opponent, King Haetion – while ministering the proceedings himself (VI-416/8). Much more important is the fact that he allowed the corpse to be buried with his – very valuable – armour (VI-418), thus considered unspoiled, a sign of the noblest warrior's death: free of the embarrassment of defeat in combat and of the shame of despoilment by the enemy. And this is attested by none other than Andromache, the wife of Prince Hector and daughter of the slain king, who lost at the same incident to Achilles her brothers, all in fair combat (VI-416/23). There is not one instance in the *Iliad* or the *Odyssey* of such chivalrous behaviour; especially if the lack of any type of ransoming is taken into consideration. And there is no indication that he ever defiled the corpse of a fallen enemy before Hector's explicitly stated intent to do so to the corpse of Patroclus (XVII-125/8), possibly as a propaganda coup for the failure of a great and risky offensive that would have caused a subpoena by the senate, which he had slandered publicly at the heyday of his success (XV-720/3), prior to the intervention of Patroclus. This double, massive and unexpected success, to mow down a powerful Greek warrior and at the same time disarm a second one (XVIII-188/93) while acquiring the fabled armour for himself (XVII-186/7), was a massive save of the last moment of a battle. A battle that had started with the best omens, then turned to disaster and then rebounding to a positive outcome. Achilles had to nullify this triple and massive success bit by bit, with the emotional/psychological element being of cardinal importance. No prisoners were taken (XXI-103/5), except for ritual execution (XXI026/31), no respect given to fallen enemies (XXI-121/5): a war of total annihilation.

Vengeful fury is as good a reason as chivalrous disposition for his direct ban on anyone interfering with his personal feud with Hector (XXII-205/7); thus it is not a safe sign of gallantry. But it does contrast with the multiple hits to Patroclus (XVI-850) and shows, once more, and in open battle, that Achilles commands the Greek army; not just leads it, but commands it and thus he is acting as lord of the host.

Although generally considered proud, if not arrogant, Achilles is more honour-bound than anything else. All his issues with his colleagues and the head of the empire (IX-315/6) originate with his – very perceptive (I-176) – impression that he does not enjoy the respect earned by his valour and his value (I-244; IX-330/45). This concept of honour includes, as in all semi-primitive societies, a very material aspect. Prizes are tantamount to respect (IX-597/601), not investment or profit. He is a very generous man, presenting unearned gifts to colleagues considered unduly bested in contest (XXIII-536/61) or too old to compete (XXIII-615/23). Despite this fact, coupled to his chivalrous magnanimity towards the slain king (VI-416/23), as described above, he has a reputation for punishing big, greasy palms. When Priam tries to present one item out of the load meant for the ransom as a bribe to the guide sent to lead him to Achilles, said man declines in terror as he considers the item earmarked for Achilles and thus belonging to him (XXIV-434/6); he obviously has a reputation for dealing with such liberties harshly. That he is *not* simply greedy is seen amply in his turning down the offer from Agamemnon, as his sense of honour is not satisfied (IX-401/5); in his sending help through Patroclus (XVI-80/2) without any prior negotiation or even thought of claiming the offered prizes extended by Agamemnon and rejected before; by his utter indifference to the story of Meleagrus (IX-602/10), which did actually reoccur; and, most importantly, by still not asking nor even welcoming the prizes bestowed upon his re-entry into battle. He did not ask, nor considered it a matter of fact. He simply passed over the event (XIX-147/8), as it was *never* about the goods. The goods were the token of respect (IX-315/9), not the purpose. Achilles went to Troy for glory, not profit, nor revenge. He felt, without actually being, duty-bound and the spoils were the proof of his valour (XVI-83/6), his value and his success in the pursuit of glory and excellence, as a true aristocrat. The Homeric apophthegm, spoken by many heroes of both sides, resounded through the ages as the motto and prerogative of the aristocrats of Ancient Greece (VI-208/9). And glory was not something abstract; it was quantifiable and determined, qualitatively and quantitatively, by proper procedure and institutions/authorities, usually personified (XVII-232).

Odysseus

Homer provides enough information for the background and the functionality within the army and its objectives for the various heroes, especially many of the Greeks, but occasionally for some of the Trojans.

Odysseus' position, role and status are peculiar. The Trojan War is of his making; it was his advice that bound the suitors of Helen in a pledge to assist, and avenge violation or insult committed against whomever was to be selected; advice that got him the bride of his choosing, Penelope, daughter of Icarius of Sparta (Paus III.20,10; Apollod III.10,9), brother to Tyndareus (Apollod III.10,4–5); and thus Penelope was a cousin of Helen and Clytaemnestra.

He rules over a rather backward island country, Ithaca, plus a number of other islands in the Ionian Sea, to the west of the Greek mainland; but his troops are named as the Cephalenians (II-631). Odysseus' grandfather, from his mother's mainland side, on Mt Parnassus, was Autolycus (xix-405/15; xxiv-332/4), the best thief ever, son or protégé of the god Hermes, protector of merchants and thieves. Being himself the personal protégé of Athena, goddess of wisdom, he is well-versed in all applications and forms of intelligence, genius and wisdom, but mainly he is devious and wily. From his father's side, he draws his pedigree from the hero Cephalus, who gave his name to the island – and the people – of Cephalonia despite his residence being on Ithaca. Although the issue of Ithaca is not within the scope of this research, the context of such an arrangement closely associates the latter with the former, rather than with any other island in the region (i-246). After all, Ithaca sends only twelve ships (II-636/7) and must be relatively tiny, but closely associated with today's Cephalonia which, however, seems to be a different isle or geographic entity (xxiv-355 & 420), possibly mostly mentioned as Samos (II-634).

This island-complex country, possibly including some estates on the mainland (II-635), was strategically located for the conduct of western trade (i-185). Odysseus is a seafarer, trader by profession, and cousin to Jason, who undertook the opening of a new eastern trade route (Apollod I.9,16). He is genuinely greedy, as seen by the lack of trust of his men (x-34/46) and by his foremost fear, not to lose his spoils and gifts (xiii-215/6).

Odysseus is one of the many characters in the *Iliad* vying for the secondary role after Achilles, but he enjoys a whole epic for himself, the *Odyssey*. His few ships are parked (or rather drawn up) in the geometric middle of the camp (XI-5/8), where one would expect to find Agamemnon's ships. This might be because the geometric middle and the centre amongst contingents differ. Odysseus is a long arm of the high king, their man for difficult tasks. He is recognized as canny, wily and wise by friends (IX-308) and enemies alike (III-200/2; III-216/24). He restores order in Agamemnon's name and is the only one who was accepted, and capable of, conversing with Achilles to re-enlist his help, despite his questionable silence (along with that of all the other chiefs and kings) during the falling out with Agamemnon. After all, his role in securing the less-than-voluntary assistance of Achilles had been instrumental and is mentioned directly and unequivocally in the *Iliad* (IX-252/5) although other traditions present the events under a different light, emphasizing the 'less-than-voluntary' part.

Odysseus does not come from the Peloponnese; he is no Danaan nor Argive: he is Achaean (Drews 1979). In battle terms, he is a gifted fighter, but no tactical mastermind. As a warrior, he cooperates smoothly with Diomedes (X-242/7) and occasionally with Ajax the Great (IX-169), none of them Danaan either, despite the former ruling over Argos proper (XXIII-471). The excellent cooperation between Odysseus and the two above-mentioned characters showcases the tactical employment of armoured infantry in a combined-arms context. Best results are expected when paired with chariotry or shielded line infantry, respectively represented by the above-mentioned heroes.

He does not own nor operate a chariot; perhaps because Ithaca is not a place suitable for chariots, as Telemachus says while declining the chariot presented to him by King Menelaus (iv-601/6). He is never referred to as an equestrian expert of any consequence, although he knows the basics, in order to lead the team of King Rhesus out of camp silently and efficiently and then mount them to escape to the Greek lines (X-498/514). He is an accomplished archer (viii-220) and the trial in the *Odyssey* says much in this respect (xix-278); but he only fights as an armoured spearman, the main heroic way; he keeps his great bow at home (xxi-36/41); and, on foot, he is fast, as an infantryman must be to survive. So fast that he wins a contest (XXIII-778/9); the win is circumstantial, to a great extent, but still rates Odysseus as a top runner.

He is good at commando and special missions; in this context he does consider the military use of the bow (X-260), which he declines to use in war as standard practice (xxi-39/42) and his performance in special warfare is stellar: from the theft of the Palladium artefact, to the night reconnaissance and assassination mission (X-242/514), to the design and execution of the mission with the Trojan Horse, Odysseus is *the* special operator. Despite Achilles being a master in ambush and raid warfare, more or less light infantry missions (IX-325/9), for serious clandestine operations and for hybrid warfare, where politics, diplomacy and cold-blooded efficiency matter, Odysseus is the right hand of the Greek high command and actually a distinct member of it. His role is very close to that of the chief of staff, which he probably inherited when he neutralized Palamedes (Phil, *Her* 20.2); still, whether such arrangements were in place before Achilles' withdrawal from action is a valid question.

Odysseus must have been implicated in the liquidation, before or after the final victory, of all the chieftains not particularly liked or trusted by the Atreid inner cycle. Being credited with the defamation and execution of Palamedes, the suppression of Thersites and the (ex)termination of Ajax the Great presents him in an awful light, especially taking his greed into consideration. Whether it is his passions and vileness that led to such entanglements, or he simply served his Atreid master, cannot be safely deduced. As prime executive officer of the arrest of the seer Prince Helenus and of the acquisition of the Palladium artefact, he qualifies as the architect of the demise of Ajax the Lesser, with whom it is obvious that he had issues (XXIII-473/90). Though, such deliberation is possible, even probable, but unproven.

Nestor

Nestor, an almost centenarian old warrior, is the King of Pylos, a small kingdom with a massive fleet and obviously thriving commerce. The patron deity is Poseidon, for his family (XIII-554/5; Apollod I.9,16) and for his realm (iii-4/9). His father Neleus was brother to the stalwart King Pelias of Iolcus and the family originated there and carved out a Pylian estate (iii-4; Apollod I.9,8–10). There are three focal points: first, it may be that Nestor ruled over (some of) Crete, if a new interpretation of the Disc of Phaestus is correct (Zangger 2016); this is corroborated by the repeated instances of Pylian and Cretan troops or commanders fighting next to each other (XIII-387/97 and XI-510).

Second, both Neleus and Pelias have bad blood with Hera (Apollod I.9,16 & I.9,8), meaning the Argive dynasties: Hera assists Jason, a man bred and trained to take from Pelias the throne of Iolcus (Apollonius Rhod, *Argon* I.5–15), strategically placed in the Gulf of Pagassai for staging naval enterprises and marine expeditions; not surprisingly, Pelias was a staunch believer in Poseidon (Apollod I.9,16). To assist Jason to this end, fifty heroes of the highest standing were conscripted for the task from the whole of Greece (Apollod I.9,16); all of them (or the surviving ones) comfortably set up with kingdoms and fiefdoms as a retirement plan or as reward, afterwards – see Telamon and Peleus – to the deep enmity of the line of Pelias, as proven by the later feud between Acastus, son of Pelias and Peleus (Apollod E.6,13). Pelias' brother Neleus was murdered by the agent of Hera – and Mycenae – Hercules (Phil, *Her* 26,3; Apollod I.9,9); or, at least, his sons, except for Nestor (XI-689/92), were.

It is very interesting that Neleus was treated with hostility by neighbours. King Augeias, who was also to be served and then deposed by Hercules (Apollod II.5,5 & 7,2 respectively), treated Neleus in a most hostile way; from an attack led by his son-in-law (XII-736/9), to the outrage during the proceedings of the games over which he was presiding: Augeias confiscated the entry of Neleus, his chariot race team (XI-695/703), an attitude discouraged by Greek ethics and thus implying either Augeias had a terrible personality, or bad feeling transmitted by Neleus to his neighbours. This report, incidentally, gives the Olympic Games a date of origin far prior to the usual mid-eighth century BC and compatible to their initiation by Hercules.

And the third point is the war council role Nestor seems to assume in the *Iliad*. He suggested the disguise and intervention of Patroclus (XI-795/800), the construction of the defensive complex of the Achaeans (VII-325/43), the chariot fighting in formation by jousting (IV-306/7) and the deployment of the Greek host on a tribal basis (II-362/8). His advice seems more important than his contingent and he clearly has assumed a peculiar position, including political and military aspects; he must clearly have the role of special adviser who stepped up as chief of staff once Achilles is missing; Agamemnon has no tactical flair whatsoever.

With Achilles absent, Nestor advises reverting to a tribal format, because nobody can pull the tricks of Achilles. What is also important is that his advice for chariot jousting is far from being in any case unorthodox (the whole of the *Iliad* makes clear that spearing with a lance from a chariot is the focal battle technique of the *eqeta*, and the dismounted cast the secondary, as discussed with references in another chapter. He advises doing so *in formation*, holding a disciplined, orderly line (IV-304/5), and not haphazardly and impulsively, with violent aggression and uncontrolled fury, as dictated by heroic instincts and prompted by the war god, Ares, but not the goddess of strategy, Athena, the patroness of the Greeks. Achilles presenting him with a gift at the funeral games perhaps shows both recognition for his effort to fulfil his role, or/and a polite scolding for his actual performance, hiding some bitterness for the sequence of events primed by Nestor's advice (and culminating in very heavy losses, a narrow escape from the jaws of utter defeat and the loss of Patroclus) in kind words, nevertheless underlining Nestor's age, incompatible with war-making and athletics (XXIII-616/24).

The Atreids

Both brothers show excellent social skills and actual caring when they stay at the side of the mourning Achilles while the army goes to sup before the battle (XIX-303/12). Their conduct in times of need is impeccable. They also assume many costs of the campaign, as they treat the other kings in messes (XVII-250), for which, of course, they demand their allegiance and obedience.

Agamemnon is an efficient king and lord and a first-rate fighter (III-178/80); however, he is a greedy king, ruling high-handedly (I-172/87), and understands policy and strategy. Tactics and operations are not his strong point, *but* he is a competent leader, inspiring his men (IV-223/49), as Achilles himself admits (XVI-76/7). It must be stressed that, contrary to Achilles' accusations, he is an acclaimed warrior, first-class in the opinion of his troops (VII-179/80), with an excellent battlefield record, once he engages in combat (IV-223/4; XI-286/9), and an accomplished, very capable spearman (XXIII-884/91).

He understands the battle as an advance, exchange and charge; applying the technique and SOPs with aggressiveness, violence and eagerness, morale and elan being of prime importance. He can command nothing more complicated than a tribal host (II-362/8) but he can fight with distinction and manage a campaign. If the word *Atarisiya* of the Hittite records implies 'Atreid' and not 'Atreus' (Giannakos 2016), his eastern adventures seem to have reborn the Arzawa at some point. It is very possible that, although he was called an Atreid, he was no son of Atreus, but a grandson, sired by the latter's son, Pleisthenes, an uncelebrated character who died early, perhaps shortly after siring him and Menelaus and at a young age (Dikt I.1); a fact that would help align chronologies and bloodlines considerably. Politician extraordinaire, chief priest of his people, unscrupulous but by no means an oath-breaker, open-minded in things his intelligence can process and apprehensive of the time and circumstances, he is open to things he understands; he clearly has issues with the comportment of Achilles, as these seem to escape his understanding in the conduct of operations and Achilles skips no chance to drive the insults home, perhaps frowning upon the annexation of his distant grand-fatherland, Aegina, into the extended Argos and actually within the realm of Diomedes (II-559/68) but also the murder of his friend, Palamedes (Phil, *Her* 25,16). In this case it is possible that the ancient sources critical of Odysseus miss the true nature of events; Odysseus may have hated and antagonized Palamedes, but it is much more probable that Agamemnon, sensing the latter's public appeal, wanted and needed him murdered, and Odysseus simply did the dirty work – not without personal satisfaction.

This becomes more plausible as Agamemnon is charged with murderous behaviour and machinations against two other warlords with whom he felt uneasy: Ajax the Great and Ajax the Lesser. The former was denied burial after his murderous frenzy that drove him to suicide (Apollod E.5,6–7; Hyg, *Fab* 107); Athena shaking his wits is a somewhat mystical argument. First, to create delusions, there is no need for a god; concoctions do that perfectly well and the priests of Apollo in the camp, Calchas if not Helenus at the time, could well have obliged. Then, it is difficult to assign losing one's wits to the mistaken slaughter of animals instead of humans rather than to the bloody frenzy one had to be under to try to murder his comrades, with whom he was bleeding up to the previous morning. Achilles also nurtured extreme bitterness for the Greek rank and file for quite some time (XVI-97/100), due to their attitude towards him when pitted against Agamemnon, and perhaps towards Palamedes. But there are several steps from this to mass murder, and pushing someone to take them sounds more convincing than anything else; Odysseus after all was not averse to poisons (i-259/62). In any case, Agamemnon, after this, denied proper burial to the man, a penalty originally imposed by Creon of Thebes and duly regulated by the Greek occult at the time; this was not to happen, no matter the reasons.

Menelaus is a capable but second-rate warrior (XVII-586/90; VII-109/12) and, like his brother, he is loyal to the men he dragged and led to death (XVII-91/105). Menelaus is continuously depicted in a positive light in the *Iliad*; he surges to the call of honour even when it is very unwise (VII-94/102), something heroic by our standards but not by the standards of the heroes; it was considered madness (VII-107/10). Resilient and determined, he does fit the family of Zeus into which he married (iv-569) by being wed to Helen. Other traditions have him instrumental in persuading Agamemnon to proceed with the sacrifice of Iphigenia, and there is an issue as to whether said niece of his was actually the bastard daughter of Helen, when abducted by Theseus (Apollod III.10,6), before her betrothal to Menelaus and then passed silently to Agamemnon and Clytaemnestra to raise. Later tradition show that Menelaus was a foreigner in Sparta, and the Spartans never accepted him for one of their own. They preferred to be ruled by the son of the Spartan Clytaemnestra than the bastard son of Menelaus from a non-Spartan woman, because with Helen he only had a daughter (iv-10/4).

Ajax the Great

Ajax was a king of small calibre, with only twelve ships, from an island near the Attic coast – an island of moderate size and great destiny – Salamis. He was a relative of Achilles; both were grandsons of Aeacus and were thus first cousins. Ajax was the second best warrior of the Greeks (II-768/9). Grandson of Aeacus and son of Telamon, he was the son of a bride from the line of Pelops and thus heir apparent of Salamis, while his brother Teukros was the son of a foreign captive princess (Apollod III.12,7). His father was credited with being the first to breach the walls of Troy under Hercules (Phil, *Her* 35,1; Apollod II.6,4) and thus received said prize princess, Hesione. The fact that Teukros was named from her people means a tender relationship between her and the hero Telamon, nothing like a captor and a captive; otherwise her origin would have not been celebrated in the name of their son. The brothers are on the best of terms (XV-471/3), although Teukros is first cousin to Hector and the other sons of Priam and their cousins. This fact is never raised in the *Iliad*, and the two cousins try to kill each other with no remorse whatsoever (VIII-309/29). Corroborating the indications provided by the name for a different, Trojan mother, Homer clearly considers Teukros a bastard (VIII-283/4).

Ajax the Great is one of the three top warriors/heroes of the Greeks in the *Iliad* who is not an *eqeta*, at least not in form. He has no chariot, as is the case with Odysseus and Ajax the Lesser, and, as with the latter, there is no hint whatsoever that he has any opinion on the issue, although one may suppose that he did; the uniform hero training includes the equestrian skills in the curriculum as standard. Ajax is unpretentious, a tamer version of Achilles, and his style of fighting, as line, not mobile, infantry with body-shield and spear(s) implies the importance the Greeks were placing onto this kind of warfare and the troops implementing it, as mentioned elsewhere. Ajax seems not to be in the good graces of Athena, thus his skills do not include tactics and flair, but he is a true leader and very eloquent, to boost the morale of the troops (XV-501/14). Actually, Ajax does not seem to be under the protection of any patron deity; perhaps he is presented as an early atheist, a sacrilegious trait he shares with Ajax the Lesser (Apollod E.6,6; iv-500). His eloquence does not extend to the assembly; he is indifferent, or his eloquence in battle is the result of all the other heroes and kings that are better orators and debaters being wounded and out of action (XIV-28/30), leaving him to assume all aspects of the conduct of the fight. Actually, he is exactly cut out for the nature of the fight by the Greek vessels, or to protect the body of Patroclus, taking place in a confined space and with no leeway for surging, storming and generally mobile tactics, but requiring unyielding, solid defence. He knows how to direct troops – not only his own – to revert to this style of fighting on the spot (XVII-354/65).

His uncelebrated death (Apollod E.5,6–7; Phil, *Her* 35,10) shows he shares the curse of rage with Achilles, something that must be running in the family: the fathers killing their brother, and then Telamon banishing Teukros because he did nothing to avenge his brother. End result: the surviving prince founded Salamis, a copy of his fatherland in Cyprus (Dikt VI.4). Still, the undoing of Ajax might have been a bit more sinister than the lore – carefully edited by the triumphant Orestes, son of Agamemnon – implies (Phil, *Her* 31.5).

The Cretans

Idomeneus is the ruler of Crete (II-645), a staunch fighter, a bit aged (XIII-512), but still ranking top. His mobility is somewhat compromised, along with his swiftness (XIII-512), but his reflexes, awareness (XIII-404/5) and aim are superior; he can still dodge a missile (XIII-503/5) and hit Hector behind the shield (XVII-605/6), a difficult cast requiring excellent aim, fast reflexes and hand-eye coordination. He uses a chariot (XVII-608/9).

Idomeneus is a direct descendant of Minos, being his paternal grandson (XIII-449/53), and does not seem to suffer being under the sceptre of

Agamemnon; he is a relative, after all, and his political affiliation might actually have been through Nestor (Zangger 2016), with whom he participated in the inner ring. Or, being either cousin or uncle to Agamemnon and Menelaus on their mother's side, he might have been an agent for the integration of Crete, the former superpower and 'queen of the waves' in the Mycenaean NATO.

But the obscure Meriones, his attendant (XXIII-124) and nephew, and also second-in-command (II-650/1), a man with pleasant character and extreme battle efficiency, is of interest. The name resounds with the Mitannian *marianu* and possible Egyptian spin-offs, the very word for the Greek *eqeta* or perhaps *hero*. He fights and competes as an archer (XIII-650; XXIII- 870/6 respectively); he gives Odysseus his bow and other pieces of weaponry for the night raid (X-260/1), while he himself is captain of the night watch, one of the seven (IX-80/6). He fights as an armoured spearman, a most distinguished one (XIII-255/8); he has his own chariot and driver (XVII-610/11) and he competes in a chariot race (XXIII-351), being the most multivalent hero of the Greeks, with Odysseus a close second.

Ajax the Lesser

Ajax the Lesser, a man with a terrible character (XXIII-473/91), but possibly focused against the minions of Agamemnon – in the case just referenced, Idomeneus – was close to Ajax the Great and thus disenchanted with the proceedings of Agamemnon and his cohort. In the epic he is a formidable fighter, a spearman. He is not an armoured skirmisher; at least not in the conventional sense. He has linen armour (II-529) and sword, but his favourite weapon is his fleetness and the *dory* spear (Phil, *Her* 31,1), both for thrusting and casting, and is never mentioned as bearing a shield or a helmet. Unlike his men (XIII-716/22), he is no missile soldier, but he seems permanently attached to Ajax the Great, especially in field engagements (XVII-719/21), thus forming a functional part of a body-shield task force – possibly similar to Assyrian arrangements (Dezső 2012). He is the pursuer (XIV-5201), while Teukros is the sniper archer.

Ajax was also rebellious and critical of Agamemnon; he must have been loath to take any pledge, and challenged his authority, at least according to other traditions (Phil, *Her* 31,1). After the fall of Troy, Agamemnon charged Ajax with religious outrage, taking Cassandra from the altar of Athena and raping her. Ajax was no fool. He noticed that Agamemnon was attracted to Cassandra; he took her for himself and carried her to Mycenae, possibly as wife and not just as concubine, thus obtaining hereditary titles to the Trojan throne and becoming the overlord of Antenor and/or Aeneas. After all, the demise of Achilles had started with Agamemnon's attraction to a woman, and the 'religious outrage' was death in the making. Not the valour of Ajax the Great nor the wit of Palamedes saved them from the murderous disposition of their overlord. Thus Ajax the Lesser made good his escape (Phil, *Her* 31,6). But the Palladium was now in Greek hands (Apollod E.5,13), and the operators too (from the priesthood of Athena, affiliated to Antenor, all the way to prince Helenus, the seer), thus 'Athena' bombed by bolt his ship – or had it mined before he boarded it and timed to explode in mid-sea (Apollod E.6,6), as will be explained in later chapters. Another bomb or bolt followed the man ashore and finished him off (iv-499/511; Apollod E.6,6). It may be important that the mother of Achilles tended the dead body (Apollod E.6,6), something she would not have done for some sacrilegious stranger, but would have done for a friend of her son.

The Argives

Last but not least in the celebrities is Diomedes and his friends Sthenelus and Euryalus, who form the regal triad of Argos (II-559/68; Paus II.20,10). Diomedes is an Aetolian, or rather half an Aetolian; his father Tydeus, a very spirited and savage warrior of little physical stature but much proficiency in arms and protégé of Athena (IV-391/7; V-809/10), was the son of the Aetolian King Oeneus (XIV-113/8).

Tydeus left, possibly under blood guilt, and resided at Argos, where he married into the royal family (XIV-119/25), and campaigned at Thebes along with the other six, where they all perished (Apollod III.6,7–8). Diomedes is nephew to the long-departed Aetolian hero Meleagrus, a most accomplished warrior, but actually his father Tydeus and Meleagrus were half-brothers (Apollod I.8,2 & I.8,4–5). Helen of Sparta and her sister and brothers are cousins to Meleagrus on his mother's side (Apollod I.7,10–8,2). With Meleagrus gone, another cousin of Diomedes, Thoas, son of King Oeneus' daughter Gorge (Apollod I.8,1), rules over the region (II-638/40; Apollod E.3,12), possibly under a mandate by Agamemnon.

Diomedes' affiliations are with Argos, where he has one-third of the throne. He is relatively young, and with an impressive CV, as he participated in campaigns against Thebes, this time successfully, into Aetolia and Acarnania and after all these he campaigns to Troy. That is much more than Achilles or Ajax the Great had to show initially, and the only reason he is not mentioned as one of the most prominent warriors of the Greeks with Achilles and Ajax must have been that this chart refers, actually, to the tenth year of the Trojan war/campaign, with the two cousins having accomplished massive feats of arms.

Diomedes is adept in chariot warfare (VIII-105/30) and chariot racing (XXIII-419513); perhaps his wounding Ares is the most direct mention of jousting. He is good on foot, an excellent spearman, a special operator and generally similar in style to Achilles – no love lost there. No archer, nor tactician, but decent in deliberation (IX-706/7). Despite his stellar performance and his excellent CV he is not in the top Greek warriors at the beginning of the campaign; that list is short and includes the two cousins, Achilles and Ajax the Great (II-768/9). Diomedes is a mainstream fighter, and as mentioned earlier a close third to Achilles and Ajax. His profile in combat is very like that of Achilles, that of *eqeta*, which is the standard for heroic warriors.

Diomedes comes to prominence as Achilles has retired from action; he proves to be a terrible surprise for the Trojans (VI-96/100), taking Aeneas out of action, and thus commands respect from the army and recognition (VII-179/80), while he bests Ajax in mock combat (XXIII-824/5), thus both challenging and taking second place under Achilles as best Greek fighter. He qualifies as the prime target for the divine Trojan weapons (VIII-133/7) but escapes – just – while he is sniped at by both top Trojan hero-archers, Paris (XI-369/79) and Pandarus (V-95/100), the former taking him out of action for good (XI-396/400).

He is a subordinate of Agamemnon and dislikes Achilles (IX-693/5) who does not wish to become subordinate to the high king (IX-388/90). The cuirass of Diomedes (VIII-194/5) is amongst the top five military artefacts in the Greek camp, along with the shield of Nestor (VIII-192/3), the cuirass of Agamemnon (XI-19/28), the shield of Ajax the Great (XVIII-193; VII-219/23) and the armour of Achilles (XVII-186/7). Still, when compared to that of his hereditary guest-friend, Glaucus of Lycia, who is second in command there, it is only worth one tenth as much (VI-235/6). This says much about the difference in wealth between the two clashing pacts, the Luwians and the Greeks; another Trojan ally is mentioned for his rich accoutrements (II-871/2). Still, not any actual Trojan or ally, but the Thracian king, Rhesus (X-439), and the chief of the Aethiopians, Memnon (Burgess 1995), are renowned for their weapons among the Orientals.

Palamedes

Palamedes was cousin to Agamemnon and Menelaus on the side of their mother; the mother of the two Atreids was sister to the mother of Palamedes and they drew their line from the kings of Crete and thus commanded a degree of protection from the sea god – along with his blessing. His father was Nauplius, son of Poseidon (Apollod E.3,7; Phil, *Her* 25,15), king of Nauplion, on the Argolic coastline, thus making a clear case for a religious split from the rest of the Argolid under Hera (IV-51/2). It is not only that he is deleted from the *Iliad*; his troops and city/realm do not figure in the Catalogue of Ships and it is an issue whether they were dismissed back to their motherland (a very risky course of action, due to the bitterness they must have nurtured for the Atreids), or somebody else assumed command, as was reportedly the case with the troops of – long-dead – Protesilaus (II-695/705). One tradition has it that he came as a privateer, in one skiff (Phil, *Her* 33,42), a strange concept. It is of importance that his realm is not assigned to Diomedes, who ruled over the whole Argolic peninsula (II-559/63); it simply does not exist. Still, his fighting alongside Diomedes on the abortive campaign against Mysia and their shared command of the same part of the army (Phil, *Her* 20,20) implies that they were cooperating closely and possibly were posted together, their contingents and vessels (if Palamedes was leading some) neighbouring each other.

Between the minions and favourites of Hera, that is Agamemnon (XI-45/6), and those of Athena, who had more than one (Odysseus, Diomedes, Achilles) on the one hand and the grandson of Poseidon on the other (Phil, *Her* 25,15), a clear interface of friction may be identified. Homer never mentions Palamedes, but the Ancient Greeks had access to other sources and knew a lot about him, paying their respects to the hero and fully appreciating the injustice imposed upon him and also his benevolent character (Xen, *Apol* 26). Since Dares and Diktys had not been among the works available to classical-period Greeks, it is obvious that epics lost to us introduced the hero and filled the gaps. Being a grandson of Poseidon, his demise due to Odysseus (this is the common denominator in all traditions) explains the wrath of the sea god against Odysseus (Phil, *Her* 25,15).

Palamedes is something of a superhero; massive, handsome, excellent fighter and also a sage (Phil, *Her* 21,6 & 23,23 & 33,1). His name implies dexterity with the hands and, actually, technology – he should have been the favourite of Athena. Amassing too many virtues to him is as suspect as Homer's total silence on the man. He is reportedly a fine tactician, a good fighter, an excellent logistician, a gifted strategist and an inventor, while his nautical skills were running in the family. A graduate of Cheiron's academy (Apollod III.13), he had in his CV the medical component (Phil, *Her* 33,2) which, out of all the heroes mentioned in the *Iliad* – except for the designated physicians – only Achilles is reportedly credited with

(XI-830/1); but then, in the *Iliad*, only Achilles is mentioned as a student of Cheiron (XI-830/1), which may imply a longer and fuller course, from early childhood to early manhood; perhaps from the age of 2–3 to 15 or so (Phil, *Her* 45,4; Apollonius Rhod, *Argon* IV.811–13).

Homer mentions nothing of the realm of Palamedes, the city of Nauplion, first capital of modern Greece, and founded by his father. This very location may have caused friction with the overlord of north-eastern Peloponnese, Diomedes and his liege, Agamemnon. Palamedes' popularity with the troops was also an issue, as, in some accounts, he really seems better suited to supreme command than Agamemnon. His abilities in solving problems and administration superseded these of Odysseus and Nestor, which would grant him at least one very determined enemy.

His battle excellence *did not* cause friction either with Diomedes, which would have been natural (Phil, *Her* 20,20 & 22), or with Achilles; on the contrary, they seemed to be friends with the latter (Phil, *Her* 25,16), which meant that, along with Ajax the Great (Phil, *Her* 20,2), they may have formed a pole of influence within the army, clearly antithetical to the Atreids. The latter trusted an inner ring, including Diomedes, who had taken the pledge, and their kinsmen Idomeneus, Nestor and Odysseus (the latter's wife Penelope was first cousin to the sisters Helen and Clytaemnestra). It is no coincidence that all three commanders of this pole were exterminated by direct or indirect machinations of the inner ring of the Atreids. Palamedes, in different accounts, was either murdered or malevolently accused of treason and publicly executed (the majority of the troops refused to participate in the execution), due to Odysseus' machinations, but under the auspices of Agamemnon. Ajax is clearly underappreciated, when he is refused the armour of Achilles, and has gone down in tradition as actually murdered by Odysseus (Phil, *Her* 20,2), his memory tarnished and his funeral rites denied by Agamemnon (Phil, *Her* 35,15; Apollod E.5,7). And then there is Achilles, who is scolded and reproached beyond any logic for no reason, other than for his aggressive character (I-176/7), which is the reason behind many battlefield successes. Whether the brains of Palamedes lay behind these successes is questionable; still, the conduct of war in the *Iliad* continues, after Palamedes is gone and Achilles seems to have been instrumental in planning and conducting the war in the tactical level, without any assistance and with the obvious negative association that, without him, the Greek high command could not manage battle and tactics.

Palamedes is supposed to have proposed, designed and overseen the fortification of the Greek camp, and given that Homer simply deletes the man, it is logical that he introduces the – known – event at some point, assigning it to somebody else; that is Nestor (VII-325/43), although one fails to see where his expertise comes from; or, if not him, who exactly is the master engineer of the Greeks assigning roles, making blueprints and supervising the work? Collective references such as 'the Greeks did that' (VII-434/42) do not accurately describe a course of action; one may think that these are deliberately inaccurate figures of speech. It must be also noted that the other Greek fortification we hear of is Achilles' residence and headquarters (XXIV-447/56). Whether Palamedes had done his friend a favour and oversaw the work may be a legitimate question, but it is a given that Achilles had no hand in the erection of the Greek fortifications as, per Homer, this happened while – and because – he was angry and sulking in his part of the camp, refusing any participation in common undertakings, especially battle. A partial reconciliation may lie in the possibility of an earlier collective and less elaborate fortification effort supervised by Palamedes and implied in the lines of the *Iliad* (Pantazis 2006) which finally, under necessity, was improved, enhanced and strengthened to the more elaborate structure mentioned in the text.

The events with Palamedes are well-suited to Achilles' bitter statements in Homer (IX-318/20), which may be seen as referring to more than himself, something corroborating ancient suggestions that his wrath was instigated over the events with Bryseis, but was brewing because of the events with Palamedes (Phil, *Her* 25.16). Whether Achilles' statements are edited by the poet to eliminate any trace of Palamedes, or were transmitted *verbatim*, is open to debate. The loss of other epics makes it difficult to follow the educative and ideological aspects; for example, the fact that a tradition contrary to the Homeric (Dikt VI.2–4) mentions all the Atreid ringleaders, with the exception of Nestor, suffering considerably on or after their return (namely Agamemnon, Menelaus, Idomeneus, Diomedes and Odysseus), may suggest a blood guilt avenged by the gods.

Chapter 8

The Heroes of the Orientals

For the Trojans things are simple; prince Hector is the commander-in-chief (II-816), while Polydamas is the operational and tactical mind; actually *the* mind (XVII-249/53). Hector is a very capable and brave warrior, true heroic style, having nothing to do with archery. He is extremely fleet of foot (XXII-193/205), very aggressive, not as brave as subsequent lore has him be (XXII-111/21), truly unscrupulous (XVII-125/7) and arrogant (XVIII-284/309); pure royalty, with excellent leadership skills and little tactical flare (XVIII-249/52). A veritable thrasher by the criteria of Ajax (Phil, *Her* 23,21).

Sarpedon and Aeneas are the two best warriors after Hector (VI-77/8 & XVI-549/51). The three Trojans are excellent charioteers and also heavy skirmishers, showing no dexterity with the bow, nor for close-quarter dense formations. They excel in the fluid tactics of the time with initiative, awareness, aggressiveness and fast reflexes; they have a good eye for exploiting an opportunity. Although also a charioteer (XVI-426), Sarpedon's performance while mounted is not mentioned and his equestrian skills and assets are not celebrated.

Paris, on the other hand, an astute political figure if nothing else, is also adept as a heavy skirmisher, since he can duel in standard attire (III-329.38) and fight with the spear (XV-341); he is mentioned combining bow and panoply (VI-321/2), but he never engages in mounted warfare; a shepherd for most of his life (Apollod III.12,5), he feels comfortable in light infantry attire, without armour (III-16/8) and with the bow (XI-580/5). He is, or was made, a *hero* in the narrow sense, of course, and thus he is versed in different modes of combat, but his personal favourites are different from the preferences of the above. His seer-brother prince Helenus seems more set on heavy fighting but with all the offensive weapons ranged in a hero's arsenal. The other brother, Deiphobus, is always mentioned as a standard heavy skirmisher, a bragging clone of Hector. He was selected to marry Helen after the demise of Paris, meaning that he became heir apparent, which did not sit well with Helenus, a pious seer (VI-76) who deserted the city (Apollod E.5,9).

1. *Axine* pickaxe, as a sidearm of a warrior with horned helmet, long later-date greaves and leather-based body armour reinforced with metal bosses – the latter are described in Homer. Copyright: Association of Historical Studies 'KORYVANTES'. (*koryvantes.org*)

2. Studded club, as a sidearm of a warrior with horned helmet, long later-date greaves and leather-based body armour reinforced with metal bosses – the latter are described in Homer. Copyright: Association of Historical Studies 'KORYVANTES'. (*koryvantes.org*)

3. Slashing axe combined with scale body armour; the latter is implied in Homer as 'copper tunic'. Copyright: Association of Historical Studies 'KORYVANTES'. (*koryvantes.org*)

4. Old-time, small metal greaves over soft fabric full-length leg-guards combined with a collection of axes (Epsilon-type, *axine* pickaxe, conventional double-headed) and the articulated model of plate cuirass. Copyright: Association of Historical Studies 'KORYVANTES'. (*koryvantes.org*)

5. Dendra-type armour with long, two-handed spear, possibly an infantry pike although shorter than the actual weapon. Note the pointed warhead, meant for perforation of soft and hard targets and thus made of iron. Copyright: Association of Historical Studies 'KORYVANTES'. (*koryvantes.org*)

6. To the left, a collection of offensive weapons, with spears and different types of axes. Note the different length of the handles of two Epsilon-axes, implying a double-handed weapon for use against heavily armoured targets or against mounted charioteers, similar to the axes of the Vikings and the Byzantine Varangian Guard. To the right, the long *pakana* longsword, combined with non-metal armour, greaves over leg-guards and a single epaulette from Dendra-type armour, a configuration reminiscent of Roman gladiators. The Dendra-type armour at the centre shows its fabric substrate to prevent heating and chaffing and how it is telescoped to more manageable dimensions for transportation and storing. Copyright: Association of Historical Studies 'KORYVANTES'. (*koryvantes.org*)

7. The Dendra-panoplied warrior carries a scaled-down naval spear like the one described by Homer for Ajax and the Greeks for naval engagements. The warhead is of bident-type, to destroy rigging with slashing attacks and recreated to original dimensions. Copyright: Association of Historical Studies 'KORYVANTES'. (*koryvantes.org*)

8. Close-quarters first-strike attack with a sidearm, here a pickaxe, once the opponent has closed with the enemy armed with a shafted weapon. Copyright: Association of Historical Studies 'KORYVANTES'. (*koryvantes.org*)

9. Close-quarters second-strike attack with a sidearm, here a pickaxe, once the opponent has thrust and missed with a shafted weapon. The warrior on the left has evaded the thrust and closed in for a downward slashing attack, most probably diagonally over the shoulder. Copyright: Association of Historical Studies 'KORYVANTES'. (*koryvantes.org*)

10. Dirk-type swords in the hands of armoured and unarmoured/light infantry. The latter re-enact the Pylian Frescoes. Copyright: Association of Historical Studies 'KORYVANTES'. (*koryvantes.org*)

11. A prehoplite/early hoplite. The armour items are direct descendants from parts used in Mycenaean panoplies, as also is the *dory* – spear. The novelty rests with the shield. Copyright: Association of Historical Studies 'KORYVANTES'. (*koryvantes.org*)

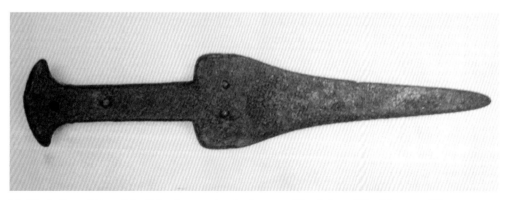

12. Find of a stabbing dirk; Pylos frescoes imply the type. The Athens War Museum. (*Photo courtesy: Maj General HA-Ret Papathanasiou B*)

13. Find of a cut-and-thrust dirk; Pylos frescoes imply the type. The Athens War Museum. (*Photo courtesy: Maj General HA-Ret Papathanasiou B*)

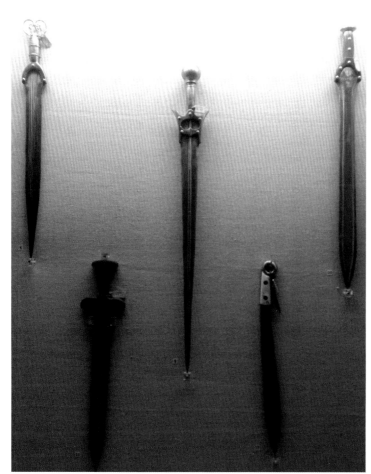

14. Different Mycenaean sword types reconstructed. Upper right, the cut-and-thrust *aor* broadsword; middle, the rapier *pakana/phasganon*, for piercing and cutting; lower right, a slashing weapon, progenitor to the classical *kopis*. On the left, different cut-and-thrust models; they might have been called *xiphe/qisipe* or *aor* as well. The Athens War Museum. (*Photo courtesy: Maj General HA-Ret Papathanasiou B*)

15. Find of a helmet; the central, longitudinal position of the crest is obvious. The Athens War Museum. (*Photo courtesy: Maj General HA-Ret Papathanasiou B*)

16. Find of bronze greaves of the early type. The Athens War Museum. (*Photo courtesy: Maj General HA-Ret Papathanasiou B*)

17. The use of the two-handed infantry pike by an unarmoured bearer of the full-size figure-of-eight shield. The Athens War Museum. (*Photo courtesy: Maj General HA-Ret Papathanasiou B*)

The Trojans, great equestrians of the time, rich and aristocratic, had a powerful chariotry, well-supplied and supported in home territory. The Greeks, due to the amphibious nature of the campaign, could not transport and deploy a number anywhere near their full levy and were thus short in this arm. Their strength lay in infantry. The rank and file infantry en masse could storm a city, disperse to pursue the defenders in MOUT (Military Operations in Urban Terrain, including street fighting, looting and incinerating buildings) much better than roaming chariots in the streets or a few dismounted nobles; it could also perform shock action in battle and assist chariotry by providing a barrier behind which chariots could find refuge after retreating and then reform to launch another attack. Some units, expert in missile warfare and skirmishing tactics, could directly engage and decimate enemy chariotry, while the dense infantry formations stopped Trojan mounted attacks. Additionally, infantry was essential for the Greek strategy: it could negotiate the mountainous terrain to raid and devastate the network of communities in the surroundings of Troy, which supported the Trojan effort with troops, supplies, intelligence and communications. The infantry were rowing the ships that projected said devastators even further, and once on the beach they doubled as assault troops to attack and plunder the targeted shore.

Thus, if given a chance by tactics, conditions and, ideally, the absence of swarms of skirmishing units, Hector would love to decimate the Greek rank and file. Destroying the heroes/knights could not conclude the issue if it did not neutralize the infantry, either by exposing it to physical annihilation or by decapitating it and degrading its battle efficiency. Slaughtering the infantry without exposing themselves to the enemy heroes was a better way for the Trojan heroes to make the Greek cause untenable.

Part II

Heroic Warfare

Chapter 9

The Homeric Art of War

Archaeology and tablet deciphering have done much to unravel the material aspect of the Bronze Age world for today's observer. But there is a discernible lack of descriptive evidence, literary or otherwise, to combine with artefacts and illustrative art of the era into building a coherent, functional picture. Especially with regard to the conduct of wars, commemorative texts on Egyptian pharaonic monuments and the like from the Fertile Crescent provide little information. The only vivid and coherent description available is the Hellenic Homeric epics; although we only possess a heavily edited, Athenian-mandated sixth-century BC version with detectable forgeries, the main structure provides a large and coherent picture (Van Wees 1994), with cases of exemplary detail usually disregarded by philologists as 'figures of speech' and by historians as 'unreliable lore'. It is true that, in the context of poetry, credibility is wanting. Aesthetic and metric concerns, always of paramount importance in poetry – both as an art and as a tool to transmit information – sap the notion of precision, especially in terminology (a problem seen with other literary forms as well, to be honest). If a figure of speech is used consistently, and thus qualifies for internal cross-reference, a philologist may say it is standard and prosaic; the more it is used, the more standardized and thus uninformative its use is considered. If not, and it is rarely used, or uniquely, it is for metric and aesthetic reasons.

Still, the massive confrontation which shook and crumbled the Bronze Age Aegean is described in terms precisely understandable by modern-day military personnel and in detail not seen in literature until the fourth century BC military treatises and historical essays written by military professionals for their kind. After all, epic poetry was not intended to amuse; the societies of the time had little use for recreation. But they did have a use for memory, as survival through memory was the main mechanism for sustaining society, by inspiring its members to altruistically take risks in battle, whenever needed, with glamorous examples.

Army organization and command

There is no question that the Trojan and allied army is a feudal conglomerate (Van Wees 1994) under the personal command of the lord of the hosts of Troy, Crown Prince Hector (who might or might not have been heir apparent). The high command, though, rests with the crown council, the king and a seven-member senate (III-146/9) which may veto his strategy or impose decisions (XV-721/3). After ten years behind Troy's walls (a time frame that is not exaggerated, if compared with the unsuccessful sieges of Tyre), allied relief contingents have arrived before Prince Hector offers major battle to the invaders (Othryoneus XIII-364, Asteropaius XXI-156); they continue to arrive by the day and are thrown piecemeal into battle, as they arrive (XIII-790/4; XXII-434). The basic administrative units are of fifty men and the total size of the army is approximately 50,000: 1,000 campfires, with fifty men sleeping, sitting or eating around each one of them (VIII-558/9). Although it cannot be substantiated, these fifty-man groups must account for the *telea* units mentioned by Hector in an administrative and logistical, as well as tactical, context (XVIII-298/300).

The Greek army had the same basic unit of fifty, because the main type of ship is the fifty-oared galley (*pentekonter*) of unknown model (II-720, XVI-170). Nevertheless there are some very large ships carrying 120 troops of a certain contingent (II-510); whether all of them were doubling as rowers or not is not stated. There were also twenty-oared galleys for other missions (I-309). But the similarities of the two armies stop there.

The Greek army in Homer is *not* a feudal levy and our understanding of Mycenaean armies corroborates such impressions (Grguric 2005). It was an integrated organization with distinct functions and specialist units, which *may* have been recruited under different local lords and fight in their customary manner. But it is the synthesis of the different arms that makes the difference, and this is much more elaborate than usually thought (Van Wees 1994); this synthesis and integration into a tactical, not a tribal, fighting force was forged at Aulis by intensive training and was the work of their best tactician, Menestheus of Athens (Phil, *Her* 23,19). In most of the *Iliad*, the Greek army also operates – and with little success – as a feudal levy, since Achilles, the mind and soul of the army and acting commander-in-chief/C-in-C (as implied in XXIV-651/8 and directly stated in iii-106) is estranged. Just before the new series of clashes, narrated by Homer in the *Iliad*, which occur during the tenth year of the war, the elderly tactician Nestor advises the high king, Agamemnon, to deploy the army in feudal/tribal fashion (II-362/8). This means that for nine years the army was *not* deployed in such a manner, and this differentiation is obviously due to the absence of Achilles. Once he is back, he clearly issues all the executive directions and orders (XIX-155, XXIV-670) and the army instantly transforms from a relatively ineffective feudal muster to a well-oiled war machine once more, operating with a plan and efficiency and not simply clashing with the enemy. There are tactical units and respective leaders/ commanders (*lochoi*, 500-strong in Achilles' own contingent XVI-168/73) although their command is not specified as being organic or ad hoc. The decimal system thus implied fits well with the ten-man *oka* of the Linear B texts. Many scholars detect dramatic effect and poetic projection in the advice of Nestor, but had it been so the poet would have easily projected it into the past, as he did in other cases, as with the pursuit of Aeneas (XX-187/91).

Both sides seem to understand perfectly well the notion of sentries doing their job properly; the Greek high command checks them *in situ* and is well satisfied (X-97/9); although this round of control may have been a pretext for a secretive meeting. Hector is just as vigilant (VIII-521), and his troops duly performed their tasks (IX-1). But not all of them, especially some of the allies; having just arrived and being very tired and lax, they pay a terrible price: King Rhesus and many of his entourage are slain in their sleep (X-559/61) during a night raid of two Greeks. Next time Hector issues such orders, he is far more explicit (XVIII-298/300).

Troop types

A. Chariotry and Cavalry

Both armies are based on the heavy armed and armoured noble warrior, owning a chariot and fighting from it (Drews 1996). The term in the epic is *hippota* (XIV-52) meaning 'horseman' and the equivalent of 'knight'; the *eqeta* of the Linear B texts, although the tablet could also be interpreted as '*epaites*', meaning 'follower' (D'Amato and Salimbeti 2011; Fields 2006).

The warriors combine heavy armour with mobility; both Achilles and Hector are fleet of foot (XIII-348), excellent charioteers, big of stature and very strong, epitomizing the heroic concept of 'tall, strong and brave', adding the 'fast'. The speed of Achilles is the most frequently used tactically orientated adjective characterizing him, instead of 'brave', 'strong' etc. Importantly, the quality and speed of his horses of divine pedigree (XVI-380/2) are also underlined (II-770; XXIII-276/8) and even more emphatically, although in far fewer cases. They were an immortal pair, a marital gift to his father from Poseidon, the god of the sea, the earthquake and horses. In general, the use of adjectives that denote an equestrian culture may underline a true dimension of chariot warfare instead of being figures of speech or descriptive relics and stereotypes. In many cases tactics, operations, orders and advice refer to matters of both horse and wheel, implying a very active role for the chariot, far more direct and diverse than the battlefield taxi sometimes understood by contemporary scholarship (Drews 1996; Smith 2015).

Other heavily armoured warriors on both sides are also notoriously fast: the Greek Antilochus, who is also an accomplished charioteer (XXIII-402/5), and the wily Odysseus (XXIII-753/6), who has no chariot; not to mention the lightly clad Ajax the Lesser (XIII-66). From the Trojans, Aeneas (XIII-482), Glaucus (XVI-597/8) and Paris (VI-512/4) are armoured fast runners. The heavily armed and excessively trained warriors, occasionally learning the trade from their fathers (XV-525/7), disembark from their chariots to fight on foot (De Becker 2009), and are supported by chariot runners (Drews 1996), possibly in the Egyptian manner (Healy 1992). Such troops may be implied twice for the Trojans (XV-516/7; XXI-90/1); the latter referring to Crown Prince Polydorus, who is explicitly identified by his swiftness as his characteristic virtue. Additionally, there is the support of the rank-and-file infantry, while the chariot proper awaits nearby with the driver at the ready to extract the warrior from the fray or to allow a hot pursuit. The Trojans have better chariotry: some of their allies use two-horse teams (V-195), but some of the Trojans have four-horse teams; the names of the four-strong team of Hector are mentioned (VIII-185). Whether they were arranged in two tandem pairs or four abreast it is not known, but the latter is more probable, especially if the Assyrian representations of three-horse teams imply rather four-horse teams, as suggested by the reins handled by the driver (Dezső 2012). The Greeks have two-horse teams (XXIII-290/305), but Nestor obviously had something more than that (VIII-81/6), although no number for horses for his team is mentioned explicitly. Achilles, the top equestrian, uses a third horse (XVI-149/53), not to drag the chariot, but to make the turns swifter (XVI-467/71), a must in mobile warfare, for both using the chariot as a means of transportation or as a fighting platform for shooting a bow or casting a javelin or thrusting and hacking with the lance or hand weapons (De Becker 2009). This again corroborates with the above-mentioned Assyrian representations (Dezső 2012), if the three-horse teams are accepted as depicted, as the real size of the team, contrary to what has just been mentioned above. After all, proper three-horse teams are mentioned explicitly (iv-590) and corroborate the above-mentioned Assyrian depictions in form.

Both Trojans and Greeks use extremely long and heavy lances from their chariots, seen on monuments and in art (Grguric 2005; Fields 2006). Perhaps they are the *'egxeiai'* of the epic (XIII-339), *ekeija* of the Linear B texts, with massive warheads reminiscent of the Japanese use of *naginata* in the sixteenth to seventeenth centuries; that is, for both thrusting and cutting. Hector is specifically mentioned as holding a eleven-cubit chariotry lance (VIII-494) while in a chariot; Ajax the Great brandishes a long naval spear, twenty-two cubits in XV-678. Hector is also mentioned as pursuing the Greek rank and file in a chariot, thrashing heads (XI-309) and wielding his spear. This adds up to the aforementioned, slash-capable shafted weapon. Most obviously, this is also the nature of the great spear donated to Achilles by his father, which could not be wielded by anyone else (XVI-140/3) and is kept in a sheath when not in use (XIX-387); not in a holder or against the wall. So heavy a weapon might not be a javelin or anything light enough for casting. An exchange of spear thrusts between Greeks on-deck – in their ships drawn ashore, using shafted weapons being intended for naval fights – and the Trojans, storming in their chariots, obviously using the long chariotry lances, is very illuminating (XV-385/9); as is the specific use of the term *xyston* for these naval weapons in both cases (XV-385/9 & XV-677), in direct contrast with the usual terms used for thrusting shafted weapons, including the chariotry lances.

It is not inconsequential that the Greeks considered lanced chariotry fighting in jousts (as Nestor advocates, IV-306/7) a thing of the past; Nestor, the Elder, is contemporaneous with the apex of such practice, as had been the father of Achilles. There is some modern scepticism on the subject (Smith 2015), although what Nestor suggests is actually 'advance in line abreast', to cover as much width, possibly without depth so as not to risk very destructive collisions whenever an obstacle surfaced. It is after all the way medieval knights, most of the ancient cavalry force, and the scythed chariots of the Persian kings charged. By keeping formation there was mutual support, to preclude infiltration by runners and the use of horse armour, or other type of protection, allows true shock action with the lance. As became clear under Alexander the Great, armoured mobility maximized such action with hand-held weapons, not with missiles. As with the Macedonian *xyston* overpowering the Persian *palton*, the *egxeia* lance of the Mycenaean charioteers must have reigned supreme in the armies of Mycenae and their enemies, especially the Hittites (Drews 1996; Fields 2006; Bryce 2007). In truth, this scepticism repeats the century-old orthodoxy, clearly misguided, which decreed that cavalry, especially ancient cavalry, was not able to charge home on unbroken infantry despite centuries of cavalry practice indicating that in principle it was quite possible, and in direct disregard or misinterpretation of ancient sources and modern expertise (Sears and Willekes 2016).

However, for dismounted fighting, the lance could prove impractical. For this reason the warrior is always equipped with a general-purpose spear, for casting and thrusting alike, and generally carried in pairs (VI-104, XIII-559). A pair of short, shafted weapons plus sword is usual in Geometric-Period Dipylon cemetery finds for both infantry and chariotry (D'Amato and Salimbeti 2017). Egyptian reliefs of the reign of Rameses III (Medinet Habu) show Sea Peoples habitually carrying pairs of spears (D'Amato and Salimbeti 2015). This reminds us of the very later Persian *'palta'* of the cavalry, much praised by Xenophon (*Cyrop* I.2,9). The pair of spears is mentioned many a time Hector jumps out of his chariot (VI-103/4), and this might imply that he changes weapons, from lance to spears. It is obvious that both lance and spears are routinely secured within the chariot (Drews 1988), as in the weapon holsters of Egyptian chariots (Fields 2006), but in an Aegean context a different arrangement is implied (D'Amato and Salimbeti 2017); the solution may be found once more in Assyrian reliefs, where long lances can be seen attached at the back of the chariot carriage at an angle, while the warrior shoots a bow (Dezső 2012).

An excellent example is Patroclus, who sets out with two spears (XVI-139) but after casting one at Sarpedon's charioteer and never recovering it, he is explicitly mentioned as fighting hence with one (XVI-733, XVI-801), which he does not cast and, for missiles, he reverts to stones while having the spear in his left hand. The dual-role *'dory'*, which can be thrown or thrust and is carried in pairs, is clearly mentioned. What is of importance is the fact that Pandarus, one of the very few Trojan allies who came on foot because he doubted the adequacy of fodder for his (two-horse) teams, has taken his bow *instead*; his phrasing points to the bow being mutually exclusive with charging chariotry (V-192/210), completely unlike the Egyptian practice – but perhaps in agreement with that of the Hittites (Drews 1996). Alternatively he was a chariot-archer by trade but left the chariot at home to fight as a field archer.

The issue of mounted horsemen in the epics is underrated and possibly overlooked altogether. There is no indication of fighting on horseback in the epics, not even of riding to battle. On the other hand, riding is explicitly mentioned: once Odysseus snatches the team of the Thracian King, Rhesus, in a raid, who is promptly exterminated along with his retinue due to lax security, he has no time to also take the chariot – light enough to lift up (X-505) – and thus, escaping with the horses to the Greek lines means inadvertently mounting the horses (X-529/30). Additionally, when Ajax the

Great jumps from ship deck to ship deck to keep the Trojans away, as they try to set fire to said vessels drawn ashore in multiple rows (XIV-30/6), he is compared to an – obviously jugglerish – rider who jumps from one horse to another in a four-horse team (XV-679/84), which implies a deep tradition in riding, although the nature and function of the horse team is withheld.

In any case, not using the horses as mounts implies two things: the available horses were rather too small and weak to carry armoured warriors; or the inability to put them in harm's way. The latter may be indirectly associated with the former; the inability of the mount to carry an armed and armoured rider plus protective gear (as armour) for itself. This can be traced back a bit: the first case of the use of a horse in war is Pegasus, a divine and winged horse ridden to adventure by Perseus and Bellerophon, a story implying that riding was understood, but fighting from horseback needed another type of horse compared to the ones existing at the time. A generation before the Trojan War, Hercules had imported a new breed of horse into southern Greece from Thrace; the man-eating mares of Diomedes, the adjective most probably indicating ferociousness in battle and a murderous attitude implying trampling/attacking with hooves and generally shock action, either as chariot teams or as mounts.

As a matter of fact, the Greeks have many first-line heroes and kings who do not possess or use a chariot. Some do fight the heroic way, an agile skirmishing fight with spear, shield and heavy armour like Odysseus (XI-435/6), while others (both Ajaxes) fight in a way unsuitable to and incompatible with chariotry, although from close range. Thus, the Greek army has more troop types than the Trojans, who operate infantry (XV-517; XXI-90), archers and heavy charioteers (knights).

B. Infantry

Similar to the description in the Hittite texts (Pantazis 2006), both armies use infantry and chariotry. The Trojans seem to rely more on chariotry than their opponents, due to their tradition and competence in equestrian matters, and since they are on their home ground, without need to transport mounts and vehicles. But they do use regular infantry (XV-516/7; XXI-90/1), not simply dismounted *eqeta*. Contrary to popular belief, archery is not attested as their national weapon in Homer. The Trojan archers might shoot from within the ranks, as Pandarus did (IV-114), covered by shields, or individually. It is a fact that they may shoot en masse, volleys, especially from their walls; the latter is stated (XXII-195/6), the former not so much, but the conjecture is secure. At least one allied contingent is identified as archers, the Paeonians (II-848), while infantry formations are identified within the Trojan forces proper, commanded by crown prince(s) and thus of high status. The mode of fighting seems to be rather fluid, mobile skirmishing with exchanges of missiles from a distance by large, linear infantry deployments, with pikes provided for countering chariotry onslaughts and opportunistic emergence of heavy armoured aristocrats, possibly on foot, to snipe at an enemy (XVI-806/13) or engage and thrust at him (XVI-820/1) or scold or encourage the rank and file (XI-64/5). Contingents of dedicated spearmen are identified amongst the Trojan allies, the Pelasgians (II-840) and the Kikones (II-846), although whether this implies pikemen, spearmen or javelineers, or all three, remains unclear. But the epic makes one thing clear: the armed forces of Troy proper include infantry but depend on cavalry, or rather chariotry, to a considerable extent (XII-60/5). They are famous horse-breeders and tamers (IV-509; V-102) and the wealth of the city allows chariots to be mass-produced, procured and maintained; princelings have intimate knowledge and skills in purely technical matters of chariot construction (XXI-34/8). Although the overall power of the Trojans is perhaps an order of magnitude lower than that of the Greeks (II-125/31), their chariotry might be superior even quantitatively; this is to be expected, as amphibious forces could not carry massive chariotry elements, especially due to the need to embark the horses. Greek chariots were rather light, since most of their chieftains had brought their own (II-763/78). The value of the arm was established and celebrated, obviously beyond its use as a means of exercising command and control functions, which is not corroborated by the descriptions, actually, but remains a distinct possibility, if one is informed by more modern practices, with commanders using horses or mechanized transportation to inspect different locations of interest.

It is very strange that the Greeks, who despise the bow, also have competent archery skills. The troops of Philoktetes are good archers and may shoot individually (II-720); Teukros exemplifies the pairing of a heavy shield-bearer to an archer (VIII-265/70) with his brother Ajax the Great, although he may fight with spear and shield, as a medium infantryman (XIII-313/4), armed with helmet, spear, shield and sword (XIII-714/5), reminiscent of dual-function archer-spearmen on Assyrian reliefs (Dezsô 2012). But Teukros has to retire to his hut to change from archer to spearman attire (XV-478/82).

The Locrian contingent shoots en masse from a distance (XIII-716/22), shirking contact and shooting some Trojan assaults to pieces from behind the storm troops' lines; but the Greek is unclear and may refer to archers paired with and taking refuge behind/beside heavy, shielded infantry, as in classical-era *parentaxis*. In addition to medium infantry, chariotry and missile troops, that is archers, the Greeks also have heavy, shielded infantry for static defence, a commodity never implied for the Trojans. The personification is Ajax the Great, a very tall and strong warrior, second only to Achilles in valour and merit, but never accused of being fleet of foot nor seen to mount a chariot. His resolve, steadfastness and endurance are admirable; his presence in a sector is a guarantee that the defence will endure (XIII-321/5). He is supported by either his brother Teukros, the archer, or another chariotless king, the Locrian chief Ajax the Lesser. Although his contingent is solely archers (XIII-716/22), Ajax the Lesser is a storm trooper, but definitively a light infantryman, as he substitutes metal armour with a linen corselet (II-529). He is very fast, an excellent spearman and offers skirmishing support to Ajax the Great's stability (XVII-719/21) and a destructive power of pursuit (XIV-520/1), more or less manifesting the combined tactics of the integrated Greek army that may have survived into evidence through similar Assyrian practice (Dezső 2012).

There are some interesting incidents in the epic that corroborate Assyrian reliefs and some Mycenaean ones as well. The first is the shield-bearer/archer combination, a very well-known Middle-Eastern pattern. In Assyrian art, the emphasis is on the archer, with one shield bearer assigned to him, using a pavise-like protective device, rectangular body-shield or any other type of shield (Dezső 2012). In a proper Mycenaean context, both the Lion-Hunt Dagger and the Battle Krater show naked, helmeted, unarmoured archers shooting from behind a line of shield-bearers, who form a rather tight formation with two-handed pikes and body-shields (figure-of-eight and tower shields); the pikemen are likewise helmeted and unarmoured. Thus the priority lies with the shield-bearers who are pikemen, and they are more numerous than the archers. The latter seem to be clearly supporting the former, while in the Assyrian context the archers are the effectors and the shield-bearers are the support element, providing protection and occasionally carrying additional arrows for them (Dezső, 2012). In the literary evidence, there are three cases: the best attested is the combination of one body-shield bearer and one archer, namely Ajax the Great and his brother Teukros (VIII-266/72). The ratio is reminiscent of Assyria, it is a 1:1 duo, but the main component is the shield-bearer/pikeman, not the archer. This is obvious, as already mentioned, from the ratio of archers and spearbearers on the Battle Krater and on the Lion-Hunt Dagger and the comparative size of the two types on sealstones and other depictions where the shield-bearer/archer pair is shown (D'Amato and Salimbeti 2013). In truth, it seems in some cases that Ajax the Great, Ajax the Lesser and Teukros are an integrated combat unit, a lethal trio (XII-335/7), where the archer supports the pikeman/shield-bearer who offers coverage also to a more mobile and agile spear-fighter, as already mentioned above. This concept is reported for Assyrian armies, with armoured spear-fighters fighting in pairs with unarmoured spear-fighters while covered by an unarmoured archer (Dezső 2012) and thus should not be considered improbable for the concept of warfare in the *Iliad*. What is not known is the support footprint of such an Assyrian unit. For the one mentioned in the *Iliad*, it is significant: Ajax the Lesser has no chaperones (XIII-712), but Teukros has one (XII-371/2), who conceivably allows the trio quite a capacity for transformation and persistence in missile warfare, and Ajax the Great several, who seem to be non-combatants; they sponge his sweat and support the great weight of the shield (XIII-709/11), without any indication that they are armed or able to engage by themselves, although this cannot be ruled out.

The second case recalls the Lion-Hunt Dagger and the Battle Krater once more; Pandarus shoots alone, covered behind the shields of his men (IV-111/4), a sniping function once more. The third case is massive archery use by unarmoured, lightly clad archer units (the Locrians) shooting en masse from behind the lines of friendly frontline troops, shielded and/or armoured (XIII-716/22). The concept is much closer to the massiveness of the Assyrian records but is not implying any degree of delegation and pairing of an archer with a line warrior. Any cooperation would be ad hoc, or simply the unit would deploy behind another unit, as ordered, with no interactions and diffusion of the synergy to the level of individual combatants. Still, things are not straightforward. The archers may spread within the lines of the shielded warriors and shoot directly, covered by the shields of the latter, or remain in a solid second line behind the first line and shoot indirectly, over the heads of the contact troops.

Another (group of) incident(s) in the epic directly implies the existence of fully armoured archers, armed with sidearms and possibly with shield and spear additionally, and not alternatively, to the bow; a direct counterpart of such armoured troops carrying all kinds of weapons (sidearm, shafted weapon, shield and bow and quiver) on some Assyrian reliefs (Dezső, 2012). Prince Helenus of Troy, fully armoured and proud owner of a Thracian sword with excellent chopping performance (XIII-576), shoots an arrow in a melee from point-blank range (XIII-585/95). It is not clear if he also has a spear and/or shield with him at that moment, but he *was* an armoured archer.

With the two Greeks, things are even more clear: Teukros shoots with his bow (XV-458/70), but with a moment's notice, he reverts to spear and shield (XV-478/83); it is not clear if he had the time to go to his hut/tent to rearm, but the heat of the moment (XV-474/7) suggests he had all his weapons nearby, thus being a very close counterpart to the armoured and fully armed Assyrian archers. Still, it is not mentioned specifically that Teukros was armoured and, once hit by a stone cast by Hector and wounded, there is no mention of armour giving way or partially resisting the blow (VIII-320/30). What *is* mentioned though is that in a case where Ajax and Teukros had to relocate to assist a hard-pressed unit, they moved on foot and Teukros had a retainer carrying his bow (XII-370/3). This suggests that the retainer was the enabler of the 'switch', holding the close-quarters battle (CQB) weapons when Teukros used the bow and passing them whenever he needed to fight with shield and spear, relieving him of the bow at the same time and possibly carrying additional quivers and arrows when his master operates as an archer, similar to additional quivers seen next to bowless Assyrians (Dezső 2012).

The foremost example of an armoured spear-fighter having a bow nearby – i.e. on his person – should the need arise, is Meriones. Coming from Crete, a culture renowned for archers in later years, he was to win an archery contest (XXIII-870/6); but he fights with spear and shield throughout the epic and is most accomplished in that (XIII-255/8). So much so that he walks away from battle once he loses his spear and is treated to one by his liege and friend, Idomeneus (XIII-256–94). But suddenly, seeing a fleeing enemy he shoots a lethal arrow (XIII-650) grasping the opportunity; it is the only arrow he fires in anger throughout the epic, implying he had bow and quiver nearby (on his person, as he uses no chariot at this point) while fighting with shield and spear, something reminiscent of Assyrian depictions; there are some of them showing armoured, shielded archers with spear and sword (Dezső 2012). Meriones is an accomplished warrior, as he is also well-versed in chariotry and competes at the funeral games (XXIII-356). As has been mentioned, his name is reminiscent of the *marianu* term in Mitanni for an armoured chariot-borne warrior, possibly the paradigm for the Hittites and Egyptians (Healy 1992).

Mycenaean infantry can be roughly divided into three categories by fusing all available evidence from archaeology and lore: heavy, medium and light, similar to Assyrian and Egyptian reliefs. This is by their kit and less so by their tactical employment, although such issues infringe upon each other. Their employment, however, is more straightforward and can be divided into two distinct but intertwined actions: first, fluid, mobile tactics, enacted by skirmishers who do *not* fight from a distance as in later years (Thuc VI.69,2), but press the attack home by engaging in CQB with similar or irregular opponents. The Battle of the Glen Ring depicts such an engagement of the first kind while the second is depicted in a fresco from Pylos (D'Amato and Salimbeti 2013). Additionally, the Agate ring shows a dissimilar engagement with a sword-bearing skirmisher engaging a heavier opponent, in this case a body-shield bearer (Petmezas 2019; Grguric 2005), although careful observation shows that the skirmisher might actually be wearing a bell-shaped cuirass.

Then there are the line tactics, with set formations reminiscent of phalanx warfare, as on the Battle Krater (Smith 2015). The heavy infantry, meaning troops shielded and armoured (by metal, soft-material or composite armour items), can be employed in both cases; chariots increase their usefulness in mobile tactics in a tactical context.

The medium troops are unarmoured, but for a helmet and, occasionally, greaves of whatever type (the latter are not only protection but an enhancer of mobility over the Greek terrain). These troops are shielded. The body-shielded ones are of limited usefulness in mobile warfare, as their shield makes running difficult due to volume rather than weight (XV-645/7). But still, they may redeploy and create nuclei of support and refuge for the mobile elements, as did the infantry for the medieval cavalry, which launched charges and returned to regroup behind infantry protection. In the ancient world, this must have been the case in numerous confrontations with cavalry-orientated cultures, possibly including the use of the imperial cavalry in the Battle of Plataea (Hdt IX.60,1–61,3).

On the contrary, medium, shielded infantry with medium and light shields, without armour, were exceptional for mobile warfare, especially the kind implied by Hanson (1999), but hardly suitable for dense formations and CQB in congested conditions (XIV-375). It could revert to such a role but was to take horrific casualties by missiles (XIII-716/22) as it was inadequately protected and a dense, static, massive target. The beauty of the system, though, was that such troops could engage the high-price chariots with low-cost outfit and arms and fight on every kind of terrain. This explains the reassignment of heavy, armoured troops to such roles, to afford better shock power, thus using the chariot as transportation (and the mount as well). The combination of mobility with protection offered a shock instrument ideally suited to storming fortifications, including walled cities; heavy infantry, and heroes at that, were reportedly very near to storm heavily fortified cities by assaulting/climbing walls: Kapaneus the walls of Thebes (Soph, *Ant* 131/3); and Patroclus the circuit of Troy (XVI-698/704). Furthermore Sarpedon did storm the defences of the Greek field fortification with his troops (XII-395/415).

And then it was the light, unshielded, unarmoured infantry, possibly helmeted and perhaps with greaves. Such troops are the Locrian archers in the *Iliad* (XIII-716/22), but, more importantly, the skirmishers with helmet, longswords (types A/C) or short swords/dirks (Types B/D) of the iconographic evidence (i.e. seal stones and Pylos' frescoes), sometimes having greaves and spear. Waistband armour belts have been found (D'Amato and Salimbeti 2017), can be seen on early Iron Age figurines and are mentioned in the epic (XXI-90/1), and this item may well have been used by medium infantry as well. It does not qualify as proper armour; Menelaus wears a plate cuirass and a belt (IV-133/5). In categorizing troops one must always face the problem of qualitative over quantitative nature: does 'armoured' means 'having armour', or 'having full armour', or 'having a set percentage of the available armour items/body coverage'? Composite and fabric/leather armour sets (II-529) are another such issue; in here they will be considered as light versions of and partial armour, thus troops equipped with these, if shieldless, are considered light infantry like Ajax the Lesser (XIII-66), obviously veering towards the mobile tactics rather than anything else.

C. Combined Arms

The picture of Homeric battle is a bit fuzzy and many scholars are bitterly trading blows as to the kind of combat it represents (Sears 2010). That is, of course, after filtering the possibility of transmitting a real picture, not a wild fantasy, from the bottom of the composer's psyche up to brilliance in mythoplasy. Perhaps something with a kernel of truth or truths, a *Lord of The Rings* or, even worse, a *Dune*. But one thing catching the eye or the brain is the integration in the use of different arms. Whether integrating and combining arms is a good thing is a matter of vogue and perspective; the cavalry-only steppe warriors had some spectacular success against more balanced armies, as did Greek Hoplites and Swiss pikemen. But this is another discussion; in Homer the fight has many stages, and the fighters seem to be well-versed. This is nothing groundbreaking: they are by choice full-time warriors for sustenance (xiv-210/25) like the Vikings. Many of them win their living by the sword and their highly centralized societies (Drews 1979) support training of both troops and officers.

A first level of combination and integration is amongst different specialities in one arm: the use of full contingents of missile troops (II-716/20) and their deployment to the rear of line troops in order to support them with missiles (XIII-716/22). Whether these troops are delegated amongst shield-bearers and shoot directly, covered by the shields of the latter, or they amass behind the deployed lines of close-range fighters, is a matter of interpretation. One, though, has to pay some attention to some signs indicating differentiation *within* a contingent. After all, tribal/national contingents were small armies that were able to engage in small wars, for their sovereign, on their own. They had to be relatively self-sufficient in some key specialities, irrespective of the basic, national arm. In a large, federal host they may have contributed their best or standard fighters (II-540/4), but they may also have contributed fully integrated, combined arms detachments. These could undertake field missions independently, perhaps the reason for only *some* chieftains (particularly Achilles) carrying out an arduous raiding campaign (IX-325/30). Alternatively, it is conceivable that the same specialities were aggregated at the army level, similarly to the practice followed for the grenadiers in large armies in the eighteenth to nineteenth centuries; concentrating them to use at a higher level and perhaps as a striking force.

The combined arms contingent can be observed in the Myrmidons of Achilles; the unit enjoys a reputation indicating renowned soldiers with *esprit de corps*, perhaps a special unit or a warband/fraternity. When cataloguing the forces of the Achaeans, Homer assigns to Achilles national units *and* the Myrmidons (II-684/5); it is not clear whether the troops from all these places, obviously levies, *are* the Myrmidons (who originate from Aegina) or *include* Myrmidon elements as special units – special in mission, raising, status, war function or origin. At the end, whether the troops of Achilles *are* Myrmidons, or *include* the Myrmidons is not very clear. They may well have been the elite part of the force, something like the Hypaspists of Philip II and Alexander, or the elite units of Classical Greece, such as the Theban Sacred Band and the Spartan 300 Knights.

Such troops in classical times were really multi-functional. They were elites and thus trained to perfection for more than one kind of combat. They were experts at warfare. In this capacity they must have had good discipline. In the case of the Myrmidons, their warlike spirit is explicitly mentioned (XVI-200/5). The discipline is pervasive but detectable (XVI-211/6); the Greek host, after all, was taking pride in its discipline and silence (III-8/9) which was proposed, imposed and introduced by Ajax the Great during the muster at Aulis (Phil Her 23,18–9) and this did relate back to their political system (I-277/81); the latter, however, was not much unlike others of the era, and Trojan autocracy was much more severe (VII-427/8).

Thus, while the rest of the host prepares for battle, the Myrmidons, since Achilles sulks in his wrath, stay put. They do not lie idle, playing dice or checkers, either. They train. They train in the discus, javelin and bow (II-773/5). This exceptionally informative piece allows for two very important conclusions: since javelin and archery are comparable, as pastimes, with the discus, the latter *is* a martial art, a war skill, perhaps applicable in throwing big stones, or, more explicitly, one type of throwing stone, of particular size and perhaps shape, to achieve and destroy some special category of targets, from shields (VII-268/72) to light fortifications. The usual throwing of the stone (today's *shot put*) was another type and skill for other applications, obviously, possibly against close-packed enemy formations and preferably

The commission of Paris

The chain of command in a feudal allied host is predictable, with the home princes occupying the highest seats. The crown prince Hector, portrayed in the *Iliad* as heir-apparent (VI-476/8), was evidently the C-in-C (II-816; XVIII-286/305), and led the main arm of Troy, the armoured chariotry (VIII-184/95). It follows that the second in the line of succession (who would be Paris) would lead the second most prestigious and important arm. And this, in the first appearance of the revamped and reinforced Trojan grand army, is the light infantry, as the equipment of Paris at his first appearance in the epic (III-15/20) fits well into this niche. Corroborating modern views (Grguric 2005) and ancient lore (Hercules), but especially representational evidence, as in ring- and sealstones, and in frescoes (as in Pylos), the light, not the heavy, infantry were of major importance. Able to engage in terrain inaccessible to chariots, able to support and exploit a chariot charge or to derail it, and also able to dislodge heavy, shielded infantry, it was the second most important arm in Troy and Paris had been heading it. His massive loss of prestige in the single combat with Menelaus (III-403/12; VI-333/6) led to restructuring the leadership, and it is possible that the very young prince Polydorus was to be found in this capacity (XX-407/12; XXI-90/1), as a direct or indirect result of Paris losing his commission; thereafter, Paris fights in armour (VI-320/40 & 512/3), as a regular, although occasionally with the bow (XI-369/77). He commands men, possibly a combined-arms force (XII-93/5), but does not lead an arm comprised of the similar units of the allied contingents.

For reasons of comparison, the Achaeans, who had a different command structure whence the high king was only C-in-C, recorded as their second best warrior the body-shielded Ajax the Great (II-768/770) after Achilles; not the only registered light-infantry-geared Ajax the Lesser, (II-527/30; XIV-519/21), who is reportedly closely coupled to the former (XII-335; XIII-126 & 701/4). This implies that the light infantry of the Greeks were assigned as a support arm to the heavy infantry, not to chariotry, nor was it used independently.

from superior positions, such as fortifications (XII-154/5). It is difficult to establish which type was used by Hector to smash the gates of the Greek fortification (XII-445/62).

The second conclusion is that archery was practised amongst the rank and file of the Myrmidons. They were not an archer contingent; they were mobile infantry and chariotry (XVI-166/7). But either they all had been taught the use of the bow, or there were specialized bowmen within their ranks. The latter is more probable, as even today special weapons require special training and specialist troops; a machine gun specialist is not, generally speaking, an expert with the mortar or the grenade-launcher or with the sniper rifle. As a result, the special unit of Achilles contained at least some specialist archers so as to conduct its operations autonomously, in the then-current concept of operations. This also implies that Patroclus perhaps led the special unit of the Myrmidons, and not the whole of Achilles' forces, in the counter-attack; a very good reason *not* to be ordered to advance far and be drawn into pursuit (XVI-83/96). In such conditions, the few troops of his would stretch thin and be exposed to counter-attacks by rallying, superior enemy forces. And, most importantly, they would betray their disadvantage, their small number. On the contrary, in the very chaotic fighting near the Greek vessels, within the camp, a very crowded area, such dangers did not exist. They would be acting fairly concentrated, not allowing the enemy the luxury to correctly assess their number, and catching the enemy by surprise at the flank; a tactical dream.

Last but not least is that the Myrmidons were able to make very dense formations on order (XVI-211/5) despite using mainly fluid tactics and surging attacks (XVI-257/67). This corroborates the ability to perform different tactical functions, as did their descendants, the elite units of Classical Greece, including the Hypaspists of Philip II and Alexander III (Kambouris *et al.* 2020).

The other level of combined arms refers to chariot warfare. Chariots were supported by runners, mobile infantry that in some cases (some chariot types) could partially and briefly mount the vehicle exterior and disembark to dispatch immobilized enemy chariots and fallen crews, broken infantry or to tackle enemy runners. But what is most important is that the use of the chariot arm is an integral part of the deployment of infantry. The charioteers can find refuge behind, charge in front, and pass through infantry lines at will, or they can lead said infantry, because they are armoured and resilient, on foot, fighting from amongst the mass or darting back and forth, during the clash. Once a decision is reached, they mount their vehicles, waiting at the ready behind the infantry screen, and launch to pursue, which they do remaining mounted; they dismount occasionally as the tactical situation dictates (De Becker 2009). After all, a dismounted hero casting javelins has a number of advantages against a mounted opposite number. He is a smaller target, not functionally or physically vulnerable due to the vulnerability of the vehicle, driver and team (XVI-378/9 & 466/71), he can dodge casts and aim much more accurately from steady ground, and also thrust more accurately, while assuming a defensive posture.

Tactics

For army tactics, Achilles favours charge and clash (XX-354/5) and Patroclus, fighting in his stead, does the same (XVI-394/8); this is not always the choice of either commander (Hector, Agamemnon), who may stop their advance at a distance and exchange missiles (XV-710), as the European armies of the sixteenth to eighteenth centuries did, while heavy skirmishers, usually the well-protected nobles, may jump in between opposing armies and strike targets of opportunity, as exemplified by Antilochus (XIII-559). The static confrontation of two lines, with a massive exchange of missiles (XI-84/7) and/or by skirmishing implies open-order and medium infantry, with enough protection to endure the exchange from some distance (a 'no-man's land') and light enough to use mobile tactics that would exploit opportunities and improve the kill probability of the shots. It is of interest that the two battle lines, contrary to some views (Van Wees 1994) were in order, allowing ingress and egress (retirement) of skirmishers, *especially* of the heavy skirmishers. This happens when the latter must convene to assess the situation and decide on the spot (XIII-750/7); or have attempted a raid (IV-494/9) and either have obtained spoils that need carrying away (V-25/5; XVI-663/5 & 129/31; XI-246/7) or have found themselves at a disadvantage (XVI-815/7). The latter may occur due to missing their aim and being subject to retaliation (XVI-806/15; XI-439/46) or to intervention by other foes (V-562/72). It is directly stated that Hector was able to pass between files of friendlies from behind the line to the no-man's-land to stab Patroclus when he realized that the latter was disarmed and stunned (XVI-818/21), or to do the opposite if he needed to call an impromptu council.

After a prolonged exchange that softens up one opponent, the other one charges to break its formation (XI-85/90) and then engage in pursuit, attempting a decisive result by attrition (XI-149/54); the defeated escape, but with the explicit intention to gain distance by trading space and eventually rally to resist (VI-103/6). The reason for avoiding the clash from the first encounter is obviously the advantage lying with the offensive weapons;

thus, rushing to contact with a large enemy body, well-versed in missile warfare, is ill-advised, which implies a generalized lack of panoplies. This, in turn, explains the paramount importance of armoured heavies and their asymmetrical importance for the mass (XVI-593/602 & 659/61): shields and helmets protect from missiles, but an armoured heavy infantryman dealing thrusts and blows with the impunity of his armour might tip the scales and shake a large part of an army single-handedly (XI-148/61) if not countered by an equal opposing number.

Shields and armour are more often penetrated in close-quarter combat than from a distance. Menelaus, an important and powerful and wealthy king, is hit by an arrow and wounded by Pandarus after the arrow head (which is explicitly mentioned as 'iron', IV-123) pierces through three successive armour components (IV-133/5); such a succession of armour parts is indicative of a Dendra-type panoply and would not have been found on other body parts, where the respective armour would have been pierced more easily. But the same warrior's cuirass deflects Helenus' arrow from point-blank range (XIII-585/95). Only Achilles (with armour made by a god) suffers no penetration – his greave even staves off a direct spear cast (XXI-591/4). But he himself is not very confident on the subject (XX-261/5). Despite this fact, he chooses to strike Hector at a spot not covered by his own, previously captured armour: as the latter charges leaning forward, Achilles thrusts at the junction of the neck and shoulder, a spot indicated as exposed, unlike to the rest of the body (XXII-322/6), and thus suggestive of a neck-guard, lower-arm-guards, possibly hand-guards, greaves and armoured skirt; the full kit of the Dendra panoply (Petmezas 2019; D'Amato and Salimbeti 2011).

Although panoplies are routinely penetrated by missiles, it is a different matter with the shields. Archery is not mentioned as piercing shields. Most lethal spear casts and thrusts are delivered around shield coverage, directly to the body armour or to unprotected body parts. The dramatic description of spear wounds may or may not reflect absence of armour. Such conclusions may only be drawn *ex silentio* in thorough descriptions. Some hits on armour are deflected, occasionally resulting in broken spear points or even spears – but the latter is considered a god-sent stroke of misfortune (VI-306, XIII-564/5) – most probably a failed weapon, or flawed in manufacture. Helmets routinely give way under direct hits (thrusts – XX-398 – and blows – XX-475), but are also responsible for some spectacular saves: Hector, Paris and Menelaus are saved from spear cast, sword cut and pickaxe blow respectively (XI-350, III-362, XIII-615). Shields, on the other hand, are just as often pierced as they repel the points (Ajax's and Achilles' shields are never pierced). Actually, this may imply an imbalance in favour of the shield: piercing it is mentioned as a worthwhile accomplishment and is not a matter of fact. The frequent remark that enemy missiles press a hero hard implies a number of them hitting the mark without piercing it (i.e. XIII-511; XV-727). Achilles' cast is legendary for piercing everything in its way (XX-99/100), a well-deserved reputation, as there is no mention of any parrying of his cast (as opposed to more than a couple of misses) and the very enlightening report that, when he missed Asteropaius and the spear was driven deep into earth, his opponent was unable to retrieve it three times (XXI-170/6). There is direct reporting of efforts to strike an opponent down with a javelin from *behind*, and not *through* the shield (XVI-312, XVI-609). This, combined with the description of warriors advancing cautiously behind their projected shield (XXII-313/5; XIII-156/8), and with the importance attested by the Greek army to the feat of Protesilaus in Mysia, where by unshielding Telephus he presents Achilles with a chance to spear him (Phil, *Her* 23,24), attests to the effectiveness and vital importance of the shields. Achilles' cast at Aeneas, which disadvantaged the latter, struck the shield next to the rim, at its thinnest (XX-274/7), begging the question of deliberate aim at that part of the shield versus a miss by the narrowest margin in an effort to target the missile past – or, rather, over – the shield.

One thing made clear in the *Iliad*, and corroborated by archaeology, is the high status/prestige and the importance of the skirmisher (Grguric 2005). Archaeology shows a preponderance of lightly clad troops, as mentioned earlier, armed with dirks/daggers, swords or javelins in both parade and action representations (the latter include combat and hunting scenes). Such light skirmishers may have been issued body tunics (*chiton*), definitely of linen (D'Amato and Salimbeti 2011; 2017; and perhaps XXI-29/31), and possibly quilted/padded (Fields 2006) to afford some protection, or short kilts. In the latter case, the black-and-white pattern of the fresco at Pylos may represent a particular colour design/uniform; or it may suggest a leather or textile overlay for protection (Grguric 2005; D'Amato and Salimbeti 2017); a precursor of the later *pteryges* (D'Amato and Salimbeti 2017), attached or worn as an undergarment with metal cuirasses by hoplites and later armoured infantry types (Snodgrass 1998). This light infantry is perhaps related to similar Assyrian types (Dezső, 2012) but is also reminiscent of chariot runners attested in Egyptian service and possibly in other cases (Fields 2006; Healy 1992).

The extreme danger of charging naked, or at least unarmoured, against a heavier, better-protected opponent with a range advantage to complement that of protection, trusting only skill, wits and mobility implies something like modern special forces' status and prestige, obvious in the representations but also in heroic lore: the foremost heroes of Ancient Greece, Hercules and Theseus, qualify as such troops. The superhuman strength of Hercules should not shadow his excellent record as a runner, as implied by his efforts to chase a stag on foot. He is not armoured, nor shielded, and uses the bow and a sidearm – in this case the club. Theseus, to qualify for the post of successor clears a swathe of land of warlords/brigands, armed only with a sword and a pair of sandals, his only fortune from his kingly father. To this kit, the essentials for a light infantryman (Grguric, 2005) he adds a mace he takes as prize from a slain opponent. Unlike Hercules, he has no missile weapon, only a sword. In this attire he slays the Minotaur.

And there is more; Jason, when he started his march from Pelion to prominence, had no armour; he only had spear(s), like the spearmen in frescoes, plus a pair of sandals (important when mobility is at a premium and reminiscent of the importance of boots in the Far West for cowboys). The said pair created the lore of the single-sandalled man. Achilles was raised as a hunter and racer. In a fake emergency he instinctively selected a sword (not a spear, an axe or anything else) and in Troy he campaigns in the suit of armour of his father (XVIII-81/5) which he lost; only then did he get one of his own (XVIII-474/613), and this sequence of events sheds a not-very-gracious light on the top fighter of the Greeks.

The *Iliad*, as mentioned elsewhere, implies such light troops, but armed with the javelin or rather the dual-purpose *dory*, and thus able to engage from some distance, but with some interesting digressions. They have a minimum of armour, at least the most prestigious ones. The examples are the waist-band of prince Polydorus of Troy (XXI-90/1) and the linen corselet of the aristocratic leader of the Locrians, the intrepid Ajax the Lesser (II-529; XIII-66). It is a matter of conjecture whether this latter has a shield of any type; he is mentioned as a spear-fighter (II-527/30; XIII-445; XIV-519/21) and occasionally a swordsman (XVI-330/3), but a shield is not explicitly mentioned for him and should not be considered a given. A somewhat vague excerpt (XXI-29/31) implies the use of jerkins of fabric for young, light troops.

But much more prominent in the epic is the similar way in which fully armoured warriors operate; their MO (*modus operandi*). The *eqeta* and the lieges are obviously trained in all applicable skills, drills and dimensions of combat (V-11; XVI-808/11), including swordsmanship, archery, spear fighting, duel, and the use of the chariot (for charge and for transportation/skirmishing), like both the pilot and weapon systems officer in modern air warfare terminology or, better, driver and passenger in Homeric parlance.

But it is the fluid fighting in skirmishing mode that is the most common, tactically relevant and prestigious, creating a surging effect in time and space (Sears 2010) that overwhelms enemy formations. Being a logical evolution of the light, unarmoured, surging infantry concept which dominated a generation earlier (and survived to allow use of different styles for different operational scenarios), the fully armoured skirmishing could be integrated with a competent use of chariots to extend the reach and save some breath for a day-long fight (Petmezas 2019). Still, its main asset was its sheer effectiveness. As correctly suggested, the cast spear, javelin or *dory* (Drews 1988; 1996) brought about a revolution. With jousting tactics and charging headlong, the chariot-borne lancer has the advantage against the infantry pikeman as he boxes the target and strikes at will, choosing to disengage or to press home, with the additional momentum of the gallop. But once missiles were introduced, and heavy missiles at that, these principles did not apply.

The impact of a dismounted javelineer was destructive for a chariot team except in the most unusual circumstances. In the *Iliad*, on many occasions, chariot crews are obliterated by heavy skirmishers that may have dismounted themselves on purpose (XI-101/46), possibly having left their own chariots behind (XI-191/2). Lopsided body counts happen mainly when a disengagement is mistimed (XI-339/42; XVI-342/4) or if obstructed by circumstances, including ground and fieldworks (XVI-368/79). But in many other cases, it is a matter of superior assets, plain and simple, leading to the slaughter of mounted warriors (VI-12/27). The dismounted warrior, especially if armoured for protection from the eventual arrow, may use his shield better, evade and parry without concern for balance and hindrance from limited space, may aim much better and apply sheer force while planted firmly on the ground. He is a smaller target and, by correct posture, may become even smaller and less exposed, and he is less vulnerable. A chariot team is a huge target and a spear cast aimed at the vehicle finds no obstacle in its structure, which affords no protection to the crew, and if it hits one of the two crewmen the team is functionally neutralized (V-580; VI-125); most probably the fall of one would compromise the balance of the other, and of the vehicle, leading to total loss. The horse-team is also a big, juicy target and, if shot, things may turn disastrous (XVI-467/71; VIII-80/90). It is possible that the horses are protected, as depicted on an ivory gaming box, the only representation of a chariot-borne archer in a Mycenaean context (Grguric 2005, D'Amato and Salimbeti 2015). The epic tacitly corroborates this: otherwise Paris would not trouble to snipe at the base of the head (VIII-81/5), he would shoot anywhere, as a wound would infuriate or collapse a horse. Still, this kind of protection, intended against arrows, might have been inadequate against javelin casts from relatively close range, with a much heavier weapon – or spear thrusts; an excellent reason for the decline of archery in Aegean chariot combat, had it ever been otherwise (Drews 1988; 1996).

It is safe to assume that there are contingents – at least of the Greeks – which, described clearly as spearmen, best interpreted as pikemen (II-542/4), still form phalanxes and engage in linear warfare with contact weapons (not really close-contact ones). The description insinuates something beyond poetic licence and thus an accurate description, perfectly compatible with the use of pikes in the Battle Krater and in the re-enactments of medieval/modern-era warfare, levelled upper-chest-high and aimed at the upper torso. But even in this case, the tribal-feudal system, especially as applied in the emergency created by the absence of Achilles (II-362/8), seems to introduce fatal vulnerabilities, as the loss of the chieftain/liege of such a contingent to mobile tactics (IV-463/9) is detrimental and the unit is never mentioned again.

From the above, the fluid fight, which may overrun heavy infantry battle lines, decimate chariotry and storm fortifications and obviously cities, had been correctly preferred to other tactics and the warriors and units excelling at this enjoyed the highest respect (Grguric 2005); discipline was for the many, the mass, the ones who could not excel and found efficiency in their numbers and mass. The very *motto* of the heroic ideal dictates excellence *and* supremacy, or better, excellence in both relative and absolute terms, with the absolute minimum being *not* to shame one's bloodline; especially the ancestors (VI-206/9); attaining glory was the logical next step (XVII-14/6; XVI-129/31; XIX -415) and booty, as both a recognition of one's value (IX-601/5 & 316/9) and an approach to secure gains, being a close third (I-161/8).

Thus close-range missile warfare, combined with technical and tactical mobility and armour protection, was the main – and the preferred – combat tactic, much like tank warfare in modern times. Still, previous or simply different practices coexist and apply in particular cases. After all, even in modern conflicts, obsolete means and practices, from the ambuscades and IED bombings of the 2010s to the pack-animal dependent Wehrmacht spearheaded by the Panzerwaffe of the Second World War, are routinely used when applicable or advantageous.

The last issue on Greek tactics is the *pyrgos/*'tower' (IV-334), an effective, mainly offensive formation. It must have been similar to nineteenth-century columns used by the Napoleonic French infantry for prompt assault, minimizing exposure to line fire and giving momentum at the point of contact, while making the advance much easier (Goldsworthy 1997). The rationale should have been similar in the Bronze Age and a kind of drill would have allowed transformation of infantry units from column (*pyrgos*) to line (*phalanx*) and *vice versa*. It is possible that this kind of formation was at the heart of classical assault formations (Goldsworthy 1997) as were the deep phalanxes of Thebans at Delion (424 BC), Nemea (394 BC), Leuctra (371 BC), and second Mantinea (362 BC). What is interesting, or even strange, is that occasionally it was used *defensively* as well, (XIII-151/3), obviously in narrow locations, so as to increase the depth of a formation and thus allow absorbing the momentum of a charge and replacing massive casualties promptly.

It might have been a Trojan tactic to aim for the lower legs when facing heavy opponents (Burgess 1995). The proverbial 'Achilles' heel' is not an isolated incidence. In XI-379, Paris' arrow nails Diomedes' foot to the ground by hitting the ankle. It might be more skill and intention and less luck to hit two prominent heroes at the same spot, heroes with highly efficient armour. One of them survived a direct hit of an iron-tipped arrow to the cuirass (V-99). Agenor shot his spear at Achilles' shin (XXI-591), which is the same concept – or it may have been a slight miss, if he aimed for the ankle and foot and missed his precise mark as Achilles charged forward. These low shots are intentional, the result of a tactical decision, well-aimed and accurately delivered. As succinctly observed (Burgess 1995), they are essentially 'mobility kills' in modern tank warfare parlance; the traction/motion element, due to the need to move, is less heavily armoured and thus more vulnerable: arrows and javelins against the leg and foot, blankets and explosives against the track, the result is the same. When immobilizing an armoured target, the actual kill, its destruction, may follow later with a repeat shot, either delivered deterministically with precision, because the target does not move or evade, or stochastically, by massive missile fire shot with accuracy against a standing, actually fixed target, thus defeating armour or avoiding it by penetrating through seams and interfaces.

The Trojans, with their intimate knowledge of the peculiarities of terrain, area and climate, seem to follow Sun Tzu and use such conditions proficiently. Their attacks under low visibility due to dust, fog, mist and wind (XV-668/70, XVI-645/50) in 'Windy Ilion' caused much distress to the Greeks (Paus II.24,2), who perform better in good visibility, due to numbers and perhaps tactical efficiency. Both opponents are more or less considered capable of expedient and massive kindling of fire for offensive use against enemy positions, ships or cities – a near fatal inability of the Athenian army at Marathon in 490 BC, where they could not burn Persian ships and had to capture them, resulting in just seven prizes – out of some hundreds ripe for burning (Hdt VI.113–15).

Deployment

Greeks have the option to revert to very tight phalanx formations (XIII-129/131 & 145/6 & 680; XVII-352/65) with high-order discipline and no room for opportunistic fluid tactics, not even individually (XVII-361/5). The Trojan infantry cannot form in any similar manner; it uses fluid, surging tactics and set lines. The Trojans were unable to break such dense formations, neither by surging infantry assaults, headed by heavily armoured heroes (XIII-143/9) nor by charging chariots (XV-405/9). Such formations may present more elaborate resistance than a plain frontal one; establishing a hedge-like perimeter to repulse attackers from many directions, like the one presented under Ajax around the dead body of Patroclus (XVII-354/5), seems perfectly possible.

Of course, such formations allow no manoeuvring and are used only as a last resort and in desperate times. It is an open issue whether this difference in formation capability is due to the shields used or to any other factor, such as training, character, morale or drill. Tower shields are not mentioned for Trojans, who do use body-shields nonetheless, as do many Greeks; Hector has a body-shield that demands dexterity in moving and handling (VII-238/9), and when thrown back it strikes the heel and neck while running (VI-118); which means that the rim reaches somewhere between the knee and mid-calf. And he is no exception, but rather the rule; a Greek warrior stumbles upon his shield and falls as he turns to flee (XV-645/7). Hector's shield is also described as symmetrical (XI-61; VII-250), the Greek wording not necessarily meaning circular, as usually interpreted, but conceivably figure-of-eight. Both sides use round shields of small or moderate size and other, non-circular shapes, especially the Trojans and their allies. There might also be double-grip shields, as circular shields with two grips are depicted on Egyptian reliefs of Rameses II in Abu Simbel, but not of the peculiar *porpax* construction, the form and function of the much later Argive (*hoplon*) shields (D'Amato and Salimbeti 2015). The only tower shield directly mentioned is the one of Ajax the Great (XVII-128), who is a most static warrior, never on a chariot or part of any manoeuvre. Homeric language is inconsistent (such pitfalls *are* indeed expected in poetic synthesis), but it is the only one that might be called *sakos* (XIV-375) *literally*, as the Greek term implies something rectangular-ish, which is not compatible with the figure-of-eight, the oblong/elliptical, or the round shields.

The Homeric *phalanx* is a patchwork of intermingled problems and doubts.

Body-shield-bearers, armed with extra-long pikes (*egxeiae*) were most probably *not* deployed in tight *phalanx*, as indicated by the fresco from Thera. First, being able to get *into* the shield is important when *not* in *phalanx*.

In *phalanx*, it was enough to keep oneself behind the shield, as hoplites would show some centuries later. A close *phalanx* would have been crushed by the leading teams of chariotry, especially if supported by powerful and accurate missile shooting and followed by skirmishers and runners. An open deployment, however, would expose phalanx troops to runners and light infantry. The Thera fresco, showing a dispersion which allows motion so as to avoid being trampled by the chariot, while remaining able to support a comrade from swarming light infantry by their pikes, is perhaps a more viable paradigm. The dispersed troops do not offer a solid target for massed archery but must be picked off one by one, which is challenging if they are not evenly spaced and in straight lines and files. The pikes create functional crossfires, and evasion of charging chariots while using the pike against the team or the crew is possible. The concept is still viable if the pike is substituted for a spear and archers may swarm within the formation. The shorter spear might make the formation a bit denser, but not too much; this might be the Homeric paradigm for both opponents' standard deployment.

The dense *phalanx* of the Greeks clearly depends on three things (XIII-131/1; XIV-371/82): men (must be sturdy and strong, not light and agile), shields and spears. Longer spears are better suited for porcupine formations and it is very probable that explicit reference to spear-fighters in both armies implies the use of long spears, or rather *egxea* pikes (tablet: *ekesi*), instead of the more typical *dory* dual-purpose spear, which was the current standard and seen arming light infantry in the Thera fresco. In one case, the text implies that different combinations of shafted weapon and shield are expected of a single warrior and that the choice is up to himself or to the commander (XIV-370/2), suggesting a full personal armoury.

For the Greeks, the contingent of Avantes sets the standard for spear-fighters, while the Kikones and the Pelasgians are the equivalent on the Trojan side (II-840/6), but also a Thracian warband is described as armed predominantly with spears (IV-533), although it is not introduced as such (II-844). It is explicitly mentioned about Avantes' men that their spears penetrate cuirasses (II-543/5) and armour; thus they are special weapons, compared to standard *dorata*. But the heart of the issue lies with the shields: Homer mentions the partial redistribution of weaponry (unevenly issued as a result of conscription practices, a millennia-old problem) to have the heavy shields reassigned in the front, for the sturdiest fighters to form a *phalanx* (XIV-375/6). This is not necessarily correct: the lighter shields, termed '*laisseia*' (V-453), allow for denser packing; and denser packing of men means a more threatening and repulsive wall of spearheads which clearly intercepted Hector and the Trojan onslaught, meaning armoured heroes on foot and regular infantry (XIII-145). The repulsive effect of a long pike, small-shield/target *phalanx* is amply demonstrated by the Macedonian phalanx (Plut, *Vit Aem* 19,1), which has been considered occasionally a resurrection of the Homeric *phalanx* (Diod XVI.3,2).

The term *laisseia* is unusual and there are different interpretations as to the meaning and nature of such items. It may refer to a particular type of light shield, like the later Thracian *pelte*, which may well have been around at the time, although the classical name was not used; or, if the term *pelte* is Thracian in origin, Homer may have failed to record it (Best 1969). If the term *laisseia* is generic, it could be meant to describe light shields such as the Warrior Vase reverse-crescent, copper-faced models; or rectangular ones as depicted in Geometric art (D'Amato and Salimbeti 2017); or circular ones, either one-handled, as the Herzsprung example (Heneken 1950) or two-handled, as in Egyptian frescoes (Abu Simbel); actually anything but body-shields. If not, it may well describe specific shield forms and shapes, with the oblong scalloped model seen in Geometric and other representations (D'Amato and Salimbeti 2011), but especially in a Hittite context (Bryce 2007), and the reverse crescent model of the Warrior Vase being strong candidates.

Formations

In the *Iliad*, there are clear signs of tactics; Achilles declares that he intends to attempt a central penetration to cut through the enemy battle line and then exploit the breach to cut off at least a part of their army (XX-360/2). He succeeds in doing that and the results are disastrous for the Trojans (XXII-104/7). The blow is decisive and could well end the war one way or another (XXII-378/84 and XXII-111/21). This practice is very different to the usual clash of battle lines, initially exchanging missiles and casualties (VIII-67; XI-85). Initiating a battle by infantry means the defeated party would have no screening force to support its chariotry and thus precipitates a decisive outcome. At this stage, dismounted charioteers could participate, either as champions (XV-572/5; XX-376) or within the rank and file (XX-377), and stiffen the resilience and defensive power of the regular infantry (XVI-363). Once a threshold is met, one line breaks the other (XI-90/2) and the exploitation by pursuit begins, the best hunting ground for mounted charioteers speeding in pursuit (VIII-185/95), while their opposing numbers usually make good their escape (VIII-157; XVI-367/8), leaving the infantry exposed to slaughter (XVI-367/9). Some sound tactics may be inferred for a fighting retreat, like the one conducted by Ajax the

Great, using stationary and mobile elements for a step-by-step rearguard manoeuvre not devolving to flight (XI-565/70).

Nevertheless, there are no indications regarding combined arms formations, and the formations in general exist but are rudimentary; the column and the line have been already mentioned, as has the dense *phalanx*, a speciality of the Greeks – or *some* of the Greeks. It seems though that actually how to form up and deploy troops (not how to move and manoeuvre them) is an almost lost art, with two old veterans bickering for the honours: Menestheus and Nestor (II-551/5). Nestor's arrangement of infantry and chariotry seems the only reasonable setup, but it is not so; posting the infantry in front (IV-293/8) had merits, as mentioned above. Setups include chariots in front, similar to the use of *protaxis* for mounted cavalry in the classical age (Kambouris 2022). *Epitaxis* (Kambouris and Bakas 2017*)*, chariots deployed behind, also had merits (De Becker 2009), and there was the *parataxis*, chariots at the side(s). But his articulation of the depth of the infantry (IV-298/300), echoing Xenophon (*Cyrop* VI.3,25; *Cav Comm* 2,2–4) raises questions: under Achilles, was the basic consideration of the troop disposition in the order of deployment alone and not in the arrangement in depth? Or was the latter uniformly accepted as an 'ability gradient', with the best troops in front and the worst at the back to add weight and not endanger the lot, especially if the fight devolved to mass *phalanx* formation?

Well, the picture in Homer may be incomplete, to say the least. Although suspect for misdating and retroprojection, the account of Diktys may be considered enlightening. No less than four different ways of ordering the Achaean army are reported: an arrangement in two divisions (the standard in Classical Greece), in four divisions (which is a spin-off of the previous), and in three divisions (two wings and centre). Achilles and Ajax are often mentioned as leading one wing each and the description explicitly implies a combination of solid, unyielding *phalanx* action with mobile tactics (Dikt II.3). This combination may clearly refer to the whole front, as was the practice of the Romans, or Greek skirmishers engaging along the line before the heavy infantry clash (Thuc VI.69). But the wording ('each of them undertook one half of the army') rather suggests an asymmetric front, with a defensive and an offensive wing, similar to the dispositions of the Thebans at Leuctra (Diod XV.55,1–2) and the Macedonians at Gaugamela (Arr, *Anab* III.9,1) almost a millennium later. This arrangement is compatible with Homer's description of the Achaean deployment, if in fact it did reproduce the order by which their vessels had beached and their camp had been established. By default, contingents under tribal allegiance would deploy in the same order they were billeted, a principle confirming Napoleon's maxim No.22 (Napoleon I 1863).

However, Achilles (or Palamedes for that matter), might have been improvising in arranging the order of the different contingents. The latter, before being liquidated by his frenemies, was distinguished for his knowledge of fortifications, for his tactical developments, especially battle orders, his contribution to communication systems especially by fire beacons (Dares 20; Gorg, *Def Palam* 30) and for organizational improvements, including training, planning, logistics and tactics (Dares 20). All these elements are not assigned to any of the Greek heroes in the Homeric account and, to some extent, seem to apply or be associated with the dysfunctions revealed when Achilles withdrew from combat.

The tripartite arrangement reported in Mysia (Phil, *Her* 23,20), which is a quantum leap from the binary ones, requires two wings and a centre, similar to Miltiades' arrangement in Marathon (Hdt VI.111,3). In Diktys' account (Dikt II.32) of a battle fought just before the wrath of Achilles, each division was under two commanders. The names of the commanders are an indication to the troop types. This may suggest that each division (or some of the divisions) included a static infantry element, that is almost certainly a *phalanx* of shield-bearers (Idomeneus, Ajax the Great), and a mobile element. The latter may be armoured infantry in loose order for skirmishing and

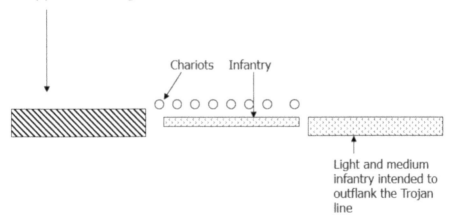

The asymmetric deployment of the Greek forces as implied by Diktys. One wing is defensive, with body-shield-issued line infantry forming phalanx and anchored to some feature of the terrain; it is the anvil. The centre is heavy with chariotry intended to attempt a breakthrough by assault and supported by infantry; it is the hammer. The other flank is mobile, with surging infantry, so as to envelope the enemy or support the centre if a breakthrough is achieved.

surging tactics (Diomedes, Antilochus, Achilles), or chariotry (Diomedes, Antilochus, Achilles). Alternatively, a massive missile element might have been assigned to the static element, to provide fire support (Ajax the Lesser's Locrian archers). Finally, although not concerning the Achaean army, the arrangement made by Panthesileia, queen (or chieftain) of the Amazons is highly asymmetrical and shows that this kind of deployment was widely known if not a common practice. Diktys reports cavalry (probably mounted) in the centre, infantry on one wing and archers on the other for the host of the Amazons (Dikt IV.2) to match the Greek asymmetrical tripartite deployment, something possibly beyond the apprehension of the Trojan high command, that had to deal with a multinational and very diverse host, but also had shown no tactical flair. The daring, violent and surging attacks against the Greek fortification were bold and competently executed in columns (XII-88/104), possibly proper 'tower' formations, which might have been a known if not standard practice at the time, as discussed before.

Personal skill and duel practices

A martial art with weapons is implied in Achilles' rampage (XX-455/89) and in Tydeus' killing an impressive forty-nine out of fifty ambushers (IV-390/6) and Bellerophon the whole lot (VI-188/90). A multitude of opponents attacking at their discretion in space and time and with a surging effect means one cannot make a solid stand using the terrain and defiles; he has to change front all the time to fend off attacks incoming from different directions. This ability to position oneself advantageously against a multitude and be lethal, as shown in the movie *Kill Bill*, inescapably implies a martial art with aspects of and skills in arms, both sidearms and polearms; and, in this kind of fight, agility is important but speed is paramount (Burgess 1995). It is *the* most important attribute, and the Homeric descriptions place it first, with lethality and armour protection being second and third; actually, the whole concept is very reminiscent of modern armoured warfare principles (with the Iron Triangle, i.e. firepower, protection, mobility) but carried out on foot.

It must be stressed that ambushing was considered a standard operation and of the highest prestige, as it tested the mettle of the warrior isolated from his comrades (XIII-276/85). This is reminiscent of current views on special operations and implies a class of professionals of warfare, where skill and initiative, not morale or anything abstract, reign supreme and the set priority is to save blood and bring effect, whatever the means; a field proper for the goddess of wisdom indeed.

The elite heroic warriors combine heavy armour with mobility; both Achilles and Hector are fleet of foot, excellent charioteers, big of stature and very strong, epitomizing the heroic concept of 'tall, strong and brave' while adding the 'fast'. The succession of offensive and defensive postures, techniques and choices in duels (both formal and informal – especially in the latter) is intriguing. Combined with the characteristics of the prominent fighters (big stature, heavy, high-tech armour and fleetness of foot), the issue is highly reminiscent of current protocols for air battles by fighter pilots, who engage the enemy successively using the longer-range weapons to gain time and advantage as they close in for shots with shorter range ones. In the Homeric duel, both antagonists start with a spear and range is essential. Thus a spear cast, especially a sudden or stealthy one, might finish the issue immediately and effectively. If the shot missed, though, the warrior is at a disadvantage. A cast spear, if perceived, can be evaded or parried and the enemy may retaliate. As the first offender is spearless, the retaliatory strike may not be another cast, which entails a very high probability of being evaded or parried as it is expected; a spear thrust is much more probable. The thrust permits better aiming, applies more strength in order to pierce shield and armour or even helmet (XX-395), retains the weapon, allowing an immediate repeat of the assault and it may allow secondary, cut/slash follow-ups if the thrust is dodged. Practically a swift close-up for a spear thrust is the best offensive option if the adversary is spearless, keeping the offender way out of secondary weapons' range. Achilles does so twice with Hector (XX-440/6) and Hector himself prefers thrusting at Patroclus, not casting (XVI-820). The reason the thrust is superseded by spear casts in terms of frequency is the inherent surprise/stealth of the latter – not to mention the distance advantage: the cast, naturally, outranges the thrust by far, thus many warriors missing their mark with a shot, easily resort to flight rather than sustain an enemy retaliation, with much better possibilities of making good their escape than if engaged in closer range.

The truth, though, is that once a spear is cast, the targeted warrior, if aware of it (not a very usual thing) must take some action. At the time he does so as to evade (Paris in III-360) or parry (Achilles in XX-261/3), the offender, if fleet and fast, has the opportunity to close the distance and position himself favourably for a second shot. This is either with the secondary weapon, delivering a blow from point-blank range, or with a second, reserve spear – which is rarely, if ever, cast. Thus, an early spear cast, even if missing its mark, may be advantageous: if hitting the shield, it may weigh it down (XX-276/83). If parried or evaded, it has pushed the target onto the defensive, allowing the offender a better footing while reverting to the secondary weapon from close range, perhaps within the minimum range of the enemy's primary weapon. In XX-259/90, Aeneas had the first cast and Achilles, after parrying it, reciprocated and followed suit with the sword. Aeneas, despite having the first shot, reverts to stone, which means he is not in a position to draw his sword and receive the attack: Achilles' cast kept him busy long enough for his adversary to acquire a definite advantage. Thus, when casting a spear, the heroes chased after their cast, using the force of the cast proper to follow the missile – and not to recoil as today's athletes do. A secondary reason for this follow-up might be to retrieve the weapon (III-529), although, the main reason is to press the attack home with the sword (as does Menelaus against Paris III-361/62, and Achilles against Aeneas, XX-283/5), before the initiative is seized by the opponent. Older veterans such as Idomeneus, who was considered ... too mature to be capable of doing this (XIII-512), relied on expertise to end the engagement with the cast.

The above sequence and its spinoffs is here called the 'DD' (see p.153), the 'duel dance', which means the almost standardized procedures in Homeric duels which, though, had tactical meaning, and may be validated mainly by reviving and re-enacting such moves with realistic weaponry.

Achilles is the perfect example in the sequence of options in a duel. He is reportedly, by the words of terrified Trojans, endowed with a murderous cast that never stops before sinking into flesh (XX-99/100). This is not so, as already mentioned; in one day's fighting he misses three times. The Trojan remark may rather imply that the cast is never intercepted by shield or/and armour but penetrates all the way. But the way he manages all enemy casts is most revealing. First, he is never mentioned as dodging or ducking an enemy cast, preferring to parry with his shield (XXII-290; XXI-164/5;XX-260/70), pushing the advantage of superior weaponry to the extreme (XXI-165). By not dodging he does not lose his composure and he remains always set and aware, not sidestepping or presenting an opening to the opponent. Additionally, he does not let lethal missiles fly around, to hit some unsuspecting friendly, found all at once exposed, as someone dodged a missile (XVII-306/10; XIII-403/12). Achilles just defeats them. When he casts, the murderous missile, even if not hitting the mark, affects the enemy's morale, seeing his defences pierced, and also pushes him onto the defensive, forfeiting the initiative. When he throws at Aeneas, the latter's shield is taken out of action, as it gets nailed to the ground, effectively restricting his moves for some vital fractions of a second as Achilles presses home his attack with a sidearm (XX-280/5). Against Asteropeus, the missile is so deeply buried in the ground that the latter cannot extract and use it, losing valuable time and thus remaining exposed for the killer sword-thrust (XXI-169/180). But the most remarkable achievement is in the duel with Hector. Achilles throws first and Hector evades (XXII-273/6), dodging out of the trajectory of the missile. By doing so he loses perspective and awareness of

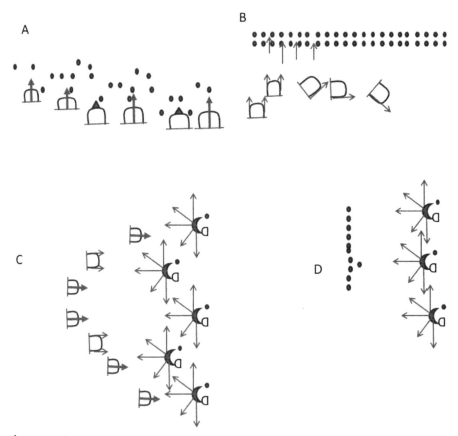

Asymmetric engagements

Against infantry in flight, or even disturbed, the chariots charge with lance (solid arrow) or even sidearm (solid triangle) effecting slaughter. (A) But against infantry standing firm (B), the chariots will not charge into contact; they will go near, cast javelins (light arrows) with the momentum of the charge and retire to repeat; a caracole of sorts, as in the sixteenth to seventeenth centuries AD in Europe.

Frescoes show shielded, unarmoured heavy infantry in relatively open order; the body-shields (solid crescents) being actually individual battle fortifications. The two-handed pike is long enough to create overlapping arcs of lethality (equivalent to crossfires of sorts) between adjacent shield-bearers, relaxing the need for very compact phalanxes that may be unwieldy in manoeuvring and solid targets for shock action and massed missile barrage. A more evolved concept, presented herein, would be to assign archer (D-shape) and light, mobile spear-fighter, with little or no armour (solid circle) to each line shield-bearer, creating a veritable task group with defensive staying power, missile element and mobile element, as exemplified by the two Ajaxes and Teukros in the *Iliad*. This concept works against chariotry (C) and surging infantry (D).

where the spent missile is. By the time he regains his footing, and elated as he is, since he has a clear advantage against a most formidable foe, Achilles obviously used his initiative to step so as to approach the weapon and retrieve it without Hector noticing; this is the most plausible explanation for the goddess Athena retrieving and passing it back to him, undetected by Hector (XXII-276/7). The skill and training of Achilles allowed him to gain a most important advantage, that of creating false hopes for his enemy's psyche who now thinks that Achilles has no spear (XXII-285) and he can thrust or cast at will, since his enemy missed his mark and also failed to follow up his cast with a rush with his sidearm.

The weapons

A. Polearms

The warrior is always equipped with a general purpose spear (*dory*), for casting and thrusting alike, and generally carried in pairs (VI-104, XIII-559). This reminds us of the much later Persian cavalry *palta*, praised by Xenophon (Xen, *On Hors* XII.12). The pair of spears is mentioned many a time Hector jumps out of his chariot, and this might imply that he changes weapons, from lance to spears. It is obvious that both lance and spears are routinely secured within the chariot. Antilochus, son of Nestor is a master charioteer (XXIII-306/8); he is mentioned as fast, agile and always eager to fight, either casting from afar, or charging to thrust with his spear (XIII-559). The spear is the main weapon, which vividly illustrates the merit of the dual-purpose *dory* that can be thrown or thrust with and is carried in pairs. It should be stressed that the *dory* is not mentioned with a butt-spike/*sauroter*, and this complies with both early Archaic Greek art and with Assyrian art where a single-hand lance is shown as the weapon of shield-bearers, with no *sauroter* (Dezső 2012). In Greek art, in some cases, as in Chigi vase, the shafted weapon is indeed carried in pairs.

The issue of the shafted weapons is a major one. It has been suggested (Drews 1996) that the javelin had been the novelty of the late Bronze Age. Probably it has been the oldest weapon in mankind's arsenal, along with the hand-hurled stone, thus it must have been some new development for such weapons in the late second millennium BC. There is an analogy with later events, when the Roman *pila*, a most evolved and dedicated weapon won the empire and outreached and destabilized the Macedonian *phalanx* (Connolly 1981; Warry 1980); but this was achieved with the *pilum*, not with other types of javelin, the Persian *palton* (Xen, *Anab* I.8,3 & 27) included. Although is not suggested by our sources, a possibility might have been the throwing-thong (Drews 1996), as described by Xenophon (i.e. *Anab* IV.2,28) for javelins – also mentioned as *akontia* (*loc. cit.*). Whether these high-tech weapons were the dual-purpose *dory* spears explicitly mentioned in Homer (XVI-139) remains an issue, for in Homer the Greek word for javelin is *akontion* (XVI-359), a noun that refers to a dedicated, throwing weapon, directly contrasted with long thrusting ones, and there is a derivative verb, denoting the cast (XIV-401). The Greek meaning of the word *egxos* (XV-707/13) means or rather implies thrusting, but the use in the epic, possibly due to poetic licence and to the needs of form is indistinguishable. The same is true for the word *xyston* (XIII-497) that implies a shafted weapon, although the term was used specifically for the long, sturdy thrusting cavalry spears of the Companion cavalry of Alexander as opposed to javelins – *palta* (Xen, *On Hors* XII.12; Arr, *Anab* I.15,5) and earlier *kamax* stabbing spears (Xen, *On Hors* XII.12). Still, the term *xyston* is mostly associated with the extra-long weapons used for naval engagements (i.e. in XV-678) as discussed later.

In any case, long spears – brandished by both line infantry (pikes) and chariotry (lances), possibly but not necessarily similar and definitely two-handed weapons – seem to account for the double-edged polearms mentioned in Homer (XV-278 & 713). The mists of centuries created inconsistencies in the composition and/or transcription of the epics even during the classical period, and poetic licence does little to fix this. Still, a long warhead with low taper (Molloy 2012), would be highly penetrative against heavy armour, body-shield and the musculature of a charging warhorse/chariot team. Similarly to the cavalry sabre of the early twentieth century, used in charges initially with the point and if that missed with the edge, which was also very handy in melees, this long weapon must have been sharp, reminiscent in use of the Japanese *naginata* (Turnbull 2003), and used also as a scythe, aiming at the exposed lower legs of horses and infantry, especially heavy infantry; thus leading to the adoption of the greave.

However, there is a second option for a double-edged shafted weapon. It is the bident (D'Amato and Salimbeti 2011), reconstructed by the Koryvantes association. The prongs are flat, curved slightly outward and imply a slashing weapon perfectly fitting the two-edged shafted *mandra* weapon of the *Iliad* (XV-278). It must have been used with a long shaft, perhaps the chariot-borne *egxeia*, and applied similarly to a *halberd*. But this item is much more likely to fit with the extra-long, twenty-two-cubit weapon (XV-678), nearly the size of the longest Macedonian *sarissas* of seven metres (Polyb XVIII.29,2). It was a special nautical weapon, used in naval warfare

(XV-677), but there is no mention of its shape or intended use or the technique and drill. Still, there are some interesting assumptions and leads.

The outline of the warhead is reminiscent of some Minoan patterns, usually thought to follow the stylized shape of the horns of the bull, the sacred animal of Poseidon, ruler of the sea, and really revered in Minoan Crete. But it could refer to a weapon that ensured the maritime dominance of the Minoan navy, as its intended use would be similar in bioergonomics to that of the double-headed axe, a clear and definite symbol of the Minoan state and its power. The meaning and importance of the latter is clearly military; it is worthless for chopping wood (Molloy 2012) or hunting, and sacred items tended to have a purely utilitarian basis. It must also be stressed that, from later art, the trident of Poseidon, the sea lord, is shown with the outer prongs curved outwards. This is most unusual and probably unwarranted for an item meant for thrusting/harpooning, as is evident from modern trident heads used for fishing. But if the representation updated the shape and form of an earlier description, as usually happened with weapons of all kinds, it makes sense. The Lord of the Sea was not brandishing an instrument of fishing, but a naval weapon, and an improved version at that; a trident, instead of a bident, with the central prong being spearlike, just like the point of a halberd, to allow thrusting and piercing

The use of such a weapon is easy to understand. The slightly curved blades could slice ropes, rigging and sails, or hack at frail timberwork, or even be thrust into planking. The narrow distance between the two prongs suggests inward-facing edges, which could capture rigging to saw gradually or simply bring within the grasp of the wielder, although the latter is less practical in a context of a boarding fight, or a close fight, from ship to ship, without boarding attempts. Sickle-bladed polearms were used by Ceasar's Romans against the rigging of Gaulish vessels (Warry 1980), by the Etruscans (D'Amato and Salimbeti 2018) and were tested by Athenian drillmasters (Plato, *Laches* 183d).

B. Sidearms

The use of secondary weapons is important, after the spear is cast or broken: there is one mention of the pickaxe, used by a Trojan ally (XIII-612), described as *axine*, instead of *pelekes*, the regular axe for tree felling (XXIII-115), and then a direct mention of both straight and conventional axes used in hand-to-hand combat (XV-710).

The usual choice though is the sword. Perhaps the first mention of a bladed weapon refers to the arch-hero Perseus, who was given a sickle-like blade (*harpe*) by the god Hermes (Apollod II.4,2). The name of the cut-and-slash weapon is similar to the musical instrument *harpa* (of Egyptian origin) and reminiscent of the shape. It could have been referring to the Egyptian *kopesh* (Healy 1992), which was possibly popular in other states as well – or evolved to similar designs (D'Amato and Salimbeti 2015). Perseus' weapon was of *adamas*, the Greek word from which *diamond* originated. Given that a diamond blade (not a blade adorned with studded diamonds) is a natural impossibility, some alloy is implied or the use of a very bright stone, such as obsidian, which makes excellent, razor-sharp blades, but is fragile and not of any particular shape. Thus, given the limitations of obsidian and the use of the material for plate items such as a helmet (Hes, *Sh* 136–7), a metal alloy is the only possibility with steel of some kind definitely not out of the question. The adamantine sickle/*harpe* is recurrent: in the other work of Hesiod, the *Theogony*, it is the weapon Cronos used to castrate Uranus (Apoll I.1,4; Hes, *Theog* 160/85), while it is used metaphorically for an unyielding heart (Hes, *Works* 147–9). The dating of Hesiod makes the reference chronologically relevant to steel; Apollodorus, being squarely into the Iron Age, is a much later source that would have found the term 'adamantine' in older material and used it without any particular scrutiny.

However, with regard to the shape, whether the *harpe* had its concave or its convex edge sharpened cannot be determined. The former would be the only possible solution for a swift strike to behead Medusa (Apollod II.4,2). The latter is perhaps the most suitable conformation to castrate Uranus (Apoll I.1,4; Hes, *Theog* 160/85). On the other hand, the nature of the weapon is of some interest. There is no need whatsoever to follow Cellini, the creator of the renowned statue *Perseus and the Head of Medusa*, who interprets the term as a sword with a hook. Curved blades, including the small, dagger-seized *xyele* (Sekunda 1998) of the Spartans, were known and the use of a special word testifies against a combined sword-sickle that would afford no real advantage for the mission at hand.

Such dagger-sized items are attested in Egypt, in Egyptian or mercenary hands (D'Amato and Salimbeti 2015), although the size in Egyptian representations might be misleading; the artistic conventions occasionally escape us and strict accuracy, preferably to scale, as with later Greek practices, is not a given, and the *kopesh* might be implied in such representations, too. Whether the *kopesh* led by evolution to the classical Greek *kopis* cleaver-like sabre, is debatable. The Greek weapon was much more robust and delivered lethal blows, rather than deep, slashing cuts. Contrary to the Carian and Lycian weapons, it was sharpened on the convex, not the concave, part of the blade, similar to the *kopesh*. The Greek name comes from the verb '*kopto*', to cut, making origination from the Egyptian word unlikely, while Mycenaean slashing blades (see below) that seem to be the progenitors of the *kopis* bear no resemblance to the *kopesh*.

Mythology does not indicate whether the sharp part was the convex or the concave side of the blade. The classical *kopis/machaira* sabres (Xen, *On Hors* XII.12), with a convex edge, have Mycenaean predecessors (D'Amato and Salimbeti 2011) with no known name (although *aor* is a possibility; see below). The Carian weapon, named *drepanon* (Greek for 'sickle') and able to shear off the forelegs of a horse with a single blow (Hdt V.112,2), is also seen in Lycia in the fifth century BC and was sharp on the concave side, similar to the Japanese *kama*. The Egyptian *kopesh*, on the other hand, is a better bet for the *harpe*, but somewhat controversial as an identification. The edge is on the convex side, as already mentioned, and it is evidently a weapon based onto the design of epsilon-type axes (Hamblin 2006) and perfectly capable of decapitating with one blow, but the origin is less certain. It might have been developed in the Levant, and more specifically Sumer, as it is seen in the Stele of the Vultures (O'Bryan 2013) and introduced into Egypt, while independently also evolving to different Near and Middle East examples, as it was used by other cultures; the Hittites are a good example. A relief from Yazılıkaya shows twelve gods of the underworld brandishing the weapon. The term *kopesh* in Egyptian means foreleg (Healy 1992), but the weapon might instead be identified as a hind leg, with the prominent curvature of the thigh. Since the Greek word *kopis* comes from the verb *kopto* (to cut), it may have been adopted in Egypt. Once the word had been imported, it was defined phonetically and the sound was written down with the most relevant symbol, that of the front, hind, ox or horse or any other leg, which, by the way, is seen in inscriptions of *circa* 2300 BC.

Homeric terminology on the subject of swords is inconsistent: there are three words for sword types and two main examples. There is the *fasganon* (XVI-339) – *pakana* in the Linear B tablets – the *xiphos* (XIV-26) – *quisiphe* in Linear B tablets – but also another word, found only in Homer, *aor* (X-489; XIV-384; XVI-473), a word denoting something lifted and thus rather implying a heavy, chopping weapon. The longsword examples found (Snodgrass 1998; Connolly 1977; Smith 2015) belong to two broad categories: the first comprises very long, almost 80 cm, rapier-like weapons (Type A and C), obviously used for thrusting at immobile targets such as body-shields, to reach the target through them, and for incision-laceration cutting wounds (slashing) of soft tissues of relatively shallow depth (Molloy 2010). The second category refers to the sturdy, dual-purpose broadsword-like weapons, which chop off limbs and heads (XX-481) and bulged near the point ('oarlike' XV-713, XX-475); a veritable cut-and-thrust model. This category mainly comprises the Naue II, but also the G-type models, that cut by incision-percussion (Molloy 2010). Such a distinguished weapon is mentioned as being of Thracian origin, imported to Troy for prince Helenus (XIII-576).

It is difficult to identify a type of artefact with a name from the ones in the literary evidence, Linear B texts and epics. A very enlightening passage (XV-711/13), in stark contrast to the usual, inconsistent use which is to be expected in poetry and some centuries' loss of terminology, the *fasganon* is described as 'oarlike', which is well-suited to the sturdy cut-and-thrust weapon, while the *xiphos* is described as 'big', which may well imply narrow, extra-long thrusting weapons; *aor* is not mentioned in this excerpt. But amongst archaeological finds there is also what looks like a cleaver-type weapon (D'Amato and Salimbeti 2011) that cuts by percussion, with or without an incision, and also delivers a murderous thrust even to bony body parts (Molloy 2010), but not necessarily through soft and flexible armour. Despite being considered an evolutionary dead end (Molloy 2010), it looks like a precursor of the later sabre used by the Greeks of the classical times, (Snodgrass 1998) the *kopis* (Arr, *Anab* I.15,7; Xen, *Cyrop* I.2, 13; Xen, *On Hors* XII.12).

In Homer, swords often break (III-361/3), something expected from the narrow, triangular, almost rapier-like blade of a thrusting weapon. However, during the Middle Ages, the main type of straight sword (the broadsword) was triangular and long. Despite this fact, it was an excellent cutting weapon, and it might well be the same with the excessively long Mycenaean examples mentioned here, whatever the exact name. The reinforcing rib, a necessity for thrusting performance, would not allow deep cuts and thus anything like chopping use, but shallow slicing attacks against soft and exposed body parts are another issue altogether (Molloy 2012). Apart from their obvious objective, to kill someone by thrusting through a body-shield – perhaps the *raison d'être* for copper-covered body-shields in the *Iliad*, like the one of Ajax the Great (VII 219–23), which are not mentioned in the *Odyssey* – the long, smart, narrow-bladed weapon might have been excellent for more elaborate uses. Finding an opening to pierce between different plates of the body armour plate interface is the obvious analogue to the rapier in fifteenth-century Europe; although other attributes, such as the balance, which would allow swordsmanship and swordfighting-only duels, do not follow suit (Molloy 2010). Another use may have been to slice at openings with precision, a good reason for neck guards (but also for arm guards) in the Dendra panoply (Snodgrass 1998; D'Amato and Salimbeti 2011; Petmezas 2019).

There is a distinct similarity with, but also differences from, the great triangular swords depicted on Egyptian reliefs from the reigns of Rameses II (Abu Simbel) and III (Medinet Habu) as weapons of various sea-peoples (D'Amato and Salimbeti 2015). The similarity is the large, triangular blades, extraordinarily large, and the shape of the hilt. In the Egyptian reliefs, the weapon arms sword-and-shield, helmeted and occasionally armoured troops, who do not carry polearms. In a Mycenaean context, the sword is a secondary weapon for body-shield bearing pikemen and the epics attest it as a sidearm of the heavy armoured knights/*eqeta*. But although some Mycenaean weapons of the type are excessively big, the archaeological finds seem longer, narrower, flimsier and with slightly concave edges.

On the other hand, the role of the broader, leaf-/oar-like weapon is straightforward: to defeat, not circumvent, any kind of armour. Thrusting (XXI-179) or chopping/cutting, it is a weapon of force rather than accuracy, but has to be combined with good technique. Its use allows breaking helmets and splitting heads (XX-475), decapitating (XX-481) or maiming (V-802) by cutting through armour plate. Straight or bulged near the point ('oar-like', XV-713, XX-475), iron or copper/bronze, it is the weapon of the stronger, not the most versatile warrior, and it is parried only by a shield.

At that time a respectful weapon was the mace or club, either as stand-alone (Arithoos, VII-137/41) or as adjacent to the bow (Hercules). Maces are pictured/mentioned as standard for Assyrians (Dezső 2012) even as late as the fifth century BC (Hdt VII.63) and also for the Egyptians (Fields 2007). The weapon of Arithoos is of iron, while one road bandit lord, Periphetes, likewise uses a bronze example, which is taken by Theseus as a prize after slaying him (Plut, *Vit Thes* 8,1). Archaeology has unearthed some samples, as well (D'Amato and Salimbeti 2011), more than corroborating the lore. Similarly, axes were in vogue, in stark contrast to Classical Greece. The *Iliad* has very few mentions of shafted blades, but when mentioning their use in melees (XV-710), it makes no distinction amongst the antagonists; amongst chieftains, there is only one such use and that is by a Trojan ally (XIII-611/3). In this case, archaeology is more enlightening, with a number of different axe blades, both cutting and piercing ones, found and restored. The Epsilon-type axe, in particular, sheds new light over the cryptic task set by Penelope to the Suitors (xxi-120/3), to send an arrow through twelve axes (D'Amato and Salimbeti 2011) although the shaft socket of more conventional axeheads might be implied as well.

Different axe heads are intended for different tasks, obviously. The Epsilon axe is cutting/crushing/slashing and causes vile wounds in unarmoured flesh, while saving weight and metal. It may be implied by the word *pelekes*, which is even today used in Greek for a cutting axe. The name may well include very different, narrower, but still mainly cutting models, more like hatchets, both single- and double-headed. The narrower and longer the blade, the more targeted and thus demanding the blow in terms of accuracy and training. Of course, it delivers the energy in a more focused way to defeat armour or destroy shields.

Whether poleaxes wielded by both hands, like those of the Varangian Guard of the Byzantines (Heath 1979) have been used is a matter of conjecture, although the double-headed examples most prominent in Minoan Crete, with their obvious usefulness in naval combat, should be considered as being either normal axes or poleaxes. Even if the item was a symbol of the power of the Minoan Regime, allegedly failing just one to two generations earlier, it might have been, even in Crete, a relic of the past for quite some time, as are the ceremonial halberds of the Swiss Guard. For double-headed weapons, it is not clear whether the second head implied some special drill/technique or was a fail-safe for battle damage or deterioration through constant heavy use. What is of special interest is the mention on one and the same line of '... ten axes and ten half-axes' (XXIII-851). Intuitively one would say that a half-axe is a single-headed one and the double-headed is the axe proper, but it may be an issue of head size, not number, and thus the hatchet-like tools/ weapons would qualify as half-axes and the broad-bladed ones, including but not limited to Epsilon models, as axes. The asymmetrical double-axe, or rather axe-pickaxe (Petmezas 2019), that integrates two different weapons in one has an obvious purpose but cannot be identified with any mention of the epic.

The plain, single straight axe/pickaxe (D'Amato and Salimbeti 2011) is called *axine* (XIII-612), a word still in use today in Greek, although rather for a piece of digging equipment, namely the mattock. It is designed to defeat armour of any kind and delivers a deep but very narrow wound, immediately incapacitating if aimed at the skull, whereas the hatchet is a compromise and incapacitates in a number of cases, limbs included. The above-mentioned passage presents us with a peculiarity, using the term *pelekes* for the handle/ shaft of the pickaxe, although in other cases the use is reserved for the full conventional axe (XV-710; XXIII-115), leaving unresovled the issue mentioned above, with the meaning of the word 'half-axe'.

It is a little appreciated fact that swordplay, as form and technique, is directly affected by other field parameters, the most prominent being the missile factor: battlefields where missile fire is abundant (not only arrows, but javelins and slingstones as well) deny the opportunity for advanced, picturesque swordplay as interpreted for the Middle Ages. The well-trained sword-fighter has to combine his blade with a shield and merit lies with swift, accurate and powerful blows while offering the least opening when moving his shield – not just to the immediate opponent, but to a hidden archer as well.

To surmise the above, if two heroes close at each other in the open for an informal duel, the duel dance occurs: each must decide if throwing a spear, to finish the engagement early on, is the best option, or charging head-on for a spear thrust. The cast is minimal danger, but in open confrontation, especially on the run, misses are often (XIII-605). If the weapon does indeed miss, or is deflected/parried by the shield (III-346/9), the opponent may return the cast at leisure (III-349/55), but this entails a high probability of missing as well; on the contrary, the only one with a spear at hand has a very nice opportunity to approach at ease with the spear as a thrusting weapon (XIII-605) and attempt any number of thrusts with virtual impunity, as any spear outranges any hand weapon (sword, mace, axe). The equalizer is the fact that, once a spear or javelin is incoming, the target must take evasive or parrying action, thus offering a minor but crucial window of opportunity

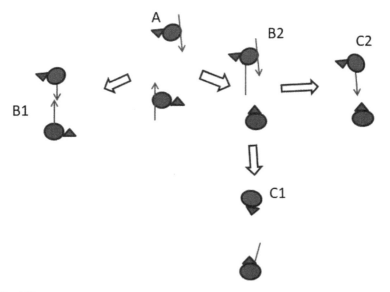

The Duel Dance
Circle: Shielded warrior; Arrow: spear at the ready for casting (side of the circle), or for thrusting (through the centre of the circle), or thrown (no point) ; triangle: sidearm.

The two opponents approach (A), spears at the ready. They might opt for a thrusting exchange (B1); otherwise, one of the two will have the first cast (B2). If he does not kill the opponent, he will revert to his sidearm and try to close the distance fast for CQB while his opponent casts and draws his own sidearm (C1). If the cast fails to make an impression, CQB with sidearms occurs. But the opponent may forfeit the cast, especially if the distance has closed fast, and rather attempt a thrust with his spear, enjoying a range advantage over the sidearm (C2).

in terms of time, posture and geometry to the attacker for drawing his sidearm of choice and pressing the assault home, retaining or seizing the initiative (III-360/2). This might lead either to delaying the cast till the last moment, which produces a quick-draw situation, eventually terminating with both opponents hit by simultaneous spear casts (V-655/60) or both opponents exchanging spear thrusts (XV-528/37); it may also lead to both opponents reverting to their sidearms in time (XIII-610/15). As the sidearm is a substitute for the spear, the same rules apply: both go for the first blow, with cases of strokes from both opponents being delivered simultaneously (XIII-610/15); otherwise, a succession of blows ensues (XVI-335/40).

C. Shields.

The first use of shields, at least on Greek battlefields, is reported to have happened during the civil strife that culminated in open battle off Argos, between Acrisius and Proitus for the throne of Argos (Paus II.25,7), possibly with Iobates' Lycian troops participating; this is two generations before Perseus, the founder of Myceneae, the grandson of Acrisius.

Both the epic and the archaeological findings imply the use of two broad categories of shields: body-shields (Smith 2015) and light shields (XIV-375). The former seem to be earlier in design and use (Smith 2015) and may be classified into three types: the tower shields, the eight-shields (actually, 'figure-of-eight') and the very big, circular body shields. In the epic, there is direct reference for the first (XVII-128) and third (VII-250 combined with VI-117/8) types; both have more-or-less close relatives present in Assyrian art (Dezső 2012).

Iconographic evidence from Mycenaean times regarding body-shields exists for the two first types. Actually, there are two different subtypes of the eight-shield, with or without a boss (Smith 2015). The usual interpretation of the epic shows no mention of eight-shield, as the standard phrase, as mentioned. For example, XIII-405 is best interpreted as 'circular', and applies to both body-shield and hand-shield categories, while being much more suitable as interpretation when metal construction is implied (XIII-803/4), which perhaps suggests either facing or an all-metal construction similar to the Herzsprung example (Hencken 1950). Still, there is a passage where the said *mandra* is combined with a construction detail, that the shield is built on a framework of two rods (XIII-407), which hardly applies to circular forms, but is depicted in findings and thus correctly interpreted by Connolly (1977) as referring to the eight-shield. Since the epic has another word for denoting circular shields (XIII-715) without any ambiguity, it might be surmised that the eight-shield is the one mostly described in the *Iliad*, and not the circular one. To support this conclusion, one should bypass the possibility that the two descriptions may refer to different kinds of circular shields (i.e. due to size, on concavity, or construction) and accept that poetic licence has its limits. The epic definitely follows no strict terminology, but since there is massive use of standardized motifs, diversions in expressive means and words, especially in technical terminology, might imply real-life differentiations or their echo, at the very least.

The bossed type of eight-shield may be more resilient, perhaps from a different era (by any account newer, a product of technological evolution), and is definitely better in offensive use. It may have been intended to create a rupture in a shield wall of tower shields. This projection may be an anachronism, from the hoplite age, as the fresco at Thyra shows a very open formation; still, the *Iliad* clearly mentions exceptionally tight formations when defending vital positions (XIII-129/131 & 145/6 & 680; XVII-352/65), where body-shields are a prerequisite (XIV-375/6). The eight-shield has no Assyrian counterpart, is amply represented in Greek art, is different from the later Dipylon shield (D'Amato and Salimbeti 2017; Snodgrass 1998) and the Boeotian shield (Snodgrass 1998) – the latter is a version of the Argive *hoplon* shield in terms of technology – but some Etruscan/Villanovan designs appear similar, being possibly spin-offs rather than paradigms (D'Amato and Salimbeti 2018). All in all, the later Boeotian shield may have been, in art or technology, an evolution of the rectangular, scalloped hand-shield seen in Geometric art (D'Amato and Salimbeti 2017) towards the technology of the Argive shield.

The body-shields hang from a belt (*telamon*), allowing soldiers to actually tuck in behind them and are perhaps handled in tilt and attitude by a central grip. They combine, in art, with boar-tusk helmets and long pikes held by both hands. Such pikes are levelled over the upper edge to engage like infantry, but kneeling positions with the pike held at a slant are also depicted, possibly to receive attacks by close-contact infantry, like swordsmen, and perhaps cavalry, mounted or chariotry. They are not represented in the hands of armoured infantry or charioteers, although this is debatable. Hector possesses a body-shield (VI-117/8) that may have been figure-of-eight shield or round; since he moves around in his chariot, like many heroes, especially Trojans, the shield must be with him, either secured in the vehicle or suspended from the *telamon* belt (V-796/7) across his shoulders and covering his back (XVI-360/1) and possibly that of the driver during the retreat (De Becker 2009); after all, the very poetic expression that 'the horses extracted Hector and his weapons …' (XVI-367/8) might imply a set of different weapons kept in the chariot and used as needed, in both mounted and unmounted engagements but definitely carried alternatively and not all at once by the warrior when on foot.

In the *Odyssey* (xxii-101/2), it is still the equipment of the unarmoured, helmeted infantryman (almost identical to the images of the Lion Hunt Dagger and the Battle Krater), but combined with a pair of *dory* dual-purpose spears (xxii- 110) instead of the pike. Of course, if one is strict, in the *Iliad*, the armament of the multitude is also repeatedly described as spear(s), shield and helmet (VII-61/2; XIII-130/1), obviously considering cuirasses and the panoply in general reserved for the knights/*eqeta* and heroes in general. It must be stressed that the representation of rectangular, or rather trapezoidal body-shields on the Thera fresco has been interpreted as flat (D'Amato and Salimbeti 2013), similar to the Sumerian models of the Stele of the Vultures (Maekawa 2003). This model is taken as an alternative or, more probably, as an additional type to the highly concave, tower-like, rectangular body-shields. The hypothesis is based on the absence of the prominent semi-circular projection on the upper side of the shield in the Thera fresco, which is defining the tower type in both full-body and shorter, half-size models in various representations (such as the Warrior Dagger and the Siege Rhyton respectively). The edges of the shield, though, if not curved backwards, do not allow handling the pike with the arms positioned as in the fresco.

Mid-sized (hand-) shields are implied in the *Iliad* as less suitable for dense, defensive formations; the very notion of such use precludes small shields. The epic is not very enlightening on the subject, but circular shields are a safe bet; especially since they are used by late Bronze and early Iron Age chariot-borne warriors (D'Amato and Salimbeti 2011; 2017). Ox-hide is one material mentioned (XIII-160/1) and bronze facing is a usual addition in the epic (XII-295/6), but finds imply frequent use of metal bosses as a usual addition too (D'Amato and Salimbeti 2015) and a central boss for protecting the centrally located handle (D'Amato and Salimbeti 2017). This concept of a central handgrip, and protected by a hemispherical, fully integrated boss, may be what is implied by the Carian invention of the shield grip (Hdt I.171,4). The reference is usually interpreted to refer to the Argive shields but the words used, and the comparison with the earlier body-shields, place the invention to the late Bronze Age at the earliest. A handgrip *should* have been added to the body-shield to guide it; similarly, a central handgrip for hand-shields should have been a given, and the mid-sized oblong/orthogonal Egyptian examples had a grip, though not central (Fields 2007). But this invention, centrally located *and* protecting the hand, while allowing space for better handling, was a quantum leap.

Central handles may also have come in pairs, with two semicircular grips on a boss, which would account for the plural in Herodotian reference. Still, an alternative presents itself once more: there are double grips, or rather bands, positioned symmetrically and off-centre in circular shields that make them arm-, and not hand-shields. Such representations are found in Egyptian reliefs of the Sea Peoples in Abu Simbel, although in the hands of *Shardana* troops in Egyptian pay (D'Amato and Salimbeti 2015). It is a long way from the asymmetrical double-grip system (*porpax-antilabe*) of the Argive shield, but this double grip is demonstrably a step in this direction and reminiscent of the double- or triple-grip system in some later Thracian *pelte* light shields.

Bosses are regularly used (XII-161), obviously to strengthen the shield to withstand specific cases of impact. Multiple such bosses may be seen on flat shields, obviously of ox-hide mostly, in Egyptian reliefs, i.e. in Abu Simbel (D'Amato and Salimbeti 2015); circular(-ish) mainly, but not necessarily. When shields are plated with (or made by) bronze or metal in general, such bosses may be decoratively represented on the bronze surface, or they may be additional items set for increased strength (XI-32/5).

There is an expression which unmistakably describes circular shields, translated as 'perfectly circular' (XIII-715), an expression not amenable to any alternate interpretation like the one previously noted meaning 'symmetrical' (XIII-405). Still, the use of two expressions might be alternating for artistic effect, and it may just as well be describing different items.

In any case, the second shield of Achilles, being of full metal construction, cannot have been anything larger than mid-sized for reasons of weight. The exquisite ornamentation, arranged in concentric rings (XVIII-478/608) and the multi-layered construction (XVIII-481; XX-270/2) imply Herzsprung-type full-metal construction (Heneken 1950; D'Amato and Salimbeti 2017), possibly a novelty at the historical time of the epic, as the type is usually associated with the Geometric Age rather than the Bronze Age. As the type did not have a rim (unlike ox-hide shields, plated with sheet metal or not), since it was of laterally homogeneous construction, it is strange that Homer describes the ornamentation of said rim; incidentally, the decorative pattern, mentioned as 'the Ocean', may well refer to the meander pattern and its different spin-offs seen on the rims of the Archaic and Classical age Argive shields (*hoplon*).

A bronze shield, perfectly polished so as to be used as a mirror, had been used by Perseus, the arch-hero of Greek lore, some five generations earlier. Whether it had been a Herzsprung, another model of plain metal

– as specifically mentioned in the text (Apollod II.4,2) – or a bronze-faced model, remains unresolved.

Had the Herzsprung type been a novelty, it would have been used at the time for the highest order of aristocrats, thus only very few would have acquired one; even Achilles got one due to the manufacture of new armour for him by Hephaestus; his original armour, the one given to him by his father, may well have not included such an item; there is a tradition of the shield of Peleus – and thus of Achilles – being made of nine ox-hides stiffened by one external layer of bronze (Ovid, *Met* 12.95–8); that of Ajax was seven to one (VII-219/23), thus that of Peleus was conventional in design and manufacture but top quality.

It is thus possible, if not certain, that the shield of Agamemnon (XI-32/40) was also Herzsprung type, for which (similar to that of Achilles) there is no mention of ox hide, as is the case for most other shields, while the reported eleven circles of bronze (XI-33) obviously refer to the standard pattern of Herzsprung shields, if not successive metal sheets hammered into one. Unlike to the shield of Achilles, Agamemnon's is made of successive layers of copper/bronze *but* there is the enigmatic *kyanio* (XI-35), which is mentioned for his cuirass as well (see below). It has recently been discovered that the dark/black inlay of Mycenaean daggers and other copper artefacts is a special alloy of copper with limited quantities of gold, with or without tin, lead and silver (Demakopoulou *et al.* 1995; Photos *et al.* 1994), and this may be associated with the cryptic *kyanio* of the armour of Agamemnon. If the black alloy is what the epic describes as *kyanio*, its use on the shield of Agamemnon is obviously purely decorative and with no tactical significance; this would suggest a similar and not utilitarian use of the alloy in his cuirass; most probably plating must have produced a highly aesthetic effect of three colours, blue-black, white-grey and gold.

It must be stressed that the shield of Achilles is described as made of successive layers of three different metals, copper (Cu), tin (Sn) and gold (Au) in 2/2/1 ratio (XX-270/2) reminiscent of modern composite armour in tanks. Here, the issue is purely tactical (XX-265/72) as the item is impenetrable. But a series of questions emerge in terms of technology: the exact order of the layers is the quintessential one, with the golden layer being in front, or, as is usually supposed by interpreting an excerpt, (XX-268/72) in the middle. If the latter is true, there are actually four plausible conformations: the *tandem*, meaning one copper-tin bilayer before, and one identical after the golden layer, giving a sequence Cu-Sn-Au-Cu-Sn (or, less probably, Sn-Cu-Au-Sn-Cu). The *palindrome* would be similar, but with the rear copper-tin bilayer inverted, producing a sequence Cu-Sn-Au-Sn-Cu or, less probably Sn-Cu-

Au-Cu-Sn. The trilayer would have same layers together and thus informing of relative thickness rather than anything else. The sequences may be Cu-Cu-Au-Sn-Sn (it may be inferred by one interpretation of XX-271) or, much less probably, Sn-Sn-Au-Cu-Cu.

But there is an alternative explanation: even the best scribe and/or poet might not be able to understand if these were the necessary ratios for forming an alloy, instead of using the ingredients in successive layers. Bronze is a disproportionate alloy of more than 10 per cent tin for high-tin bronze and ~5 per cent for low-tin alloys (Demakopoulou *et al.* 1995). It is possible that when the epic mentions tin weapons, as in greaves (XVII-613), it is high-tin bronze compared with low-tin bronze for other pieces (i.e. cuirass). This, although literarily plausible, most probably is not the case.

Non-circular shields safely include the half-tower-shield, seen primarily on the Siege Rhyton (Smith 2015) and also found in Assyrian reliefs (Dezső, 2012) and possibly referred to explicitly (XIV-375) as smaller shields of rectangular shape or, rather, projection. Again, artistic licence must be taken into account, but the literal meaning is 'shouldering a smaller, orthogonal shield' and should be considered at face value, as describing precisely a known item. A second candidate is the strictly rectangular and demonstrably flat item seen on Geometric pottery, even arming chariot-borne warriors.

The double-scalloped rectangular shields of Geometric representations, if indeed flat and scalloped (this might be a perspective of curved shields, rectangular in projection) occasionally used by chariot-borne warriors as well (D'Amato and Salimbeti 2017) are not in context in the epic and their identification with the above is a possible third candidate, but not a plausible one. These rectangular, double-scalloped, medium shields, obviously hand-held (suspension straps should not be excluded for any medium and small shield) may indicate enemies rather than Greek Geometric Age warriors. In theory they could be the object of the description in V-453, but the latter is probably better identified as an early description of the Thracian *pelte* buckler (Best 1969), as it reads 'winged shields' and the *pelte* is surely reminiscent of the open wings of a bird, and in many cases a bird was the preferred blazon/emblem (Webber 2001). The item known as *pelte* during the fifth and fourth century might have been called something else some centuries earlier, and the Thracians, who fought as allies of the Trojans, may well have introduced it into the battlefields of the Troad. Alternatively, the light scalloped-off sub-circular shield of the Warrior Vase might just as easily have been implied (Snodgrass 1998; Grguric 2005). The structure must be of ox-hide, with or without a boss, and faced with bronze – or not. The scalloped shape allowed improved mobility of the lower body when the shield hangs from the belt for assault or flight, indicating an item designed for mobile tactics more than anything else.

The *Iliad* clearly mentions Ajax, with his tower shield (XVII-128) made by a master craftsman, with seven ox-hides and a facing layer of bronze on top (VII-219/23). There is no reason to assign the quality of 'tower' to metaphor (Howard 2011; Van Wees 2009), once other descriptions for shields abound and describe or imply mostly circular shapes. After all, such a metaphor is routinely applied to Ajax when another word is used; the *Iliad* prefers stereotypes for ease of memorizing rather than a wealth of synonyms for effect. Full armour for Ajax may be implied (VII-206/7); but that is in the context of a duel or, rather, single combat (Molloy 2012). There is an indirect indication of the battle use of such gear *without* armour; Ajax is struck by Hector's cast behind the shield and the spearhead stops not at the cuirass, but because of the overlap of the shield suspension strap and sword baldric (XIV-403/4); excellent examples of the latter, being wide and decorated, obviously thick too, have been depicted on stone reliefs (D'Amato and Salimbeti 2011). Similarly, after the death of Patroclus, Achilles says he has no weapons with which to arm himself, in order to assist the hard-pressed Greeks, as the only weapon he could have used except his own panoply, passed on to him by his father (XVII-194/7), entrusted to Patroclus (XVI-130/8) and now possessed by Hector, was the shield of Ajax (XVIII-192/3); spears were obviously no problem and abounded in the Greek camp, but defensive weapons *were* a problem as they are size-sensitive. It is directly implied that he could fight with the said shield if need be, without further defensive items. These two instances corroborate the impression from the epics mentioned above and the iconographic evidence unearthed up to now: all three main representations of pike-and-body-shield Mycenaean infantry (the fresco at Thera, the Lion-Hunt Dagger and the Battle Krater) show no body armour except, provisionally, for a helmet.

Small, not medium-sized, circular shields are seen is an Assyrian context (Dezső, 2012). There is no reason to suppose such shields were adopted into Mycenaean use, although the repeated mention of *smaller shields*, unsuitable for dense phalanx formation (XIV-375), might actually refer to *small* shields and the reference in V-453 could be interpreted as *lightweight*, not as an attribute of shape.

The known passage where the Greeks are redistributing shields (XIV-375/6) has not received the attention it deserves: first of all, it implies that different shield types exist and that would be due to personal preferences; but this is a retroprojection of classical warfare to the past. If the assignments were centrally managed, as is the case today, with central conscription and standard issues, then one may hypothesize that either of two eventualities were happening: either the Greek system tried to maximize numbers of decently war-capable troops, assigning lighter equipment to better warriors, which would be properly used and best exploited, while inferior troops, to be of use were issued superior equipment, to make up for their own low quality. In this case, the urgency of the situation required a rapid reboot, giving precedence to qualitative edge rather than quantity: maximizing the fighting power of fewer troops that were posted in the thick of the fighting, so as to attain a favourable decision; the rest of the troops were not expected to assist in the decision, and may have been unengaged and remaining in second echelon, or even uncommitted, when the fighting was dispersed along the line to specific hotspots (XIII-737/9), as determined by the Trojan assaults. The defensive formations of the Greeks, the dense phalanges, would not allow local counter-attacks and flanking, as would have been the case with more fluid tactics. The phalanx, once formed, allowed only forward frontal counter-attacks – as happened once Patroclus' flanking action gave some respite (XVI-356/7).

The other possibility, exclusive to that mentioned above, is that the good troops were assigned to lighter infantry units, leaving inferior troops for the heavier shields and more static fights. This scheme would require both categories to have been drilled in the basics of defence (not necessarily of offence, for the inferior troops) and suggest that mobility and fluid tactics were paramount in the conduct of war. This agrees with the pictorial and archaeological evidence, where light infantry seem more prestigious (Grguric 2005), as is the case with special forces even today. Thus, the elites, used for the mobile phases of the fighting and occasionally expected to seek respite behind the static, lesser troops (older, like the Roman triarii, or simply inferior), were issued lighter gear for surging combat, in repeated attacks and possibly repeated hit-and-run strikes (XIII-794/800).

D. Armour

Three different words are used in the Homeric text for the suite of arms, or panoply: *teyxea*, *telea* and *entea*. The second word is also used for the tactical or organizational units of troops (XVIII-298/300). The terms are indiscriminate and do not entail any detail or implication for the number of items of the kit. It is a kit, be it shield and spear, or panoply.

The armour of the nobles is described as plate bronze or copper, but the mention of a 'copper tunic' (XIII-439/40) for one – rather elderly – Trojan also implies a panoply of scales. A derivative adjective is used for both Greeks (XIII-255 & 272) and Trojans (XVII-485). Whether this literally means scale armour, similar to the standard in a Hittite context (Bryce 2007), contrasted with the plate-type cuirass explicitly mentioned occasionally (XIII-507 & 587; XVII-314), or it is a figure of speech to denote 'bronze body armour', cannot be determined. Still, the unique reference to the item proper implies an accurate record/remark for XIII-439 against the figurative use of the derivative adjective(s) for the other cases.

The Dendra panoply is the role model for such sets of armour; a rather early model, offering excellent coverage if not protection. On first sight, it seems cumbersome and has thus been considered chariot armour, or duelling armour, or infantry-only armour (Bakas 2018). The first sounds logical; a heavy set would make striding difficult and thus external mobility would be needed, and similar practices are attested for other chariot forces (Wise 1981; Healy 1992). Experiments regarding balance and stability indicate challenges to the point of operational inefficiency (*ibid*), but do not take into account a long training programme that would have been prescribed for such elite warriors in equestrian issues, balance included (XVIII-808/11; XXIII-306/15; Apoll II.4,9), nor possible provisions built into the chariot to allow for better support. A central rail, dividing the space in two could suffice. The right leg, possibly intentionally left without a greave (Bakas 2018), would be wrapped around or planted against it. The third sounds absurd, but in the context of a static fight, as if with body-shields, it makes sense, and the ground is a much more stable fighting platform than a moving chariot, especially if the chariot was used for moving this trooper around, to fight dismounted, as mentioned in the *Iliad* (III-29) and practised by mounted infantry throughout the ages (Van Wees 1994), with Alexander the Great not being an exception (Arr, *Anab* I.6.5).

The second suggestion, that it is duelling armour (Molloy 2012), is interesting: maximum protection is needed in formal single combat, because time and space allow full use of one's dexterity with weapons. The *Iliad* suggests that Ajax put on armour to face Hector (VII-206/7), which may imply he had usually been fighting without it. He also put on armour for a mock fight with Diomedes in the Funeral Games of Patroclus (XXIII-8011/4). Similarly, Paris was given armour by his friends and brothers to challenge Menelaus (III-329/36), because on this particular day he was clad as light infantryman, without armour (III-16/9), although he clearly had a full set and wore it when needed (VI-321/2 & 512/3). It follows that a hero was expected to own full armour but use it at his discretion. He might find himself assigned to a battlefield role, or select it himself, where armour was not an asset but a liability, as when operating with light infantry (or perhaps over broken ground). Even in open combat, there might have been instances where armour was still a liability: possibly the use of full-size body-shield and pike was such a case; there is no illustration from frescoes or gemstones where a full body-shield is combined with armour, except for a helmet, and the basic kit of war in both the *Iliad* and *Odyssey*, as referenced elsewhere, supports this possibility.

However, in single combat, dexterity and mobility are needed to get into an advantageous position so as to land a blow, or to parry one, and, most importantly, to evade one; Paris' ad hoc acquired equipment, referenced above, includes basic items and definitely nothing as complete and heavy as a full panoply of the Dendra type. And this brings us to the important part of the discussion. Medieval knights, armoured as heavily, if not more so, were perfectly able to fight on foot in battle and in jousting contexts. They were not as free-moving as other troops, but the balance was favouring protection, as the richest, noblest and best troops craved armour and not lightness. And, when tried, the Dendra panoply was not particularly cumbersome, and at some 15kg (Molloy 2012), not very heavy, especially compared with the gear of today's professional soldiers, which can weigh at least 18kg. This depends of course on the reconstruction and the re-enactment, that differ wildly (the neck guard and the shoulder guards are usually exaggerated in size), because different reconstructions weight 18kg (D'Amato and Salimbeti 2011) or up to 25kg (Petmezas 2019) or even 30kg (Bakas 2018), possibly by varying not only the size of the individual pieces, but the thickness of the plate and the padding. That it is not ritual but fully functional there can be no doubt: being found with one arm-guard (implying the use of a shield), and presenting a wider arm-hole to the right, to allow freer movement to the strong right hand, brandishing a shaft or blade, implies battle use (D'Amato and Salimbeti 2011). In general, assigning functional objects to ritualistic use is somewhat of a pandemic in archaeology (Molloy 2012) and should be discouraged as a line of thought. An $8 million modern tank (or ten such, for $80 million) are excellent for parade and show, but they are not purchased for show and parade, nor *designed and built for* such use.

As surmised from the above, the *eqeta*, whether he is perceived as follower or as knight, would find his armour perfectly functional for duelling, infantry and chariotry uses (Molloy 2012; Petmezas 2019). Whether its use made the shield redundant is a matter of conjecture, but also of vogue. In a two-wheel chariot, there could be little room to accomodate such an armoured passenger; 'passenger' being the direct translation of the Homeric term *parabatai* (XXIII-132). In effect, a hollow body-shield, plus the armoured passenger and the driver, irrespective of the latter's kit (Connolly 1977), is a bit too much for Mycenaean chariots, which had to be robust, due to the ground in the motherland, but light, to be transported easily onboard for raids and expeditions. And the driver may have been fully armoured (XIII-394/8), as many times an *eqeta* could function in either capacity, warrior or driver (V-226/8). But the medium shields, round, scalloped or rectangular, shown in much later art for differently armed and armoured passengers with new equipment, would not be a problem; and a body-shield would not necessarily have been so in the context of a four-wheel chariot (D'Amato and Salimbeti 2017).

Hand- and forearm-guards/bracelets have been found, compatible with holding reins (D'Amato and Salimbeti 2011), although not necessarily from the same set of armour, or even from similar ones. On the other hand, the existence of the armoured skirt and neck guard is securely attested by finds (Snodgrass 1998) and iconography and may well explain why Achilles, when his previous, older-model armour was taken by Hector, had to think and observe the enemy's posture so as to detect an exploitable weak spot in the otherwise complete protection afforded by the suit (XXII-320/5).

Late Mycenaean armour is very different, because tactics, vogue and technology all evolved (D'Amato and Salimbeti 2011; 2015; 2017). Still, two main characteristics of the Dendra suit continue to eternity. The first is the plate cuirass, formed by breast and back plates that fit the torso and are self-supported at shoulder level. These may be lined/padded by leather/fabric substrate for the comfort of the wearer but are not supported by it, like some triangular plates and other items, including pectorals (D'Amato and Salimbeti 2018), that have been discovered. The difference for this cuirass is that it is self-supporting, with the two plates directly attached to each other (and not hinged by additional parts, like the articulated cuirass – Connolly 1981), although securing by pins or laces is to be expected. The new cuirass shed any number of attachments, such as the skirt, the neck guard and the shoulder guards and soldiered on in the new era; it will evolve to the early hoplite bell-cuirass, the late hoplite muscle cuirass and as such will change era in the arsenal of Roman (Connolly 1981) and Byzantine generals, only to be reverse-evolved in medieval and modern Europe all the way to the cuirassier cavalry – some 3,000 years! The new panoply of Achilles was of this newer kind, as it comprises greaves, helmet and cuirass (XVIII-610/3), and leaves the forearm naked (XXI-166/7) possibly, as already mentioned, in contrast with his original suit (XXII-320/3), which was his father's (XVII-194/7).

The other feature, moving directly to the new generation, is the concept of semi-overlapping attached metal bands that formed the armour skirt below the cuirass. This concept will evolve in size and detail to become the main feature of body armour (Snodgrass 1998; Connolly 1977), thus affording ease of manufacture and excellent flexibility, while combining with leather or fabric substrates that function as padding and also as soft armour over more exposed body parts to create composite armour. It is possible that this kind of armour made of overlapping bands, reminiscent of the human rib pattern and shown on the Vase of Warriors and in Egyptian reliefs (D'Amato and Salimbeti 2015), is described in the epic as the cuirass of Agamemnon (XI-24/5). The concept of banded armour, historically, concluded with the Roman *lorica segmentata* (Connolly 1981).

In the *Iliad*, a cuirass (*toraka* in Linear B texts, *thorax* in the epic) is occasionally described as *polydaidalos* (XI-436) and this implies exquisitely crafted, either in terms of decoration or of manufacture. On top of the improved plate armour and the metal bands – *oimoi* – almost all conceivable armour solutions had been tried by the later Bronze and early Iron Age: scale, composite (metal parts attached on perishable substrate) or metal items tied by strips over the body, as seen in older and recent finds (D'Amato and Salimbeti 2011; 2015; 2017). The epic clearly mentions the linen corselet, with no mention of metal parts, used by Ajax the Lesser (II-529), and probably jerkins of cloth (XXI-29/31) as well. The composite models refer to a perishable material substrate reinforced with scales, chain mail, bosses or partial plate parts, such as upper-body items, including shoulder guards (Linear B texts: *epomijo*), pectorals, waist bands/belts (D'Amato and Salimbeti 2011). The cuirass of Agamemnon is, as mentioned, an interesting issue; a wholly metal artefact, a masterpiece, made from forty-two *oimoi* parts, an even number, allowing for left and right sides. These parts are grouped in three by the metal they are made of: tin, gold and an unknown metal or alloy called *kyanio*, a word associated in Greek with the colour blue, but here described explicitly as black (XI-24/5). The latter term is usually interpreted not as 'black' but as 'deep', for 'deep blue' and the whole description points not to an account of the structure of the cuirass, but of its decoration, as mentioned earlier. Nevertheless, whether the analysed alloy (Demakopoulou *et al.* 1995; Photos *et al.* 1994) is endowed with as-yet-unknown mechanical qualities, making it suitable for tactical, not decorative, purposes cannot be surmised by available data.

Copper armour belt/waist bands are reported in the epic. They are used without further body armour by some light infantry (XXI-90/1) or whenever full panoply is impractical (X-75/80), and there are numerous archaeological finds (D'Amato and Salimbeti 2011). In such cases they were the only protective equipment for the torso, as helmets and greaves may have been issued; but the belt could also be used to enhance or complement other protective solutions, functioning as additional armour for better-armoured warriors. One approach to such an end would be as a metal piece of armour added to a protective suit made of perishable material, such as a leather jerkin or a padded tunic (D'Amato and Salimbeti 2011; 2015; 2017); another would be to complement short or extra-short metal cuirasses, which allowed body motion like that needed for ducking or riding or climbing, as used by Samnite Italians in the fourth century BC along with articulated cuirasses (Connolly 1981). In this light, one may also expect the use of a belt as an obviously superfluous item to afford added protection by wearing it *over – or under –* the breastplate of a conventional or composite cuirass. This may be the case for the armour of Menelaus, which saved his life by intercepting the iron-tipped arrow shot by Pandarus (IV-132/7).

The Greeks use greaves (XI-17) and this is an item which characterizes them both in frescoes and within the *Iliad*. Their greaves are characterized as well-made (V-668), bronze (VII-41), white and in some cases special attention is given to their attachment around the ankle (XI-18/9; XVI-130/2), which might imply something elusive, undetected in the frescoes; possibly ankle-guards (Van Wees 1994; D'Amato and Salimbeti 2011). The pair made by Hephaestus for Achilles is allegedly made of tin (XVIII-613), which implies a colour different than copper and perhaps similar to iron. The latter is a safer bet, given that they stave off a direct hit from a cast spear (XXI-556–60).

By contrast, the Trojans are seldom mentioned as using greaves (e.g. Paris against Menelaus III-330/1). The description in the *Iliad* is not clear: it may imply the Bronze-Age double arrangement seen in the frescoes: a tall, flexible, close-fitting cloth- or leather-made inner one, actually a leg guard (Fields 2006) and possibly similar in construction with the *linothorax* (D'Amato and Salimbeti 2017), plus a metal, canted-disc, ovoid or curved trapezoid-shaped shorter item for the shin, tied by wire or laced in position. Alternatively, some form of flexible bronze protecting both shin and calf may be implied, as is attested early on, being the type found with the Dendra armour. Such items that encompass the lower leg all round and are kept in position by the elasticity of the metal (D'Amato and Salimbeti 2011) are the antecedents of the hoplite panoply greaves represented in art and found in Archaic and Classical Greek contexts (Snodgrass 1998). Early examples seem to be low, while classical-era models project to form a kneecap, to extend protection to the knee, and the same is seen in the perishable, fabric or leather inner leg guard in the fresco from Pylos. Later representations, like that on the Warrior Vase, clearly show different leg guards, fluffier like long socks or padded substrates (D'Amato and Salimbeti 2017).

The helmets are of many models and designs or materials, including, but not restricted to, composite, padded, metal, boar-tusk, leather, or formed by stretched leather-bands (Grguric 2005; Connolly 1977; D'Amato and Salimbeti 2011; 2013). Different terms in the *Iliad* perhaps imply different types (XII-257/8). Crests with horsetails (XI-41/2) and horns (XIII-614) are the usual decorations, possibly used in combination as seen in the Warrior Vase or separately. They may be indicative of rank or of unit/contingent. Metal discs/bosses (XI-41) were rather to improve resistance to smashing and chopping blows than to decorate further. Their prominence in iconography, especially of the later boar-tusk ones, which are of extremely high cost, because they require massive amounts of tusks precisely fit on a substrate of leather bands (X-261/5), suggests a kind of uniform, but also a propensity for weapons aimed at the head, from stones to clubs, maces, hammers and chopping polearms, swords and axes.

The elaborate and ornate metal or metal-reinforced helmets in the *Iliad* make nice poetry and perhaps art; a wide variety have been unearthed, suggesting many options, but whether this is by unit, troop type, locality/palace of manufacture or era and fashion, it cannot be determined. Two cases, though, stand out: the non-reinforced ox-hide one, suitable for commando and guard missions, as it is noiseless and not reflective (X-257/9), and the boar-tusk. The latter is also used in such a raid (X-261/5), possibly because it is relatively stealthy/low-signature compared to metal-made items, but it is the standard issue of light Mycenaean infantry in the frescoes of Pylos. This does not mean it is reserved for these troops only: found with the panoply at Dendra and shown in representations of body-shield bearers, it seems to have been the most celebrated item on top of the most expensive ever, due to the number of boars needed for its manufacture, as already mentioned.

Given that, in iconography, similar troops are almost identically clad, except for the usual variations, such as the arms afforded to different troop types and the patterns of ox-hide, a notion of uniform can be suggested, possibly in addition to artistic convention (Papadopoulos 2012). In this light, the exceptional variety of similar weapons and armour may imply something more than personal preferences, especially in a highly bureaucratic and centralized system; namely different palace preferences, artisan practices and standards (Grguric 2005), a reference with multiple attributes running exclusively or inclusively. For example, the temporal issue, relating to material availability, evolution/technology and also the vogue of the time, should be taken into consideration, but then so should local preferences and the expertise of the available workshops, especially regarding technologically similar but morphologically different items. Last, but not least, semantics are also important, as different equipment might indicate different missions/ troop types or ranks, as might have been the case with similar but slightly different helmets.

There seems to be, by merit of archaeology and especially its experimental constituent, an interplay between arms and armour. The rapier-like longswords were able to kill behind a body-shield, but when the latter was plated by bronze it became necessary to go for attacks over the rim, as shown on the Agate ring. The single-edged chopping sabres could deliver murderous thrusting blows (Molloy 2010) and strike the head behind the body-shield and defeat felt caps, leather and padded helmets that were adequate against cuts of the rapier sword and perhaps against some clubs and maces. The boar-tusk helmet changed that, and the bronze-reinforced (by bosses or studs) leather or felt, simple or padded, models offered a marked improvement, which might have included protection against some axes as well, as is the Epsilon type and the usual double-axes (D'Amato and Salimbeti 2011). Hatchets and pick-axes offered a much improved offensive option, and the flexible use of the medium-sized shield became a must. This allowed more elaborate tactics for bladed weapons; the short swords/dirks allowed more room for dexterity and were effective in stabbing soft body parts, if unprotected or protected by soft armour, such as leather, or linen, even if padded (Molloy 2010). The use of the bronze waist belt was the remedy for this liability, but the advent of the broadsword (Type G and Naue II) brought the advantage to the offence, until the emergence of the *hoplon* shield.

Something similar may be seen with shafted weapons. Spear points of pikes are attested, as in the Battle of the Glen (Grguric 2005; D'Amato and Salimbeti 2013), with rings around the socket. These may be interpreted as handles for easily affixing the head to the shaft; but much more probable is that their purpose was to stop ingress of the shaft into the body of the target in order to make extraction from the victim easy, especially if the latter was naked and impaled at high speed (XVI-862/3).

E. Archery and missiles

Hercules, son of Zeus, is an outcast prince whose scheming parents are exiled to Thebes from Tiryns, whence they claim rights to the throne of Mycenae. He enjoys an excellent education and is protected by Athena, the goddess of wisdom, warfare and deviousness. He lives in the highlands of Thebes for quite some time and associates with mountaineers and hill people. He wears a lion skin, he is proverbially strong and fleet enough to try to hunt stag or boar on foot during his renowned Labours and uses a club or a mace along with his bow, with which he shoots venomous arrows. There are a few, later (but possibly based on early) traditions with Hercules fighting conventionally and owning an almost full panoply, being an armoured archer with two sidearms, a sword and a club (Apollod II.6,11), similar to some Assyrian depictions (Dezső 2012). In other instances he also brandishes a shield and full panoply; his shield is the subject of a small epic poem (*The Shield of Hercules* by Hesiod), possibly echoing the earlier Homeric description of the shield of Achilles (XVIII-478/608), but in the context of the Boeotian hero, and in that case he fights as a Homeric hero. This implies a warrior fully trained in all the martial skills and arts.

In the *Iliad*, the bow is despised by the leading Greek heroes, but not by the high command. There are two archer contingents and four renowned archers in the Greek force. First is Philoktetes, the follower of Hercules, who inherited his notorious bow and arrows and leads an archer contingent numbering 350 men in seven fifty-oared ships (II-718/20). Then there is Odysseus, the most prominent, along with Philoktetes (viii-220); he has kept his own – just as renowned – bow, a gift of friendship at least two generations old, at home (xxi-39/41). The weapon shoots extremely straight; so straight that the arrow passes through the holes of twelve axes (xxi-75/7) but its penetrating power is questionable, as Odysseus becomes anxious once his hitherto trapped and unarmed enemies get proper body-shields (xxii-146/8) but no body armour. These two archers have highly celebrated bows, both linking their pedigree to Apollo, the archer-god.

Then there is Teukros, who is the most efficient archer during the events of the *Iliad*. He is adept in fighting in conjunction with his brother Ajax the Great, taking refuge behind his large body-shield before and after shooting his arrows with excellent accuracy by direct aiming (VIII-265/72). Last is Meriones, the Cretan second-in-command, a much acclaimed shielded spearman (XIII-255/8) and competent charioteer (XXIII-351). He only shoots in anger once, at a fleeing opponent (XIII-650); however, he outdoes the most lethal Teukros in an archery contest (XXIII-870/6), shooting with a rather unimportant bow. His own bow is also nothing special and he lends it to Odysseus for his scouting mission, along with a helmet and sword (X-260/1).

The second archer contingent is the Locrians of Ajax the Lesser, explicitly mentioned as carrying no armour and shooting from behind friendly troops (XIII-716/22); this is usually considered to mean behind friendly lines, i.e. indirectly and en masse – in a high arc. But it may mean that each of them is covered behind the large shield of a heavy infantryman, much like in the *parentaxis* pattern of classical times (Kambouris and Bakas 2017) and the pattern showcased by Ajax the Great and Teukros (VIII-265/70). Their leader, though, Ajax the Lesser, is no archer; he is a nimble and accomplished light-armoured spearman (II-529/30), illustrating the importance of light troops (XIV-519/21), their prestige (he is a king), their mode of employment and perhaps their kit: light body armour and perhaps no shield.

The overall picture is that there was an era of great archers who were also the greatest of heroes: Iphitus, who gifted Odysseus his bow (xxi-22/33), and his father Eurytus are mentioned as such; the latter taught archery to Hercules (Apollod II.4,9), who was to murder his son (xxi-22/40), but relevant lore is lost to us. They are protected by two archer-gods, Apollo and Artemis, before these mutate into sun and moon deities respectively. This era was less civilized, definitely rural and the best warriors were not armoured but clad in skins, as were Roman standard-bearers; light, independent, on foot and wielding powerful hand-weapons for close combat. These hero archers had no hesitation or restrains in the use of poison, as evident by the endorsement of the practices by Hercules, who used such commodities (Apollod II.5,2). But this culture of the bow was a thing of the past for the Achaean heroes of the *Iliad*, considered unheroic and uncivilized although tactically useful. Odysseus had failed to procure poison for his arrows from the son of King Mermerus of Ephyra (i-259/63). This Ephyra is not to be confused with Corinth and was located opposite the island of Corfu, on the mainland, and the name of the king coincides with the son of Jason and Medea (Paus II.3,9) – who are supposed to have retired to Corinth (Apollod I.8,28), but since the other name of Corinth is Ephyra, there might have been some confusion and the alternative tradition referring to Jason and Medea retiring to the whereabouts of Corfu be more accurate (Paus II.3,9).

It is possible that the intended use would be hunting, since Odysseus never used his bow for war (xxi-39/41). Trojan nobility, though, persisted with the bow in skill, form, function and mentality, although they also avoided the use of venomous arrows. In the whole of the *Iliad* there is not one mention of a poisoned arrow by any contestant. The rules of engagement in the issue will be relaxed once Paris uses such a missile against Achilles; then Philoktetes will be accepted back into the host and will shoot and wound Paris mortally with a poisoned arrow from the quiver of Hercules.

Paris, on the Trojan side, is adept with armour, shield and spear, but when shooting his bow, he does so while hidden, like a sniper (XI-379). In his first battle appearance, he brandishes bow and spears, leopard skin and sword, similar to Hercules, a character hated and despised in Troy. Thus, a category of warrior, lightly armed for missile warfare with bow and hand weapon (Paris opts for sword, Hercules for club/mace) and clad in skins, is implied. Dolon, a Trojan scout captured by the Greeks, is armed with bow and spear and is dressed in a wolf skin (X-333/6). Paris' brother Helenus shoots while in a melee (XIII-580/96), wears full armour and reverts to sword for close combat (XIII-576/7). But the most prominent archer is Pandarus from Lycia (V-172/3), belonging to a contingent which fights conventionally, and the Paeonian contingent, composed of archers (II-848).

Massed archery to repulse the Achaean landing is attested by the defending Mysians in the abortive Mysian campaign (Phil *Her* 23,14). Densely falling missiles are described in the *Iliad* time and again, but this does not necessarily mean massed, concerted archery – and is not always attributable to archery. Javelins and stones are just as common as missiles, if not more so.

Mention of the bow in the *Iliad* is usually in the plural, possibly meaning bows consisting of two parts. The bow of Pandarus is made of horn (IV-109), which rather implies a bow consisting also of horn parts – though not necessarily, as the American bowyer John Farrell proved with an all-horn-and-tendon bow in 2014. Pandarus' arrow is feathered, iron-tipped and rather short (IV-123) and pierces three plates of armour when wounding Menelaus (IV-133/5). The rear of the shaft is carved (IV-122) to allow better grip, especially for fingers becoming slippery due to blood or sweat or less firm due to exhaustion. It is important to remember that the armour of Menelaus deflects an arrow shot by Helenus from point-blank range (XIII-585) – and Helenus, a royal prince, is not supposed to have an inferior weapon. In the *Iliad*, the bow can be carried slung from the shoulder (X-333), straight or diagonally; it may also be carried in a bow case, like Pandarus', but this is separate from the quiver (IV-105 & 116), in stark contrast to the Scythian *gorytos* which is a later invention.

The *Iliad* recounts many cases where stones have been used as missiles, thrown by hand and not by sling, and that by some of the most prestigious heroes, including Ajax the Great (XIV-408/12), Hector (VIII-320/30) and Aeneas (XX-259/90). This is a recurrent issue in Ancient Greek warfare (Plato, *Laches* 184a; Plut, *Vit Aris* 19,1). Stones cause crushing wounds behind bronze plate armour and break the frame of shields made up of wickerwork and/or curved planking, while they may knock down a warrior by sheer impact (VII-270). Stone-throwing (shot put) thus naturally made it as an event in the sporting contests such as the Olympic Games, where all events were war-related, either as practice for, or as a relic/reminder. In the funeral games of Patroclus, there is a throwing event described with the Greek word *solos* (XXIII-839), which might imply a lump, in this case explicitly mentioned as made of iron. The object is described as 'made of iron sufficient for agricultural needs for five years' (XXIII-826/31). A discus, occasionally identified with '*solos*', cannot be considered to be simply a deposit of iron for prospective uses; thus, this case may refer rather to the shot put of today and to the martial skill of throwing large stones and not discus.

In the Homeric epics, there are some incidents usually considered to refer to the discus: the said Greek term can be found in two of them (I-774; viii-186) *verbatim* and thus there is no question of the accuracy of the identification. In the first instance, it is one of the pastimes of the Myrmidons, along with throwing the javelin and archery (I-774), making the conclusion it is a martial event inescapable. The other case refers to a gaming contest and the description of the object corroborates the identification (viii-186). The discus, invented by Perseus, the focal person in the Argolid-related Greek epic cycle, son of Zeus, and blooded immediately by the – accidental – slaying of his wicked grandfather, Acrisius (Paus II.16,2–3), is never mentioned as a weapon. The form and style of the throw, as well as its shape, made a very potent weapon of it against the heads and shields of a *phalanx* of body-shields, including the more advanced figure-of-eight-shields which were capable of rupturing an enemy shield wall, especially in their bossed version.

The Siege Rhyton unmistakably shows a helmeted slinger in action near an archer (Grguric 2005) and archaeology corroborates this, from very early times, by unearthing stone slingshots (Grguric 2005; D'Amato and Salimbeti 2013). The many representations (and of armoured slingers at that) in Assyrian contexts (Dezső 2012), along with the plentiful supplies of lead sling bolts in late classical Crete (Kelly 2012), corroborate such use, despite the fact that, in the epic, the Greek word for the sling appears only once and should rather be interpreted as a bandage (XIII-599/610).

Casting or Jousting?

The obvious battle technique in the *Iliad* is the casting of missiles, either en masse by the conscript branch of an army or individually by heavily armoured and fleet-of-foot professional fighters (XVII-631/2; V-618/9); tanks of sorts. Mobility (XIII-502/3) was as important as armour (XVII-605/7) for survival. What is in the epics but seldom mentioned is the alternative method, massed chariot charges, with the fighting conducted from the chariot. At Troy, such fighting seems chaotic, with violent charges, but charges nevertheless (XV-258/9), with arms made for chariot-borne fighting and such events accounted for chariotry charges. Such charges were expected to break enemy

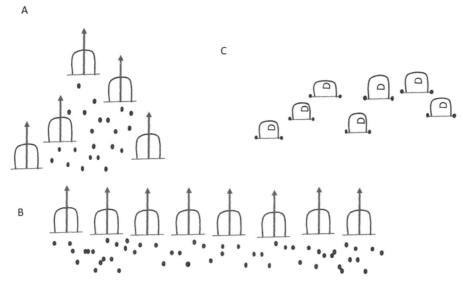

Chariotry employment.
The 'D' symbol denotes archer charioteer, the solid circle the surging, light infantry and the solid arrow the chariot-borne lancer.

The tactical employment advised by Nestor was a well-dressed line of jousting chariots supporting each other as they advance in line (B); infantry is following from behind. This is in stark contrast to the usual charge of chariots in the *Iliad* (A) shooting javelins and thrusting with lances, as they advance intermingled with surging infantry, favouring elan rather than discipline. The Egyptian way was for archer chariots to charge, carrying a couple of chariot runners on the axle, who dismount just before the impact (C).

lines, if disorganized, and disperse enemy concentrations, preferably after the loss of their cohesion. In the latter case, repeated charges (XVII-459/62; XV-615/6) could disperse successively several different enemy groups, allowing for a much easier pursuit by both mobile infantry and chariotry; groups of enemies were always a potential risk, due to the inherent threat of a volley or a massive thrusting effort delivered in a concentrated manner (XIII-146/8); this implies physical shock combat.

Earlier, it seems that chariot-borne fighting was following other rules: there are two experts in tactical disposition in the *Iliad*, both veterans: Menestheus the Athenian, the best tactician in the army (Phil, *Her* 23,19), and Nestor of Pylos. They excel in deploying the different arms of an army and in tactical dispositions (II-551/5), which implies that it was a declining art during the Trojan War. The renowned passage where Nestor gives orders for chariot jousting (IV-306/7) is usually interpreted as a different style of fighting, as he himself underlines it is the Old Ways. It is not the jousting he refers to; it is the disciplined fighting in formation, in an orderly line (IV-301/5), to provide cover for runners in between the chariots and cover predictable sectors with their weapons, so as to create a lethal killing front that may exterminate, not simply conquer, an enemy (IV-308/9). In the days of the *Iliad*, the surging fight was normal (XIII-795), with initiative, opportunism, awareness-reaction and violent aggression. It was an undisciplined, individualistic setup for both chariotry and infantry: a knightly endeavour. Nestor's advice implies that chaotic charges were then the norm for charioteers (XV-269/80); for infantry, descriptions abound (XVI-257/77), and such surging could dislodge enemy infantry or overwhelm and disintegrate chariot masses and their runners, especially if (a) the latter are caught before accelerating to full gallop or while stationary; (b) when mass infantry assault is assisted by a missile barrage, especially by archers; and (c) in difficult, broken or prepared terrain.

In this scenario, once bows were no longer the preferred weapon, chariotry was focused instead on lances. Casting javelins from a speeding chariot could be less accurate and effective than desired, but Diomedes tried it against Hector (VIII-116/22), rather successfully killing the driver and thus neutralizing the whole weapon system for a while. The best case of a lance strike from a speeding chariot is the description of Diomedes spearing the god Ares (V-855/9) so violently that the shaft breaks after penetrating the (not so divine and unconquerable) armour and the body of the god! The lance is the preferred weapon for pursuit by chariot, the means to turn a successful charge into a gory triumph and the weapon par excellence for killing fugitives (XVII-459/65; XIX-71/3). The lance spares expensive missiles, such as arrows or javelins. Allowing different techniques and angles of strike, with a long reach and excessive flexibility, targeting different anatomical spots, and used by both hands, the lance is the most feared weapon of the mounted *eqeta*; the description that 'the lance is frantic in his palms ...' (XVI-74/5) means the delivery of multiple blows in quick succession, most probably by diverse and different techniques.

Once on foot, though, and that would be a reality dictated by both the tactical situation and terrain, the javelin provided much greater reach and was very accurate from a standing posture. Depending upon the thrower, it was not simply the penetration – Achilles being notorious on the subject (XX-98/100). It also packed considerable stopping power; a direct cast by Ajax at the shield, although it failed to penetrate, sent Hector off balance (XIII-191/4), rendering him momentarily vulnerable and shaking his confidence, while missing casts ending in the ground show massive amounts of kinetic energy (XVI-610/5). Diomedes makes a point of the issue that a direct hit is not always fatal; the impact depends on the thrower, meaning his strength (XI-388/92), as much as on the marksmanship.

Combined with the tactical mobility of the chariot, a kind of manoeuvre warfare, in depth, was possible, where a fighter might joust mounted, be transported by his mount to and from spots, where he was to dismount and fight with the spear as a missile and as a close quarters weapon, and secondarily with a sidearm, such as sword of any kind or axe. The chariot must be there, at the ready to pick him up for transportation, either in pursuit or in flight. Failure of the charioteer to be close and ready might be fatal (XI-338/42).

The assault use of the chariot is definitely included: there is a nice passage in the *Iliad* where a Trojan charioteer, Asius, chooses to charge over a smooth chariot corridor to break the defences of the enemy, whose reaction is two dismounted heroes standing in the way and casting their spears, causing havoc to the task group (XII-110/94); but the *equeta does* burst through eventually – to be killed dismounted (XIII-384/8). The sound advice of the Trojan chief of staff, Polydamas, that Trojan *eqeta* should dismount before the Greek ditch and press home their attack on foot, while their drivers stay at the ready to extricate them if need be (XII-76/7), is very reminiscent of medieval warfare, where the decision was with the cavalry which, though, had to charge through and retreat behind an infantry line in repeated attempts. This practice was also followed by heavy skirmishers, as it was with Roman legionaries. The *triarii* spearmen afforded the successive lines of heavy skirmishers a refuge, if repulsed (Connolly 1981). Thus, a hero would gallop and fight mounted with any available weapon, especially in pursuit, dismount to storm a position or surge against an enemy weak point, and remount his waiting chariot nearby (operated like a modern armoured personnel carrier-APC) to give further chase or retreat to rearm or find refuge and draw breath behind a friendly infantry screen.

Fieldworks and Fortification

There are interesting details in the construction of the Greek camp defences that exceed the strategic and operational level – such as the reason this precaution had been taken at that point in time rather than years before, as Achilles succinctly observes (IX-348/50). The fortification expert was Palamedes (Dares 20), disposed of due to jealousy and internal conflicts in the Greek camp, as mentioned earlier. This did nothing to deter the efforts of the Greeks, nor did it compromise their performance. The Homeric tradition links the fortification with the Wrath of Achilles (IX-348), puts it to the tenth year of the war and, most importantly, due to the above-mentioned reasons, dissociates it from Palamedes and assigns its blueprints to Nestor (VII-325/43). According to other traditions, Palamedes considered it a priority to secure the anchorage and camp, and this did indeed take place just after the landing (XIV-30/6). There is one more memory of this, or an indirect corroboration, *within* the Homeric text (XXIV-455): Achilles is said to live in a hut made of fir trunks and a roof made of thatch from the meadows, a rather elaborate structure, surrounded by a courtyard fenced with closely set stakes and a door with a large latch, which required (his) considerable strength to operate. This is an elaborate, semi-permanent fortification, meant from the beginning to protect the most-feared warrior, as it was constructed beforehand, possibly immediately after the landing (XXIV-448/9), as a standard operating procedure, and not in view of the new risk assessment update brought about by battlefield reverses.

The work of the Greek wall and ditch was elaborate (VII-436/41; XII-257/60, 454/6, 397/99) and progressed fast (VII-433/42), which means expedience, know-how and a ready supply of wood. The fortification pattern must have been a circuit resting on the seashore, from where infantry assault would lose momentum and chariotry charges would be unable to negotiate the mud and may get stuck. The circuit might have been an open one, with one side resting on the beach and the other on some inland feature of the Sigium promontory. The exact conformation depends on where the Greek anchorage had been. The two different positions, Beşik Bay and the Gulf of Troy, dictate very different fortification orientations. The former means a circuit resting on the beach at both ends would be an option, perhaps the only one. The Gulf of Troy means that one extremity of the fortification was resting on the beach and the other either on the opposite beach on the other side of the promontory, or to some prominent land feature, such as a glen, some hills, or mountain range.

The Trojan line of advance was parallel to the shore, one wing resting there (X-427) and the other inland (X-430/1), implying a line of advance along the shore of the Gulf of Troy. Had the Greek anchorage been at Beşik Bay, the usual guess of modern scholarship, the Trojans had to move inland. The Trojan advance would have never been able to approach it from the seaward; it would have developed head-on to the line of the drawn ships. Only this arrangement, an open circuit at the Bay of Troy, allows for the two ends of the Greek anchoring order to be one nearer (Ajax) and one further (Achilles) from the Trojan aspect and line of approach. The trek of Priam (XXIV-437/46), Achilles' confidence that his vessels are not in danger from the Trojans (IX-646/51) and the fact that the Myrmidons did not participate in the fortification of the Greek position, all may be interpreted to corroborate such an arrangement and location, usually ignored by scholars who suggest Beşik Bay as the landing zone of the Greeks. Ajax, on the other hand, was on the other side of the coast. Clearly his ships were very close to the fortification wall, as Teukros came and went, in the middle of the battle, in his hut to change weapons. Also very close to him are the ships of Protesilaus, which suffer battle (fire) damage. Additionally, all this probably means that the wall was perpendicular to the line of the landed ships and was breached by the Trojan assault at a position allowing them to access directly the ships of Ajax and the Cretan ones, since it is reported that the ships of Idomeneus and Ajax were in the same direction (X-112/3).

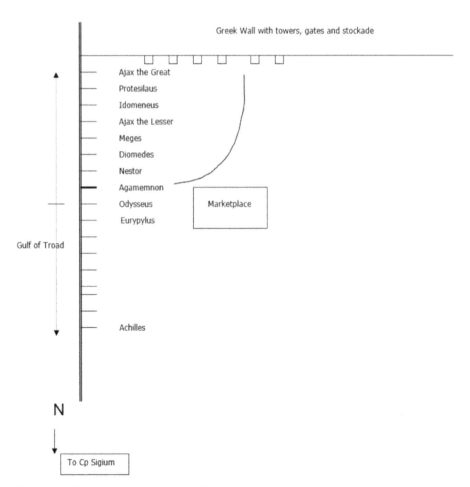

The order of the Greek anchorage and force deployment.

On top of the above-mentioned argument, the proposition of Besik Bay is contradicted by the fact that, when considering a total, strategic withdrawal, Achilles clearly says that his vessels will sail to the Hellespont and, from there, west to Greece (IX-357/63). An anchorage at Beşik Bay does not lead to sailing down the Hellespont; sailing from the beach leads directly to the Aegean. Additionally, the grave to be constructed, according to Hector, by the Greeks for their fallen champion, should he be vanquished in the duel, was to be near the Hellespont (VII-84/7).

Digging a ditch (VII-440) and using the soil from the excavation to erect a rampart is standard wisdom. Erecting a wall/fence on the rampart, reinforced with towers (VII-436), is a step further, affording protection from enemy missiles while friendly missiles would have a clear kill zone and overlapping sectors of fire as implied by the mention of back wounds (XII-427/9); the towers, more explicitly, allow observation, further range due to launching from an altitude and enfilade shooting as they project from the curtain wall. But there are more advanced features, like the width of the ditch and the stakes in its base (VII-441), making surging by infantry a challenge and by chariotry suicidal, along with any need for retreat under pressure (XII-61/74). There were gates in the circuit guarding wide, flattened passages that allowed access for friendly chariotry and massed infantry (VII-438/9), either for ingress or egress. Up to this point, it is nothing wildly different than Roman arrangements (Connolly 1981; Warry 1980), and perhaps later classical Greek, including, but not restricted to Alexander's time (Arr, *Anab* III.9,1).

The most interesting tactical feature is the comfortable space between the ditch and the wall (IX-66/7). This arrangement means two things: a killing zone for missiles, once the enemy bursts through the ditch; meaning, in turn, massed missile fire, including archery, stones and perhaps slings – and, of course, javelins. Additionally, this arrangement allows the defending army to line up between the wall and the ditch, to push back enemy storm troopers attempting to negotiate the ditch – a very tell-tale arrangement, intending to bring into play all of the infantry, irrespective of shield size (XII-426) and especially their pikes, to intercept en masse a literally uphill enemy charge, with the stakes interrupting any notion of formation by the attackers. Thus, the fortification was no precaution, no mere deterrence or psychology and morale booster, providing a sense of confidence and security, but an integral means of a battle strategy and planning, shaping a prospective battlefield if things were to go south.

Medical corps

The Greeks have a well-organized medical Corps, with two Asclepiad brothers (IV-193, XI-833), Machaon (surgeon) and Podaleirios (internist). They tend both the wounded and the sick and are much admired and valued (XI-514), but their humanity is not in question. Nothing divine or miraculous. Other medical doctors are directly but anonymously mentioned, specialists in tending a wound and restoring a lightly wounded warrior to operational status (XIII-212/4). Moreover, many a warrior, such as Achilles, Patroclus, Sthenelus and others are adequately trained in first aids and wound care, extracting arrowheads and dressing the wound (XI-830), while also offering analgesic medication, as was the case of the treatment of Eurypylus by Patroclus (XI-843/5). Having been tutored by Cheiron the Centaur (XI-830/31) seems to equal more than a basic knowledge of wound care medicine, at least at the level of first aids. The alumni have more than know-how; they possess, or know how to make, rudimentary drugs and ointments (XI-827/31) for painkilling, faster wound healing and perhaps for preventing infection.

No such thing was the case with the Trojans. There the gods, within their temples or ad hoc, offer miraculous treatment (XVI-528, V-447/8), implying that the healthcare is in the hands of the priesthood, mostly that of Apollo, the patron deity of doctors par excellence. The best a Trojan noble or retainer can do is to bandage a wound with a woolen band or strip, to stop the bleeding or any major mechanical deterioration; Agenor was well-provided with a number for such an emergency and used it on Helenus (XIII-599/610).

Chapter 10

Unconventional Warfare

Any serious discussion on the historicity of the epics – and there have been precious few attempts – always refers to the everyday presence of the gods in events, drawing the conclusion of a mythoplacy and thus unworthy of further study but for the artistic value. This may be so, but such conclusions are ill-advised. Religiousness and a tendency towards the supernatural are neither indicative of untrustworthy reporting, as the history of the Middle Ages implies, nor exceptional. In particular, fighters and warriors, living at the edge and under the shadow of death, have a greater propensity towards the divine and the occult and take seriously the divine and luck, much more so than civilians. Thus, the dialogues with the gods would be an easy projection of the protagonists, *not* the poet, to express inner dialogues, doubts, fears or determination. What is even more explainable is to attribute everyday fully explainable events to the divine. It is not a goddess that sends a javelin or arrow a bit off target, or makes the cast less determined and powerful; a gush of wind or anxiety or fatigue may do that. But, on the receiving end, that this happened at this particular cast may well be attributed to a guardian angel or god (IV-128/34; XX-438/41). A spear breaking on impact (XIII-160/2) may be of flawed manufacture or due to a previous event that damaged its integrity; no god in there. That it happened in a given instance is easily attributable to the Providence's favour for the warrior who survived (XIII-554/65). And this works well the other way round, if one accidentally loses his footing and gets stabbed in the back, while stumbling (XXIII-780/5).

In this light, regular mention of the gods in the epics makes them no less reliable than the Arabian historians who dwell upon the wrath of Allah for his believers, as the reason for the failures against the early waves of crusaders. It follows that the conduct of war may well build upon such religiousness in at least two divergent and discrete ways: the first is ritualized combat, the battle by convention; a broader version of the trial by combat which became a standard institution in Europe during and after the Middle Ages. Battle by convention may take several forms, but, in the *Iliad*, it is usually a battle between champions – or rather a duel between two champions – and not a clash between groups, as in later times

(Hdt IX.48,4). The other way is to engineer physical results, or the semblance of physical results, of supernatural power, by using methods and technology unknown to the enemy, or to the rank and file, or in an innovative way. This approach rests intentionally upon religiousness for several reasons: first, by assigning a deity as the perpetrator, one discourages the enemy from seeking countermeasures; second, it instills fear and a lack of confidence, in battling against the supernatural; and third, such capabilities were vested in nuclei of accumulated knowledge, that is the priesthood(s), that would impersonate the gods and speak their divine will. It is exactly this latter attribute, that the gods are rather inconsistent in their preferences and allegiances or even their calls, if not outright temperamental, that suggests foul play of human making instead of divine will and gimmicks.

Under the auspices of Zeus: Decision by ritualized duel

In the *Iliad*, a duel between leaders or champions was an acceptable way of deciding a conflict based on a clash of principles with minimal bloodshed, as is always the case in aristocratic/feudal societies. The same happened in the time of Alexander in Persia (Arr, *Anab* III.28,3), later in Greek history and during the European Middle Ages, etc. On the contrary, where the ideology and the identity of the citizen is strong, as in Classical Greece, it was discontinued as a practice, since the fortunes of all cannot rest on one person's skill and fate. One must therefore concentrate on the two formal duels that were intended to decide the issue during the uncertain heavy fighting of the massed battles of the *Iliad*; such duels were in essence wildly different from opportunistic single combat events occurring spontaneously, more or less formally between two rival warriors of similar class and prominence who ran into each other and decided to fight it out with minimal interference. Why did the two opposing armies consent, twice in some days, to decide the issue that way? Could they not have done so in earlier years?

The Greeks had several reasons to accept such proceedings. For whatever reason, they fought in a different way without their best warrior and tactical genius, Achilles. An all-out battle with a default battle plan was not the best, nor the most promising, prospect against a reinforced and renewed enemy who had gained sufficient confidence to try to fight it out after refusing open combat for quite some time. The Greeks might have not known that Troy received allied contingents and was to receive more; but the mere sight of coming out to meet the great Achaean host in open battle was revealing about the improved morale of an enemy who could not have known that the Greeks were missing their top fighter and commander. Therefore, the Greek leadership clearly wanted a settlement by duel, as battle(s) were fought at a double disadvantage: their weakened state against a much reinforced enemy, who was pushed but showed no signs of breaking, and enjoyed a prospect for better luck in any subsequent encounter, even if further reinforcements were not imminent, which could not be assumed, of course. All in all, defeat (or rather strategic failure to achieve the original goal) was now a distinct possibility, unrest at home even more so, and if there was a pretext of victory – a solution to the claims on the sovereignty of Sparta arising from the abduction of Helen of Sparta (who was the holder of the crown by right of blood) and a good compromise on expenses (and the stolen Spartan treasure) could be achieved – the outcome would be acceptable. The campaign had severely weakened Troy so as to make it less of a threat, and the destabilization at home was suddenly becoming an issue with which to reckon. If they withdrew after a formal defeat on the battlefield, or voluntarily without any settlement, the reputation and self-confidence of the Trojans would greatly increase, that of the Greeks would plummet and Trojan power would be restored, if not quickly multiplied, while Greece would become the target of constant aggression from different directions but mostly by Luwians.

For the Trojans, things were different. In the first instance, the size of the Greek host in full array, perhaps seen for the first time fully deployed in battle order, was something of a shock (II-796/800). In the second, the Greeks were winning (VI-73/5), which reveals the main Trojan motive. The Greeks showed that they had not lost their mettle, nor their aggressiveness. A prolonged struggle would bleed Troy of its wealth, and strip it of its power and sway, the retention of which was the very reason for its resolve to resist and endure the siege. If sustaining its allies was to impoverish it any further (XVIII-288/92; XVII-220–8), then the double jeopardy was not worth the risk. Hector did not have much confidence in his 'new' army and had twice seen the battle turning against him in one day, while his deputy Aeneas was seriously wounded. It is no coincidence that, from the moment the Trojans began to wrest the advantage and to threaten the Achaeans, he does not favour similar arrangements, despite no shortage of opportunities. He knows that the penalty for defeat is the obliteration of the city, but he prefers a complete victory, which will ensure for Troy a long-standing deterrence unachievable by convention or compromise (VIII-515/6).

Hector repeated the attempt to secure a formal duel only after he had lost half his army to Achilles and felt his position back in Troy to be in peril (XXII-99/101). He proposed an 'honest duel' to Achilles, something he did not suggest to Patroclus or any other Greek chieftain, whom he considered within his abilities to overcome. This automatically reveals the motive for such a proposal: to gain time anew and/or to drag his opponent 'somewhere' where a warm reception with some archers could be arranged. After all, in one version of the conclusion of the war, this is exactly how Achilles was finally slain, not to mention that ambuscades by archers were a tactical choice the Trojans seemed to favour (XI-370/6). Achilles, being a very vindictive man, remembered that such niceties had not been extended to his slain friend Patroclus or any other Greek chieftain. Additionally, he might have been informed about the previous arrangements with the Trojans and their destructive effects on the Achaean army. He would have nothing to do with such proposals and went for a 'gloves off' duel, without conventions, but – very important – without anyone else interfering (XXII-205/7).

Hector is not against the war. It is clear that he is trying to build the future power of Troy through awe and deterrence (VIII-510/6), based on the success of the repulsion of the Achaeans (or, to be precise, their extermination). He is opposed to the way Paris handled the issue as reckless and indecent. Not to the aggression, but to its implementation, with a small measure of residual success and profit largely balanced by the international outcry for the behaviour of Paris and his followers. Hector never applies any measure of pressure for the return of Helen (VII-362.4); he most probably would not have a problem if Paris had destroyed Sparta and thus left no loose ends. He has a problem because Paris incites the masses, underestimates the noble warriors, and avoids following the code of the heroes, as he skips battle once reprimanded after defeat. But, mostly, for dragging the whole of Greece under Mycenae in his wake, due to the issue of succession he attempted to create, because he actually gave the Peloponnesians some measure of their own medicine; Pelops was the first to teach such matrimonial approaches. Hector considers Paris incompetent militarily and capable only of small-scale naval operations, actually raids. The political personality of Paris in the Hittite archives (if he can be identified with Alaksandu) is very reminiscent of Pericles and Greek myths. If, instead of Homer, Thucydides had recited the events, we would have had a different impression. Both the American and the Italian movies of the *Iliad*, with the possible exception of *Troy* by Petersen, apprehend this point quite clearly, but prefer the easy way of falsifying the narrative instead of reconstructing the facts it alludes to.

Thus, when Hector consents to such an arrangement, he has a clear agenda in his mind; even more so when he does it himself. It is possible that Hector would not really mind Paris being slain, as it is possible that he was second in line to succeed Priam and perhaps not his true brother; many Trojans definitely would not (III-450/4). The Trojans twice chose to propose a duel, because they had little self-confidence, faced reverses on the field and defeat meant annihilation. The Achaeans twice accepted it, despite the bad faith shown the first time, because they were even less confident, and under weak incentives, in continuing the war (II-149/55) and securing with a duel sufficient deterrence to ensure the safety of their empire from Trojan aggression (Hdt VII.20,2) suddenly became an acceptable deal.

If the newly arrived allies could shake the confidence of the Greeks enough for a formal duel to be agreed upon as a battle by convention, it would be a great comparative advantage, as their opponents would forfeit their advantages of numbers and possibly cohesion, tactics and battle experience. If, under the pretext of duel, there was the possibility to deliver an asymmetric, lethal blow, so much the better. Such things were not unheard of: the Thebans won the first war against the Argives precisely by playing their cards well, after the draw in the settlement by duel between the two warring sons of Oedipus.

The first formal duel was fought between Menelaus and Paris. No champions here, as would have happened before, just the two actual antagonists, as it should have been since Day 1. As discussed, the Greeks beforehand had no reason to accept, because they considered total victory within their grasp. Why would the Trojans, with their new-found advantages, risk such a solution? It could have been to pressure Paris, but this was never of any serious consequence, as is obvious from some excerpts (VII-354/64). True, the Trojans would love to get rid of the invasion, and of the expense of supplying their own allies, with a ten-minute ordeal of their foremost culprit. But, what would happen if he lost? The war was not of his making, but was the strategy of the city, or at least of Priam and his council, not the result of a love affair. If Helen and the treasure were returned, Troy would be considered formally beaten.

Hector's attempt to parley or rather bargain with Achilles may shed some light on the Trojan motives – sanctioned by King Priam himself, who took the vows, since Agamemnon insisted on the issue, considering his word alone as binding (III-105/10). It all refers to the episode with Pandarus, which destroyed any goodwill between the opponents, as he sniped at Menelaus (IV-116/40) when he had prevailed in the duel with Paris (III-456/60; IV-13), a most heinous act of sacrilege (IV-157/60). Given that the settlement by duel was conceived favourable for the Trojan leadership only if it emerged victorious, a contingency plan was put in place. If Menelaus was slain, it was a breach of the consent and the oaths, for sure. Agamemnon would stress this and there would be outrage amongst the Greeks. But, on the other hand, the motives of the great majority would be undermined. With Menelaus gone, there was no oath to bind them to pursue the war; the oath was to Menelaus, not to his offspring, friends, brother or relatives. Thus many contingents reluctantly joining would retire to Greece immediately, especially in the light of the greatly reinforced host now defending the city and taking the field, and after the impression left by the quarrel of Agamemnon with Achilles (II-239/42) and after a massive pestilence that depleted their ranks (I-52/6). It could also be the perfect time for a slaughter of the invaders, as happened with the Seven against Thebes.

Parts of this plan were definitely laid by the party of Paris, a prominent member of which, Antimachus, had suggested the lynching of the Greek ambassadors, including Menelaus (probably for the reasons just mentioned) before the initiation of hostilities (XI-138/41). Paris' political prominence and power base depended on the huge successes of the Trojan expansion and the prestige and wealth it brought, which was partially diffused and distributed to the Trojan masses, as was the case with the looting of Sidon (VI-290/2). Hector and the main governing faction were no real opposition; he never speaks a word against the breach of the vows by the sniper and he had politely welcomed Helen, thus embracing the abduction.

If the Trojan War ended in formal – though not utter – defeat for the Trojans, then Paris, as well as his own faction, and possibly Priam, who accepted such policies, would have faced terrible repercussions as the casualties and damage would have been for nothing; no grandeur to ease the loss and pain. In order not to have the Trojans as enemies, they needed external enemies in the face of the Achaeans and in order to survive they needed to defeat them, so as to acquire the halo of the victor(s). The similarities with the Peloponnesian War are obvious (Plut, *Vit Per* 32,3).

Therefore, Pandarus, who shot Menelaus, knew very well what he was doing. The same with his men who covered him. The fact that Athena, the personification of destructive temptation for the Trojans, advised him maliciously by stressing possible honours bestowed upon him by Paris if he did something so disgusting (Thucydides would consider it 'realistic' and 'bold') means that there was talk in Troy that gave him reason to assume as much – if not direct instigation by Paris' faction and operatives. Any charade the previous day, before the major battle, advancing a 'relentless spirit' of resistance to the final victory against the invaders who wanted to dictate to the Trojans how to live, who to annex and whose womenfolk to abduct under the guise of rights in love, would have done half the trick.

With the assassination of Menelaus, if successful, discord and doubt would have been nurtured in the Trojan camp, along with deterrence: in order for the gods not to punish such ungodly people, the Achaeans should have insulted them more, perhaps by simply assaulting the city which was under the patronage of such powerful gods. The occult/psychological dimension of Paris' politics, i.e. the official policy of Troy fully supported by Priam, even with Paris gone, seemed perfectly attuned with a force who knew religion and could handle prejudice, and this reveals, once again, the Trojan priesthood.

And here lies the Trojan motive for the second duel by convention, between Hector and any Greek champion (Achilles had been perceived absent by the Trojans by then), which ended with Ajax the Great being his antagonist (VII-211/5). Gaining time to deploy some wildcard, something that lies in the realm of special and secret warfare under the mantle of the religion and the supernatural.

In this case, the Greeks were clearly winning, after the flight of Paris from Menelaus in the duel, and Trojan morale collapsed. The Trojans urgently need any divine help they can get, because they are on the verge of total defeat. Hector, at the bidding of Helenus, his brother who was a seer, falls back into the city to require his mother, the queen, to appease the goddess Athena by some symbolic and valuable gift from the womenfolk of the city (VI-86/91), plus lavish sacrifice. Clearly the priesthood of Athena had to be placated, due to the previous attitude of the city towards the deity and its ministers. The high priestess was the wife of the leader of the anti-war faction (VI-298/300 & VII-345/54), while the city was religiously taken under the protection of Aphrodite, the patroness goddess of Paris and mother to Aeneas (XX-209), and of Apollo (XVI-92/4; XVI-698/704), and placating the most estranged Athena seemed important. As the hatred of the goddess, which is described in the epic as deep and virulent (IV-20/3), could not be satisfied easily, it becomes obvious that the know-how of this priestly faction somehow became relevant, but time was needed for the preparations. Time a formal duel could provide no matter the outcome.

Hector greets his wife and son, as he knows that gaining time requires personal risk this time; no more proxies. He will issue a challenge (VII-73/91). If the Greeks, cocky as always (VII-93), take the bait, the fighting pauses. Then, it is the duel, and no matter what the outcome, the truce, for the winning side to celebrate and for the defeated one to mourn and perform funeral rites. Since the duel actually ended in a draw (VII-287/91), the ceasefire proposal (VII-365/74) secured some of the extra time, and then more for the cremation of the dead (VII-375/7). The Achaeans use this time to build fortifications (VII-435/42), as they had met with a nasty battlefield surprise; the Trojans, having actually seen their hopes of battlefield supremacy dashed (VII-401/2), use it for the acquisition and deployment of divine weapons, a process reminiscent of the Battle of Blackwater River in *The Game of Thrones*.

The realm of Metis: Special and Secret Warfare

The night raiding/commando operations are an integral part of Homeric warfare, as are ambushes in general. It is remarkable that the basic units (*company*-level) in all Greek armies to the present day are called *lochos*, the Homeric term for ambush; obviously the standard unit needed for such actions is implied, and this operation is highly prestigious, more so than open combat (XIII-177/87). The Homeric term *euzon* is used for light troops (IX-586), literally meaning 'fairly belted/banded'. This link conceivably stems from the use of waist-bands or protective textile/leather overlays over their kilts/*chiton* (Grguric 2005; D'Amato and Salimbeti 2017) as sole body protection, obviously decorated to regimental/unit patterns, although the interpretation of 'slim-waisted', alluding to body physique, may be a valid option. The term was used for the infantry attire of the irregulars/militia of the Greek revolution and for the elite battalions/light infantry of the modern Greek army until 1941, equivalent but not similar to the European grenadiers.

Night reconnaissance and strike are attested for both enemies but the Greeks seemed better attuned to such operations (X-305/12 & 204/26). The archaeological evidence corroborates the high importance of such methods of warfare in the Mycenaean world, with the preponderance of light infantry evident in warrior graves but, more importantly, in representational evidence on frescoes, gemstones, daggers and other artefacts (Grguric 2005; D'Amato and Salimbeti 2013). In such cases, one has to concentrate on the pairing of helmet and blade. Greaves are attested in the fresco of Pylos, but the gemstones of the Battle of the Glen Ring show nothing of the kind. A shield is out of the question, so too a cuirass. Some waist protection, as a fabric or leather overlay in the Fresco of Pylos or a – metal – waist band (XXI-90/1 & XX-414/5) would be quite appropriate for the ones that could afford it. The illustrations do not exclude a shafted weapon; but in the *Iliad* it is directly attested, in order to give some reach, obviously, and it may be supplemented or exchanged for a bow (X-333/5 and X-260 respectively). This light kit could well apply in day ambushes. The mention of ambush in the *Iliad* (XIII-276/86) never suggests night or day, nor anything concerning the equipment used; although it *may* be implied that wearing one's armour does not apply to ambuscades (I-226/7). Metal armour would be gleaming by day and noisy by day and night and, thus, counterproductive. So, non-metallic items would be preferred instead, where applicable; the special operators in the *Iliad* use non-metallic helmets by preference (X-261/6 & X-257/9). The similarities between the kit of the night raiders in the *Iliad* and that of the Fresco of

Pylos are many and very important and suggest that they refer to the same warrior type.

Besides raiding, which is a straightforward mobile warfare setting that may just marginally be considered as 'special', there are four distinct cases of unconventional/secret warfare from both state and non-state actors in the lore of the Trojan War: the use of explosives by the Trojans, the use of biological/biochemical agents by different branches of the priesthood against the Greeks, the ingenious use by the Trojans of both a doppelgänger service to protect leadership targets and of reduced visibility conditions to mask an attack and cause chaos and disruption to an enemy dependent on command and control by its chain of command and, last but not least, the flooding of the plain by the Trojans by the use of river water to literally drown a most successful enemy offensive, along with remnants of their own side, of course.

Spit – or cast – fire

The use of fire to burn enemy vessels (XVI-122/4; XV-731 & 716/8) is not something special and thus is not included in the list. The prompt kindling of fire to light prepared incendiary torches (burning high for relatively short time, as opposed to lighting ones, burning slow, low and bright) for the moment the enemy ships would be reached upon is also rather simple. Raisin torches are a safe bet on the subject, as was later practice (Partington 1998). Still, one has to remember the abject failure of the Athenians to do so at Marathon after their astounding battlefield success (Hdt VI.113/5), which led to the capture of only seven vessels out of some 600 at the very least. The Trojans, with a much lower degree of attained battlefield superiority (XV-415/20; XV-704/16) posed a far greater threat to the survival of the Greek expeditionary force, precisely because of their ability to deploy incendiary equipment (highly combustible torches) and make them available to troops in contact (XV-743/6), albeit not in great numbers, nor in any form to be cast/thrown from a distance (shafted missiles, sling bolts or even torches resilient enough to be thrown by hand). The truth is, though, that there is not one description suggesting what this equipment really was; the Homeric word is always 'fire', without any indication as to its nature and the proposal that highly combustible, special-purpose torches were used is an assumption based on a single reference to torches (XV-421). The only fact is that to burn an enemy vessel, close contact was needed, since a defender with a shafted weapon had to be neutralized, instead of casting torches from a distance out of spear-range (XV-415/20). Thus, devices or packaged incendiary mixtures like those suggested in *circa* 360 BC by Aeneas Tacticus, non-extinguishable by water (Partington 1998), is a possibility, but not very probable; the Greeks had no problem in extinguishing the fire once the Trojan infantry retired (XVI-293/4).

Stealth in daylight

Daylight operations in poor visibility cause chaos and are a distinct advantage for a force with knowledge of the terrain that fights in looser order, with higher initiative and personal motivation. The Mycenaean fascination with light infantry would suggest decent abilities in such conditions, but such loose order requires good situational and tactical awareness, to the point where a side deprived of these faces annihilation; better-ordered and close-ordered settings that allow mutual support and collective defence are rather more resilient. Attacking through the fog, dust and mist, or with the wind behind would be easy for a native host (XII-253/5), and such fighting in low visibility – especially at the spot where decision was likely to occur (XVII-370/7) – repeatedly proved detrimental for the Greeks (XII-255;XVII-634/50), neutralizing their numerical advantage (XIII-738/40) for as long as such conditions lasted (XV-668/70; Paus II.24,2). It could have been spontaneous, on the plains of windy Ilios (XII-115), but man-made devices cannot be ruled out, such as raising dust with fast, horse-drawn bunches of green branches, or with smoke generation by kindling and feeding fires with highly moist, combustible material or the like, to produce abundant smoke; the latter could be combined with incendiary equipment for burning enemy vessels.

Deception supreme

A special category of divine interventions refers to identity deception. In several cases, the patron god of the Trojans, Apollo, disorients the Achaeans either by impersonating a Trojan warrior (XXI-566/70) or by constructing an effigy, according to Homeric accounts (V-449/53). The goal is to relieve key personnel from hot pursuit (XXI-563/4) or lure away enemy elements (XXI-569), but the former case is not at all mysterious or miraculous; locals can extricate themselves, occasionally disappearing from the sight of their pursuers by using terrain features (XXII-7/9). In other cases, with major Trojan heroes making miraculous comebacks after being severely wounded with debilitating, crushing wounds (Aeneas: V-446/7 and V-512/5; Hector: XV-286/90), another mechanism is implied. The medical abilities of priestly medicine are not factually miraculous to ensure extra-fast turnovers, comebacks and healing, despite drugs and painkillers. But the existence of a number of lookalikes operating as stuntmen, possibly individuals of physical similarity if not true doppelgängers complete with identical armour suits, could well account for these events. It is a practice that will find its best expression in the Japanese Middle Ages, with the Kagemusha lookalikes, as is shown in the homonymous epic film of Akira Kurosawa (1980), while Pyrrhus used a similar trick against the Romans (Plut, *Vit Pyrr* 17,2) and there is also a precedent in the Bible with Ahab (I Kings 22,30). Trojan familiarization with the practice is evident in their seeing through the disguise of Patroclus as Achilles after brief observation of his behaviour in battle (XVI-721/5), the giveaway possibly being Patroclus' choice of spears instead of the signature jousting lance of Peleus (XVI-139/44) or his less impressive stature and physique.

Explosive supremacy

However, what is one to make of the pinpoint accuracy with which Diomedes is assaulted by lightning bolts – which defy natural laws and, when they strike, produce flame, a blast effect and they smell of sulphur (XIV-413/6; VIII-133/6) instead of ozone? It was a turning point in the battle, and although Diomedes survived, he retired, thus breaking the morale of the Greek army and exposing it to further attacks. The storyline is reported later; briefly, after a distinct but not decisive Greek advantage, the formal challenge of Hector results in a draw in his duel with Ajax the Great and a ceasefire to allow funeral rites to the dead of both camps.

As battle is joined anew in some days, and after some fighting, thunderbolts incoming from Mount Ida land within the Achaean army, forcing it to retreat in disarray (VIII-75/8). The excellent timing of the attack, in the middle of a long battle, for maximum psychological effect on both sides (VIII-66/77), must be noted. A first-class hero, King Diomedes of Argos, tries to stem the tide and counter-attack (VIII-109/31). At this point, a lightning bolt narrowly missed Diomedes, but spooked his chariot-team and made him retreat in confusion (VIII-132/58). The detailed description of the event, with flame, a smell of sulphur and smoke, as the shot hit the ground, is revealing! Three more thunderbolts come in, again from the direction of Mount Ida (VIII-170). There are two more instances in the *Iliad* where powder-like explosives are implied, although with different descriptions. One is against Patroclus (XVI-790/806). It is not at all out of the question for Hector to stand up to Achilles in order to expose him to another such attack. The other case is the sudden removal of an obstacle (XV-353/67) in the Greek fortification which opened a broad path for the Trojans to deliver a chariot attack against the Greek camp and anchorage. The detailed description is easily understood and interpreted by any field officer/sapper of the Engineer Corps. In both these cases, blast effects with minimal flame are reported, in the latter case possibly buried under earth for maximum removal, while with Diomedes it was a surface blast with visual footprint, odour and blast effect, thus implying a surface, possibly hand-tossed weapon.

Basic technology for such amenities is neither exotic nor beyond the reach of the sages of the day. The use of sulphur for cleansing is attested as standard (xxii-493/5; XVI-228), its combination with charcoal provides two-thirds of the formula for gunpowder and the need for incineration both for burials and for sacrifices would mean that priests had centuries of experience of this; Fire Magic was within the playbooks of many priesthoods in the Middle East and the scientific level and horizon of the Chinese when inventing gunpowder is by no means higher. With the known ingredients of the period, can one be so bold as to assume the use of gunpowder, which is easy to make and smells of sulphur, while producing the noise of the thunder? Similar weapons had been used in the past in Thebes, just one generation previously, against Kapaneus, Sthenelus' father (II-564), thus claiming victory for the besieged (Soph, *Ant* 129/35). They would be used in the future by the Greek priesthood, possibly against the Persians in 480 BC (Hdt VIII.37,3), and almost definitely against the Gauls in 279 BC (Paus X.23,2), while their use in a biblical context has been suggested before, and persuasively at that, in the case of Jericho (Kalopoulos 1998).

The other such blatant case of battlefield use was against Patroclus, and twice at that; he was first pushed back while charging the outer circuit; something unseen, and of divine origin, pushing against his shield (XVI-702/4). This is reminiscent of a blast effect from a near miss of an explosive weapon. It did not achieve a direct hit so as to burn the target as well, as happened with Kapaneus in Thebes (Soph, *Ant* 129/35). Ultimately, Patroclus was disarmed by Apollo's strike on his back and the description is reminiscent of a blast (XVI-790/806). As a result, his spear is broken, his shield and armour blown away and he emerges stunned and disorientated (XVI-805/6); much like the victims of seventeenth-century grenadiers.

The description of Patroclus' undoing implies a similar weapon to that used against Diomedes; there is better aim (Patroclus is on foot, not on a speeding chariot) and no flash (XVI-791/4), which could be a glitch in the account. Moreover, a dense, dark entity whence the strike came is directly implied (XVI-790), possibly dust from a gust of wind, but more probably smoke from the blast of an explosion. Especially of something leaving residues after combustion, as with gunpowder. The blast stuns him, like a concussion grenade, and strips him of his armour, since the blast wave blew away the metal parts of the panoply – a panoply probably too large for him, as Achilles had abnormal physique, which is not how Patroclus is described and this might well have – partially – given the ruse away. Perhaps it was one lucky shot after a number of failed ones; there is no other way to interpret the immense pressure/thrust exercised by a god in order to intercept a charging, fully armoured hero as he tries to breach the enemy fortifications (XVI-703/4). Bolts exploding nearby push him back with their blast, an excellent account for defences/walls/cities guarded by gods.

The lightning bolt that destroyed and sank – with all hands – the ship of the ungodly Ajax the Lesser after the fall of Troy could have been a similar, timed and primed, contraption – a bomb, mine or other IED of sorts, made and planted by the same priesthood; in the *Iliad*, Athena detested the man (XXIII-774/83).

If the evidence is taken and pieced together, one sees a string of events: the ceasefire asked for by Priam secures time, but also access to Mount Ida for the Trojans; an access the Greeks were in a position to harass, if not to block altogether (XXIV-661/3), as it was on the other side of the Trojan plain to the city. Ida is the epicentre for thunderous events (VIII-75/7). This follows the appeasement of the priests of Athena (the goddess of inventions) in Troy, proposed by Hector's brother, the seer Helenus, with direct reference to Diomedes – perhaps naming him as a priority target (VI-86/101). The said priesthood might have acquired or developed, or otherwise been endowed, with the technology of explosives and its secrets might have been kept in the Palladium (perhaps the formula), an artefact that ensured the survival of Troy, even though it was a totem of Athena, the goddess most hostile to the city. Small statuettes used for concealment are attested in other cultures at the time, oriental cultures at that (Kalopoulos 1998), suggesting such a use by the like-minded Trojans.

If one looks at Greek art, the appearance of a thunderbolt of Zeus in a fifth-century BC artefact from Dodona, is nothing like the normal shape of lighting as depicted today. Since some natural phenomena have not changed in the last 3,000 years, the bolt represented is symmetrical and could be interpreted as either a tube with a missile in it, similar to modern rocket launchers or recoilless rifles; or, a hand-thrown bolt intended to make contact with three prongs, either to stick or to explode – a grenade of sorts, perhaps reminiscent of similar devices of an incendiary nature described by Aeneas Tacticus and containing sulphur (Partington 1998). Later, Hellenistic art suggests flamethrowers, as in the case of the torch of Phoebe in the Gigantomachy on the altar of Pergamon, where a tube spitting flames is clearly visible.

The role of Athena in this issue has to be stressed (Kalopoulos 2014). The use of explosives is implied time and again, in direct or indirect applications (as a weapon or engineering tool), but although such uses are attested twice in interventions by Apollo – against Patroclus and to demolish the Greek fortifications – the connection with the thunderbolt is reserved only when Zeus himself intervenes, as against the army of the Greeks and against Diomedes in person. For Apollo, it is explained away differently, although the results as described in detail tell a different tale.

Still, the keepers of the secret, at least in Troy, seems to have been the priesthood of Athena, as already mentioned, a fact corroborated by standard Greek lore (although the independence of such corroboration is not a given). Athena is credited later with being the keeper of the secret – and magazine – of the bolts of Zeus (Aesch, *Eumen* 827), uses them herself on occasion, in order to destroy the ship of Ajax the Lesser (Apollod E.6,6) and she is presented in art (i.e. on coins struck by the Macedonian King Antigonus of the second century BC) brandishing them, in full panoply. Thus, despite the manufacture of said bolts being securely credited to Hyphaestus, the priesthood of this goddess is implicated in the use of something akin to the thunderbolt and not only in Troy; it is a widely accepted endeavour and prerogative of the goddess for something like a millennium.

Given that Athena is a bitter enemy of the city of Troy, the use of 'her' technology time and again is difficult to explain in a myth, where the patron god of Troy is Apollo, a divinity having nothing to do with the issue of thunderbolts, thus resulting in inconsistencies in the storytelling. Later, such details seem to be of less importance; in Delphi, where the shrine of Apollo was located, two different invaders in 200 years, both prone to loot and ravage, are intercepted by lightning bolts, as mentioned above. First, in 480 BC, a detail from the host of Xerxes specifically dispatched to plunder the shrine (Hdt VIII.35,2), and then in 279 BC a massive raiding army of Gauls under Brennus (Paus X.23,2), also attracted by the fame of the accumulated wealth (Paus X.19,8). It should be remembered, though, that in the first case the interception of the marauders is explicitly associated with the local temple of Athena (Hdt VIII.37,3), located a small distance from the main complex that was dedicated to Apollo; the location of the temple of Athena is highly reminiscent of an outpost relevant to the core facilities of the shrine, if one visits the area. An outpost strategically located to guard the approach, and armed with divine weapons – lightning bolts – to deny access to it.

Drowning an attacker
The epic fight between Achilles and the river Scamander (XXI-234/327) is a very strong poetic text, full of emotion, and reads like pure fiction and

drama, not even metaphor. Still, there might be something more, a notion of factuality. The proceedings read strikingly similar to other, similarly obscure, or slightly less so, cases where floods favour one side. The biblical record of the Egyptian host drowning in the Red Sea (Kalopoulos 1998; Exodus 14,23/31), the much less known case of ditches employed by Hercules against the pursuing Thracians after stealing the man-eating mares of King Diomedes of Thrace (Richepin 1953) and, much later, in the sixteenth century AD by the Dutch against invaders, as in the siege of Leiden (Motley 1855; Henty 2002). The latter were using dams and it is conceivable that the Trojans could have done something similar on the slopes of Mount Ida, because the level of technology was by no means extraordinary; one generation ago, Hercules was a top engineer of such projects, including land improvement and irrigation applications, as explicitly mentioned by the feat with the stables of King Augeas of Elis, where he diverted the bed of two rivers to clean the said stables (Richepin 1953). It is very difficult to interpret the details of this incident of the *Iliad*, if one does not extend beyond Homer to other sources, both literary and material, that report extensive hydraulic projects in the Trojan plain, beyond simple irrigation and perhaps drainage, and in the city itself (Zangger 2016); works that could well allow individual infiltrations in the city, as the tradition reports, for stealing the Palladium artefact. These works would most probably have a security valve for critical conditions, to flood the area; or it may have been an emergency, desperate measure.

More troubling is the possible interpretation (other than the obvious poetic licence to use the antithesis) of massive incinerations as the only applicable measure to contain the threatening flood, by instantly evaporating large masses of water. The incineration by non-extinguishable agents (Kalopoulos 1998; Mayor 2003; *Partington 1998*) of material used ad hoc by the Trojans to dam and divert the flow of rivers and channels may be inferred, but this is highly speculative. Although in Homer incendiary technology is only implied, as mentioned earlier, by the 430s BC a massive, siege-grade conflagration by tar and sulphur had been tried at the siege of Plataea by the Peloponnesians (Thuc II.77,2); by 424 BC the Thebans had a massive, siege-grade flamethrower mounted on a wheeled platform (Partington 1998). By the time of the Hellenistic Kingdoms the technology had made quantum leaps (Partington 1998), as evident by the details in a supposed torch (which is more like a portable flamethrower) at the hands of titaness Phoebe, as shown in the gigantomachy presented at the altar of Pergamon built during the second century BC – or such knowledge was transferred to public/scientific knowledge from the 'black world' of divine arsenals.

Still, one has to presume Trojan forces cut off by the Greek offensive on the flooded part of the plain as KIA (Killed In Action); the poetic report that the river god was hiding and protecting them from pursuit by their enemy (XXI-238/9) does not mean they survived the flood. Technically, they were spared from the violent death by the Argive blade, but, especially as many were allies coming from far away, with the Paeonians being a prime example (XXI-154/9), they were expendable and not privy to possible safe zones. The natives, on the other hand may have identified such zones, such as dykes, for example, and thus actually survived, as reported in the epic (XXI-238/9).

Biowarfare

In Homeric theology, Apollo is the god of sudden death (I-39), of divination (I-69/72) and of medicine (V-400), not of the sun. This is easily interpreted as a priesthood excelling in medicinal and public health arts. By the same token, the former quality may be traced to the use of poisonous or germ agents deployed in original or conventional ways to cause targeted or massive killings. Chemical poisons were known and biotoxins as well, since poisoned arrows were a known commodity (i-259/62). Microbial theory was not known, but this by no means precludes the empirical knowledge of infectious agents, mostly but not exclusively by using parts and products of infected/diseased animals (Mayor 2003); the generation zero of bioagents (Kambouris 2021). The latter is the usual choice for causing massive health casualties due to the self-replication of the microbes, which amplifies their virulent activity.

The disease that decimated the Greeks (I-51/6) at the beginning of the *Iliad* is of course attributed to Apollo (I-10), but the issue is whether a human agent had been involved. The coincidence of the outbreak with the disrespectful arrogance of Agamemnon to a minister of Apollo (I-26/32), to the point of sacrilege, might have caused other powers (that be) to act: these powers were not Trojan, as they would not have stopped once satisfaction had been exacted; they would persist to end the war. It is much more probable that ministers within the Greek camp decided to put the fear of god into their own leadership, which was openly critical to the verdicts of sages and oracles, like the seer Kalchas (I-102/8); seers after all, were by definition under the protection of Apollo in his guise as the patron god of divination, with the oracle of Delphi (in Homer, *Python*, II-519, from the same root as the name of the oracle, *Pythia*). Poisoning by hand would be much easier in this context and there is an interesting remark that the dogs were early casualties (I-50). One could seek similarities with the plague upon the firstborn in Egypt (Kalopoulos 1998). One should consider that an epidemic, caused by live agents, is very difficult to contain so as not to be blown out of proportion, nor is it easy to abort according to the perpetrators' whims, i.e. once the insult has been exonerated and the deity placated (I-457). Such a succession of events implies, rather, a steady spiking of supplies, preferably by a poison or by a non-transmittable pathogen as in *Bacillus anthracis*. Corn, wine or water would be the obvious objects of spiking, with the latter being the easiest and the one accounting for the early loss of domestic animals/dogs (I-50). The said diviner might have perceived the arrogant behaviour of Agamemnon as detrimental to the international law of the day, or for his standing, or both. It is perhaps a good reason for the Greek gullibility later in formal proposals for ceasefires and conventions by the Trojans, as mentioned earlier.

Part III

The Epic Campaign

Chapter 11

The Nature of the Affront

The crown of Sparta belonged to the family of King Tyndareus. He was a crown prince, though not heir apparent. He was in line to succeed after Hercules high-handedly cleared the line of succession, bloodily and promptly (Apollod II.7,3). Tyndareus was duty-bound to Mycenae because of this and gained the gratitude of the two Atreids by assisting them in their dynastic rivalry with Thyestes (Apollod E.2,15). He married a princess from abroad, Leda, daughter of Thestius of Pleuron (Paus III.13,8) and sister to Althaea (Apollod I.7,10), who was married to Oeneus of Aetolia and gave birth to Meleagrus (Apollod I.8,2). How exactly the crown of his kingdom then passed to his daughter Helen, and through her to Menelaus and not to his male descendants, the Dioscuri, is a true mystery that has never troubled the historians; unless the said male offspring had died *before* the betrothal of Helen. However such a sequence of events is not supported by any account.

Thus Paris abducted not the queen, but the heir of the throne of Sparta. By wedding lawfully, under Trojan laws and the auspices of the sovereign of Troy, the abducted queen, Paris and the Trojans directly denied (or cast into doubt and questioned) the legal status of her wedding with Menelaus; a lawfully wedded woman could not be wedded again if her husband was alive – or if he had not divorced her, as Odysseus did with Penelope according to some lore (Paus VIII.12,6).

As a consequence, Paris could claim the throne of Sparta; if not for himself, then for his offspring with Helen, who only had a daughter (Hermione) by Menelaus. It must be noted that later tradition has it that Menelaus was considered a foreigner in Sparta, when it came to the succession (Paus II.18,6); this hardly implies a good opinion of the populace for their sovereign. Had this been the case, the loss of Helen to Troy could invalidate his rule over Sparta. If Menelaus was not appreciated and loved by the Spartans, an issue over which Homer's *Iliad* is suspiciously silent, they would have no problem in accepting a sovereign residing far, far away, paying him due dividends, and be left alone rather than suffer the hot breath of the Atreids – and of Argos – on their necks.

The two novels of Parotti (*The Greek Generals Talk, The Trojan Generals Talk*) present an excellent grasp of the ideology of the Greek invasion. It was a D-day. The Greeks did not go in for looting, because for many years the war was, in financial terms, a huge liability, disrupting production, transportation and commerce. In the end there were not many spoils to be shared among the victorious Achaeans, as many a Trojan reports with broken heart in various dialogues in the epic (XVIII-288/92). But even when it became obvious that Troy was exhausted (IX-401/3) and loot became uncertain, the Achaeans did not leave for more lucrative enterprises.

Re-opening the shipping lanes through the Hellespont was not the main issue, either; if it was, they would have installed a fortress. Nor was it an issue of natural resources, because in that case they would have colonized the region massively. The Greek persistence, combined with low profitability, the terrible deterioration of any aspect of sustainability, the endangerment of the rear and the fact that, after their departure, they allowed both the escape of many Trojans for relocation under Aeneas and the resettlement *in situ* of a selected sub-population under Antenor (Dikt V.17; Dares 44), indicate that the aim of the campaign was basically to destroy the Trojan power. The latter had reached a peak in terms of aggression when the royal house projected sea power with enough temerity to endanger the vital dynastic interests of Mycenae and began to creep much further south than might have been expected (VI-290/2). Helen's abduction was, for the most part, a valid cause.

Contrary to some scholars, who understandably see pastoralism as the main economic and social activity, it was neither the only one, nor the main. The names and, most importantly, terminology that implies familiarity with livestock is not a good indicator. True, the princes are herding their own flocks, herds and stocks, as did Aeneas when pursued by Achilles (XX-188/9); but they also have cattle-, swine-, goat- and shepherds, as did Odysseus, some of them slaves, other dependants in the truest sense (xvii-247; xvi-156; xx-235).

In the Far West, steers and cattle were the prime business before oil and the Gold Fever; this does not mean they had no telegraph, medicine, gun powder, steam power, or electricity after a point in time, and dollars for their transactions. The great landowners were working with their cowboys, not studying management. This is the correct way to view the Homeric society. Food production is of paramount importance and, in pre-industrial societies, livestock was also instrumental for transportation, energy and other amenities; thus the use of such words, figures of speech and names was warranted: even today, the name Georgia, meaning husbandry, is in use;

the same with Georgios/George (farmer). Thus, it is not a simple pastoralist setting (Pantazis 2006). It is an almost industrial-scale society, with massive livestock exploitations to support the population of the urban centres, a profitable industry, vital for the state. True, the use of currency seems not to have been discovered. But pricing items by the standard value of a steer, means a currency unit. Not necessarily an abstract one; this requires some abstract thought unattainable by the level of sophistication of these societies. It may refer to an *actual* currency, real money, similar with our talking in Lincolns etc instead of the $5 bill upon which he is depicted.

And there was proper, mass industry. To a level much plainer than that of the seventeenth century, but quite structured. Women were not captured for breeding and sexual purposes; they were pressed into service en masse, especially for the weaving industry (IX-128/30), but also for housekeeping and other urban and rural services (VI-456/8).

Chapter 12

The Mycenaean Reaction

A) The muster(s) and the foreplay

The launch of the Achaean campaign is inextricably linked to the events of Aulis, a muster with some interesting public aspect and a much enlightening hidden dimension, despite the seeming controversy. Whether the ten-year campaign as foretold by the seer Calchas referred to the duration of the war or to the time spent before the walls of Troy is unclear. Homer (XII-13/5) suggests instead that the episode took place at the gathering at Aulis and was referring to the true duration of the main campaign, from muster to return; this muster was effected ten years after the abduction of Helen (Apollod E.3,18) and eight years after the auspices taken in Aulis and the invasion of Mysia (Apollod E.3,15).

In any case, the first campaign hit the beach at Mysia, indifferent whether on purpose (Phil, *Her* 23,5) or by navigational error (Dikt II.1; Apollod E.3,17). The locals presented stiff resistance under their sovereign Telephus, son of Hercules (Apollod E.3,17), adopted by the previous, native, King Teuthras (Dikt II.3; Hyg, *Fab* 100–1), a name highly reminiscent of the other national name of the Trojans, Teucrians. It was the exact pattern of acquisition of soon-to-be vacant thrones, as with Theseus, Peleus, Telamon etc. Greek lore has a series of misunderstandings prompting Telephus to defend his shores in strength and actually beating the attackers, up to the moment Achilles wounded him and the battle paused.

Homer does not describe the battle – he is not engaged with the Trojan War *sensu lato* as a whole (Phil Her 24,2). Later sources assign some interesting episodes, although they do not agree with each other, such as, *inter alia*, the accounts of Diktys Cretensis and Philostratus. For example, the latter reports that the Mysians had amassed quite a host, with many allies from afar, allegedly from the valley of Ister in Europe (Phil, *Her* 23,12–13) as it would have been impossible to face the massive Achaean army otherwise. The vanguard of the Mysians was shooting arrows at the first wave, the Arcadians, who by enthusiasm and lack of skill assaulted first and clumsily (Phil, *Her* 23,14); Achilles and Protesilaus assaulted second and together, routing the opposition and establishing a bridgehead (Phil, *Her* 23,16). With the Achaean disembarkation completed and their host deployed into battle order, the Mysian and Allied host came up. The Mysians proper under King Telephus were posted against Achilles and Protesilaus (Phil, *Her* 23,20), which means the two Thessalians were routinely operating together, and this explains the events in the beach of Troy; they were sailing together and fighting together. This is not corroborating Homer who reports the vessels of Protesilaus on the beach of Troy, near those of Ajax (XIII-681/2) and thus far from the ones of Achilles (VIII-224/5).

Near the Mysian charioteers and infantry were their womenfolk, armed as mounted cavalry (Phil, *Her* 23,26); against these, the Achaeans deployed their more feeble and younger, inexperienced warriors (Phil, *Her* 23,27). Another part of the Achaean army was under the Argives, Diomedes and Sthenelus and Palamedes (Phil, *Her* 23,20). This nicely fills the gap in the Homeric report on the Greek contingents which does not mention Palamedes, nor his national levy and city. It also implies that Diomedes was a warrior with seniority similar to that of Achilles. And there was another part of the Achaean army, implying a three-part division of the front (although which was the centre and which the wings cannot be determined). This third part was under the two Atreids and Ajax the Lesser (Phil, *Her* 23,20); but the report makes obvious that Ajax the Great was also there, as he single-handedly slayed the two commanders of the European allies of the Mysians (Phil, *Her* 23,22), who fought from a four-horse chariot, as did Hector – a remark made by Philostratus (*Her* 23,22). Palamedes and Diomedes working well together, dispatched the commander posted against them, Haimus (Phil *Her* 23,23), and Achilles performed similarly with Protesilaus; Protesilaus unshielded Telephus and Achilles speared him at the thigh (Phil, *Her* 23,24); the wounded king escaped, thanks to the self-sacrifice of his guards and retainers, but the Mysians paid a hefty price in blood (Phil, *Her* 23,24). The only commander of the Mysians that survived was Telephus; his wife Hiera, commanding the mounted women, was slain by the Greek Nereus (Phil, *Her* 23,26) and the other three allied commanders were slain by Diomedes and Ajax the Great as mentioned above.

Next day an armistice was declared and the 'misunderstanding' resolved, thanks to the intervention of the Heraclids present in the Greek army (II-655/8 & 677/9; Dikt II.5).

Being to the south of Troy, the Greeks recoiled back to the mainland, as the time of the year was inopportune for sailing north (Dikt II.7). This is the official story and oared galleys do not require the wind; but, especially when fully loaded for an invasion, they *do* need the weather not to be opposite or opposing, especially in the case of a grand fleet, which must maintain cohesion in order to achieve a bridgehead on a potentially defended enemy shoreline, and to disembark all the mustered forces and the support materiel.

The abortive operation brought some strategic benefit by detaching Mysia from the Trojan alliance, at least to some extent; the *Iliad* reports Mysian contingents fighting for the Trojans (II-858). This may be explained easily: Telephus was *a*, not *the*, king of Mysians, not *the* Mysians. Other Mysian communities, under different kings, existed (Phil, *Her* 23,10) and had not pledged neutrality. But Telephus did, and it is worthwhile to remember that his son broke faith and reinforced the Trojans only after the death of Achilles (Dikt IV.14), which may not have been coincidental, but rather signifying a personal pledge of the King *to* Achilles, or *through* Achilles.

This contribution of Achilles explains his later fame. But it is perhaps not the end of the beginning. Now the Trojans are notified, and a counterattack would be in order; the sequence of events of the surviving lore that the Trojans waited for a decade (actually eight years) for the Greek attack after the events at Mysia (Apollod E.3,15) is somewhat faulty. Thus, some time – after two years, according to Apollodorus – following the abduction, the Greeks achieved a muster and attempted an invasion, but were repulsed for all practical purposes. At this stage, it is possible that the Trojans launched a counter-attack, a two-pronged one. One by land, through the allied – or subject – lands of Thrace, all the way to the Ionian Sea – a continuous land corridor or belt, last used by their Amazon friends to seek vengeance against the Greeks and Athens in particular, under Theseus. The other prong of the attack would have been an amphibious one, more disruptive than destructive but intended to assist the land operation. The seaborne attack was led by Hector. The land attack would have been headed by none other than Prince Alexander, a.k.a. Paris (Plut, *Thes* 34,2), a strange proposition, as he was the spiritual father of the Trojan navy. Other combinations are possible, but this version corroborates the report of some sources (Hdt VII.20,2) and explains Menelaus' aversion to the aggressiveness and bellicosity of the Trojans (XIII-634/9). Moreover, it does not contradict the existing – and incomplete – Homeric tradition at all. Achilles was seemingly instrumental in fending off this Trojan attack, as his father's kingdom includes the most vital junction southwards: Thermopylae itself! The region of his realm (II-681/5) is literally located around the pass and it is perhaps some kind of border between his realm and the next one to the south-east, probably Locris of Ajax the Lesser (II-527/30). As a result of such repulse, Achilles' fame and prestige would have skyrocketed, much more than his performance against Telephus would have allowed.

This version proposed herein is literally incompatible with Achilles' assertion that he was fighting at Troy even though the Trojans had not attacked him, nor hurt his family, people or realm (I-152/7). This could be interpreted more liberally: that *before* engaging with the cause of the Atreids and siding with them, he had no quarrel with the Trojans. Once he led the Greeks – and with distinction – he, and everything of his, were fair game, of course, but the fighting ever since had neutralized the Trojan capacity to project power and thus his own kingdom was safe, should he decide to leave.

This previous Trojan operation may account for some unspoken, but apparent, disaster of the Trojan navy; although some Luwian states still operated vessels in the war (XI-221/30) and Aeneas used some to make his exodus (Ovid, *Met* 14, 527–45), the Trojan navy is never mentioned during the main phase of operations and his physical father, the chief-shipbuilder Phereclus, was an early casualty fighting on land, slain by Meriones (V-62). This is really difficult to swallow: he was an invaluable human asset that should have been protected at all costs, if there were any functional and operationally relevant remains of the Trojan navy.

A sinister backstage: the tale of Iphigenia and her sacrifice

Having beaten back the Trojans, the Greeks, similar to the Allies after Dieppe, took the lesson to heart and did it better next time, with due diligence: they assembled, possibly using a larger force, at Aulis. Why Aulis was chosen will be discussed in a while. The discrepancies between Homer in the catalogue of ships and other sources, like Diktys, may stem from different time frames: Homer supposedly describes the tenth year of the war. Other sources (Apollod E.3,11–14) may refer to the original fleet from Aulis, or, more importantly and plausibly, to the fleet of the first campaign.

Then, during the muster in Aulis, Achilles was something of a celebrity. Despite his young age (not so young actually, he is in the war for 8 years at that time!), his lustre and fame is used to lure Iphigenia, Agamemnon's daughter, from Mycenae for a betrothal – along with her bitter mother, Clytemnestra, who somehow, being the queen of Mycenae, would consider for her son-in-law the lord of the hosts and heir-apparent of a relatively small and marginal region of the Achaean world. Both his performance and the dirty business in Aulis explain to a degree his later – mutual – aversion with Agamemnon.

The story of the sacrifice of Iphigenia is known and does not need to be followed or explored here, except for an obvious question. Why was she the designated sacrifice to placate Artemis, a goddess not supportive of the Greek cause and having little to do with weather and seas? Is it likely that the lord of the seas, Poseidon, wanted the Greeks to go to Troy to exact vengeance for the impiety shown towards him (XXI-441/50) by the Trojan royal family, and the goddess of hunting, wild game, virginity, the Moon etc overrules him in issues of weather overseas? In which pantheon would this have been anything but material for comics? Why was *nobody* in the *Odyssey*, not even Zeus, able to do so and Poseidon had to be persuaded or taken unaware (i-65/79)?

It is possible that the issue here was another aspect of the raging social and mostly religious upheavals. Matriarchy in Greece was recent, and the concept of the Olympians shows an almost hopeless effort to manage the war of the sexes. On Crete, Minos was probably the man who abolished political matriarchy and became king, not the male consort of a queen (and leader of the state army), possibly of yearly tenure and probably ending with his sacrificial death, as dramatically narrated in *The King Must Die* of Mary Renault. This change probably coincided with Zeus being declared the lord of heaven and god of lightning, a god reared on Crete, incidentally. Just as in the time of Hercules, many regions have queens without kings, a direct insinuation of matriarchal constitutions, the practice might have been widespread still. Hercules survived the company of such queens and this probably means the overthrow of the respective regimes. Although patriarchical regimes are many generations earlier and matriarchy is perhaps the Silver Age (Hes, *Works* 121; Ovid, *Met* 1,113–24), the importance of Minos may be deduced from the fact that he was the senior of the three judges of the afterlife; the areas referred to in Greek lore under the Olympian pantheon must have been the original enclaves of patriarchy, the new emerging religion and social reality, whereas areas of matriarchy were black holes and blanks on the map of the lore, until such regimens were overthrown. This procedure must have taken centuries, to judge from the generations between the Deluge and the Trojan War and taking into consideration the existence of unnamed natives in different areas of Greece, and the silence concerning other such areas (as is the island of Euboea) until very recent times, some two to three generations before the *Iliad*.

Thus, a 'conspiracy of queens' is nothing outrageous as a concept: an effort of networked, highly placed and ambitious women, especially if bitter with their spouses and fathers, to regain prominence and power in an otherwise simmering society. Dissent in these societies is a given; Sarpedon implies its detrimental and imminent effect (XIII-310/21), while popular leaders such as Thersites (II-212/42) and Polydamas (XII-211/5) were taking the stage against the ruling aristocracy, heroes or not. The fact that such trouble was detected in both sides of the Aegean may imply a systematic liability of this political and social system, or mirror the previously strong influence of the Greek character and morals in western Asia Minor. The massive scale of events reported by Greek lore suggests the second possibility; the fact that Queen Semiramis was one of the greatest conquerors in Asian history and her exploits were unique, but not unprecedented, supports the first. And there are indications aplenty to show an international, diverse pattern. Ishtar was a female deity of both lust and war, Queen Tomyris of Scythia conducted war against Cyrus II the Great and slew him, the Amazons of the Euxine haunt the lore to this day, along with at least three more female warrior peoples; one seen in Africa (in Libya, under Medusa) and one south-eastern Europe (the Maenads of Dionysus of Naxos). Likewise, Egyptian history and religion have their share of female prodigies in politics and war.

It goes without saying that a very pernicious situation would develop during the absence of the enforcers of the new social architecture, the fighting element, if it was to stay away for sometime. One should not forget a numerous, basically female slave population in the Mycenaean centres; women that were the object of raids, not just a juicy but opportune prize. After their menfolk were slain by the raiders, they were captured and brought back, not just for sexual exploitation, but as the workforce of the heavy industry of Mycenae, textile production (VI-454/6).

Since, in Aulis, the imminent character of a multi-year campaign was accepted by all the leaders that were present and participating, precautions were in order for such contingencies – and the very story of the *Odyssey* shows the sagacity of such projections and their eventual failure, as in the case of Agamemnon (xi-404/30).

Nobody liked multi-year campaigns; they were causing civil unrest, diminishing the productivity of the agricultural sector, unsettled commerce in all its guises (plundering raids included) and entailed personal cost in terms of family ties. It was, though, an inflexible need. The respective decision may have been taken mainly to deny opportunities for the Trojans to reciprocate, after enduring or repulsing a short raid. The comparison with the yearly incursions during the Peloponnesian War is revealing: utterly destructive for both belligerents but indecisive.

Thus the Greeks decided to use a massive force and attack the nest of the vipers, Troy. They understood that this effort would perhaps take time and crossing the Aegean on a yearly basis was not a good or sustainable idea. It was a bad idea: the Trojans could regroup, rearm and perhaps reciprocate once the raiders were to retire. By staying there, the Trojans proper would not dare to counterattack in strategic terms and the defence of Troy would absorb resources from other members of the Assuwa alliance.

And, of course, the Trojan fleet would be pinned down or destroyed and its strategic potential neutralized – a Pearl Harbor of sorts. They were also notified that the conditions and build-up of such an enterprise presented special requirements: they had to act proactively and develop answers for any surprises and special assets the Trojans were likely to present, some of them from up their sleeves. The greater minds of the Greek world would be needed. Superior tacticians were the number one prerequisite: this is why Achilles was considered essential in the first place (Apollod III.13,8); so essential as to scout for him all over Greece and lure him from his hideout at Scyros (Hyg, *Fab* 96; Apollod III.13,8). Then, the Greeks had to plan in advance to be able to respond in kind to any Trojan initiative, including unorthodox setups and prohibited means and practices. Philoctetes was carrying poisoned arrows inherited from Hercules. This was unacceptable at the time, but, when facing existential risk, the Trojans might forget the pleasantries and fair play, and the Greeks had to be able to respond in kind, fielding poisoned arrows in response, which made Philoctetes just as important (Apollod E.5,8). Last, but not least, the Palladium artefact had to be retrieved (Apollod E.5,13), because the Trojan mystical/scientific wonder weapons were causally associated with it, as discussed elsewhere.

Being understandably unsure about their rear (after all, among themselves the chieftains had no bonds of trust: Agamemnon overran the kingdom of Argos as Diomedes was leading his host against Thebes and Aetolia) the Greeks, or some excellent and shadowy advisor, identified the greatest risk factor: Agamemnon's firstborn daughter, Iphigenia. She was a tool at the hands of her mother, always bitter for her lost love and child, murdered by Agamemnon (Apollod E.2,16), and with the tacit consent of her father, Tyndareus, who validated the union with the Atreid (the Dioscuri initially had vindictive dispositions towards the outrage, but this came to naught under fatherly advice).

Clytemnestra had no claim whatsoever over the throne of Mycenae, matriarchal or otherwise. She was a foreigner, a Spartan – a fact that led her to take a native consort, Aegisthus, later on. But her daughter, carrying the blood of Atreus, designated/elected king after the demise of Eurystheus (Apollod E.2,11–12), was another thing altogether: under matriarchal rules, easy to enforce upon a society where most of the men were far away or dying in combat, Iphigenia could usurp the throne without violating the dynastic rules of patriarchy, as she was of the blood of the king and her mother could serve as regent or counsellor. Taking her out of the picture swiftly and promptly would disarm Clytemnestra and other wives of likely intentions and inclinations. It was vital; the example of Lemnos one generation beforehand, where the womenfolk murdered all the males and almost wiped out the Argonauts, had raised flags. Agamemnon disliked the idea and this was a time he was on the same page with Achilles, although for all the wrong reasons. But the scheme was put into effect, possibly because Agamemnon had to accept its wisdom: such dynamics required that the male offspring of the ruling king may be underage or removed, and young Orestes was at the epicentre: his mother would not hesitate to remove him to accomplish her plans, thereby killing two birds with one stone: stage a coup and get even with Agamemnon for the murder of her child with Tandalus the Younger (Apollod E.2,16), by depriving him of his legitimate son. His aunt Anaxibia, sister to Agamemnon and Menelaus, saved him, taking him with her and raising him with her own son Pylades, son of the King of the Phocians, Strophius, reigning on the north shore of the Gulf of Corinth (Apollod E.6,24; Paus II.29,4).

The conclave of the kings established or recognized by Agamemnon in the Peloponnese was particularly vulnerable to such machinations. It was not just his own maverick of a wife. Two of the most important kings of the Peloponnese, Diomedes and Menelaus, were outsiders marrying into their thrones once the male heirs had perished under questionable circumstances.

The successor of Argos, Aigialeus, was the only one of the Sons of the Seven who perished in battle. Adrastus, his father and king, died from sorrow, and Diomedes ascended to the throne of Argos as husband to Aigialeia, sister of Aigialeus (Apollod I.8,6) and (co)guardian of the minor Cyanippus, son of Aigialeus. The queen may have got rid of her nephew while the two regents were in Troy, as she was instrumental in the 'conspiracy of the queens' (Apollod E.6,9–10).

Menelaus, on the other hand, was more than a number two in a *duetto*: he was a passionate man (III-205/15) and a decent, although second-rate, fighter (XVII-586/90; VII-109/12), but an astute politician. He survived the upheavals that ravaged Mycenae and other centres; he also recovered his wife, prestige and property. Marrying to Helen made him an in-law to Zeus (iv-561/9). Together with Nestor, with whom they shared matrimonial relations in one secondary tradition (Dikt I.1), they carved up most of Messene between them: Oitylon and Messe were under Menelaus (II-581/6), while other Messenian areas like Arene, the seat of Aphareus, kin to Tyndareus and Ikarius and father to Idas and Lynceus, were annexed by Nestor without much ado (II-591/601; Paus IV.3,1).

At the time of the Trojan War, human sacrifice was not practised by the Greeks in a ritual context. It could perhaps happen as a function of punishment or deterrence (XXIII-19/23), but not for placating a deity.

For placating the gods, such practices were most probably discontinued. Still, under duress, nothing can be excluded and there were incidents both shortly before, as with the Theban blood sacrifice to appease the gods at the campaign of the Seven (Paus IV.25,1), and after, with the drawing of lots to select one Dorian Messenian virgin for human sacrifice to appropriate divine help against the invading Spartans in the First Messenian War (Paus IV.9,4).

In this light, modern scholarship considers the lore of Iphigenia being snatched by the goddess and substituted by a deer (Paus IV.19,6), while the damsel was carried miraculously to the northern Euxine, an effort to amend the myth to a less gory version, suitable for the more civilized later morals. It is a very logical interpretation, but unwarranted. Dislocation and displacement were already taking over as a means to resolve proactively dynastic rivalries, as is obvious from the catalogue of ships in the *Iliad*, with the many fugitive/displaced princes and heroes. Additionally, the Greeks of the Trojan War followed the ideology and carried the standards of Hercules, known for his intolerance to human sacrifice and resolving, bloodily or not, several such issues: from the murders of Bousiris in Egypt, Cycnus son of Ares and Agaeus son of the Earth (Gaea), to the rescue of the Trojan Princess Hesione from the sea monster (Apllod II.4,10–6,4). Similar, although less celebrated amongst the would-be invaders, was the career of Theseus, highlighted by the slaying of the Minotaur (Apollod E.1,1–10). So, a bloodless solution was definitely preferable to a human sacrifice, especially since Hera, the deity of familial life and sex, had Agamemnon as her personal favourite; slaughtering one's daughter for the second-rate huntress-virgin deity spawned by her rival (for the affection of Zeus), Leto, would not have sat very well with the Queen of Olympus, would it?

The Byzantines would have sent the girl to a monastery and made her a nun and be done with it. With the Olympians, this was more difficult. But a geographical exile, to some faraway and trusted partner, a trade partner deeply annoyed by Priam's practices and dues, that was another matter. The dwellers of the northern coast of the Euxine, trade associates at least since *Argo* and the Argonauts, would oblige. Scythians – at that time – or not, the princess was snatched during the sacrifice ceremony and transported, most probably overland and/or by the riverine network to a faraway but friendly and trusted land; a backwater but plentiful land, where she received priestly office to ensure her safety, dignity and well-being. Her proceedings there could be dramatized to taste some centuries later.

Diktys' account (Dikt I.22) expressly refers to the secret exile of Iphigenia in Scythia (Apollod E.3,22), with a clear connection with the hunting divinity Artemis; goddess of the hunt, Artemis (or, actually, a homologous deity) was revered on the steppe and the whole story with Artemis being enraged with Agamemnon nicely puts the issue into context: the lady was asked for (or sent to) Artemis the huntress, i.e. to her people far to the north. Herodotus corroborates (Hdt IV.103,2) and so does Pausanias, quoting Hesiod, who says Artemis requested (or was presented without solicitation; these are open to interpretation) Iphigenia as a *Hecate* (Paus I.43,1), the latter name obviously being a priestly title for the worship of Artemis.

All the above may be linked with one more peculiar line of events in Greek lore: many a queenly wife commits suicide after the demise of her beloved heroic husband. Not meaning to deny such touching demonstration of love, the issue is reminiscent of Indian ceremonial cremation of female spouses whenever their husbands die, to dissuade the women from poisoning their husbands to inherit them and remarry.

Marpessa, the Aetolian wife of the Argonaut Idas, son of Aphareus of Messene, committed suicide after the death of her husband during the engagement with the Dioscuri over ... cattle (Apollod III.11,2). Her daughter Cleopatra did the same when her husband Meleagrus of Calydon perished; and her granddaughter Polydora after the death of Protesilaus in Troy (Paus IV.2,7), a suicidal trait running in the family and coinciding with the Trojan War. During the previous generation, Alkestis, daughter of Pelias, king of Iolcus (Apollod I.9,10), gave up her life voluntarily – this time to save her husband Admetus, king of Pherrai, and she was in turn saved by Hercules (Apollod I.9,15). Their son, Eumelus, was fighting at Troy (II-714/5) and was considered the best charioteer, with the best team, after Achilles (II-763/5; XXIII-276/8). It was happening in Troy as well: Oinone, the first wife of Paris, committed suicide by plunging into his funeral pyre when Philoctetes killed him. This development would have delighted Priam, as there were no loose ends with his deceased son – or 'son' – and the assets of Helen could pass on to Deiphobus (Apollod E.5,9). So much so that helping the despairing widow to be gallant may be suspected ...

Intricacies of the locality

Another matter is the reason for assembling the fleet at Aulis. For a massive invasion force, a staging area was the only workable concept, as tens of different naval detachments with some thousand ships could not rendezvous at sea or on the enemy shore; the weather would delay some of these contingents, as they were coming from all over the compass, and thus some should wait for some others – even if they were all trying their best to be on schedule, which was not a given, as there were recalcitrant masters and commanders. Thus, a staging area, and a rather advanced one at that was needed; but why Aulis? Present-day Aulis seems an incomparably stupid choice, since one would have to sail in either opposite direction initially, to then change bearings to Troy. The axis of the two Gulfs of Euboea is north-west to south-east (a south-easterly egress route would take the fleet straight into Cape Caphereus, a *very* inopportune occurrence), while Troy lies north-east of Aulis. Why increase the distance?

The Greek needs were quite clear: a safe coastline was required for mooring a fleet of 1,000 ships for a long time. A beach, spacious but protected from the elements and from Trojan incursions, easily accessible and providing the necessary supplies nearby, especially fodder, water and food; but also easy communication with the mainland and the main administrative centres of the Mycenaean empire. Also wide, spacious areas for camping, drilling and exercising the army were imperative. Although there are many areas that meet some of these requirements, only Aulis satisfies them all. It is quite close to a number of Mycenaean centres. The island of Euboea and Boeotia were known for their herds. Boeotia had agricultural surplus, as Orchomenus, the fabled city was located there, and Euboea had massive copper mining and industry facilities; the city of Chalcis translates from Greek as 'Copperland'.

By comparison, the Gulf of Pagassai was rather isolated and with no copper-working facilities on a massive scale. The opposite was true of the Saronic Gulf coast: it was close, there were several anchorages and facilities, the nearby areas could supply the army, but extended open areas for camping and drilling were not at hand – not to say anything for security and the ability to keep away from prying eyes.

Staying for a time in the same staging area was beneficial. The contingents could be forged into an army (Phil, *Her* 23,18–19). Organizing the expeditionary force from feudal-type troops into a single, perfectly articulated force, as presented in the *Iliad*, with dedicated, separate commands and ad hoc organized staffs for defence, offence, intelligence and logistics was no mean feat and not a short process. It required time under joint command and hard training for the units to adapt, combine and attune with each other so as to present a cohesive, coordinated force rather than a muster.

The equipment and materiel, especially weapons and tools, could be repaired and upgraded and kits completed from the local workshops as mentioned; vessels could be serviced, horses broken, trained and groomed and chariots inspected. But the most important issue was the planning, convening and in general determining and hammering the formation of an army out of a host. Large-scale training was indispensable, and this was the prerogative of Menestheus of Athens, who integrated the various parts into a cohesive whole (Phil, *Her* 23,19); nevertheless, it was Ajax the Great who proposed the silent advance (Phil, *Her* 23,18–20), the characteristic feature of Greek discipline (III-8/9).

Palamedes was allegedly instrumental in this function as well, and in many other vital aspects of the support and logistics requirements. Communication systems for such a host were necessary, otherwise the battle would be anarchic and without direction. From the issue of an order centrally until it was transmitted to 100,000 warriors, the execution would have become history. Signalling by fire was known (XVIII-210/3) and essential for the final fall of Troy (Apollod E.5,18), but whether this method was Palamedes' invention, or any kind of sound-based signalling, with instruments like trumpets, is not attested. Inventing additional letters of the alphabet (Phil, *Her* 33,1; Gorg, *Def Palam* 30), for better written communication (a must for diplomacy and dealings such as selling slaves/captives and purchasing supplies from allies or neutrals) and pastimes for the rank and file to have something to do – other than bickering – was vital. The *Pessoi*, the signature table game of the Greeks, was his invention (Phil, *Her* 33,2); believed to be checkers but for some researchers better suited to chess (Plevris 1993).

B) The Invasion

The Greek effort to assault Troy by disembarking a massive force within striking distance focused on stepping stones nearby: Lemnos was instrumental, probably favourably neutral, due to the reign of the son of Jason of the Argonauts (VII-467/9), and thus available for unofficial trade-offs, such as captives and hostages (XXI-40/4). Tenedos was the second, visible from the shore. Tenedos was hostile, ruled by Tenes, son of Apollo, who conquered and named it (Apollod E.3,23–5). The place was stormed and subjugated by Achilles, who slew Tenes and incurred the wrath of Apollo, despite lavish sacrifices for atonement (Apollod E.3,26). Imbros and Samothrace are mentioned as landmarks but not as theatres of operations. Thasos must have belonged within the Trojan sphere of influence, because of its proximity to the shoreline of the European allies of Troy.

The landing of the Achaeans was the most important event of the war. The Trojan army was by then at the highest level of readiness, fully mobilized and most probably reinforced by some allies, like King Cycnus of Kolonai, and tried to repel the landing, which turned into a contested issue, a violent amphibious battle (Apollod E.3,29; Ovid, *Met* 12,70–140). This implies, beyond any doubt, that the Trojans had adequate early warning.

It is very likely that the Trojans had no idea exactly where the landing of the Achaeans would take place, and therefore could not deploy accordingly. There are examples from the classical era of the superior mobility of a naval force compared to a land force. If the geography of the area at the time offered more than one suitable beach, the Trojans would logically cover any eventuality with a screening force and would maintain a sufficiently large, mobile reserve force for committing at the point where the landing would eventually take place. Not surprisingly, the Trojan general (i.e. Hector), would have to command the reserve, while other commanding officers, allies and Trojans, would assume command over the various advanced/screening contingents. The latter would play for time until the intervention of the reserve, and the redeployment of the whole force to the endangered sector.

The story of Protesilaus (Apollod E.3,30–2) corroborates the above. Not surprisingly, Achilles was one of the first to land with Protesilaus (Apollod E.3,31; Dikt II.11). The story comes in various versions, but the point is that, as Protesilaus hit the beach, Cycnus, son of Poseidon moved to repulse the Greeks headed by Protesilaus, and Achilles to intercept Cycnus, implying Achilles sailing close to Protesilaus, which corroborates their previous close cooperation and deployment next to each other in Mysia (Phil, *Her* 23,16). The engagement ends with Achilles dispatching Cycnus with a stone (Apollod E.3,31) or his bare hands, grabbing his helmet and throttling the man with the strap (Ovid, *Met* 12,128–46), because no metal weapon could wound him (Ovid, *Met* 12,64–115); another case of invulnerability that might be interpreted as due to a panoply, despite gory details of perforation. While Achilles, by either breaking the neck or skull of his opponent or throttling him with the strap of his helmet, provides a model for Menelaus in his duel with Paris (III-369/73), Hector kills Protesilaus (Apollod E.3,30), possibly leading the reserve to the counter-attack.

Despite the loss of Protesilaus, the Greek landing succeeded, the Trojans were pushed back and pursued and the Greek force landed on the captured beach (Dares 19; Dikt II.12). Once the Greeks established themselves on Trojan soil, they became organized. A camp was set up, the ships were beached, many of them hauled onto the sand to make room for more in the rather narrow shoreline and huts and tents or other quarters were established, occasionally of very elaborate design and construction, exemplified by fences and gates for the lodgings of a king (XXIV-448/56). The procedure was planned, supervised and organized, as evidenced by the controversy over who would anchor his ships on the most exposed sides of the naval camp. The two extremes were occupied by Achilles and Ajax (VIII-224/5), while

Odysseus' ships were right in the centre (VIII-223), something one would expect for Agamemnon's unit. Whether this implies a special advisory/administrative role for Odysseus or is explained by different notions of 'centre' (measured by distance as opposed to vessel numbers or contingent numbers) cannot be surmised.

After the first battle, the verdict of which was probably disheartening for the Trojans, a truce is made to collect the dead and offer funeral rites, while a Greek embassy goes to Troy. It has two assets for the negotiation: the support of a huge expeditionary force nearby and a victory. Paris' faction (under Antimachus, who is not a member of the senate) threatens the ambassadors (XI-123/41; Dikt II.23–4), who are saved by the second most powerful man in Troy, Antenor (Apollod E.3,28–9). After that, the Achaeans assault the city unsuccessfully and lay waste to the surrounding area (Apollod E.3,31; Dares 19).

At this point, the siege of Troy begins; it *is* a siege, because the invaders threaten the city and actively limit the movements of the defenders (XXIV-662/3). It may not have been a very tight investment, or rather no investment at all, but it is a siege.

The operations are not covered, except for the very compact, and highly abstract in nature, pair of narratives in the Homeric epics, and this allows very few useful conclusions on the issue. What can be presumed is that an indirect strategy resulted in the destruction of the Trojan network and administration in some depth.

The expedition of Achilles, who conquered twenty-three enemy cities on the coast of Asia Minor and on numerous islands (IX-328/9), obviously including Lesbos and Tenedos, but not Imbros, is the Homeric mainstay. Other sources are more revealing, mapping this action all the way to Smyrna to the south (Apollod E.3,33). The equally astonishing successes of Ajax mentioned by Diktys take place on both continents: Thrace, in Europe, and Asia Minor. In the latter case, his footprint is towards the hinterland (Dikt II.18). This pair of expeditionary events, being either a single, consecutive, two-pronged campaign, or a series of successive raids and operations, shapes the nine-year-long siege. It weakens the Trojans in terms of manpower and resources, foodstuffs included, it batters their morale and it helps to sustain the Greeks psychologically and materially.

Somewhere in this campaign one may discern the shady figure of Palamedes. In terms of operations, Palamedes is definitely credited with huge success in support operations, a prime example being the resupply of the army with corn, at a time when Odysseus had failed. Whether the campaign is his plan or of Achilles cannot be established, as the sources referring to Palamedes overcompensate by far for his eclipse from the Homeric epics.

Unfortunately, only the Homeric references, especially due to their extent, allow some glimpse into the nature of warfare. For example, it is obvious that amphibious action was at a premium, along with raiding-type warfare based on swiftness and surprise. This explains well why light infantry tactics, even among heavily armoured warriors, had been at a premium. It also begs some questions: whether, in amphibious raids, the *equeta* were carrying their chariots with them; if yes, whether their intended use was that of an assault or a forward command vehicle and what kind of panoply they were using. Full kit, a modular approach in a case by case basis, or the most basic and light kit? This refers to the heroes, trained to all types and approaches of warfare, as the rank and file might have nothing but the basic kit – which, on the frescoes at Pylos, seems to include as standard issue greaves and helmet, implying that the former were also used as boots, to protect the leg from non-battle wounds. The prominence of the latter may imply a more direct set of risk factors referring to head blows, especially from stones thrown or slung, and more so in broken ground and/or urban operations.

The demise of Palamedes due to the machinations of the *evil trio* (Agamemnon, Odysseus, Diomedes) is attested by diverse sources, but not Homer, an issue compromising the authority, objectiveness and credibility of the poet since ancient times (Phil *Her* 24,1–25,17), although a poet is not characterized by such virtues in the first place. This chain of events, and especially the raiding warfare, is causal to the plot of the *Iliad*, which is based on a … reshuffle of the prizes of the plundering operation that turned against Achilles, after the commander-in-chief Agamemnon had to return his share (the captive beauty Chryseis), to exonerate a very destructive curse – pestilence. But some quintessential issues for the Homeric description seem to evade most scholars.

The first is that, most probably, this series of campaigns, possibly taking something like eight to nine years, must have had a causal relation with the massive reinforcement of Troy, which is evident in the *Iliad*, with a number of contingents specifically mentioned to have been freshly arrived and continuing to do so during the action. Whether this is regarded as a reaction, delayed due to the terror and damage in the support and communication networks of the land by Ajax and Achilles, or, on the contrary, as a delayed reflex to the widespread disaster they cause campaigning, making other unenthusiastic allies ponder over their fate, is open to debate. But the 50,000-strong Trojan allied army mentioned in the *Iliad* (VIII-558/9) could not easily have been present – brought in, billeted – and sustained for the duration of the siege;

the burden on the besieged city would have been catastrophic. Indeed there are direct references that this assembly of allies was an event of the final year (Apollod E.3,34).

The second is the nature of the presence of Aeneas. He is heir apparent, if not reigning king of the Dardanians, who *are* Trojans; the Homeric adjective '*bouliphore*' (XIII-463), literally translated as 'bearer of the communal will', means a civil/administrative function parallel to the purely military one, if poetic licence is excused. What is he doing in Troy and why is his regal father (reigning king or not) along, so that he enjoys praise for not leaving him behind after the fall of Troy? Is it possible that the most unfortunate and almost fatal encounter with Achilles in his realm actually resulted in said realm passing to Greek control and thus he found himself a refugee of sorts in the court of his – not-that-loving – uncle (XIII-459/61)? Aeneas was accomplice to Paris (Dares 38) and his friend; he vehemently opposed any peaceful resolution (Dikt II.26) and was eager to support the cause of king Priam (not just of Paris; it was sustained and sanctioned by the sovereign). The man was there to assist with the abduction of Helen (Diktys I,3), so why would he not be enthusiastic to assist?

The only explanation for this dynastic bickering and the open hostility, or at least suspicion by Priam (XX-178/86) could be that Aeneas, son of Aphrodite, was behind the radical beliefs of Paris, who reformed Trojan religion in favour of Aphrodite, a more oriental model than Athena, who had been well-respected and revered before, ministered by the Theano, wife of a most respected and powerful Trojan, Antenor (VI-296/300). Priam was an adherent of Zeus; or, rather, of his Luwian counterpart. It is his statue he reveres in private (Paus II.24,3) and he considers the deity as residing on Mount Ida, not on Olympus (XXIV-308). He did endorse the cause and policies of Paris, but perhaps not wholeheartedly; and he may have identified Aeneas as behind his need to do so, his beliefs and perhaps a reckless nature that would eye his throne in some scheme or other (XX-180/3) and definitely a land grant for his support (XX-184/6). Perhaps this is the reason that Aeneas is assisted in his command by two sons of Antenor (II-819/23), the most devoted Trojan. Homer assigns them to the leadership of the Dardanians, *under* Aeneas (II-819/23).

And the third is that, if Homer did edit things so as to have Palamedes vanish from the record, Achilles' wrath with Agamemnon might have been instigated by the demise of Palamedes. It is a very interesting aspect. They were close friends, and it seems that there are pairs of top fighters and top thinkers; the light, Achilles and Palamedes, and the dark, Diomedes and Odysseus. If the wrath of Achilles was sparked by the events of commandeering his prize,

Bryseis, but simmering for the institutional murder of his friend, engineered by Odysseus and sanctioned by Agamemnon, a relative of the murdered hero (no matter which way the murder was effected, as there are again different traditions), then the events of the *Iliad* beg an alternative interpretation altogether. If the event was prior to the start of the plot of the *Iliad*, then the extremely aggressive tone of Achilles against Agamemnon (I-90/1) *before* the latter delivers any offence to the former may well be understandable.

Actually, Homer's introduction in the *Iliad* implies some facts: the Greeks have just finished a series of raiding operations with great success. 'Finished' is substantiated by Achilles' aversion that Agamemnon will be reimbursed for the loss of Chryseis, whom he returned to her father, from the spoils of Troy (I-125/9). This means there are no other prospects for acquiring booty. '*Just* finished' because the whole event with the plague occurred due to the dismissive treatment of the priest Chryses, who came to ransom his daughter (I-11/23); which means that the capture and the respective raid were current, not long past, events.

C) The 3 Great Battles of the Iliad in a Summary Description

After the Greek landing and their possible catastrophic defeat on the beach, the Trojans follow the strategy of exhaustion, and the Greeks, as mentioned, an indirect approach striking at vulnerable minor Trojan allies, taken by surprise or with a fraction of their hosts in readiness, as they had sent troops to Troy – and obviously high-readiness, elite and dependable troops, thus presenting themselves a qualitative depreciation of their combat value. The above accounts for two parallel strategies of attrition followed by the two sides. But, as if by convention, the two opponents almost simultaneously change course towards a 'strategy of overthrow', resulting in three great battles, from the time following the wrath of Achilles to the death of Hector.

First battle
After twelve days had passed from the events that led to the wrath of Achilles, Agamemnon personally assumes command of the Greek army. His intention to test their mettle (II-73/5) and the mess that followed, an almost spontaneous massive desertion (II-142/54), shows his feeling was amiss and perhaps had not taken the trouble to feel out to his troops, something in line with Achilles' accusations (I-148/71). The crisis is handled and averted by his staff, especially Odysseus (II-182/211), and Agamemnon resets the whole thing with more-or-less inspiring harangues (II-369/80). And, by

leading in person (II-474/83), he deploys the army and offers battle to the enemy; the Trojans accept the challenge and reciprocate (II-802/10).

This is not as simple as it reads. There are issues aplenty to ponder upon.

The obvious question is why did Agamemnon do this, and at that time, twelve days after falling out with Achilles and thus without his top tactical mind and the most effective warrior. Why not before, or later? And the same with Hector: why, since he had been shirking open confrontation, did he accept the challenge; more to the point, why had he been prepared and ready to do so, as the Trojan sally (II-795/810) was no spontaneous reaction to the Achaean deployment but an obviously prepared and premeditated move.

The Trojan forward observer who spotted the Greek deployment and sounded the alarm (II-791/5) implies two things: the first is the Trojan interest in the proceedings of the Greeks, which is very understandable, but one may wonder if it was standard practice or some special measure – and if the latter, why then. The second implication is that the Greek camp and thus the beach was not visible from Troy; it was beyond or out of the line of sight from the elevated viewpoints of the Trojan walls and towers. This may have been due to distance (beyond the line of sight) or due to some terrain feature, like a depression or a range hiding the Greek camp.

Agamemnon had a deadlock to break. The actual campaign was lengthy and tiresome, creating longing and disappointment amongst the men. There had been a successful and profitable set of raids; but also a series of reverses: an important and very popular commander had been eliminated, accused of treason and executed with great indignation – or murdered. It is important that Homer, in the catalogue of ships, does not mention Palamedes' troops and vessels, as if they were absent, non-existent, liquidated or assumed by some other chieftain. Then there was the plague, and after that the explosive fallout with Achilles. He had to prove him wrong by participating in a battle royal; nay, by assuming command and leading out the army. If the Trojans passed, morale would be restored. If not, he had every reason to believe he could win the encounter.

But there is no answer to the temporal question: why then? Why twelve days after falling out with Achilles. Why not three days before or after the designated D-Day?

With Hector things are more straightforward: the enemy was showing no appreciable loss of determination; they were nailed to his doorsteps, and ravaging the whole region. This could not continue; the Assuwa alliance was crumbling and metropolitan areas were turning to cinders. He needed a decision, and he had been assembling reinforcements from everywhere, even the furthest allies and sympathizers. The siege was never particularly tight: reinforcements arrived unhindered from land and equally unhindered from Propontis and the Hellespont, as the current hampered Greek naval surveillance. Rhesus and Asteropeus somehow crossed from Europe to Asia, while Iphidamas (XI-230) came with twelve ships from Thrace to Perkote, high in the Hellespont, which suggests he started from the whereabouts of Propontis. From Perkote he reached Troy by land.

Obviously the grand muster could not stay indefinitely for reasons of logistics if nothing else (XVII-225). To curtail sustainment costs, allies and mercenaries (Homer does not ever mention the latter) would have assembled at a specified time to swell the Trojan force to a manageable size, comparable if not equalling that of the invaders. That, coupled with an intimate knowledge of the land and some other advantages, like non-conventional weapons, could turn the tables. Possibly the non-conventional weapons were not the first, nor the best, choice: imperial policy had estranged the priesthood of Athena that excelled in such amenities and favoured conventional forces, much better suited to imperial endeavours and high prestige. Thus, Hector was preparing at the time for a face-off. He was not ready: some of his reinforcements had just arrived, like Asteropeus (XXI-152/6), but not yet Rhesus (X-434/5) and Othryoneus (XIII-363/4), although their arrival was imminent. Hector could not pass on it; although not fully ready, he had to accept the challenge and raise Trojan morale. It was also an opportune moment: it is not certain, and rather improbable, that he knew about the wrath of Achilles, although a god mentioning it implies a whistle-blower or another kind of HUMINT/human intelligence (IV-507/13); even without such connivances, the plague and the massive death toll would have been obvious to observers/pickets from the massive funeral pyres and the commotion.

In these conditions Hector had to attempt a sally, but would rather settle the issue without risking a battle. A duel between Paris and Menelaus would do just this. If Paris won, the war was won; the ravaged morale of the Greeks may also afford an opportunity for a surprise attack, as the Israelites did to the Philistines after the victory of David. If Menelaus won, he would have rid himself of his 'brother', and Plan B would be activated. By sniping at Menelaus, the issue was resolved; no interested, molested party, thus a nice opportunity for the Greeks to fall back and go home in front of the reinforced, impregnable and confident Troy. Things did not play out his way: Menelaus won the duel but Paris did not perish; Pandarus sniped at Menelaus, infuriating the Greeks, but failed to kill him; thus, the issue was not resolved. In the battle that ensues, and is pursued by collision, a violent clash, the Achaeans prevail. Among the casualties are the master shipbuilder

Phereclus (V-59/63) and Pandarus (V-290/4), the master archer (II-826/7); Aeneas is wounded (V-302/10) – less seriously than originally thought (V-512/6), and lost his chariot and team (V-319/26), which implies he is no longer a full *equeta*, but survives almost miraculously (V-313/8.). Despite the massive loss of prestige – he is practically demoted and stripped of command – his fortune and royal standing would make up for the damage once he recuperates, and this happens fast (VI-77).

Hector and his advisors must have noticed, during the duel, as they were arrayed against the Greeks, that Achilles was absent. This made the opportunity even more irresistible. After all, the Trojans seem to perform decently; the god of war seems to favour them (V-590/5), and the most prominent descendent of Hercules, Tlepolemus of Rhodes, is killed by Sarpedon of Lycia, who suffers a minor wound (V-655/62). But then the evil duo, Diomedes and Odysseus, jump into action and cause mayhem and havoc; Diomedes reaffirms his name and fame, becoming even more feared than Achilles (VI-96/100), and turns the tide; somehow Ares left the Trojans (V-860/8). The Trojans rally before their gates; this is the point where they usually do so, perhaps supported by missiles shot from the walls. Hector twice more was to stop his flight at the same spot; before Patroclus, when he also rallied his troops (XVI-712/4) and before Achilles (XXII-5/6).

At this point, the Trojans have forfeited the initiative. Prince royal – and seer – Helenus suggests that his brother forgets the conventional approach and, since Achilles is missing, he issues another challenge for a duel. The idea is to gain time in every way possible so as to once more befriend the priesthood of Athena, estranged, especially after one of its favourites perished stupidly, if not by malice; a master shipbuilder fighting with shield and spear (V-59/63) is a moronic endangerment of valuable human assets and resources, reeking of an effort at atonement by combat, and thus a falling out of favour must be understood. Once the priesthood of Athena is placated, the Trojans can enjoy divine support on an unprecedented scale.

This second duel takes place late in the day; Hector, to make the plan work, just had to survive until dusk, and he does so (VII-307/10). As the Greeks do not settle – after a betrayal in a formal duel under oath they occupy the moral high ground and are optimistic (VII-399/402) – a ceasefire is agreed upon, to bury the dead (VII-408/10); events show that the battle ethics are civilized and that it is quite some time since the two opponents have met in combat and need to attend to corpses on the plain of Troy. The Trojans use the lull to develop a divine arsenal, while more reinforcements are expected to pour in (Rhesus, Othryoneus); also to restructure their command team and rethink their strategy and tactics. The sons of Agenor stepped up into the command structure and assumed responsibilities on an equal basis with the other ad hoc members of the Trojan panel of field commanders (XI-56/60), thus safeguarding the position the family held before the wrath of Paris and his crew and the open threats he made (VII-357/60) due to the senator's proposal: to return the abducted queen and the stolen property, instead of pushing for a decision after committing a further impiety in the duel between Paris and Menelaus.

The Achaeans use the lull to throw up an elaborate fortification (VII-436/41). This Homeric tradition contradicts the one that reports that this arrangement was an early precaution, shortly after the establishment of the Greek bridgehead and camp, suggested and overseen by Palamedes (Dares 26).

Second battle

The second battle of the *Iliad* may be called 'Troy Victorious'. It features interesting parts, its duration being one of them. At a time when a battle lasts one day, this is a multi-day battle, as the events of each day were starting exactly where the ones of the previous had paused, due to the night-time lull. The fighting was paused, not stopped; the ground was held; the two opponents were not recoiling to their bases to meet anew. They were continuing the fighting from where they had left it.

The first battle was the opposite: after ebbing and flowing many times, it had nonetheless ended, and in a truce. The Achaeans had fared better, but the Trojans were the victors: they were able to stand and look their opponents straight in the eyes. They were a match, although not superior by any metric. They also had seen the great weakness of the Greeks: they had reverted to tribal deployment and tactics and brute force, and they were not good at it – or, at least, *that* good. After learning to function like an army, they were back to being a host, and a host missing its greatest warrior, as much as the army was missing the sense of tactics. They were more, many more; they were better, but the odds were much more even. Both opponents read the same line of conclusions and the fortifications erected were a sign that the Achaeans had started doubting their supremacy (VIII-529/34), and Achilles was not expected anytime soon.

On the contrary, the Trojans had much more to expect than a boost to their morale. More allies poured in, and their piousness and devotion, as instructed by the prince royal, Helenus, was expected to bear fruits, despite their continuous offences; after all, they were fighting for their homes and lives (VIII-56/7). They were also fighting for dynastic rights at Sparta and for their empire of sorts, but this was a backthought.

The issue of the allies is important: after many years with not a single arrival, suddenly they just do not stop coming. It may have been a problem in timing, as they were coming from afar, but it may have been intentional and the Trojan requests may have been timed so as to ensure successive waves that would ease logistics and support and would act additively against the Greek army. The latter was not to receive any replacements or reinforcements and thus wear and tear and casualties steadily undermined their tolerance.

In any case, the second battle opened conventionally, with the enemy lines staying at a distance and exchanging missiles. Somehow the prayers and atonement to Athena prescribed by Helenus (VI-75/101) are answered by Zeus. Lightning strikes, a barrage of them from the direction of Mount Ida (VIII-75/6) breaks up the Achaeans, who flee (VIII-78/80). Diomedes alone tries to change the course of the battle, as the Trojans press home their advantage by conventional means; it is a stunt he had most gloriously performed during the previous battle. This was almost his undoing; the Trojan deities were ready for him and he becomes the target of individually aimed lightning bolts (VIII-133/6).

The thunderbolt stopping Diomedes struck open ground (VIII-134)! But true thunderbolts are attracted to something, the warrior clad in copper or his team. Gods do not bypass the laws of nature; they make and enforce them. Gods also do not miss their mark. But priests and men begotten by gods (temple personnel) occasionally do, but do not admit it; they declare that the god, in his wisdom, simply sent a message (VIII-140/1). After all, Diomedes retreated in terror, his team in fright (VIII-136), and the Trojans carried the day (VIII-212/9). If Diomedes had been struck by the bolt, the drama of Thebes might have been replayed.

The Achaeans are routed and they regroup far away from the field of fire of the divine weapons of their enemy, between the ditch and the fence/ wall (VIII-213 /5). The wisdom of the engineering is manifest. Away from the divine intervention and supported by said works, the Greeks hold their opponents (VIII-251/2) and, fired up by Agamemnon, who saw it fit to intervene personally (VIII-218/30), counter-attack, following Diomedes (VIII-253/7), and overthrow the Trojans, with Agamemnon participating (VIII-261/2); the Trojans, in turn, rally, regroup and carry the day. The Greeks are routed and find refuge *within* their wall (VIII-335/6), not in front of it. Trojan morale skyrockets, one additional ally arrives in the night, King Rhesus, and Hector bivouacs the army in sight of the enemy camp (VIII-502), to continue next day from where they stopped. At this point the army of the Trojans is estimated at 50,000, i.e. 1,000 campfires for each fifty-man tactical unit (VIII-558/9). There is no opportunity for the Greeks to deploy and deny the Trojan advance. Trojan logistics and support elements are rearranged to make this show of persistence possible (VIII-505/9). Hector also issues strict orders for vigilance and night watches with many sentries in the city (VIII-521/2), as a strategic counter-attack on the empty city, denuded of defenders, was a risk (VIII-517/22). After all, Hercules took and pillaged the city by circumventing the standing army that was away attacking his ships and, after trapping it and destroying it, he sacked the city (Dares 3). But the Trojan vigilance is not as good in the field; they are too elated by their imminent victory and too tired.

The Trojan allies were successively deployed, from the seashore inland (X-428/31), with the Thracians of Rhesus at the extreme inland wing (X-432/4). This seashore-to-plain arrangement means the Greek mooring and camp was not at the Beşik Bay; if it were there, the Trojan line of advance would have been straight to the centre of the beachhead and both Trojan wings would be by the sea, in a horseshoe formation.

At the same time, the Greeks first try to placate Achilles, who feels vindicated (IX-603/6). His refusal to accept any gifts shows that it is not greed; the personal issue is much more severe, to the point of hatred for Agamemnon. He includes Menelaus in the picture (IX-338/41) but never pronounces a bitter word about him; and he demonstrably feels that his fellow Greeks, chieftains and heroes first, but not alone, have tacitly sided with Agamemnon in what was an obvious transgression of authority and common deliberation: the spoils were attributed as a communal, almost

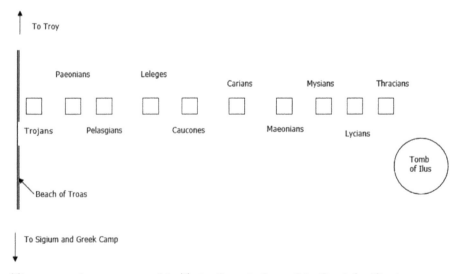

The nocturnal encampment of the Trojan forces in front of the Greek fortification.

democratic, decision in open proceedings. This bitterness comes to stunning levels (XVI-97/100).

Diomedes' harangue is appreciated (IX-706/7), but actually does little to lighten the spirits, and a midnight council meets out of the camp, beyond the ditch (X-194/200). The main issue is reconnaissance, and its strategic aspect at that, not to understand the strength, condition and disposition of the enemy, but his intentions (X-204/10). Diomedes and Odysseus volunteer, are armed at short notice from the guards of the camp, and show the Greek superiority in nocturnal and special missions: they detect, neutralize, interrogate and liquidate their Trojan counterpart, Dolon (X-339/456). They learn the disposition and the new arrivals on the Trojan side (X-432/4) and assassinate Rhesus and a number of his *eqeta* (X-494/6), actually neutralizing the newly arrived contingent by wrecking its morale and decimating its natural leadership. To add insult to injury, they steal the team of Rhesus (X-498/500) and escape riding it (X-512/4) – which shows that riding a horse was a well-practised skill, but fighting from horseback was not.

The council meeting that decided the Odysseus-Diomedes mission took place outside the fortification. It is strange that it did not take place in the hut of Agamemnon, as Hector expected when dispatching Dolon to learn the Greek conditions, circumstances and intentions (X-308/12). Checking the vigilance of the sentries (X-180/2) is hilarious as an excuse. Instead, counter-espionage practices, directed towards their own traitors and possible enemy reconnaissance, or the desire to keep as discreet as possible the dispatch of their own mission, which seems to have been in the thoughts of all before they even met, may be suggested as reasons for such a exceptional arrangement.

Next day, Day Two of the second battle, the Achaeans emerge with restored morale due to the night raid; the mounts and perhaps other spoils of the Thracian King must have been paraded to bolster morale. Additionally, Agamemnon decides to join his men from the very beginning (XI-15); this was not attested the previous day, when he appeared only when things were going particularly sour to inspire them – with great success, as already mentioned. The Achaeans deploy in front of the trench, all *eqeta* on foot, set to enhance the infantry formations to fight it out (XI-49/50). Horses and chariots are held behind the infantry (XI-47/52), as the distance from the Trojans is short and the chariots cannot develop speed or assume and keep formations. Chariots are clearly waiting to exploit success and load and carry the warriors to give chase, once an opportunity presents itself. They go for a conventional battle, undeterred from last day's events.

The Trojans project a first line under six commanders, all Trojans, (XI-56/60), implying a basically tertiary division of the front to two wings and centre. Allied units having lost their natural leadership, i.e. the men of Pandarus or Rhesus, must have been absorbed by other contingents. After the usual exchange, the Achaeans dislodge the Trojan line by delivering an assault (XI-84/91) and pursue, causing great slaughter, with Agamemnon performing brilliantly (XI-91/263) and proving Achilles wrong; he was a very capable fighter after all, once he decided to engage.

Once Agamemnon is required to retire due to wounds (XI-267/74), the Greeks have an unavoidable drop of morale. The Trojans, having regrouped in front of the Skaean Gates (XI-170/1), as they did in the first battle, experience a boost in morale, with Hector firing up their spirits by moving back and forth along the files (XI-64/5), which implies rather loose formations. This springs them to counterattack. Agamemnon's words sound pessimistic: he seems to realize that the battle was to develop badly, with the salvation of the ships being the ultimate prize, not the victory (XI-276/9). Perhaps he realizes that he has probably been lured into a trap; during the counter-attack, Hector uses words that suggest springing a trap (XI-286/90). Until that moment, he had not been seriously engaged; moreover, Paris is explicitly mentioned as lying in ambush behind the monument of Ilus, from where he shoots at Diomedes (XI-369/78). The monument might have been a tumulus in the custom described by Homer (XXIV-797/801) and seen in Russian Kurgans. The ambush must have included some strength and the Greek natural leadership was eventually decimated, with three top performers, members of the inner ring, Agamemnon, Diomedes, Odysseus, being taken out of action. Paris was the hero of the day, personally bowing down three key enemies and he must have led the ambushing force. This is the only good reason for him not to have been included in the original six-strong battlefield command panel, all of its members being Trojans and not one ally (XI-56/60). The allies, subsequently seen to fight with distinction, must have been kept in reserve or ambush.

The onslaught of Hector and the Trojan chariotry (XI-289/90), which wreaked havoc on the Greek rank and file (XI-304/5), literally thrashing heads (XI-309) and 'slaying by spear and horse' (XI-503), implying mounted engagements and physical contact at the charge, meets some resistance. Diomedes, assisted by Odysseus, had momentarily checked it by scoring some kills (XI-315/42). Additionally, Diomedes hit Hector, almost knocking him unconscious (XI-349/55) before being shot at by Paris (XI-376/9). Riding back, he left Odysseus exposed (XI-401/6). The latter fought desperately and brilliantly, practically isolated and also wounded (XI-456/60), but is finally saved by Ajax (XI-485/88).

The Trojans carry all before them and eventually pursue the Achaeans to their camp (XII-4/5), although Ajax the Great, after saving Odysseus, momentarily repulsed Trojan onslaughts, exterminating 'men and horses' (XI-496/7), a clear indication of the vulnerability of charging teams in front of steadily set, line infantry. Hector moves along and across the battlefield (XI-64/5), exercising tight, centralized command; he seems to have an issue with delegating tasks, perhaps to be expected in multinational and multilingual forces with little or no cohesion. Starting from the Trojan left, near the bed of the Scamander (XI-498/500), where he was engaged against Nestor and Idomeneus, who command the forces deployed there, after Diomedes had been wounded and evacuated, Hector moved against Ajax, at the other side of the front (XI-496/532). The proximity of Pylians and Cretans is recurrent (XIII-400) and perhaps implies an interdependency, as supposedly mentioned in the Phaestus Disc (Zangger 2016).

Hard pressed by masses of enemy missiles, Ajax fights competently a rearguard action (XI-565/70), occasionally assisted by Eurypylus (XI-574/9), also to be shot at by Paris (XI-580/3). Retiring wounded, Eurypylus reports back to the camp a clear Trojan victory, made even worse by the neutralization of the most resolute Greek heroes and kings (XI-821/6). At his point, Nestor, evacuating the wounded medical doctor Mahaon (XI-649/50), another victim of Paris (XI-505/9), finds an opportunity to suggest to the worried Patroclus the idea of leading Achilles' troops mounted on his chariot and in his armour, as a surrogate, to dishearten and also surprise the triumphant but exhausted Trojans (XI-795/800).

Once behind their wall, the Achaean forces seem formidable, their defence led by the two Ajaxes and Teukros (XII-3357). This scheme implies instead the rank and file of light, heavy and missile infantry but without armoured heroes; a very logical setup in the circumstances, with no mobility and the advantage of an elevated position.

This forces Hector to follow the course suggested by Polydamas, probably the chief of staff and definitely the best tactical mind amongst the Trojans, and explained in detail (XII-60/79). The assault against the Greek fortifications will be conducted on foot, and the Trojan *eqeta* dismounted to do so (XII-76/9). The force structure is reshuffled ad hoc to comprise five assault columns, each under three leaders (XII-88/102), the additional commanders implying uncommitted forces that may well have been used in an ambush or as a planned reserve.

Hector, with Polydamas and his brother Kebriones, most probably led the central column, and definitely the best one, in qualitative and quantitative terms (XII-88/91), where the decision was expected. Two other columns

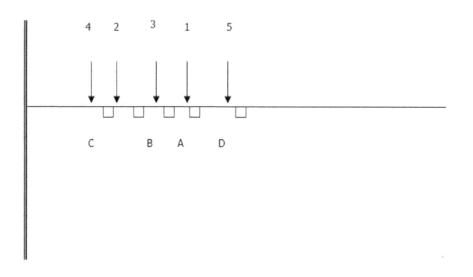

1. Hector, Polydamas, Kebriones	
2. *Paris*, Agenor, Alcathous	
3. *Helenus*, Deiphobus, Asius	
4. Aeneas, Acamas, Archelochus	
5. Sarpedon, Glaucus, Asteropeus	
A. **Ajaxes**, *Teucer*	
B. **Idomeneus**, *Meriones*	
C. Menelaus	
D. Menestheus	

The disposition of the attackers and the defenders of the Greek fortification.

are headed by commanders of the morning line-up, assisted by one more colleague per pair. But the rightmost column, next to the sea, is commanded by the crown princes and siblings of Hector, Helenus and Deiphobus and the ally Asius (XII-94/5), none of which was present at the first lineup (XI-56/60). The column furthest from the sea was the only one commanded exclusively by allies and/or mercenaries: Sarpedon with his lieutenant Glaucus and Asteropeus (XII-101/2); they were also missing from the early day command structure (XI-56/60). They have the most dangerous mission, as they operate in the vicinity of the troops of Achilles, which explains why Sarpedon was well-positioned to intercept Patroclus (XVI-419/27), and also a quintessential one. Sarpedon's attack draws Greek forces, thus acting as a distraction; Ajax the Great, for example, originally deployed opposite Hector (XII-154/92) and hurried to assist the local commander, Menestheus of Athens (XII-370/3). As the sector where Hector attacks was far from the ships, he expects, correctly, less resistance; the Greeks would spontaneously move as near to their ships as possible, to defend them and to be able to launch and board them if need be.

The Trojans use all their mettle and arsenal to breach the Achaean fortification. From standard, modern-day sapping (XII-256/62) to attacking under low visibility (XII-253/5), so as to deny to the enemy commanders awareness in the conduct of battle, the Trojans show ingenuity and determination, along with resilience.

The attack of the Trojans, though, as advised by Polydamas, is dismounted (XII-76/8), since the Trojan mounts decline to attempt a crossing of the ditch (XII-50/5); with one exception. One of the Trojan leaders, Asius, named after Assuwa/Asia, charged with his chariot directly through the enemy chariot-lanes and open gates (XII-109/14), kept open to receive retreating friends (XII-118/23). Two dismounted Greek heroes wreak havoc on the mounted attack (XII-126/32 & 182/95), Asius is repulsed and wounded (XII-162/73), but survives only to be slain by Idomeneus while fighting dismounted later (XIII-387/8).

The rest of the Trojans have left their vehicles at the ditch, at the ready, and stroll through it, and against the wall, in five attack columns (XII-83/104) as already mentioned. The attack develops decently; despite the signs, prompting Polydamas' advice to fall back (XII-223/9), Hector declares that defending one's fatherland is the best sign (XII-243) and presses home, fully exploiting the fact that Ajax had moved to repel Sarpedon at the right edge of the Greek fortification.

The Trojans breach the wall in many places; Sarpedon shatters the rampart battlements (XII-395) at the position of elder Menestheus (XII-330), despite Ajax the Great and Teukros arriving to assist the hard-pressed Menestheus (XII-370/5). They do repulse the Trojan onslaught, wound Glaucus, Sarpedon's lieutenant (XII-387/90), resist the Lycian infantry in bitter fighting, and a spear thrust sends Sarpedon himself some steps back (XII-404/7); but it is Hector who shatters a gate with a stone, allowing his infantry to burst through and, in effect, also overwhelm the wall, routing the defenders (XII-445/70) and deploying in fighting formation within the Greek circuit.

Nevertheless, Idomeneus and some others, offering stiff resistance, decimated the commanders of the other three assault columns, also inflicting devastating casualties on the troops. At this point, and for reasons of personal allegiances and vengeance, Aeneas intervenes (XIII-463/8), although still bitter (XIII-459/61), due to the contempt he obviously received from the king after his near-fatal encounter with Diomedes in the first battle (V-302/16), where he lost his precious horses (V-319/27) of the famous, divine breed (V-163/73). These were now available to the Achaeans for breeding and fighting. This was a fitting sequel to his even worse experience with Achilles in his home territory (XX-186/91). At this point, more or less, Hector restructures his force once more (XIII-789/92) to face the Achaean line-up and to balance the massive casualties at his right (XIII-674/6).

On the other hand, the injured Achaean leadership intervenes to lead, encourage, advise and command (XIV-378/83). Competently led and with restored morale, the Achaeans counter-attack successfully, driving the enemy back through the ditch with crippling casualties (XV-1/4), including the badly wounded Hector, struck with a stone by Ajax the Great (XIV-408/19).

The sudden return of Hector (XV-269/70) may be attributed to a service of duplicates or some concoction combining painkillers with dope – something like the potions used by the Celts of the Gaulic Wars of the Romans and the berserkers of the first millennium AD, who fought manically and with no fear or sense of pain (Paus X.21,3). Or it may have been a ruse; by a retreat, paid for with some – or many – casualties, the Achaeans open their stiff phalanxes to give chase, spread across the plain, and are vulnerable to a chariot counter-attack, which would find them exposed in the field, and would press home the advantage by launching a new mounted attack against the Greek defences; in this way the defenders will be too depleted and out of both breath and time to reform to a new defensive line. Thus, no matter whether due to a duplicate/surrogate, or a fake injury, Hector may have been intentionally withdrawn from the battle. His return (XV-279/80) signals the offensive comeback of the Trojans, while Greek morale plummets for many reasons: false hopes being dashed, divine intervention imagined (XV-292/3), or being caught off position by a chariot offensive (XV-269/70). The surprise and the desperation of the Achaeans, met by the massive boost to morale of the Trojans, as they saw their top fighter and commander alive and kicking, sent the former running back (XV-295). This time the Trojans pursue and mount an attack on chariots; Apollo obviously has a degree in engineering and levels trench and fence/wall to a width of some tens of metres (XV-355/9), paving the way for the Trojan chariotry, who gallop full speed to the beached Greek vessels (XV-384/5) through their crippled wall. Still, somehow, possibly due to exhaustion and failure or disinclination to join the chase at the previous turn, there are Greek warriors aplenty there, and they joust from the decks of the beached vessels against the Trojan mounted lancers (XV-385/9). This, plus the Trojan focus to charge, not exterminate fugitives, allows the rallying of troops in retreat to form once more in a close-knit *phalanx* which again repels the attackers, now mounted (XV-405/9), just off the sterns of their vessels. As the Trojan infantry arrives and rallies, it becomes obvious that the Trojan attempt at a surprise charge to the Greek vessels failed and once more conventional confrontation ensues, where the Greeks have numbers and better-suited formations to their advantage. Heavy fighting ensues (XV-569/95), with the Trojans being formed around Hector. The Greeks rest their hopes with the inspired and deadly conduct of defence by Ajax (XV-501/14). Initially exchanging missiles, the fight comes down to hand-to-hand combat and the attack stalls (XV-617/22), but the Trojan pressure mounts, especially on Ajax. Paying dearly in casualties (XV-745/6), Hector at last makes headway against Ajax the Great, the foremost defender, destroying his pike (XVI-114/6), while massed shooting and exhaustion pushes him back (XVI-119/22) and allows the Trojans to burn the exposed stern of the vessel he was defending (XVI-122/3 & 285). At the same time, visibility is restored (XV-668/70), whatever the reason for the previous low visibility/ low awareness conditions – spontaneous or engineered.

The intervention of the Myrmidons under Patroclus takes place at this point, catching the Trojans within the Greek camp at their exposed left flank held by the Paeonians (XVI-284/7); something corroborating the earlier detail that, at this location, the allies were deployed, under Sarpedon and Asteropeus (XII-101/2), which explains why the former was in a more favourable position, compared to other Trojan champions, to attempt an interception. The flanking explains why such interception took some time, until the retreat of the Trojan army brought Sarpedon in line with Patroclus.

Achilles has specifically ordered repulsion of the enemy, not pursuit, nor an attempt to suddenly occupy Troy (XVI-80/96), due to the divine overwatch of the city (XVI-94) and obviously having some idea about its nature, including the targeted thunderbolt strikes. The Myrmidons counter-attack in five phalanxes, with their local aristocracy commanding each (XVI-171/97), but overall command has been assigned to Patroclus (XVI-256/7). The attack, by surging infantry (XVI-259) headed by chariotry, if not intermingled with it, is decisive: the Trojans first step back and relax the pressure (XVI-305), and thus the defenders deliver a head-on counterattack in the respite (XVI-356/7) against a startled, if not panicking, enemy (XVI-280), already engaged on the flank, who resists briefly, due to inertia after their previous success, but then give way (XVI-357). Because of the trench at their backs, the Trojans are decimated; chariotry can hardly retreat (XVI-370/1) while Hector for a time continues on foot, saving the infantry that had kept fighting under his personal command all this time from slaughter (XVI-363), but then understands what is in the making, mounts his vehicle and leaves them to be massacred (XVI-367/9). The divine horses of Achilles allow Patroclus to deliver successive charges against massed enemies in order to disperse them (XVI-376/7), and once the route is complete, he easily crosses the ditch (XVI-380/1), overtakes the enemy and cuts off a portion, especially infantry, denying retreat and sealing their fate (XVI-394/7).

The condition being critical, Sarpedon, for the reasons mentioned above, finds himself suitably placed and hurries to intercept Patroclus, as the others seem disinclined to do so. He dismounts (XVI-426), thus imposing a difficult decision on Patroclus: to do the same, thus relaxing the pursuit and allowing a window of escape for the Trojan army, or to clash mounted against a dismounted armoured warrior. As the dismounted armoured javelineer has a distinct advantage in accuracy, flexibility and survivability, Patroclus reciprocates in order to duel (XVI-427) and emerges victorious (XVI-480/91), but by stopping the pursuit briefly, he allows a Trojan disengagement and subsequent rally over the body of Sarpedon. The Greeks, with the momentum of deliverance and of the counter-attack, overpowered the Trojans in the struggle for the possession of the body (XVI-656/65) and the latter are routed all the way back to Troy, under hot pursuit (XVI-684/711). As was his standard practice when Achilles was active (IX-352/5), Hector rallies his troops under the walls, in front of the gates, for a possible counter-attack but also ready to order them into the circuit (XVI-712/4); he will try the same routine with Achilles (XXII-5/6). Being under the protection of conventional and unconventional defences and weapons deployed on the walls, Hector learns/notices that the pursuer is *not* Achilles (XVI-715/25), possibly by the less-than-perfect conduct of the operation, or by the use of spear and not of the signature lance when mounted (XVI-139/44), or by some other sign. Such may have been the physical size of the figure or some indication of loose fitting of the panoply, that would expose the surrogate Patroclus if compared with the very characteristic body form of Achilles.

Patroclus, being repulsed by the divinity and his mystical works in his effort to take the walls of Troy by assault (XVI-700/6), receives the counter-attack of Hector, who correctly focuses on him and not on any other enemy troops (XVI-731/2). Still, the engagement goes to Patroclus, who kills crown prince Kebriones, the driver of his opponent, thus briefly neutralizing his team, and after stiff fighting for the corpse, the Greeks triumph (XVI-781/2); Hector obviously retreats, because he is seen behind the lines when he reappears in the narrative (XVI-818/20), while Patroclus presses home the advantage and causes considerable casualties (XVI-785). Being even closer to the walls, he is struck by divine will/unconventional weapons and is unarmed and stunned in the thick of the fight (XVI-791/806). Euphorbus, a Trojan hero and brother of Polydamas, the chief of staff, wounds him while naked with a spear in the back (XVI-806/8) and Hector emerges on foot to deliver the lethal thrust to the abdomen (XVI-820/2).

At the time, many thought that the head of the charge was Achilles; only the Trojans witnessing the disarmed Patroclus could have had any idea that Achilles was not there. Thus, Trojan morale skyrockets, that of the Greeks plummets and it becomes a focal issue to take possession of the body; Hector has lost his chance to win the war and his casualties are horrific. His window is closed as Achilles is to reappear soon and the allies are decimated, especially their leadership, including but not restricted to Sarpedon. Moreover, it is possible that the divine arsenal is exhausted; it will not emerge in the following encounters – but Hector may have had no idea about this. He collects the weapons of Patroclus, i.e. of Achilles, dispersed by the blast and fallen all around (XVII-125), and puts them on immediately (XVII-189/95), something begging questions on the quality of his own set and thus of the Luwian armourers, despite his body armour (helmet and cuirass) having repeatedly stopped enemy spearcasts: from Ajax on the shield (XIII-191/4), Diomedes on the helmet (XI-349/53) and Idomeneus on the cuirass (XVII-605/6).

The senate, with which he is routinely at odds (XV-721/3), will subpoena him for not taking heed of the acting chief of staff, Polydamas (XVIII-254/81), to fall back before the imminent re-emergence of Achilles. He would have had the enemy crippled and his morale broken, and now it is the opposite. Thus he needs something spectacular; Achilles will be in the fight the next day and the Trojans have lived the horror already. They need a boost, and savage treatment of the corpse (XVII-126/7) may balance the lower significance of the kill.

Menelaus is an astute politician and a decent companion. He is also a realist. He understands the above and also that, after partly avenging the dead man by dispatching Euphorbus (XVII-59/60), he will earn the eternal (figure of speech) gratitude of Achilles (XVII-104/5) and the respect of the army for standing by his comrades (XVII-91/3) by rescuing the body. That is the reason, along with the amicable nature of the deceased (XVII-670/2), that makes the fight over this particular corpse so important.

As the battle was seemingly going to bring about the fall of Troy, the Greeks have once more deployed all of their forces forward, including their heavy infantry elements. Thus, while the loss of Patroclus brings about a local defeat and Hector fails to capture the team and dispatch the driver of the deceased (XVII-525), Menelaus has the perfect man to call upon, Ajax the Great (XVII-114/6), while the close friend of the deceased, Antilochus is summoned, briefed and sent as a messenger back to camp to notify Achilles (XVII-685/90). Once more Ajax had been posted on the left (XVII-116) and Antilochus, a mobile warrior, similarly (XVII-682), showing the cooperation between different troop types.

The battle develops under curtains of smoke or dust, a Trojan ruse or natural events (XVII-366/74 & 649/50) and the tide changes three times (XVII-242/4 & 319/22 & 593/6), finally favouring the Trojans. The Achaeans, defeated, retreat under pressure but in relatively good order (XVII-730/4), but the Trojans overtake and overwhelm them just before the ditch (XVIII-148/55). As if by a miracle, Achilles appears. His war cry (XVIII-221) and imposing stature in the dusk (XVIII-205/6) create an eerie combination and cause deadly panic with some fatalities amongst the exhausted Trojans (XVIII-228/31). As a result, they retire (XVIII-241/2) and the body comes back to the Greek camp with honours (XVIII-233/5), marking the end of the day and the battle. The tides of this battle had changed seven times during this one day!

Third battle

Although nominally starting the next day from where the two enemies had left it, this is not in fact the case; it is a whole new setting, in terms of tactics, morale, aims, objectives and combatants. The Trojans felt uneasy; they had panicked and lost an opportunity to end the war by the simple notion of the arrival of Achilles. It was not so, but the damage done by the mere notion, and the late appearance indicating an imminent participation, were not good indices. The Trojans were undoubtedly the victors of the previous day; they had carried it. Operationally this meant they had the choice of the battlefield and the initiative. Hector restored their morale with his pep talk, and they opted for advanced deployment. The moral issue notwithstanding, this meant that keeping the conquered/liberated terrain, they had two advantages: they did not allow a decent deployment of the larger enemy army, and they had much space behind them for fluid tactics for their chariotry. Hector passed this choice to public vote, his arguments reminiscent of Hitler in the USSR: his estimation and situational report (SITREP) was based on the facts of the previous day, not the prospects of the next. He hoped to go on once more from where he had stopped, keep his territorial and moral gains and, suddenly, he was appreciative of wartime economics; the crippling costs of war (XVIII-288/92). Just as Hitler knew about a wartime economy and did not withdraw from Russia.

Polydamas had a better reading of the situation (XVIII-254/83). Achilles was coming and the Trojans had shown they were not ready. The opportunity to win the war was gone. Patroclus, at the end of the day, restored Trojan morale and donated an excellent set of armour to the Trojans with his death (XVII-130/1), meaning that Achilles had no armour at the moment (XVIII-82/5). And this was all; Patroclus had, on the other hand, wrecked the established Trojan victor mentality, their morale was *restored*, not genuinely *high*, and this meant it was fragile. He had caused crippling losses, including the No. 3 warrior, Sarpedon. He almost stormed the city fortifications and resolved the existential issue for the Greeks. No matter what, the next battle was not to be for their vessels and camp; it was a clean slate. All these, plus the guarantee of Achilles' return, for a second-rate hero, actually Achilles' driver (XVII-475/8; XXIII-279/84) and a couple of Myrmidon *eqeta*. The casualties of the Trojans were crippling; they wanted and intended to but they could not threaten the Greeks any more. Patroclus was, by his deeds, a Greek hero in the modern sense.

The Greeks were delivered; they were defeated, but were delivered. The threat was removed, they had a respite and a new hope. What Achilles' impact was to be was clearly demonstrated from the success of Patroclus and the terror that closed the previous day. They themselves had high morale. The fight would be between two spirited opponents. The Greeks were down just one suit of armour.

The very few, very fresh and very aggressive Myrmidon troops Patroclus had led almost won the war. They were not supposed to; they were tasked to repulse the attackers (XVI-80/90), who were deployed in difficult terrain, overstretched, badly led and tired. Patroclus tried to press home the advantage and cut off (some of) the enemy army to exterminate it and remove the threat for good (XVI-394/8). Sarpedon (XVI-419/27) nullified his effort: not only did he have to stop his galloping charge to dismount and fight, losing time, but the delay allowed for more Trojan chieftains to gather and fight over the dead body, which amounted to a delaying action. The Trojan army was routed, indeed, but not trapped. The emerging Greeks pushed back the Trojans at that point, and Patroclus reverted to the next best thing: he took up the pursuit, which was bloody. Within the chaos, once more he tried to capitalize on the opportunities: he caused mass casualties, terror and panic. The Greeks almost stormed the city by exploiting the fact that the Trojans were off balance, a low blow to Trojan morale. But his troops, and his skill, were insufficient for the task he took upon himself.

Hector could see and count. Achilles was coming. He played the card of his opponent being deprived of his weapons, and thus somewhat of a window of opportunity was perceived. He had to capitalize, as strategically things were not as promising as he would like to think. His new army was broken in a matter of days. The Trojan command on the morning of the second day of the second and toughest battle numbered six Trojan and Dardanian commanders: three sons of Antenor, Aeneas, Hector and Polydamas (XI-56/60). When the Trojans attack the fortress of the Achaeans in five columns, a total of fifteen commanders appear (XII-88/102), three in each. Five were the same as in the morning, as one was killed in action. The other ten included four of the Allies, three of which commanded by themselves one attack column; one, Archelochus, replaces his slain brother. Another four were Priam's sons, and two more were other sons of Antenor. Of the new structure, there are two groups of three that had no part in the first phase of the battle, implying that the Trojans had deployed 60% of their strength, keeping the rest out of sight, to intervene and surprise.

A brilliant choice. Still, the leaders were decimated: three dead, Alkathous, Asius, Archelochus and three wounded, Glaukus, Deiphobus and Helenus. A total of six out of fifteen (40 per cent) out of battle before Patroclus' attack, with only Hector's task group sustaining no leadership casualties; one of the task groups, headed by Deiphobus and Helenus is completely leaderless. Patroclus will slay two more, Kebriones and Sarpedon, bringing the total to eight out of fifteen.

If one excludes true divine intervention, it must have been the Lemnian workshops, possibly deployed in the Troad with the Greek fleet, that have worked miracles. The task of making an excellent new set of armour overnight for Achilles was undoubtedly divine, although details are hazy. Lemnos would have some involvement: the island of Hephaestus (I-590/5), god of the coppersmiths (XVIII-400/5), was held firmly to provide a logistics base including hostage ransoming (XXIV-751/3; XXI-39/45), fencing, purchase of supplies, especially wine (VII-467/75) and – apparently – arms maintenance and repair, as no coppersmiths are mentioned in the Achaean camp.

Unlike the obscure but magnificent armour of Peleus, this one was tailor-made for Achilles and is described in detail (XVIII-478/613) – or it was highly adjustable, to fit him like a glove (XIX-384/6). And this removed the only liability inherited by the previous day: Hector would have a most unpleasant surprise the next day, as Achilles would not be unarmed.

Achilles was set on receiving the indemnity from Agamemnon (XVI-84/6); he was not indifferent to material culture. He simply considered it a distant second to the moral value of such items. Now he would not fight for glory, a metric of which had been the material goods extended. He would fight for vengeance, and he says so (XIX-67/73). He does not care a bit for the indemnity any longer (XIX-146/52). And despite this turn of events, Agamemnon pays it to the full. Contrary to the profile of the profiteer, greedy and exploitative high king, he does not exploit the moment and Achilles' feelings and decision to shirk payment. He could; he made an offer at a time and under a given set of conditions, temporal, moral and tactical. His offer was rejected impolitely and with disgust; he had no obligation. And it does not even cross his mind not to pay in full (XIX-140/2). He, his brother – and some other chieftains – also stay with Achilles in his fasting (XIX-305/7) before the next battle, while the army sups (XIX-309) at the – correct – insistence of the wounded Odysseus (XIX-230/4); and they abstain as well, as a matter of support and empathy to stand by Achilles in sorrow. This is the Greek heroes at their best. For the sake of history, these Greek heroes were the inner circle of the Atreids: their loyal minion and long hand, Odysseus of Ithaca, their trusted advisor Nestor of Pylos and their uncle- from their mother's side – Idomeneus the Cretan (XIX-310/11).

Achilles puts on his new armour and tries it to see how it feels and if it fits (XIX-384/5). Obviously some adjustments to the harness would have been possible; Hector had to make some when putting on the armour he acquired by despoiling Patroclus (XVII-210). When the two forces are set against each other at a distance, as if in a battle by convention, Achilles rides in his chariot to deploy (XIX-424), as expected of all *equeta*; but when Aeneas emerges from the enemy line to intercept him, he dismounts too (XX-158/60). It is clear, from the fact that in front of him was Aeneas and not Hector (who was on the right), that Achilles aimed at the centre, or, to be precise, to the left of the Trojan centre, possibly himself launching from the Greek right wing.

After some taunting, where he directly accuses Aeneas of opportunism and aspirations to the Trojan throne (XX-179/82), they engage in spear casting, where Achilles is true to his fame for his murderous, unstoppable cast (XX-99/100). He emerges victorious, although Aeneas is saved by a sudden, god-sent, very focused screen of smoke, hiding him from the site and the onslaught of Achilles (XX-321/2) while at a disadvantage. This is reminiscent of Ninja disappearance techniques under flash and smoke grenades.

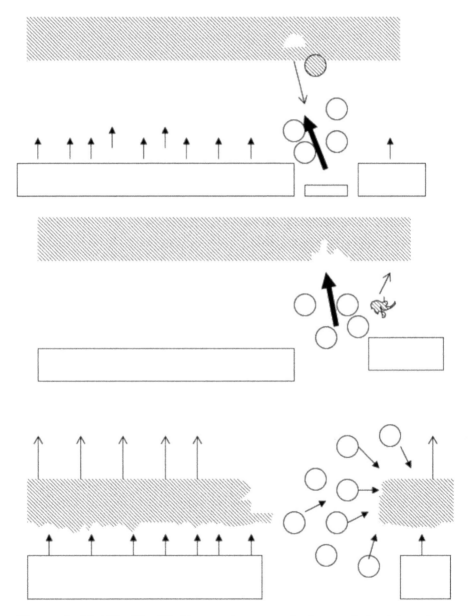

The attack of Achilles. The failed interception attempt by Aeneas, the breakthrough and the extermination of the left flank of the Trojan army.

After this *brief* introduction, Achilles orders a general assault, instead of the usual exchange of missiles from a distance (XX-354/5) and himself is set on a central penetration, and makes it obvious to friend and foe (XX-361/3). This is not some game of attrition or other niceties. Hector does not move to intercept due to a god's advice (XX-376/8) and remains, prudently, within the mass of the army; Aeneas' example must have been persuasive. Unobstructed, Achilles starts a true rampage, exterminating a series of Trojan *eqeta* (XX-382/405) and breaking the Trojan lines (XX-354/5). As he slays one young half-brother of Hector (XX-413/5), the latter in anger moves to vindicate but the result is once more a miraculous, smoky disengagement of a Trojan champion in distress (XX-443/6), indicating another gimmick of Trojan unconventional (a.k.a. divine) tricks with conventional impact. With both Trojan top fighters summarily sent to the rear to lick the wounds of their pride, Achilles concludes the rupture of the enemy formation and is speeding in mounted pursuit (XX-498/502). It is an early, fast and decisive defeat.

The conventional impact, but for the salvation of the Trojan natural leadership, is decisive; the early and sudden collapse of the Trojans spells carnage during the pursuit (XXI-493/4), but, on top of this, a large part of the Trojan army is cut off. Practically the same as the plan of Patroclus, but this time, the attack is properly executed and with sufficient forces. It is an outstanding success.

Achilles correctly prioritizes the most vulnerable of the two parts – or fragments – of the army, the one away from Troy and near the Scamander. It is separated from the rest, thrown into the river (XXI-3/11), boxed and slaughtered, while the rest of the Trojan army is routed (XXII-1/3). This limited entrapment, contrary to Patroclus' effort to cut off as many as possible, leads to clear results. A substantial part of the enemy is eradicated, as their smaller number does not allow a fighting escape, while their comrades make good their own. Away from the walls of Troy and possible divine weapons, Achilles wins the war. After days of crippling casualties sustained in the hope of stealing the victory, this time the exchange is one-sided and massive: the Trojans lost the war on the spot.

The ultimate humiliation and last hope is to take a page from the book of Hercules, their arch-enemy, and use their hydraulic engineering to flood the area near the river, hoping to drown Achilles and his troops (XXI-240/71), while some of their own may find refuge on dykes (XXI-238/9) as they know the area and are familiar with its peculiarities. Even if not, their sacrifice is acceptable; they are already considered killed in action (KIA), while the rest of the army make it to the city.

Somehow the Greeks nullify the Trojan scheme and the Homeric tradition suggests the use of fire. If it is not poetic licence, as fire and water are eternal enemies or opposites, and something like this really happened, it is interesting what the engineers, or even the priesthood of the Achaeans, devised, that would be associated with fire in form or function (XXI-342/55).

Achilles, after making short but bloody work of the Trojan – and allied – force thrown against the river, and their third-best captain, King Asteropeus (XXI-161/82), is saved from the wet trap and returns to the main theatre of the fray to fall upon the larger part of the routed army. A third Trojan hero moves to intercept; a second-class one this time, young Agenor (XXI-545/7), son of the wise Antenor. A second-class but shrewd warrior, casting below the armour and shield at the lower leg, and with great accuracy, but the new greaves of Achilles deflect the blow (XXI-556/60) and once more a miraculous escape is effected (XXI-563/4), this time not by a sudden smokescreen, but perhaps with hide-and-seek into broken, uneven terrain and hidden entrances and crypts.

Hector is once more set before the main gates (XXII-5/6), the ultimate rallying point, as he did by standard operating procedures (SOPs) whenever things were going south. But this is no south; this is hell. The army is destroyed and the war is lost. He knows that unless he resolves the issue then and there his immediate future would be bleak in Troy, as his chief of staff had informed him time and again, Aeneas looks for an opening for the throne and the Trojans, perhaps fed up with Priam's arrogance, now that they have someone of pure blood to blame for broken promises, may well react violently. Hector is very keen to offer a compromise to Achilles and the return of Helen and an indemnity (XXII-1114/21), meaning that by choice the Trojan government had undermined all previous efforts to resolve the issue (IV-87/103; VII-368/78). But he is shrewd enough to understand that wearing the panoply of his opponent, which he took from the dead body of his best friend, whom he wanted to desecrate in death, guaranteed a swift execution as had happened repeatedly with surrendering members of the royal family during the day. Achilles took no prisoners from this day except for ritual execution, and with Hector even 'ritual' would have been too lenient.

Thus he fights. Well, actually he challenges the fastest Greek warrior to a sprint match around the circuit of Troy (XXII-136/7). This is a ridiculous proposal as it stands; it must have been meant to expose him to some intervention from the walls, by missile fire (XII-196) or by divine fire. But the Achaean army being there, the Trojan troops prefer not to irritate the monster. The divine arsenal possibly exhausted and nobody coming to the rescue, Hector turns and fights (XXII-248/52). And despite the scarcity and laconicism of the poetic description (XXII-273/330), the superiority of Achilles is evident. It is evident in the strategic evolution of the fight, with the manipulation of the space and the psychology of the opponent (XXII-273/86), the cold efficiency in executing said manipulation (XXII-276/7) and the skill in the kill, with a high-precision thrust (XXII-322/7). With the entire Greek army there, ordered by nod not to intervene (XXII-205/7), Achilles delivers vengeance and breaks the Trojan spirit (XXII-392/415). It is in the back of his head to press the advantage home, the triple advantage (of killing Hector, despoiling and mutilating him in front of the wall and in public view and of destroying the battle-worthiness of the entire Trojan army after eliminating physically a large part of it) and storm the city (XXII-378/84), but considers it proper to return to pay homage to his dead friend and all the friendly casualties beforehand. This piousness is his ultimate undoing; he could have ended the war then and there, and victoriously at that, perhaps thus surviving it. By not doing so, he would be dead shortly (XII-365/6).

D) After the Iliad

Pentheseleia and Memnon

In a sense, the Trojans were not much worse without Hector. Supplies must have been replenished in the days of their supremacy, few as they were. After all, the siege was never too tight (Thuc I.11,2). The massive casualties, especially allies, who were not familiar with the terrain, reduced the number of mouths (XVII-225/6), while the Achaeans had taken quite some beating, with massive casualties and less propensity to intercept incoming supplies. If the Trojans reverted to waiting it out, it may have turned to their advantage. Additionally, further reinforcements were to arrive.

The arrival of the Amazons, old frenemies from the time of the Amazonian war but also from Priam's common operation with the Phrygians (III-184/9), was no surprise, but for the timing. They arrived during the truce for the rites of Hector (Dikt IV.2), while the Greeks were confident that the bruised Trojans had no nerve – or troops – to assume the initiative. Perhaps originally Penthesilea was supposed to arrive in time to participate in Hector's great offensive and missed it by a few days. In any case her arrival did much to restore the spirits of the Trojans. Her bragging, on the other hand, gives away her status. Hers was a warband, possibly more mercenary (Dik IV.2) than official help, as their leader was banished for accidental murder (Apollod E.5,1); after all, a hefty amount of precious metals was provided by Paris to persuade her to stay. After this renegotiated deal, the Amazon task force, men included, selected an opportune time to deploy – alone, no Trojan or other allies, they were too broken – and charged a hastily assembled Greek line with devastating efficiency (Dikt IV.2). The surprise was total. Achilles and Ajax were playing checkers while it was happening and rushed to the rescue. It is possible that the Amazons were fighting from horseback. In any case the scene where Achilles pierced the queen and her mount by spear rather implies a lance thrust, from chariot or on foot, than any cast (Dikt IV.3). The Greeks did not take it well when women were facing them in battle, Thersites requested the mutilation of the body, Achilles denied such affront (which implies he still is the C-in-C), and when Thersites scolds him, he summarily murders the man (Apollod E.5,1), which brought him into blood feud with Diomedes, the deceased man's cousin. There was no love lost between the cousins; the fathers were undermining and fighting each other, but this was family and a foreigner dispatching blood was another issue. Another account, charging Diomedes with the outrage of the – still alive – Amazon (Dikt IV.3) is a bit less satisfactory, but the common denominator exists: after the Amazon, Achilles and Diomedes where in even worse terms than before.

The massive army of Memnon, with troopers from the Far East of the time, a truly multinational host from the fertile crescent, arrived just after the conclusion of the Amazonian intervention (Dikt IV.4); by 'just', the next day is meant. The important thing is that Memnon's army is supported by a navy, or rather cooperates with a navy in the strategic sphere, as they have to approach from different routes, each arm moving individually. The navy is Levantine, with many Phoenicians, who do not really like the allegiance of this fleet, as they had been raided by Paris; as a result, in the first instance of resistance, they mutiny at Rhodes and the fleet completely disperses (Dikt IV.4), a nice example for similar endeavours by Themistocles against the navy of Xerxes some centuries later (Hdt VIII.22). Whether this naval campaign has something to do with Asian kings projecting a clear preference to conquer the Greeks at sea to assume maritime dominance as found in inscriptions (Haubold 2012) may be debated; it may well be a pattern or a causative relation. The sure thing is that the overlord of Memnon held the Levantine naval areas as subjects and sent a full expeditionary force west, not some relief or volunteers. It is the prequel of the Persian Wars.

The arrival of the Aethiopians and others mobilized the Trojans themselves, who came out to fight once more, after a massive session of training and perhaps reshuffling of Memnon's army in full sight of the citizens, to raise their spirits (Dikt IV.5). The process sounds similar to the one the Greeks underwent in Aulis and perhaps suggests the proceedings of the host of Xerxes when wintering at Sardis during the winter of 481–480 BC (Hdt VII.32). The battle cost some good Achaean warriors and Antilochus, son of Nestor (iv-185/9; Phil, *Her* 26,17–8; Apollod E.5,3; Dikt IV.6), who died defending his father from Memnon's attack. Either during the battle (Apollod E.5,3), or the next day and with the help of Ajax (Dikt IV.6), Achilles killed the Aethiopian king, destroyed his host and sealed his own fate.

Demise of Achilles and Ajax

Either after slaying Memnon and during the pursuit, or on some other occasion, Achilles was killed by Paris, allegedly with an arrow, poisoned or not, to the heel, guided by Apollo. There are alternative traditions, which implicate Achilles' passion for Priam's daughter Polyxena (Dares 27; Dikt III.2; Phil, *Her* 24–57; Hyg, *Fab* 110). Whether Paris sniped at Achilles in a secret meeting, which would have made the girl his accomplice, or stabbed him during a parley, at the temple of Apollo (Dikt IV IV.11), the common denominator is that Paris had slain Achilles in a way discouraged by the customs of war and religion and somehow there was some involvement of Apollo. The main tradition, of Aethiopis, with the bow and Achilles' heel is more convincing and Petersen's *Troy* develops it superbly: fully armoured, Achilles had a weak spot at the heel. Once hit there, his famous speed was gone and with much or even more effort and casualties, he was killed conventionally. But the decisive wound was at the heel. Still, the issue of an ambush holds water (Dares 34; Diktys IV.11); if not, the Greeks would not have sacrificed Polyxena, the daughter of Priam and the object of Achilles' love at his grave (Phil, *Her* 44–57; Dares 43; Hyg, *Fab* 110). This implies they believed she was guilty of baiting the trap.

The Trojans were too elated, grew some spine and tried to take possession of the corpse, but this was not to happen (Dikt IV.12). After a gruesome battle, the Greeks took possession of the body, with Odysseus covering it and Ajax carrying it (Apollod E.5,4). After the funeral rites and the funeral games (Apollod E.5,5–6), the armour of the fallen warrior was to be passed to his successor. Contrary to all expectations, this was not Ajax, but Odysseus, which enraged the former (xi-543/9) and definitely has the signature of Atreid malice in the proceedings (Dikt V.14). The official story was that Ajax, in his rage, decided, in the middle of the night, to murder the Greeks for the affront (all of them? Alone?), but Athena took his wits and he mistook livestock for humans and slaughtered it. In the morning, he understood what had happened and in disgrace he committed *sepuku* (Apollod E.5,7; Phil, *Her*

35,10; Hyg, *Fab* 107; Palaeph, *De Incred* 12); the Samurai would have few amendments to make to the technique. His murderous intent was punished by Agamemnon by denial of a proper burial. He was buried in a coffin and far from the camp (Phil, *Her* 35,15; Apollod E.5,7).

To say that Ajax, cousin to Achilles, had succumbed to rage, like his cousin, is all well and good, although in the *Iliad* nothing indicates this to the reader. Their characters were very different (Phil, *Her* 35,5). But to say that in full possession of his faculties he was going to slay the Greeks (Apollod E.5,6), and not *some* of the Greeks, is ridiculous. Saying that he took leave of his senses not for the murderous intent, not for the stupid idea that he could murder by himself so many men as if cattle, but for the selection and misidentification of the targets seems, though, pure malice. The Aeacids where exterminated with the exception of Teukros, who, wisely, chose never to return to *Agamemnonland* and founded Salamis in Cyprus (Dikt VI.4).

Demise of Paris and Eurypylus

With Achilles and then Ajax dead, the Greeks were at a loss. They only had one good, top fighter, in the guise of Diomedes. The Trojans had Aeneas and Deiphobus. The Greeks needed more, and especially they needed an Achilles, an aggressive man-at-arms. Perhaps the need for shield-bearers was now lower, because the Trojan field army was destroyed. They also needed more archery and, once the war had become total and the gloves were off, the poison arrows of Hercules were cleared (Apollod E.5,8).

There are different traditions as to how Philoctetes came in, along with Neoptolemus, the son of Achilles. The latter filled the bill for an assault fighter. Neoptolemus was raised on Scyros (XIX-330/5), in line to succeed his grandfather king Lycomedes, but was fetched to avenge his father (Apollod E.5,11). He was to reign over both kingdoms, but had not properly taken on the mantle of Peleus (XIX-330/5). He was not a graduate of Cheiron's academy, obviously. He was 18 years old at the very least. Achilles left Scyros to participate in the attack against Mysia, and eight years after this operation the landing on the Troad took place, while the *Iliad* develops ten years after the landing. Achilles did not return to Scyros to reside after he left. He started for Troy from the realm of his father, Peleus, who bade him farewell (IX-438/40; XI-780), although whether these events refer to the first campaign against Mysia or the second cannot be deduced. In any case, Achilles must have called to Scyros at some occasion or other after the first campaign (Apollod E.3,18; IX-663/4; Hyg, *Fab* 96).

A warrior is nothing without his weapons and Odysseus had to part with the armour of Achilles (Apollod E.5,11). Obviously the Myrmidons

– and the cherished vehicle and team of Achilles – were placed under the new leader; it is not known who had been the commanding officer in the meantime. Neoptolemus was every bit like his father and brought a fresh breeze of optimism to the army and a renewed determination for vengeance and victory (Dikt IV.15–16), a will to win, along with reinforcements (Dikt IV.16). He dispatched the son of Telephus, Eurypylus (Apollod E.5,12), who had brought havoc to the Greeks with his forces of Mysians and Hittites (Dikt IV.14) enhanced by Trojan veterans (Dikt IV.17), and slain the elected leader of Thebes, Peneleus (Dikt IV.17) – ironically the constitutional successor of Thersander, son of Polynices and king after the fall of the city to the gang of Diomedes; Thersander was slain by his father Telephus in Mysia (Apollod E.3,17). And in this way the very last shipment of assistance expected by Priam was liquidated, while a first shipment of reinforcements had come for the Greeks. The Trojans were dismayed, and Aeneas had already started thinking the next day; he did not participate in the offensive of Eurypylus (Dict IV-17).

The later of the late arrivals was not a new one; Philoctetes participated in the original expedition but did not land in the Troad with the others. He had stayed in Lemnos, (II-718/22) the actual logistics base of the Greeks, despite its partial neutrality as a fencing and slaver centre (XXIV-751/3; XXI-40/4). Was he left there due to injury, as the lore has it (II-721/4; Apollod E.3,27)? Or as a reserve and rearguard, given that a small, selected crew stayed with him (Dikt II.14), and his main force deployed to Troy (II-726/7)? Or was he, personally, left behind due to the intervention of the Apollonian priesthood of the Achaeans under some memorandum to banish poisoned weapons? The mediator of such an understanding must have been Odysseus. This is the man Philoctetes hates and blames for his exclusion from the war, whether due to a poisoned wound or not. Odysseus was well informed on poisons, as he was a user himself, seeking such in Ephyra in Thesprotia, opposite Corfu (i-259/63), the main source of venoms and their know-how at the time. After all, Odysseus abstained from the martial use of bow in battle (xxi-39/41).

The Greek Apollonian priesthood healed Philoctetes by the hand of an Asklepiad (Apollod E.5,8). Why this had not happened before is a valid question. Obviously the healing refers in occult terms to Philoktetes and his poison arrows being reinstated; to a ban or curse or taboo being lifted. Thus, roughly in the same time frame, possibly after the neutralization of the Mysian and Hittite reinforcements under Eurypylus, Philoctetes slew Paris slowly and painfully (Dikt IV.19), in order to make it clear to the Trojans that the Greeks had similar weapons and their own 'gods'.

Paris' demise left the warmongering party headless. It was a nice opportunity for peace. But adding affront to avarice, Priam remarried Helen to one of his sons, Deiphobus, showing who was behind Paris' policies after all (Apollod E.5,9). The Trojans obviously refused to listen to reason, and by this marriage proved that it was not the policy of Paris, but of Troy – perhaps of the popular party – that he was enacting. Helen is not returned, even now that Paris was not present to veto it, and with Achilles, who at some point developed an existential and personal enmity against Troy (XXI-128/34), dead. On the contrary, they decide, like the Athenian democrats in 425 and 409 BC, to fight on.

Deiphobus was automatically selected for the succession, once in the bed of Helen (iv-276), and Helenus, the runner-up, decided to become a hermit on Mount Ida (Apollod E.5,9); this tradition is more believable than the one that he retired after the murder of Achilles due to the sacrilege committed by his brothers in the temple and during a truce in honour of the God (Dikt IV.18). Calchas, remembering his (alleged) Trojan roots and contacts (Dares 15), but also the privileged intelligence of the priesthood internationally (be that divine or not) was quick to tip off the Achaean supreme command, and Odysseus (Apollod E.5,9), possibly assisted by Diomedes (Dikt IV.18), led a select task force to capture the man, bring him in and debrief him over the oracles of Troy (Dikt IV.18; Apollod E.5,9–10) – meaning all the secrets of its defence. And thus the Greeks learnt of the Palladium artefact, its whereabouts, its significance (occult and tactical) and, most probably, the secret entrances to the city by the sewage channels.

Chapter 13

The Day has Come

A) The Palladium

Few things are stranger in the story of the Trojan War than the famous Palladium. Manfrenti (2004) believes that this artefact, a source of mystical power, was the real cause of the war. The controversy surrounding it should have produced heated contest; that it did not, is a proof of the minimal scholarly attention paid to the ethical, moral and socio-religious character of the epics, i.e. in sectors beyond historicity that is usually taken as non-existent.

Controversies abound. The Palladium is in honour of Athena and yet, if not captured by the Greeks, the city cannot fall, due to the protection of Athena, who is set to destroy it (XX-313/7)! After the procession of the queen and her companions to placate her, as instructed by Helenus (VI-86/98), which almost won the war, the issue of the Palladium is the second case where Athena seems to play a role in the protection of Troy (Dikt V.5); an involuntary role casting doubt on the power of a goddess. This suits the Christian view of impotent and non-existent pagan gods, but how exactly did it sit with said pagans? How was it that Athena eliminated two major Greek heroes for minor offences? Violating the sanctuary of a temple is bad, and Ajax the Lesser by doing so against Princess Royal Cassandra, junior daughter of King Priam and Queen Hecuba, was impious. Seeking sanctuary in a temple of a goddess almost expelled from the city pantheon is, though, hypocrisy. Why not presuppose that the goddess, in her deep and proven enmity against the city, had not considered her abode there to be profane and any divine protection to such offenders, especially the royal family and the accursed Princess Cassandra, forfeited?

A possible answer (Kalopoulos 1998) may be that the artefact was used for the safekeeping of mystical, divine weapons such as poisons, potions, explosives and, most likely, their formulas. The Palladium fell from the sky; then why give it a name referring to Athena, if the association of the Palladium with Athena is not on the basis of knowledge/science and simply religion/worship? Its size is not ascertained: the one implied by Diktys (Dikt V.8) must have had ample internal space allowing for powders and

raw materials. If it was a statuette, as often depicted in art, a folded recipe/
formula could be the answer.

The Palladium cannot have been associated with the plague that befell
the Achaeans (I-50/3). Had it been so, the plague would have persisted until
the utter, or at least functional, extermination of the invaders, as happened
to armies besieging Jerusalem a few centuries later. The divine bolt weapons,
on the other hand, used repeatedly against the Achaeans at Troy (VIII-75/8
& VIII-170), such as the thunderbolt of Zeus that stopped Diomedes' attack
by impacting in front of his horses (VIII-132/58) – in fact better understood
as a near miss of a targeted strike – might have been connected to this
artefact. After all, there was the precedent of Thebes where Kapaneus, father
to Sthenelus, assaulted the wall and was thunderstruck by Zeus because of
arrogance and presumptuousness (Soph, *Ant* 129/35; Aesch, *Seven* 422/34).
As mentioned before, something similar will occur in Delphi against the
Persians in 480 BC and the Gauls in 279 BC. It is tempting to suggest that
the priests of Troy decided, like their Theban colleagues before and the
Delphians later, to enact the will of the Gods by throwing lightning bolts
themselves.

When the Greeks learned of the artefact and its significance (not its
exact function), a special mission was organized, to steal and perhaps use it
themselves, by the usual pair of special operators, Diomedes and Odysseus,
who infiltrated, possibly from the extended sewage or watering duct networks
(Zangger 2016) and were successful in obtaining the artefact and carrying it
away (Apollod E.5,13).

B) The Trojan Horse

Unlike the Palladium, the Trojan Horse is well known and, from ancient
times, caused considerable deliberation. It might have existed as the legend
has it (Hyg, *Fab* 108), a hollow artefact presented as a religious offering
with a task force of commandos in its bowels, towed in by unsuspecting,
jubilant Trojans as a token of victory. Or, in a different form but of the same
function, i.e. some contraption to assault a fortified city, as a siege device/
engine (Paus I.23,8). Or it may refer to something loosely associated with
'horse' and detrimental for the survival of the city.

Taking the third possibility, the horse was the symbol of a gate at Troy
(the Gate of the Horse) opened to the Greeks by a group of traitors (Dares
40), although it could just as well refer to the gate the invaders assaulted
successfully after all. Other interpretations are possible, as the metaphor for
an earthquake (Murphy 2017), since both the horse and the earthquakes are

directly associated with Poseidon, especially given the role of earthquakes to facilitate, at the opposite side of the straits, the Turkish conquest of the Kallipoli Peninsula in the early second millennium AD. Still, the Greeks being so lucky, after a ten-year siege, as to be assisted by an earthquake, or being there hoping to get one of the proper magnitude and focus, sounds a bit stressed.

The first possibility leads to rather simple conclusions. The Greeks constructed a wooden artefact shaped like a gigantic horse, hid some elite warriors in it, wrote a dedication (one must note that there was again a written piece of information) to Athena, and sailed away by night, not to be obstructed by the Trojans, especially vindictive ones, following Hector's line of thought for deterrence (VIII-512/6). The amazed Trojans find the Greek camp deserted but for the artefact, and one mutilated poor bastard left behind, perhaps to die; he gives the name Sinon. The survivor, now that he was delivered by the Trojans, reports gratefully that the Greeks left the artefact to appease Athena for a good sail home (why to appease their patroness, or how she had anything to do with sea-weather are open issues). A priest of Troy, Laocoon (Apollod E.5,17), does not buy the story and proposes burning the wretched thing, but he is eliminated, with his sons (or followers/ministers) by (sea)serpents, sent by Poseidon against his minister and to favour the Greek ruse. After these events, the Trojans are persuaded to bring the artefact into the city, and tear down a part of the wall as the height of the artefact was intentionally too high, to discourage exactly such proceedings – or so says Sinon.

The victory dance – and feast – leaves the Trojans in a drunken stupor, Sinon signals to the raiding party, who come out of the horse, while sending a fire signal, seen by the Greek fleet hidden in the shores of the island of Tenedos. The raiders open the gates, slaughter any half-asleep sentries and occupy strategic locations in the city. When the army arrives, the city falls in a blood orgy, the inhabitants suddenly waking into a nightmare and in some cases fighting with desperation. The Greeks burn the city, slaughter or enslave much of the population, slay the king and his successor Deiphobus, release Helen and pay their debt from ten years before: they do not touch a hair, or a fabric, from the house of Antenor and everyone and everything in it, as signalled by a hide. How did the patriarch know *when* to deploy said hide? In the midst of savage retribution, where Priam is slain by the son of Achilles, Neoptolemus (Dares 41; Dikt V.12; Apollod E.5,21), and Deiphobus, the heir apparent by Menelaus (Dikt V.12; Apollod E.5,22), Aeneas packs his family and friends and leaves, not undetected but unmolested by his enemies (Apollod E.5,21).

This version has been questioned since antiquity for being implausible (Paus I.23,8). It is, but not that much. This is not the only time in history that some people, out of relief, made a disastrous security miscalculation. Why did the priests detailed to guard the Palladium raise no objections to the acquisition and endorsement of the horse, once the city had lost its occult/mystical arsenal? And why did a priest of some deity, Laocoon, got involved in the case (Apollod E.5,17)? The Trojan horse was dedicated to Athena, not Poseidon; Poseidon was the lord of the horses, but Athena presided over chariotry. It is possible that Laocoon was, or was appointed ad hoc (Hyg, *Fab* 135) minister of the water deity protecting Troy, as mentioned in the Alaksandu treaty (Pantazis 2006) and his involvement was exactly due to the fact that the city was under the protection of his divine overlord. He was institutionally involved in the security and safety of the city.

The third issue is the reason Aeneas was allowed to depart, more or less comfortably, and definitely with his father, his comrades and all the tokens of the home deities – a true, official onset of a colonial mission (Apollod E.5,21).

The Greeks had enough chivalrous spirit to literally keep the promise they made to Antenor after more than 10 years (Paus X.26,8) for his support of their cause and the deliverance of their delegation from the outrages perpetrated by the Paris faction (III-203/7; Apollod E.3,28–9). But they had no reason to treat Aeneas particularly well, no matter where his father was located.

The existence of accomplices from within the city is a favourite component for interpreting the lore (Franklin 2002); Dares used it in antiquity (40–1). A recurring issue over the centuries, it may fill some strange gaps in the narrative. Aeneas is the best candidate for the role of traitor. Diktys records the Greeks suggested him coming to Greece, where he would be given a fiefdom but he refused (Dikt V.16).

Antenor, personally insulted and bullied by Paris (VII-354/64), was a senator and Priam did nothing to save his dignity – he had lost many of his noble sons in the service of his homeland. The disenchanted priestess of Athena, Theano, was his wife (VI-298/300). Panthus, father of the chief of staff Polydamas, was not royalty and, together with Antenor, was against the war (Dikt II.23–4).

And then there is Prince Helenus, a seer, if not a priest, possibly disgusted with the behaviour of the partisans of Paris, especially if poison or the pretext of an oath had been employed to bring down Achilles. Helenus corroborated Calchas.

Aeneas' motives may not be known, but they might have had something to do with the prospect of succeeding Priam, as eloquently noticed by Achilles (XX-178/83) when Hector and Paris were still both alive and well. His sights might have been set after the demise of Paris, but his hopes dashed as Deiphobus stepped in line – and into the bed of Helen. Or maybe he understood, at some time, that utter defeat was near and wanted to survive; both the enemy and Deiphobus. In any case, he was not able – or inclined – to live in post-war Troy and Dardania and sailed away, either immediately or after some effort to adapt to the post-Priam Troad.

What could his role have been? To suggest bringing the artefact within the walls; a hand in liquidating the meddlesome priest Laocoon; lax security for the night; suggesting where to place the artefact and possibly signalling to the enemy fleet are all possibilities. Drugging the wine, to incapacitate the celebrating populace fast, is another. The night is not long, and to row from Tenedos to Troy, land and go into the city on foot, and all this after everyone is dead drunk, is a bit challenging in temporal terms … especially if followed, as legend has it, by a vicious assault and a stiff fight during the fall.

But it is very likely that there was another Achaean agent in Troy, who could have done some of the above. Helen, possibly bitter at being passed to another Trojan royalty as if an inheritance; she might have escaped with her life from the encounter with her cheated husband Menelaus for good reason.

And third, but enjoying a lower degree of freedom of movement, was Sinon, the agent Odysseus planted to manipulate the Trojans to transport the horse within the walls instead of destroying it.

The Trojans were quick to believe the Greek retirement was for good. Was it because they *wanted* to believe it? Or did they have good reason to expect such developments? They could have staged unease and riots back on the Greek mainland, as was standard Persian practice later, against Agesilaus the Spartan and Alexander of Macedon.

The second possibility suggests that the Trojan Horse was in fact a siege engine (Paus I.23,8), incidentally shaped to the rough lines of a horse, as depicted in Assyrian reliefs (Connolly 1977). The assault tower and the battering ram, or a combination of the two, are the most probable devices to mistake for a horse. In this case it is obvious why the Palladium, if of the nature mentioned above, had to be taken out of the equation, even if the Achaeans had established dominance over the battlefield. Its secrets could destroy the contraption. The only objection one can have is that sapping is explicitly mentioned in the *Iliad* (XII-256/62) and, if there were such machines, other uses would have been reported, as in Thebes. With the first campaign a generation before, and the second some years before that against Troy, the means, especially those requiring extensive know-how and ample resources, could not have changed a lot. Secondary but obvious developments, such as the massive Trojan celebration, or the absence of the Greek fleet, if not invented to explain the mutated lore of the Trojan horse, cannot fit with the narrative of a siege machine.

Another machine, not conventional siege contraptions, may be suggested, but with less persuasive arguments. The horse was dedicated to Athena, possibly implying the application of science/technology, especially since she was the inventor of the bridle and the use of horses in chariotry. On the other hand the horse was an animal sacred to Poseidon, god of the earthquake. For Athena, any other animal would do; but the Trojan Horse was a double dedication: to Athena, by the inscription, and to Poseidon by shape. This would better suit, at least in part, the issue of earthquake. Remembering the walls of Jericho (Kalopoulos 1998), the wooden horse might have been the instrument of an event producing a direct or indirect effect reminiscent of an earthquake. It could have been used as a bomb, filled with explosives – given that the secrets of the Palladium were now in Greek hands – to tear down the walls, or as a vehicle/vector to insert the bombers/sappers.

Chapter 14

The Next Day

The Trojan War was the first known intercontinental war. It had it all: a galley D-Day, the Trojan von Rundstedt/Hector, the Greek Patton/Achilles and a veritable cast of ancestors of history's most well-known personae fighting with vigour and determination, in cases with gallantry as well. The impact was just as apocalyptic. Whether migration movements to the north of the Euxine had occurred, and dismantled the established trade networks, cannot be proven. It remains open to question, who were duelling the coasts of the Euxine, forming the farther part of the trade network of the Mycenaeans; was it the Scythians, or some predecessor that was pushed out, possibly the Cimmerians? But what happened in the far north is difficult to follow, and has no causal relationship with the Achaean campaigns. Orestes' adventures in Scythia (Taurus), which inspired the famous tragedy (*Iphigenia In Tauris*), suggest that the trade route between the Euxine and the Mediterranean did not re-open automatically with the fall of Troy, as huge social and political upheavals had taken place and trade may have been deregulated for years. The direct and indirect results should be classified by geography in the following categories:

- What happened in the Troad, the main theatre of war;
- The impact to the wider theatre, practically Asia Minor and (part of) the Aegean;
- The impact on out-of-area but affected geographical units, including Egypt–North Africa (taken as a whole), the wider Mediterranean, especially to the west, and the Levantine coast;
- What happened in Greece.

The Troad

After the fire and fall, Troy did not disappear or be abandoned. It was completely destroyed as a political and military force, but not as a residential and cultural complex, no longer posing any threat for Mycenae. The fall of Troy saw slaughter, arson, looting and enslavement; but not extermination. Similar to practices mentioned by the Hittites (Pantazis 2006), much of the population, the productive and potentially troublesome elements, were carried away, and the rest were ruled by some converted local, occasionally of the ruling dynasty. This sounds very like Hercules' practice, and the Mycenaeans particularly favoured women slaves for their industrial (IX-128/30) and domestic tasks (VI-456/9), but also men for rural/agricultural tasks, especially concerning livestock handling (xv-403/14). This pattern may have been universal and possibly followed by the Achaemenid Persians in their conquests, where stormed cities were reduced to insignificance, but not erased from the face of the earth, the obvious example being Miletus.

Both Diktys and Dares accept that, after the fall of Troy, the place was not completely levelled, but that several survivors gathered under Antenor; both imply a rather massive population of survivors (Dares 44; Dikt V.17) that had escaped annihilation and assembled for the next day in inglorious existence in terms of sustenance rather than imperium. A coup may have been attempted by the other Dardanian traitor, Aeneas; but he failed (Dikt V.17) and then he left the Troad for Italy by ship with his followers; possibly he used (some of) the (few?) vessels built and pressed into action by Paris (Dares 44).

It is not very probable – but it is possible – that the Greeks offered Aeneas a large fiefdom in Greece, which he refused. It was a steep price for a confirmed traitor; where exactly would Aeneas settle and what would he do in the continuous local brawling due to rivalries between priesthoods and regions? It cannot be substantiated, but he probably would have liked such an arrangement and was denied it, but allowed instead to settle in the West on his own terms and means. Even if the presence, rule and prestige of the Achaeans was not firmly established in the West, the course from the Troad to Italy allows for much Mycenaean leverage.

Antenor and his people (more like a clan, possibly augmented by partisans of the same political views) were spared because they had treated the Greek envoys properly; the traitors, if any, would have been equally favoured both in staying and in migrating.

The Mediterranean and the Levant

The fall of Troy was not an isolated event. It occurred to several other cities and many of them Trojan allies. The period was very turbulent, as corroborated by archaeology, and one may suppose either that the destroyed cities succumbed due to a common cause, as the mainstream theory of the Sea Peoples suggests; or there might have been a common denominator (perhaps another interrelation of the Sea Peoples). But a massive flow of populations clockwise is obvious: the Luwians moving toward Egypt and the Levant,

Kaska (Kaukones) dislodging the Hittites in a north–south direction and massive Thracian migration from Europe to Asia (Strab, *Geog* XII.8,3), to create Bithynian Thrace (Hdt VII.75), possibly through the Bosporus, are eloquent enough. A period of instability and chaos, with one city burning the other and in turn falling victim to other states, raiders or invaders, would perfectly match the scene. For example, in Classical Greece, Athens and Thebes razed several cities and in turn were defeated: Athens twice survived, thanks to the magnanimity of the Spartans and the Macedonians, while Thebes was annihilated by Alexander the Great.

It seems that, after the fall of Troy, the Thracians cross to Asia to form Bithynia, possibly accounting for the Cimmerian invasions in all but name. The Luwians, thus pressed, move south-south-east, to become the Sea Peoples (Zangger 2016; Giannakos 2016) but also west, especially after being repelled in Egypt. The Cilicians move from NW Asia Minor, near Troy, to the other, SE corner of Asia Minor (Strab, *Geog* XIV.4,1). The Kaska move south, sweeping the Hittites and possibly initiating the whole domino (Zangger 2016).

The Greeks seem to move radially: some to the western Asian coast, which will be the primary destination of their first colonization wave, perhaps one or two generations after the conclusion of the war. Some others to the southern part of Asia Minor, as in Pamphylia. Cyprus, which could easily have raised fifty ships to participate in the Trojan campaign, but did not (Apollod E.3,9), was colonized at least in two places: Keryneia in the north is named after the area in the middle of the northern Peloponnese shore and mountain range. And Salamis, named after the island in the Saronic Gulf, founded by Teukros, who did not return to be scolded by his father for failing to avenge – or protect – his brother from the malice of the ringleaders (Dikt VI.4). The adventures of the Cretans and the turmoil in the island (Apollod E.6,9–10) perhaps explain and definitely corroborate Cretan colonization in Palestine, possibly as part of the Sea Peoples, which may have resulted in the foundation of the Philistine cities.

Some others, like Diomedes, go to Italy (Ovid, *Met* 14, 455–60), following the Luwians. The migration of the latter to the West is exemplified by the Lydians colonizing Tyrrhenia in Italy (Hdt I.94,2), and the colonization of Sardegnia by the Satrdana of the Sea Peoples, possibly Lydians too, from near Sardis (D'Amato and Salimbeti 2015). Nearer Greece, the Carians seem to have colonized islands of the Aegean, once Mycenaean seafaring collapses, along with the palaces. When the Athenians consecrate Delos (late fifth century BC), they find many Carian graves, recognizable by the burial customs, posture and armour (Thuc I.8,1). The latter implies a knowledge of

Carian armour and this must refer to relatively recent models, like the early hoplite gear, dated to comfortably after the Trojan War, rather than Luwian models that would apply to dates before and after it. This presence of the Carians corroborates the Sea Dominance (i.e. Thalassocracy) catalogue and gives proper meaning to the Egyptian narrative that 'the Sea Peoples conspired against me at their many islands…'.

Whether the founding of Carthage by the Phoenicians has anything to do with this westward movement after the Trojan War cannot be substantiated. Carthage was founded considerably later, and perhaps the association is restricted to the direction of the colonial operation, following an established course, set by others, some centuries earlier.

In this pattern, there is a very interesting question. What happened with Egypt? The Sea Peoples invaded there, to be repulsed – or so says the Pharaoh. True, they did not colonize it as they did the southern part of Asia Minor: many toponyms there are similar to the ones of the northern part (Pantazis 2006) and although chronology may be an issue, this could be explained by northern Luwians moving southwards, as did the Cilicians (Strab, *Geog* XIV.4,1 & XIII.3,6). Some Greeks would be among the Sea Peoples, no doubt: the Cretans, for example, landed and colonized Palestine, and Odysseus told a perfectly believable tale of a Cretan raid against Egypt, that was repulsed bloodily (xiv-245/72).

What does this say about Menelaus? Menelaus spent some time in the Levant. He was a guest of the Egyptian sovereign. This has different interpretations: he might have offered assistance against some of the invasions; the Egyptians did use mercenaries of tribes and peoples that were their enemies to counter their unaffiliated siblings that were attacking. Many Egyptian mercenaries were Sea Peoples (D'Amato and Salimbeti 2015) and this may not refer to former captives, but to actual war bands seeking employment. The other possibility was that Menelaus was implicated in the different events of the Sea Peoples' invasion, and his sojourn in Egypt was rather 'hospitality' to a defeated and captured foreign attacker. Odysseus' *Avatar*, having been captured and enslaved in Egypt once defeated in the raid, he was persuasive that he was once more free. Being captured in Egypt as an enemy did not mean one was erased from the face of the earth. After faithful service, he was redeemed.

Greek mainland and the islands

Similar movements on a much smaller scale occurred in Greece: land was at a premium within the Greek peninsula, and social friction occurred. The legal offspring of the warriors had grown up in a power vacuum and had stepped in. There was no way to make them step back or down to make room for their returning fathers/elders/veterans. It was a generation gap, just as destructive as the one of the late twentieth century; and due to more and better reasons than the latter. It is the generation of Orestes, Telemachus and Neoptolemus, although the latter, baptized in the fire of the Trojan War, was a different case after all. It must be underlined that not all the others felt the need to man ships and assist their fathers in the war, but preferred the niche they had carved for themselves back home.

The greater part of the returning Greek armada was destroyed at Cape Caphereus, during a storm; King Nauplius, father of Palamedes, lights fires on the steep rocks to deceive them, since they would mistake the lights for safe heavens and ports. It is the first part of his revenge for the murder of his son. The 'conspiracy of the queens' was the second, which ignited the generation gap.

Nauplius took some time to travel the Greek mainland and entice disenchanted queens to move in unison to take back or assume the authority of their realms. Whether this was based on a previous matriarchal background is open to debate. The implicated queens were the wives of the inner ring: these of Diomedes, Agamemnon, Idomeneus and Odysseus. The former seduced the son of Sthenelus, who had a third of the kingship of Argos; the youngster, though, after assuming the throne, dispatched the queen summarily, along with the young lad Cyanippus, whose guardians were Diomedes and his own father Sthenelus, and kept the power for himself; Diomedes thus migrated to Italy, while what happened to the usurper's father, Sthenelus, is a mystery.

Odysseus' wife had been unfaithful, but kept faith in terms of authority. Pausanias mentions her grave on the mainland, where she died after being cast out and divorced by Odysseus precisely because of her faithlessness (Paus VIII.12,6). But the fact that the suitors are infuriated by her attitude in the *Odyssey*, usually taken to mean her marital faith, is easily interpretable as a matter of institutional authority: whether she was at last making one of them her official consort and regent to Telemachus, or king by matrimony. The language does not imply marital faith (ii-85/114)!

Agamemnon's story is well-known, but there are details of importance. Clytaemnestra had no entitlement to Mycenae, since her firstborn daughter was removed; this is irrespective of whether Iphigenia was hers and Agamemnon's or Helen's and Theseus' (Paus II.22,7). She was adopted/recognized by the regal pair of Mycenae and was their firstborn for any legal purpose. Aegisthus, the son of Thyestes and possibly uncle of Agamemnon had, though, such claims. Orestes was an exile to his aunt Anaxibia, the sister of Agamemnon, in Phocis. Once Agamemnon returned from Troy with Cassandra, the last heir of the throne of Priam – and thus overlord of Agenor – he intended to marry her, and thus take formally the throne of Troy; a name reminiscent of his is in a diplomatic letter of the Hittites and refers to him ruling over many islands as dowry (however involuntary) due to a dynastic marriage with a princess of Assuwa (Giannakos 2016). This means that the 'many islands over which Agamemnon rules over' (II-108) may have been an anachronism in the Homeric text; but, contrary to the above, he definitely returned to Mycenae *already married* to Cassandra, evidently by the new sovereign Antenor and his priestess wife Theano, as a ceremony in Mycenae would have no meaning; in Troy it would fully confer the titles upon him. He was going to rule a superpower! The family of Palamedes, father and sons, had every motive to help Aegisthus, and Clytaemnestra, seeing herself utterly ejected from her seat, decided to act swiftly and at the same time exact vengeance for her daughter and her first husband and child (Apollod E.2,16). The Mycenaeans had no particular problem and, once Orestes brought Phocian help to overthrow Aegisthus (Paus II.18,5), the brothers of Palamedes provided the usurper with every possible assistance (Paus. 1.22.6).

With Cassandra out of the picture, Orestes moved in to create a more limited, local superpower, by directly incorporating different realms under his sceptre (Paus II.18,5), while the Dorians were lurking, waiting for their chance. Orestes took Sparta by consent; the Spartans preferred the nephew of Helen over the bastard son of Menelaus (Paus II.18,6), and it must be noted that, in the *Iliad*, Menelaus is never mentioned as fighting with his home troops. His absence in Egypt weakened his grasp of the populace even further; no one knows who the regent had been. The other kings campaigning at Troy in person had left their wives. The sailing of Orestes to the Euxine, to track his sister Iphigenia, means the straits were under Greek authority, indirectly of course. This attests to the rule of Antenor or his offspring. Venturing into the Euxine implies a revival of the trade routes disturbed during the war. Orestes seems to have realized his father's dream of conquest and prestige. Still, the veterans of the Trojan War were sorely missed. Although fighting did occur, it was a given that, with a missing generation, the quality of the home troops was diminishing; when, in the next generation, the Dorians invaded, the son of Orestes was unable to stop them.

The Dorian invasion was a massive revenge of the Apollonian priesthood upon Greece. The cities dear to Hera succumbed to the invaders, vowing to

Apollo and less so to Athena – and thus implying a double origin, Heraclids and Dorians, the former devoted to Athena (their clan leader's guardian) and the latter to Apollo, the god of rural communities and pastoralism.

In here, there was a small problem for the brave new world created by Orestes. Neoptolemus had not been affirmed in the kingdom of Peleus and, once the old man was overthrown and usurped by his unrelenting neighbour Acastus, son of Pelias and sworn enemy to the comrades of Jason, he had no institutional rights to the throne of Phthia. Achilles did not have time to introduce and prepare him for succession in the realm of Peleus – or, rather, the realm acquired by Peleus. Thus Neoptolemus moved west, to the Ionian coast, possibly to lands known by the Trojans through their earlier campaigns. Helenus advised him on the subject. Neoptolemus had some other loose ends, as with the family of the Atreids: he was a war hero, and he would have appreciated a nice throne, as his participation in the war (being the only one of his generation to enjoy this honour) resulted in losing his paternal realm. He was promised the hand of the daughter of Menelaus and Helen, Hermione (Apollod E.6,13), which was highly advantageous for Menelaus, having the son of Achilles to stabilize his own throne in Sparta.

But events were running faster, and Orestes got the bride first, as the heir elect by popular vote. It is possible than Neoptolemus veered to Delphi to set the matter before the judgment of Apollo, as was standard practice in such events. Hercules had done the same, Orestes too. But in here there was a danger: Apollo was hostile to his father, and Neoptolemus was supposedly guilty of atrocities in Troy. This is ridiculous; but Orestes had two allies: the first was the duo of the king and the heir apparent of Phocis, meaning his uncle Strophius and his cousin Pylades, who had a blood feud with Peleus (Paus II.29,9) and some leverage with the oracle. The second was Helenus, a priest of Apollo. Thus Neoptolemus was murdered under some pretext or other – traditions are really varied, indicating perhaps different public versions of the events. But it all comes down to Orestes being left in possession of his gains, territorial, matrimonial and perhaps in cash as well; Pylades being the best friend of the most powerful ruler and Helenus inheriting everything Neoptolemus had obtained, first amongst which was the widow of Hector, Andromache.

Epilogue

The Greeks did not consider the end of the Trojan War anything like an end. It was transitional, an era of turmoil, that led without any pause to their then-past, what is now known as Archaic Greece and, possibly mis-stated, Dark Age that preceded it. The heroic lore survived in many versions – something other, strict oral cultures deem unacceptable and thus suggesting a more easygoing, hybrid method of temporal transmission of data.

But the heroic age did die out after the war. Agamemnon was a most powerful ruler, an emperor in all but name. Neither he nor his minions and champions were to enjoy their victory; as was to happen with the Scythians and the Spartans in later centuries, they were away for too long and the new generation did not acknowledge their niche, nor their glory. They had to migrate and thus enlarge the Greek footprint, but not the empire. They were too bitter for this, whereas Orestes, the son of Agamemnon, consolidated his authority. He ruled a super-kingdom, much bigger than anything Agamemnon had under his direct sway, from Sparta to Phocis. But this was all. The empire was short-lived, even more than the one of Alexander the Great. Lurking in the north, the Dorians – already known to the Mycenaeans, as Homer mentions them, and in Crete nonetheless (xix-177), although it is always possible to have been an intentional later corruption – were unimpressed by Orestes' power projected to the north of the Gulf of Corinth. They were allied to Hercules and thus to the Heraclids from days past (Apollod II.7,7), and their combined forces took their time and the chance and invaded, this time successfully, the land of Orestes. Somehow his rule seems to have been either unappreciated by his subjects, or inadequate and unable to inspire and prepare them for the incoming threat. As a result, his kingdom collapsed after him, giving precious little fuss to the invading Dorians. Theoretically, before entering Peloponnese, the Dorians could not have colonized Crete and thus have been there at the time of Agamemnon (xix-177). In any case, two generations after Agamemnon, the victorious Dorians from the arid lands appropriated the fertile and rich areas of the Peloponnese, thus fully rearranging the distribution of Greek tribes there and triggering the massive colonization to the areas emptied by the Luwians after the fall of Troy. As the Luwians moved south to Egypt and west to Italy and the Aegean, the Greeks established themselves first in western Asia Minor, with its fertile valleys, and then infiltrated into the Black Sea, following routes known through Mycenaean explorers and merchants, this time to plant colonies on the shores of fertile prairies and vast, open plains. The lore of the Trojan War was used to ignite the colonists' interest in this New World. It was the nexus, not a reset, to Classical Greece.

Bibliography

References

Bakas S 2018. *The Mycenaean Dendra Panoply. Experimental Reconstruction and Interpretations*. Masters Thesis in Archaeology, University of Warsaw, The Faculty of History, The Institute of Archaeology.

Best JGP 1969. *Thracian Peltasts and their Influence on Greek Warfare*. Groningen: Wolters-Noordhoff.

Brown A 1998. Homeric Talents and the Ethics of Exchange. *The Journal of Hellenic Studies* 118: 165–72.

Bryce T 2007. *Hittite Warrior*. Warrior 120 Osprey.

Burgess J 1995. Achilles' Heel: the Death of Achilles in Ancient Myth. *Classical Antiquity* 14(2): 217–44.

Burkert W 1985. *Greek Religion*. Wiley-Blackwell.

Castleden R 2005. *The Mycenaeans*. Routledge.

Connolly P 1977. *The Greek Armies*. Macdonald Educational.

Connolly P 1981. *Greece and Rome at War*. Greenhill Books.

D'Amato R and Salimbeti A 2011. *Bronze Age Greek Warrior*. Warrior 153 Osprey.

D'Amato R and Salimbeti A 2013. *Early Aegean Warriors 5000–1450 BC*. Warrior 167 Osprey.

D'Amato R and Salimbeti A 2015. *Sea Peoples of the Bronze Age Mediterranean*. Elite Osprey.

D'Amato R and Salimbeti A 2017. *Early Iron Age Greek Warrior 1100–700 BC*. Warrior 180 Osprey.

D'Amato R and Salimbeti A 2018. *The Etruscans*. Elite Osprey.

De Becker F 2009. Evolution of War Chariot Tactics in the Ancient Middle East. UF 41 Available at: https://www.academia.edu/768238/Evolution_of_War_Chariot_Tactics_in_the_Ancient_Near_East.

Demakopoulou K, Mangou E, Jones RE and Photos-Jones E 1995. Mycenaean Black Inlaid Metalware in the National Archaeological Museum, Athens: A Technical Examination. *The Annual of the British School at Athens* 90: 137–53.

Dezső T 2012. *The Assyrian Army*. Eotvos University Press.

Drews R 1979. Argos and Argives in the Iliad. *Classical Philology* 74(2): 111–35

Drews R 1988. *The Coming of the Greeks: Indo-European Conquests in the Aegean and the Near East*. Princeton University Press.

Drews R 1996. *The End of the Bronze Age: Changes in Warfare and the Catastrophe c.1200 BC*. Princeton University Press.

Fields N 2006. *Bronze Age War Chariots*. New Vanguard 119 Osprey.

Fields N 2007. *Soldier of the Pharaoh*. Warrior 121 Osprey.

Franklin SB 2002. *The Daughter of Troy*. HarperTorch.

Giannakos K 2016. Cutting-edge Technology and Knowhow of Minoans/Myceneans During LBA and Possible Implications for the Dating of the Trojan War. *Talanta* 46–7: 51–80.

Goldsworthy AK 1997. The Othismos, Myths and Heresies: The Nature of Hoplite Battle. *War in History* 4(1): 1–26

Graves R 1955. *The Greek Myths*. Pelican Books.

Grguric N 2005. *The Mycenaeans*. Elite Osprey.

Hamblin WJ 2006. *Warfare in the Ancient Near East*. Routledge.

Hanson VD 1999. *The Wars of the Ancient Greeks*. Cassel.

Haubold J 2012. The Achaemenid Empire and the Sea. *Mediterranean Historical Review* 27(1): 4–23.

Healy M 1992. *New Kingdom Egypt*. Elite 40 Osprey.

Heath I 1979. *Byzantine Armies 886–1118*. Men At Arms 89 Osprey.

Hencken H 1950. Herzsprung Shields and Greek Trade. *American Journal of Archaeology* 54(4): 294–309.

Henty GA 2002. *By Pike and Dyke*. Robinson Books.

Howard D 2011. *Bronze Age Military Equipment*. P&S Books.

Kalopoulos M 1998. *Biblical Religion Vol 2*. Thessaloniki.

Kalopoulos M 2014. *Athena-Metis and Ulissean Spirit*. Thessaloniki.

Kambouris ME 2021. Chapter 8: Black Biology. In: Kambouris ME (ed) *Genomics is Biosecurity*. Elsevier.

Kambouris ME 2022. *The Rise of Persia*. P&S Books.

Kambouris ME and Bakas S 2017. Archery in Ancient Greece: Operational Practice and Tactics *Arheologija i Prirodne Nauke* 12: 159–70.

Kambouris ME, Heliopoulos GZ, Bakas S 2020. The Hypaspist Corps: Evolution and Status of the Elite Macedonian Infantry Unit. *Arheologija i Prirodne Nauke* 15: 19–30.

Kelly A 2012. The Cretan Slingers at War. *The Annual of the British School at Athens* 107: 273–311.

Knight WFJ 1933. The Wooden Horse at the Gate of Troy. *The Classical Journal* 28(4): 254–62.

Maekawa K 2003. Battle Formation of the Sumerian Phalanx. *Bulletin of the Society for Near Eastern Studies in Japan* 46 (2): 28–51.

Malloy B 2010. Swords and Swordmanship in the Aegean Bronze Age. *American Journal of Archaeology* 114(3): 403–28.

Manfredi V-M 2004. *The Talisman of Troy*. Pan Macmillan.

Mayor A 2003. *Greek Fire, Poison Arrows and Scorpion Bombs: Biological and Chemical Warfare in the Ancient World*. Overlook.

Mayor A 2014. *The Amazons*. Princeton University Press.

Molloy BPC 2012. Martial Minoans? War as Social Process, Practice and Event in Bronze Age Crete. *The Annual of the British School at Athens* 107: 87–142.

Monro DB 1884. The Poems of the Epic Cycle. *Journal of Hellenic Studies* 5: 1–41.

Moreu CJ 2003. The Sea Peoples and the Historical Background of the Trojan War. *Mediterranean Archaeology* 16: 107–24.

Motley JL 1855. *The Rise of the Dutch Republic*. Harper.

Murphy L 2017. Horses, Ships, and Earthquakes: The Trojan Horse in Myth and Art. *Iris Journal of the Classical Association of Victoria (New Series)* 30: 18–37.

Napoleon I 1863 *Maximes de Guerre*. Adamant Media Corporation 2001.

O'Bryan J 2013. *A History of Weapons*. Chronicle Books.

Pantazis V 2006. *Homer and Troy*. Kardamitsas [In Greek].

Papadopoulos A 2012. Dressing a Late Bronze Age Warrior: The Role of 'Uniforms' and Weaponry According to the Iconographical Evidence. In: *KOSMOS: Jewellery, Adornment and Textiles in the Aegean Bronze Age. Proceedings of the 13th International Aegean Conference 2010. Peeters*: 647–53.

Papasavvas G 2014. Warfare and the Cypriot Kingdoms: Military Ideology and the Cypriot monarch. In: Iacovou M and Hadjopoulos M (eds), *Basileis and the Poleis on the island of Cyprus*, Cahier du Centre d' Études Chypriotes 44: 153–90.

Parotti P 1988. *The Trojan Generals Talk: Memoirs of the Greek War.* University of Illinois Press.

Parotti P 1986. *The Greek Generals Talk: Memoirs of the Trojan War.* University of Illinois Press.

Partington JR 1998. *A History of Greek Fire and Gunpowder.* John Hopkins UP.

Peacock M S 2017. Wealth and Commerce in Archaic Greece: Homer and Hesiod. In: Eugene Heath E, Kaldis B (eds) *Wealth, Commerce, and Philosophy: Foundational Thinkers and Business Ethics.* University of Chicago Press: 11–17.

Petmezas SV 2019. *Introducing Archeophysiology. Studying the Tactical Athlete of the Ancient World: Physical Performance and Comfort of a Bronze Age Panoply Wearer Warrior, During Different Combinations of Weapon Fighting Techniques in a Stimulated Combat Environment of the Trojan War.* Postgraduate Thesis for Master's Degree in 'Military Fitness and Wellbeing' of the Department of Physical Education and Sport Science, University of Thessaly, Greece.

Photos E, Jones RE and Papadopoulos, Th 1994. The Black Inlay Decoration on a Mycenaean Bronze Dagger. *Archueonierry* 36 (2): 267–75.

Plevris K 1993. *Chess, Nature and History New Position.* Athens [in Greek]

Richepin J 1920. *Mythologie Greque.* 1953 DAREMA Athens [in Greek]

Rutherford I 2020. Chapter 5: Anatolian–Greek Religious Interaction in the LBA. In: *Hittite Texts and Greek Religion.* Oxford University Press.

Scott JA 1909. Homer's Estimate of the Size of the Greek Army. *The Classical Journal* 4(4):165–74.

Sears M 2010. Warrior Ants: Elite Troops in the Iliad. *Classical World* 103(2): 139–55.

Sears MA and Willekes C 2016 Alexander's Cavalry Charge at Chaeronea, 338 BCE. *JMH* 80: 1017–35.

Sekunda N 1992. The Persian Army 560–330 BC. Elite 42 Osprey.

Sekunda N 1998. The Spartan Army. Elite 66 Osprey.

Smith AJC 2015. *Mycenaean Warfare and the Mycenaean Tower Shield.* Alan Smith.

Snodgrass AM 1998. *Arms and Armor of the Greeks.* The Johns Hopkins University Press.

Turnbull S 2003. *Japanese Warrior Monks AD 949–1603.* Warrior 70 Osprey.

Van Wees H 1994. The Homeric Way of War: The Iliad and the Hoplite Phalanx (I). *Greece and Rome, Second Series* 41(1): 1–18.

Van Wees H 2009. *Greek Warfare Myths and Realities.* Gerald Duckford & Co Ltd.

Watkins C 1984. The Language Of The Trojans. In: Mellink MJ (ed) 'Troy and the Trojan War'. Bryn Mawr, 1986 pp.45–62.

Warry J 1980. *Warfare in the Classical World.* Salamander Books Ltd.

Webber C 2001. *The Thracians 700 BC–46 AD.* Men-at-Arms Osprey.

Wilkens IJ 1990. *Where Troy Once Stood.* Rider/Century Hutchinson.

Wise T 1981. *Ancient Armies of the Middle East.* Men-at-Arms 109 Osprey.

Zangger E 2016. The Luvian Civilization. Ege Yayinlari.

Abbreviations

Aesch, *Eumen*	Aeschylus, *Eumenidae*
Aesch, *Seven*	Aeschylus, *Seven against Thebes*
Apollod	Apollodorus, *Biblioteca, Epitome*
Apollonius Rhod, *Argon*	Apollonius Rhodius, *Argonautica*
Arr Anab	Arrian, *Anabasis Alexandri*
Dares	Dares Phrygius, *De Excidio Troiae Historia*
Dikt	Diktys Cretensis, *Ephemeris Belli Trojani*
Diod	Diodorus Siculus, *Bibliotheca historica*

Dion Hal	Dionysius of Halicarnassus, *Antiquitates Romanae*
Gorg, *Def Palam*	Gorrgias, *Defence of Palamedes*
Hdt	Herodotus, *Histories*
Hes, *Sh*	Hesiod, *Shield of Hercules*
Hes, Theog	Hesiod, *Theogony*
Hes, *Works*	Hesiod, *Works and Days*
Hyg, *Fab*	Hyginus *Faboulae*
Ovid, *Met*	Ovid, *Metamorphoses*
Palaeph, *De Incred*	Palaephatus, *De incredibilibus*
Paus	Pausanias, *Graeciae Descriptio*
Phil, *Her*	Philostratus, *Heroica*
Pind, *Od*	Pindar, *Odes*
Plut, *Vit Aemil*	Plutarch, *Life of Aemilius Paullus*
Plut, *Vit Aris*	Plutarch, *Life of Aristides*
Plut, *Vit Artax*	Plutarch, *Life of Artaxerxes*
Plut, *Vit Lyc*	Plutarch, *Life of Lycurgus*
Plut, *Vit Per*	Plutarch, *Life of Pericles*
Plut, *Vit Pyrr*	Plutarch, *Life of Pyrrhus*
Plut, *Vit Solon*	Plutarch, *Life of Solon*
Plut, Vit Thes	Plutarch, *Life of Theseus*
Soph, *Ant*	Sophocles, *Antigone*
Strab, *Geog*	Strabo, *Geographica*
Thuc	Thucydides, *History of the Peloponnesian War*
Xen, *Apoll*	Xenophon, *Socrates' Apology*
Xen, *Cav Comm*	Xenophon, *Cavalry Commander*
Xen, *Const Lac*	Xenophon, *Constitution of the Lacedaimonians*
Xen, *Cyrop*	Xenophon, Cyropaedia
Xen, *On Hors*	Xenophon, *On Horsemanship*

Index